ROTH FAMILY FOUNDATION

Music in America Imprint

Michael P. Roth
and Sukey Garcetti
have endowed this
imprint to honor the
memory of their parents,
Julia and Harry Roth,
whose deep love of music
they wish to share
with others.

The publisher gratefully acknowledges the generous contribution to this book provided by the Music in America Endowment Fund of the University of California Press Foundation, which is supported by a major gift from Sukey and Gil Garcetti, Michael Roth, and the Roth Family Foundation.

THE SAN FRANCISCO TAPE MUSIC CENTER

THE SAN FRANCISCO TAPE MUSIC CENTER

1960s COUNTERCULTURE AND THE AVANT-GARDE

EDITED BY **DAVID W. BERNSTEIN** FOREWORD BY **JOHN ROCKWELL** PREFACE BY **JOHANNES GOEBEL**

UNIVERSITY OF CALIFORNIA PRESS BERKELEY LOS ANGELES LONDON

EXPERIMENTAL MEDIA AND PERFORMING ARTS CENTER **RENSSELAER POLYTECHNIC INSTITUTE**

The first printing of this book was issued with a DVD included. The contents of that DVD can be accessed at www.ucpress.edu/go/tapemusiccenter.

University of California Press, one of the most distinguished university presses in the United States, enriches lives around the world by advancing scholarship in the humanities, social sciences, and natural sciences. Its activities are supported by the UC Press Foundation and by philanthropic contributions from individuals and institutions. For more information, visit www.ucpress.edu.

University of California Press
Berkeley and Los Angeles, California

University of California Press, Ltd.
London, England

© 2008 by The Regents of the University of California and Rensselaer Polytechnic Institute

Frontispiece: Tony Martin at the Trips Festival. Photograph © Susan Elting Hillyard.

Library of Congress Cataloging-in-Publication Data

The San Francisco Tape Music Center : 1960s counterculture and the avant-garde / edited by David W. Bernstein ; foreword by John Rockwell ; preface by Johannes Goebel.
    p. cm.
Includes bibliographical references and index.
ISBN: 978-0-520-24892-2 (cloth)
ISBN: 978-0-520-25617-0 (pbk.)
  1. San Francisco Tape Music Center—History. 2. Electronic music—History and criticism. 3. Avant-garde (Music)—United States. I. Bernstein, David W., 1951–.
ML33.S3S36 2008
786.70973—dc22   2007040979

17 16 15 14 13 12 11
10 9 8 7 6 5 4 3 2

CONTENTS

Foreword
    JOHN ROCKWELL   vii

Then, Now, and Then Again (A Preface)
    JOHANNES GOEBEL   xi

Introduction
    DAVID W. BERNSTEIN   1

The San Francisco Tape Music Center: Emerging Art Forms and the American Counterculture, 1961–1966
    DAVID W. BERNSTEIN   5

    Lee Breuer, "When Performance Art Was Performance Poetry"   15

    Robert R. Riley, "Liquid to Light: The Evolution of the Projected Image Light Show in San Francisco"   21

    Scott MacDonald, "Canyon Cinema"   35

The San Francisco Tape Music Center—A Report, 1964
    RAMON SENDER   42

An Overview of the Tape Music Center's Goals, Autumn 1964
    RAMON SENDER   47

Ramon Sender and William Maginnis
    INTERVIEWED BY DAVID W. BERNSTEIN AND MAGGI PAYNE   50

Memoir of a Community Enterprise
    PAULINE OLIVEROS   80

Pauline Oliveros
    INTERVIEWED BY DAVID W. BERNSTEIN AND MAGGI PAYNE   95

Music as Studio Art
    MORTON SUBOTNICK   112

Morton Subotnick
    INTERVIEWED BY DAVID W. BERNSTEIN AND MAGGI PAYNE   117

Composing with Light
    TONY MARTIN   136

Tony Martin
    INTERVIEWED BY DAVID W. BERNSTEIN AND MAGGI PAYNE   146

Don Buchla
    INTERVIEWED BY DAVID W. BERNSTEIN AND MAGGI PAYNE   163

    Morton Subotnick, Ramon Sender, and Maggi Payne, "The Genesis of the Buchla 100 Series Modular Electronic Music System"   166

Michael Callahan
    INTERVIEWED BY THOMAS M. WELSH   178

The Great Grand Kludge!
    WILLIAM MAGINNIS   198

Terry Riley
    INTERVIEWED BY DAVID W. BERNSTEIN AND MAGGI PAYNE   205

    Fred Frith, "The 1958 KPFA Tapes"   208

Anna Halprin
    INTERVIEWED BY DAVID W. BERNSTEIN   222

    Janice Ross, "321 Divisadero: A Staircase to 1960s Dance Experimentation"   225

Stewart Brand
    INTERVIEWED BY DAVID W. BERNSTEIN   239

    David W. Bernstein, "San Francisco Underground Rock"   245

Stuart Dempster
    INTERVIEWED BY THOMAS M. WELSH   252

Chronology
    THOMAS M. WELSH   265

Archival Recordings   283

DVD Program Notes   289

Bibliography   303

List of Illustrations   309

Index   313

FOREWORD

JOHN ROCKWELL

They say that if you can remember the 1960s, you weren't really there. I do, and I was. I grew up in San Francisco and returned to the Bay Area in 1963 to get my doctorate from the University of California at Berkeley. My interests overlapped in myriad ways with those of the subjects of this book, the composers of the San Francisco Tape Music Center, which shared a building at 321 Divisadero Street in San Francisco with the choreographer Ann (now Anna) Halprin and the listener-supported Bay Area radio station KPFA. I danced with Halprin and collaborated as a ghostwriter on her speeches and articles; did all kinds of programs at KPFA; and attended Tape Music Center concerts at the San Francisco Conservatory of Music, at 321 Divisadero Street, and at Mills College. In January 1966, I even went to the first night of that "re-creation of a psychedelic experience" called the Trips Festival.

History notoriously belongs to those who write it. The principal narratives of mid-twentieth-century contemporary classical music have been written in Europe from a European perspective, and in the United States, from an East Coast perspective. In other words, either by the mandarins of largely academic, largely serial composition, or, less commonly, by admirers of John Cage (a Californian, born in Los Angeles, who moved to New York in 1942) and the "downtown"—meaning lower Manhattan—school he spawned. In portraying the remarkable new music scene in the San Francisco Bay Area in the 1960s, this book should thus help redress a historical imbalance. For the period it documents was remarkable, and not just because of the hippies and flower power and drugs, sex, and rock 'n' roll.

What makes a "scene"? This is a different question from why the San Francisco Bay Area has been the epicenter, if one may use that word, for scenes as diverse as the beats, the hippies, campus protests, the regional cuisine movement, gay culture, and the computer and Internet revolution, notwithstanding the self-satisfied, provincial indifference of much of the local ruling class (to which I belonged, although as a rebellious offshoot).

I played a peripheral role in some of these creative scenes, and in the "downtown" and punk scenes in New York, the latter based at that archetypal dive on the Bowery, CBGB. Most likely, scenes self-generate, the result of a serendipitous coming-together of like-minded artists and cheap real estate, only later reinforced institutionally (or by institutions the artists themselves create, like the Tape Music Center) and a sympathetic press. As a member of that press, I have always been fascinated by the role played in the fostering of the new music scene in San Francisco by Alfred Frankenstein, music and art critic of the *San Francisco Chronicle.* He left his music post about the same time the scene was breaking up, with composers leaving Mills College in Oakland for the University of California at San Diego and beyond, nesting and seeking security as they grew up. I always felt that the sudden loss of Frankenstein's advocacy hastened the end of this particular scene, and I took his example as an inspiration to try to encourage creativity wherever I could find it.

And what a scene this was while it lasted! There were other focuses of new music creativity in the United States, not to speak of Europe and Japan: New York, of course, but also Ann Arbor and, with the lingering influence of the German and Russian immigrants, Los Angeles. But San Francisco was unique.

Maybe I feel that way because most of us think fondly of our youth, when hopes and energy and optimism were high. Certainly, there's a lot of nostalgia in this book, in the articles and interviews with individual composers. But in this case, I think the Bay Area was strong and important and influential in ways that still haven't been fully understood, or recognized on the East Coast.

Some of the key composers have indeed made major careers, among them Steve Reich, after he moved back to New York, Terry Riley, Morton Subotnick, and La Monte Young (who preceded this scene by a few years). Pauline Oliveros is still regarded fondly by her admirers (like me). Lou Harrison as twinkling godfather is important, though still derided as a maker of too-pretty music. Robert Erickson is another father figure, but his music has not traveled widely beyond his students and contemporaries. Donald Buchla and John Chowning are best known for their pioneering work in audio technology and electronic music in Oakland and Stanford. Ramon Sender, who plunged deepest into the hippie ethos, is not heard often today, nor (to my regret) are Loren Rush, Douglas Leedy, and others, such as Stuart Dempster, Robert Moran, Charles Shere, and Charles Amirkhanian, who were active mostly later. The European teachers and mentors of this loose group—Darius Milhaud, Luciano Berio, Karlheinz Stockhausen—are well known today, of course, but they are not primarily associated with the Bay Area.

What I remember most fondly about that time was first of all the music itself. Reich's *Four Organs,* echoing grandly in the churchy acoustics of the Pacific Art Museum in Berkeley; or Oliveros's haunting transmutation of *verismo* opera into cosmic electronic flux in *Bye Bye Butterfly;* or Riley's joyful, communal *In C*—these and many other pieces created an excitement when they first appeared akin to the broader passions provoked by every new release of Janis Joplin or Bob Dylan or County Joe or John Fahey or the Beatles. They were cultural moments.

A lot of this music involved live performers; the dividing lines between performance and unsullied electronic music were always vague, and productively so. Still, aside from the beauty and liveliness of so much of what these composers made, they pioneered in another way, too. Along with the rock musicians and engineers like Buchla, they helped inaugurate the era of inexpensive yet sophisticated electronic equipment. No longer tied to gigantic computers that only universities could afford, composers could make electronic music anywhere, anytime. One didn't have to be a professor or indebted to the academy; anyone, given the talent and the ambition, could make electronic music. And they did.

Reading about the Tape Music Center in this book, one is struck by how modestly funded it was, how much they made of so little. But sometimes penury can be a spur to creativity, however romantic that may sound. Maybe had these composers had all that institutional equipment, they might have been subtly—or unsubtly—undermined, denied the stimulus of bohemian penury.

Beyond the music, I recall the openness. There is a hint of sniffiness about rock 'n' roll in some of these interviews, but I remember concerts in which rock experimentalists shared the stage with all manner of classical musicians, with no one feeling that any one else was out of place. Uptown vs. downtown, West Coast vs. East Coast, Asia vs. Europe, high vs. low, dissonant vs. consonant—it was all met with open ears. That was the way I learned to love new music, so imagine my shock when I moved first to Los Angeles and then to New York, where polemical scorn was presumed to be the norm.

The openness transcended this scene, or even music, and so sometimes this book on the Tape Music Center quite rightly finds itself spreading out to encompass the whole Bay Area artistic scene of the 1960s. Gerhard Samuel was a friend of new music, and his Oakland Symphony, then a sort of glorified community orchestra, was a source of lively concerts and chamber-music spin-offs, mostly at Mills College. KPFA's live concerts and tapes from all over the country and the world served as an invaluable corrective to self-contented provinciality. KPFA held live concerts at its San Francisco studio on Divisadero Street.

The openness also extended to arts beyond music. It was no accident that Halprin shared the Divisadero space, since she used Tape Music Center composers and they used her and her dancers to enliven their concerts, not least at the Trips Festival. Her excitement about broadening the means and the ends of dance, about exploring the body and the spirit and the community, helped define a decade.

Stan Brakhage and the local experimental film scene were also close to these composers, as were commercial film young Turks like Francis Coppola, George Lucas, and Walter Murch. So too were jazz musicians and theater people and poets and artists and all-purpose hipsters and pranksters like Stewart Brand and Ken Kesey. Chet Helms and Bill Graham hovered on the sidelines as enablers, and the nascent rock-critic scene took an interest in this music, too (Ralph J. Gleason on both jazz and rock at the *Chronicle,* Jonathan Cott at *Rolling Stone,* later myself). I have long argued that new music is most vital when it appeals to artists of all kinds, not just to a closed circle of like-minded composers and their students, dragooned into attending their teachers' concerts. I got that idea from the San Francisco scene in the 1960s.

By 1966, the original San Francisco focus of the Tape Music Center had begun to blur. Sender followed his hippie dreams, Subotnick moved the center to Mills, and by the next year, the exodus to San Diego and beyond had begun. But of course life and art in San Francisco went on, mutating constantly into whatever scenes flourish there now. (I know about some of them, but, as a critic working in New York, I am naturally constrained by distance.)

I can only hope that this book, with its jostling together of essays and interviews and observations, will serve to remind people today what a lively, wonderful kind of new music existed in the Bay Area forty years ago. Oliveros calls it a haven, a community. That's not just youth, or her youth, or my youth, talking. As this book reminds us, it all really happened, and it was really great.

THEN, NOW, AND THEN AGAIN (A PREFACE)

JOHANNES GOEBEL

The San Francisco Tape Music Center happened in the 1960s. Before, during, and ever since their collaboration back then, its members have all pursued, shaped, and lived their individual artistic directions. Today, they remain active and "doing their thing." So it was wonderful to invite them and produce a festival in 2003 entitled "Wow & Flutter," featuring works from their collaborative times and some new works as well.

"Wow & Flutter" was the first major artistic initiative by the Experimental Media and Performing Arts Center (EMPAC) at Rensselaer Polytechnic Institute. Dr. Shirley Ann Jackson, president of Rensselaer, conceived of EMPAC in 2000, together with the faculty of the institute, and with the full support of its board of trustees. EMPAC will be launched with its new building in 2008. In anticipation of the opening, the program of EMPAC is ramping up, and "Wow & Flutter" set a tone for the multiphonic chord to come.

One of the five members of the former San Francisco Tape Music Center, Pauline Oliveros, is now a professor in the Arts Department at Rensselaer. Meeting her when I joined Rensselaer in 2002 as the director of EMPAC rekindled our relationship from times past and reminded me of an idea I had proposed to the San Francisco Museum of Modern Art about a year earlier: a festival celebrating the diversity of electronic/computer/experimental music in the Bay Area. My impression was that the rich tradition of musical innovation in these fields in this part of the country is not widely recognized. When I began working at Rensselaer, guiding EMPAC as both a building and a program, I saw the opportunity to follow up my original idea with a festival featuring the San Francisco Tape Music Center.

Another motivation to produce this festival was the perception that even arts students were not really aware of the rich gold mines of experimental and interdisciplinary practice in the United States. They see teachers who are so much older than they are, and it is almost impossible for them to imagine that some of them were actually once as young and crazy as they are. Or to put it in other words: "arts and technology" are not an invention of the digital age, and growing older and getting more mature is not bound to becoming dull and petrifying and repeating oneself. On the contrary, there are actually people of age who are flexible and open-minded, who have been interested in new ways and directions their entire lives, creative artists who started out with analog electronics and now use the latest laptop, or who may not need anything but a clarinet, a drum set, an accordion, and an overhead projector. It's not the advancement of technology that is driving their art, which can absorb any tool that they see fit for what they want to do.

Art, music, technology, nontechnology, and the "unexpected," performed for the young and the old by the old and the young, condensed into two evenings, also created a dynamic link between twenty years of integrated electronic arts (iEAR) taught in the Arts Department at Rensselaer and the first steps toward a brand-new center for experimental and performing arts on the campus of the oldest existing engineering school in the English-speaking world. Now that was a long sentence. And the path toward EMPAC has been equally long.

As we were working on the program for the festival and were looking for material for the program booklet, Pauline pointed out to me that David W. Bernstein was writing an article on the Tape Music Center, and, with Maggi Payne, had already interviewed its members. So out of this grew this book with its DVD companion, its form and direction being developed in close collaboration with David, Thomas M. Welsh, and Mary Francis. I hope that the publication of this book will lay the foundation for many publications to emerge from EMPAC in the years to come.

History is interpretation. Interpretations change with time. History is changing and changed over time as we are changing over time. History is the expression of interests; history is a projection from a past through the lens of the present into a future, with its focus in the present. You are holding this book in your hands, reading these words at this moment, and when you read this book you will have your own thoughts added to what you read. And then was then and now will be then, and there will always be a new then.

This book may serve different desires, approaches, and perspectives. It may create a vivid picture of what happened "back then." It may shed multicolored lights on the actors involved, on creativity and technology, on fantasies beyond superficial consciousness and on the never-ceasing fire to move on in the now without getting stuck between the then of a past and the then of a never-to-be-reached future. It may serve as foundation for musicologists and art historians who are interpreting the past for us. It may be a good read. It may be generating energy for the new and coming, since there is so much new to be discovered in the past. And may it also serve as a celebration of "The Five"—the wonderful creative artists to whom it is dedicated: Bill Maginnis, Tony Martin, Pauline Oliveros, Ramon Sender, and Morton Subotnick.

Introduction

DAVID W. BERNSTEIN

In February 1965, the *New York Times Sunday Magazine* featured an article by the poet Kenneth Rexroth entitled "Thar's Culture in Them Thar Hills."[1] Noting that the San Francisco Actor's Workshop had recently moved to New York, Rexroth was not surprised that the nation's largest metropolitan area had looked across the continent to a small city for a theater company to reside in Lincoln Center. San Francisco's cultural scene, he said, although on a smaller scale, was "incomparably richer and of higher quality proportionately than New York's."[2] Rexroth's claim resulted to a certain extent from a frustration with the parochialism present, not only in New York and other East Coast cultural centers, but also in San Francisco itself. The achievements of San Francisco's writers, artists, dancers, and musicians, he felt, were too often ignored, even by the city's own mainstream institutions.

The history of the San Francisco Tape Music Center is a case in point. Although the Tape Music Center was at the forefront of advances in musical aesthetics during the 1960s, scholars, for the most part, have devoted little attention to its contributions.[3] This book provides a history of the Tape Music Center, examining its subject from a variety of perspectives. At its core stand vivid personal accounts of this history through interviews with and essays by the Tape Music Center's founding members. These materials provide insights into the origins and manifestations of Ramon Sender's highly original musical voice and his role in the San Francisco counterculture. They show us how crucial the Tape Music Center was for Pauline Oliveros's compositional career and her continuing dedication to art as a community enterprise. They document Morton Subotnick's pioneering work in mixed media and his collaboration with Sender and Don Buchla, which led to the creation of the Buchla 100 series Modular Electronic Music System. They help us understand how Tony Martin's magical real-time compositions with light led to the development of a new interdisciplinary art form. And they document how the wizardry of the Tape Music Center's technical directors Bill Maginnis and Michael Callahan opened up unlimited creative possibilities with limited resources.

The Tape Music Center was part of a larger avant-garde artistic scene that included such groups as the San Francisco Actor's Workshop, the San Francisco Mime Troupe, the Committee Theater, the Dancers' Workshop, and the Open Theater, as well as a diverse community of independent writers, artists, musicians, and dancers. Although it is not possible to cover this rich cultural environment without losing the book's primary focus, it would be a mistake to present the history of the Tape Music Center apart from its exciting artistic context. We have therefore included interviews with creative artists and visionaries who played important roles in the San Francisco avant-garde during the 1960s and who also had personal connections with the Tape Music Center. In this portion of the book, Terry Riley discusses his free improvisations with Pauline Oliveros and Loren Rush during the late 1950s and the genesis of his monumental work *In C*, first performed at a Tape Music Center concert in 1964. Don Buchla talks about his invention of the "Buchla Box" and his ongoing interests in instrument design and multisensory art. An interview with Stewart Brand covers the Trips Festival and his interest in the consciousness-expanding potential of LSD. Stuart Dempster sheds light upon the San Francisco new music scene from a performer's perspective. Anna (formerly Ann) Halprin, founder of the Dancers' Workshop, discusses her collaborations with La Monte Young and Terry Riley and her early interest in crossing disciplinary boundaries, which inspired composers at the Tape Music Center and generations of creative artists in the Bay Area to do the same.

The larger portion of this book consists of oral history, a genre that creates a degree of immediacy, bringing the reader close to what happened by sharing the experiences of those who were there. This method is richly informative, and its results are often far from passive, objective accounts. With this in mind, we have included Thomas M. Welsh's detailed chronology, a systematic examination of the Tape Music Center history based on archival research that complements the more subjective approach in the interviews. Our book contains photographs, illustrations, a list of archival recordings (transferred from reel-to-reel tape to CD by Maggi Payne) available in the Archives of the Center for Contemporary Music, F. W. Olin Library, Mills College, Oakland, California, and a DVD documenting the "Wow & Flutter" San Francisco Tape Music Center retrospective presented at the Rensselaer Polytechnic Institute on October 1 and 2, 2004. We have also included several short essays that cover the Tape Music Center's broader context: Janice Ross on Ann Halprin's Dancers' Workshop, Scott MacDonald on the Canyon Cinema, Fred Frith on the seminal 1958 KPFA improvisations, Lee Breuer on his early work in experimental theater at the Tape Music Center, Robert R. Riley on the development of the light show in

San Francisco, and my own essay on interactions between the San Francisco experimental music and rock "scenes." The book begins with a cultural study in which I examine the history of the Tape Music Center in light of the political and social upheaval that occurred during the 1960s, particularly in the San Francisco Bay Area.

This book began as part of a larger project, an oral history of experimental music at Mills College, which I started with my colleague composer Maggi Payne more than ten years ago. Maggi introduced me to the wonderful community of composers and performers associated with Mills, of which she has been a member for almost thirty years. This community includes the founders of the San Francisco Tape Music Center, who all had strong ties to Mills.

Our research on the Tape Music Center began in the home of Bill Maginnis, where we first interviewed Bill and Ramon Sender in December 1994. I clearly remember talking with Ramon and Bill, looking over a box full of Tape Music Center programs and other ephemera, immediately realizing that something unique had happened in the San Francisco new music scene between 1961 and 1966. Subsequent interviews with Pauline Oliveros, Tony Martin, and Morton Subotnick confirmed this initial impression. Our contact with the founding members of the Tape Music Center exposed us to their creative achievements. It also led us to understand the underlying strength of the group as a whole—its communal spirit based on unwavering friendship and a shared commitment to artistic and aesthetic goals rather than the advancement of individual careers.

Our investigations have come a long way since 1994. Several years ago, Pauline Oliveros introduced us to Johannes Goebel, director of the Experimental Media and Performing Arts Center (EMPAC) at Rensselaer Polytechnic Institute. Johannes is a visionary, an innovator in the field of computer music, a pioneer of free improvisation in Germany, a writer on aesthetics and technology, and the leader of an institution dedicated to extending the potential of the arts through technological innovation. He has never hesitated to push boundaries when necessary, and he also has the wisdom to understand that artistic innovation, in his own words, "does not fall out of the sky"; it depends upon human creativity, both past and present. It was Johannes's appreciation of the relevance of the past that led to his interest in and support of this book, which has greatly benefited from his guidance and feedback.

Thomas M. Welsh was another integral member of our team. The founder of San Francisco–based Elision Fields artist management and independent recordings,[4] he has an exhaustive knowledge of Bay Area culture. Thomas has a voracious appetite for accumulating documentary evidence and a genuine passion for getting the facts straight. As his finely honed chronology demonstrates, he contributed invaluable research to our book. Thomas helped curate some of the photographs that appear in the book and suggested that we consider a joint publication arrangement with the University of California Press, a strategy that fortuitously resulted in its music editor, Mary Francis, joining our team. Mary quickly recognized the significance of our book. It was a great pleasure to collaborate with an editor so familiar with its subject matter. This book owes a great deal to her unwavering advocacy and editorial expertise. It was also a pleasure working with senior editor Dore Brown and copyeditor Peter Dreyer; their editorial acumen made it possible for this book to reach its final form.

A complex project invariably involves contributions from many people. I would especially like to thank Renee Jadushlever (head librarian at Mills College), Janice Braun (special collections librarian), and Nancy Mackay (who prepared an extensive catalogue of Tape Music Center archival recordings) for their advice and support, and Ralph Johnson and David Kwan, who helped prepare some of the book's illustrations. Tony Martin's images are courtesy of the artist and the Fales Library, New York University.

I would also very much like to acknowledge my colleagues in the Mills Music Department, whose creative work continues to inspire me, and to thank the Mills poet Stephen Ratcliffe for his critical insights. Finally, special thanks as always to my family (Jamie, Jeremy, and Beverly) for putting up with me during another writing project.

NOTES

1. Kenneth Rexroth, "Thar's Culture in Them Thar Hills," *New York Times Sunday Magazine*, February 7, 1965, 28–29, 78–80.

2. Ibid., 80.

3. There are several noteworthy exceptions. Joel Chadabe discusses the history of the San Francisco Tape Music Center in *Electric Sound: The Past and Promise of Electronic Music* (Saddle River, N.J.: Prentice-Hall, 1997), 85–91. See also Thom Holmes, *Electronic and Experimental Music*, 2d ed. (New York: Routledge, 2002), 206–8, and Trevor Pinch and Frank Trocco, *Analog Days: The Invention of the Moog Synthesizer* (Cambridge, Mass.: Harvard University Press, 2002), 36–41. Ramon Sender's unpublished novel "Naked Close-Up" contains accounts of events that took place at the Tape Music Center.

4. See www.elisionfields.com (accessed July 4, 2007).

The San Francisco Tape Music Center

EMERGING ART FORMS AND THE
AMERICAN COUNTERCULTURE, 1961–1966

DAVID W. BERNSTEIN

More than six thousand people attended the Trips Festival, a series of concerts that took place at the Longshoremen's Hall in San Francisco, January 21–23, 1966. The producers, Stewart Brand and Ramon Sender, promoted the event as "a nondrug re-creation of a psychedelic experience," featuring "the Trip—or electronic performance—a new medium of communication and entertainment." They hoped to create an "electronic art happening," the sort of sensory overload envisioned by Marshall McLuhan, whose work was in fashion at that time.

The festival was a crucial moment in the evolution of the American counterculture. It was also a watershed event in the history of the underground arts scene in San Francisco, which brought together experimental theater, dance, and light shows. Several rock bands performed, including the Grateful Dead, Big Brother and the Holding Company, and the Loading Zone. Ken Kesey and his Merry Pranksters distributed LSD throughout the crowd and performed their *Psychedelic Symphony*—free improvisations by both musicians and nonmusicians playing flutes, guitars, an old Hammond organ, and noisemakers made from found objects such as auto parts and piano strings, which they called "thunder machines." Films by Anthony Martin and Bruce Baillie and projections from a Vortex Light Box added visual stimuli. There were even plans to use Don Buchla's newly invented modular synthesizer to manipulate music performed by Big Brother and the Holding Company.[1] Additional events were held at other venues during the festival: a "Worship Service" with the dancer Chloe Scott and Lou Harrison, and a collaborative work entitled *A Theater Piece* (1965), created by Pauline Oliveros and the dancer-choreographer Elizabeth Harris. Virtually the Bay Area's entire avant-garde arts scene was involved: the Committee Theater, the San Francisco Mime Troupe, the Open Theater, the Dancers' Workshop, and the San Francisco Tape Music Center.

1 TRIPS FESTIVAL PROGRAM COVER BY WES WILSON. © WES WILSON.

this is the FIRST gathering of its kind anywhere. the TRIP -- or electronic performance--is a new medium of communication & entertainment.

FRIDAY, JANUARY 21
america needs indians, sensorium 9 - slides, movies, sound tracks, flowers, food, rock'n'roll, eagle lone whistle, indians (senecas, chippewas, hopi, sioux, blackfeet, etc.) & anthropologists. open theatre - "revelations" - nudeprojections. "the god box" by ben jacopetti. the endless explosion, the congress of wonders, liquid projections, the jazz mice, the loading zone rock'n'roll, steve fowler, amanda foulger, rain jacopetti, & the unexpectable.

SATURDAY, JANUARY 22
ken kesey, members of the s.f. tape music center, big brother & the holding company rock'n'roll, the don buchla sound-light console, overhead projection, anthony martin, ramon sender, bill maginnis, bruce baillie. "the acid test", the merry pranksters & their psychedelic symphony, neal cassady vs. ann murphy vaudeville, the grateful dead rock'n'roll, allen ginsberg, roy's audioptics, movies, ron boise & his electric thunder sculpture, the bus, hell's angels, many noted outlaws, & the unexpectable.

SUNDAY, JANUARY 23
high energy experiments conducted in the cyclotron of dome-shaped longshoreman's hall by america needs indians, open theatre, s.f. tape music center, the merry pranksters, gordon ashby (light matrix), henry jacobs (air dome projections), kqed, don buchla, the grateful dead, the loading zone, big brother & the holding company, & many others still being assembled. since the common element of all shows is ELECTRICITY, this evening will be programmed live from stimuli provided by a PINBALL MACHINE. a nickel in the slot starts the evening.

the general tone of things has moved on from the self-conscious happening to a more JUBILANT occasion where the audience PARTICIPATES because it's more fun to do so than not. maybe this is the ROCK REVOLUTION. audience dancing is an assumed part of all the shows, & the audience is invited to wear ECSTATIC DRESS & bring their own GADGETS (a.c. outlets will be provided).

design:
Wes Wilson

TICKETS — $2 PER EVENING
— $5 FOR SERIES
AT CITY LIGHTS, S.F., ASUC
AND CAMPUS RECORDS,
BERKELEY; HUT-T-I, S.F.
STATE- INFO: 392-5489

printing:
Contact Printing Co.

The Trips Festival was evidence of an escalating movement culminating in 1967 with a migration of thousands of young people from all around the country to Haight-Ashbury, the Human Be-In, and the Summer of Love. This movement, which the social historian Theodore Roszak termed the "counterculture," inspired an ambitious reassessment of cultural values, an "effort to discover new types of community, new family patterns, new sexual mores, new kinds of livelihood, new aesthetic forms, new personal identities on the far side of power politics, the bourgeois home, and the Protestant work ethic."[2] Although the events in San Francisco were joined by parallel developments around the world,[3] California, and San Francisco in particular, provided fertile ground for the emergence of the American counterculture. Its relative isolation on the western edge of the continent has traditionally provided fertile breeding ground for "rascally and anarchistic types" from a variety of political, social, and artistic circles,[4] a phenomenon noted by both nineteenth- and twentieth-century writers. As Frank Norris, describing San Francisco at the turn of the twentieth century, observed: "Perhaps no great city is as isolated as we are.... Isolation produces individuality, originality.... Other cities must grow by expansion from without; San Francisco must grow by expansion from within; and so we have the time and energy to develop certain unhampered types and characters and habits unbiased by outside influences, types that are admirably adapted to fictitious treatment."[5]

During the late nineteenth and early twentieth centuries, the city and surrounding areas were home to such writers as Joaquin Miller, George Sterling, Gertrude Atherton, Frank Norris, and Jack London. San Francisco's thriving bohemian community of painters, poets, and musicians were all rugged individualists, yet often similar in their shared interest in mysticism, experimentation, and non-Western cultures.[6] During the 1930s, the city was known for perhaps the most militant labor movements in the United States, a political environment reflected not only in the many public murals in the style of Diego Rivera and José Orozco but also in drama and music created at the time.[7]

Although the Beat Generation was born in New York, it later moved to San Francisco. In the 1950s, poets and writers such as Jack Kerouac, Allen Ginsberg, and Gary Snyder formed an intellectual community that protested against the oppressiveness and homogeneity of postwar American society. Presenting their poetry during public readings at coffeehouses, jazz clubs, and venues such as the Six Gallery, a converted auto repair shop, the beat poets also sought to break down boundaries between mass and elite culture. Their ideas exerted a direct influence on the 1960s counterculture; many of the beats—Gary Snyder, Neal Cassady, and Allen Ginsberg, for example—

were active participants in such events as the Trips Festival and the Human Be-In. This merging of radical and popular culture was an important social development during the 1960s. In general, the intellectual framework developed in the avant-garde arts communities, which endorsed antiestablishment and experimentalist agendas, later took root on a much larger scale. And, as Richard Cándida Smith has observed, it was in California that the dividing line between artistic radicalism and popular culture initially began to disappear.[8]

During its five-year existence, the San Francisco Tape Music Center provided an ideal environment for a significant interaction between the counterculture and the West Coast avant-garde. Founded in 1961 to provide a group of local composers with a studio and a venue for the presentation of their works, the Tape Music Center began at a time when composers increasingly recognized the enormous potential of electronic music. In the 1950s, this new and exciting musical resource captured the imagination of composers active in Milan, Paris, and Cologne. By the 1960s, electronic music studios had been established not only in Europe and the United States but in Japan and South America as well.[9] With the refinement of magnetic tape in the 1940s, recording technology had taken an important step forward, making it easier for composers to explore the virtually infinite expressive possibilities of electronic music. "It used to be said," the composer Ramon Sender wrote in 1964, "that every composer must confront Arnold Schoenberg's 'Method of Composing with Twelve Tones' and come to some sort of working agreement with it. Today the composer cannot afford to ignore the experience of working with tape."[10]

It was Sender who in 1961, while studying composition with Robert Erickson at the San Francisco Conservatory of Music, took the initial steps toward the establishment of the San Francisco Tape Music Center. The conservatory had a two-channel Ampex tape recorder, which provided Sender with his first opportunity to experiment with "sound on sound" recording.[11] This led to the composition of *Four Sanskrit Hymns* (1961), a work for four sopranos, instrumental ensemble, and three tape recorders, first performed at the conservatory's Composers' Workshop concert on June 13, 1961. The workshop, organized by Erickson, was a forum for student works and also included performances of a broad range of twentieth-century music by such composers as Cage, Harrison, Partch, Krenek, Stockhausen, Varèse, and Berio.[12] The June 13 concert featured Morton Subotnick's *Three Preludes* (1956, 1961) for piano; *Composition for Synthesizer* (1961) by Milton Babbitt; *Electronic Composition #3 "Birds and Bells"* (1960) by Istvan Anhalt; and Richard Maxfield's neo-dadaist *Piano Concerto,* in which the pianist (Terry Riley), "dressed in a tuxedo and wearing a stocking cap and dark glasses, poured marbles into the piano, set its strings

```
                THE SAN FRANCISCO CONSERVATORY OF MUSIC
                          1201 Ortega Street

                               Presents

                               SONICS I

                     Monday, December 18, 1961, 8:30 P.M.

SOUND: STUDY NUMBER ONE                        TRAVERSALS
           Philip Winsor                             Ramon Sender

M... Mix                                IMPROVISATION FOR MIXED INSTRUMENTS
           Terry Riley                              AND TAPE
                                                Laurel Johnson
TIME PERSPECTIVES                               Pauline Oliveros
           Pauline Oliveros                     Ramon Sender
                                                Philip Winsor

                     Intermission

                          Technical Assistance
                               Ellis Gans
                             Charles Shaefer

       We are happy to welcome you to this first of a series of concerts
       of electronic music at the Conservatory. Eight weeks ago work began on
       the building of an electronics laboratory for the production and playback
       of electronic compositions. The admission charge will assist in the
       continued improvement of the studio facilities. Donations of technical
       skill, electronic equipment and/or money will be gratefully accepted.

                     You are invited to tour the laboratory
                     Coffee will be served in the lounge.
```

3 **SONICS I PROGRAM (DECEMBER 18, 1961).**

vibrating with a child's gyroscope, and dropped all manner of objects into some sheets of foil over the strings."[13]

After composing *Four Sanskrit Hymns,* Sender decided to create an electronic music studio in the conservatory attic. He and Pauline Oliveros, who was also attending Erickson's composition seminar,[14] began a series of concerts, which they called "Sonics," the first of which took place on December 18, 1961, and featured compositions created in the new studio by Sender, Oliveros, Riley, and Philip Winsor.

The facilities in the studio were modest; this led the composers to invent new sounds from everyday objects, often enhancing their acoustical properties with contact microphones and a piano soundboard for reverberation. Two tape compositions performed at the first Sonics concert, Sender's *Traversals* (1961) and Oliveros's *Time Perspectives* (1961), demonstrate that elegant music could be created using limited technical resources. *Traversals* used modified accordion sounds as well as sounds made by Sender's baby son bouncing in his crib; in *Time Perspectives,* Oliveros's first tape piece, the composer's source materials included sounds made from small found objects resonating in wooden apple crates, as well as vocal sounds. Cardboard tubes served as filters and a bathtub functioned as a reverberation chamber. Hand winding a Sears Roebuck SilverTone tape recorder while in record mode made it possible to do variable speed recording that modulated the frequencies of Oliveros's sound sources. *Time Perspectives* was recorded in real time; as was the case with her other early tape compositions, Oliveros avoided cutting and splicing tape as much as possible.

Riley's interest in tape music dates back to his *Concert for Two Pianos and Five Tape Recorders* (1960), which he performed with La Monte Young,[15] while they were both graduate composition students at the University of California, Berkeley, and working together as co–music directors for the Dancers' Workshop. Sonics I featured Riley's *M . . . Mix* (1960–1961) (also known as *Mescalin Mix*), originally a tape piece written for Halprin and created with a thirty-five-foot tape loop that extended all the way around the studio, using several wine bottles as "spindles." Riley's early work with repetitive music using tape loops anticipated the modular structures that are hallmarks of his minimalist style. The title shows the influence of John Cage's tape compositions *Williams Mix* (1952) and *Fontana Mix* (1958), as does Riley's use of chance to select tape segments from his source materials, which include a blues piano riff and the famous laughing woman ("Laughing Sal") from the funhouse at Playland at the Beach in San Francisco.[16] *M . . . Mix* is a tape assemblage composed without sophisticated equipment. It was recorded in mono, sound on sound (a technique that accumulates distortion and background noise), the composer changing the tape speed manually to create special effects.

The initial Sonics concert concluded with a free improvisation with tape featuring Sender (piano), Oliveros (accordion), Winsor (trumpet), and Laurel Johnson (percussion). Group improvisations, later termed "Opera," were featured on every program in the Sonics series. The nucleus of composers who formed the San Francisco Tape Music Center shared a predilection for spontaneous music making. Oliveros's interest in improvisation dates back to the 1950s. In 1958, along with Riley and Loren Rush, she formed an improvisation group that met weekly and recorded their improvisations for KPFA, a Bay Area listener-sponsored radio station.[17] Initially, Riley had received a commission from the sculptress Claire Falkenstein to make a soundtrack for a film entitled *Polyester Moon.* He invited Oliveros and Rush to record an improvisation for this project in which Oliveros played the French horn, Rush koto (a zither-like Japanese stringed instrument) and bass, and Riley the piano. According to Oliveros, their improvisations began without predetermined guidelines or structures.[18] They recorded each session, later listening critically to the results in order to improve their improvising skills. As Riley recalled, their improvisations reflected "the kind of compositions we were doing in those days . . . [and] were quite free," comparing them to a form of "musical abstract expressionism rather than jazz."[19]

The three young musicians were all students of Robert Erickson, who, sharing their interest in improvisation, began working with combinations of improvisation and conventional notation in his *Chamber Concerto* (1960). Interest in free improvisation was also part of a larger trend in the new music scene, which started to take root in the 1960s, inspired by the indeterminate scores and "open forms" of John Cage and others, as well as by the omnipresent background of the jazz tradition. The 1958 KPFA improvisations anticipated subsequent developments, and interest in free improvisation later gained momentum during the 1960s.[20] Other groups and ensembles such as Franco Evangelisti's Nuova Consonanza, AMM, Joseph Holbrooke, Larry Austin's New Music Ensemble, and Musica Elettronica Viva cultivated various forms of free improvisation, paralleling and interacting with the revolutionary free jazz of such giants as John Coltrane, Ornette Coleman, Cecil Taylor, and Albert Ayler.

The Sonics I concert was announced as a "bring your own speaker" event. As speakers arrived, they were dispersed around the auditorium and wired to a specially configured keyboard. This allowed the composers to "play" their works spatially throughout the room and the adjacent corridor. There were also plans for Milton Cohen (a member of the Once Group from Ann Arbor, Michigan) to project special lighting effects during the concert.[21] At that time, Cohen was living in San Francisco and giving public performances in his studio. Some of the composers involved with the Sonics concerts improvised for his light shows.

The Sonics series continued into the spring of 1962. A concert on March 24, 1962, featured recent electronic music by Bruno Maderna, Luigi Nono, and Luciano Berio, composers from the Studio di fonologia musicale in Milan as well as Henri Pousseur's *Trois visages de Liège* (1961, composed at the APELAC studio in Brussels). Maderna's contribution to the program, his *Serenata à 3* for flute, marimba, and tape (1961), was a work for live musical instruments and tape, a genre the composer initiated with his *Musica su due dimensioni* (1952), which would later become a focus of the composers working at the Tape Music Center. The program also included American composer James Tenney's *Analog #1* (1961), his first composition using digital synthesis, which he created at Bell Labs.

Composers participating in the Sonics series collaborated with dancers and challenged traditional distinctions between performer and audience. In one concert, John Graham and Lynne Palmer, both members of the Dancers' Workshop, moved from room to room accompanied by tape music from a variety of sources. At one point in the performance, Graham wandered down a hallway followed by a rumbling Maytag washing machine (with a long extension cord) filled with stones. The final

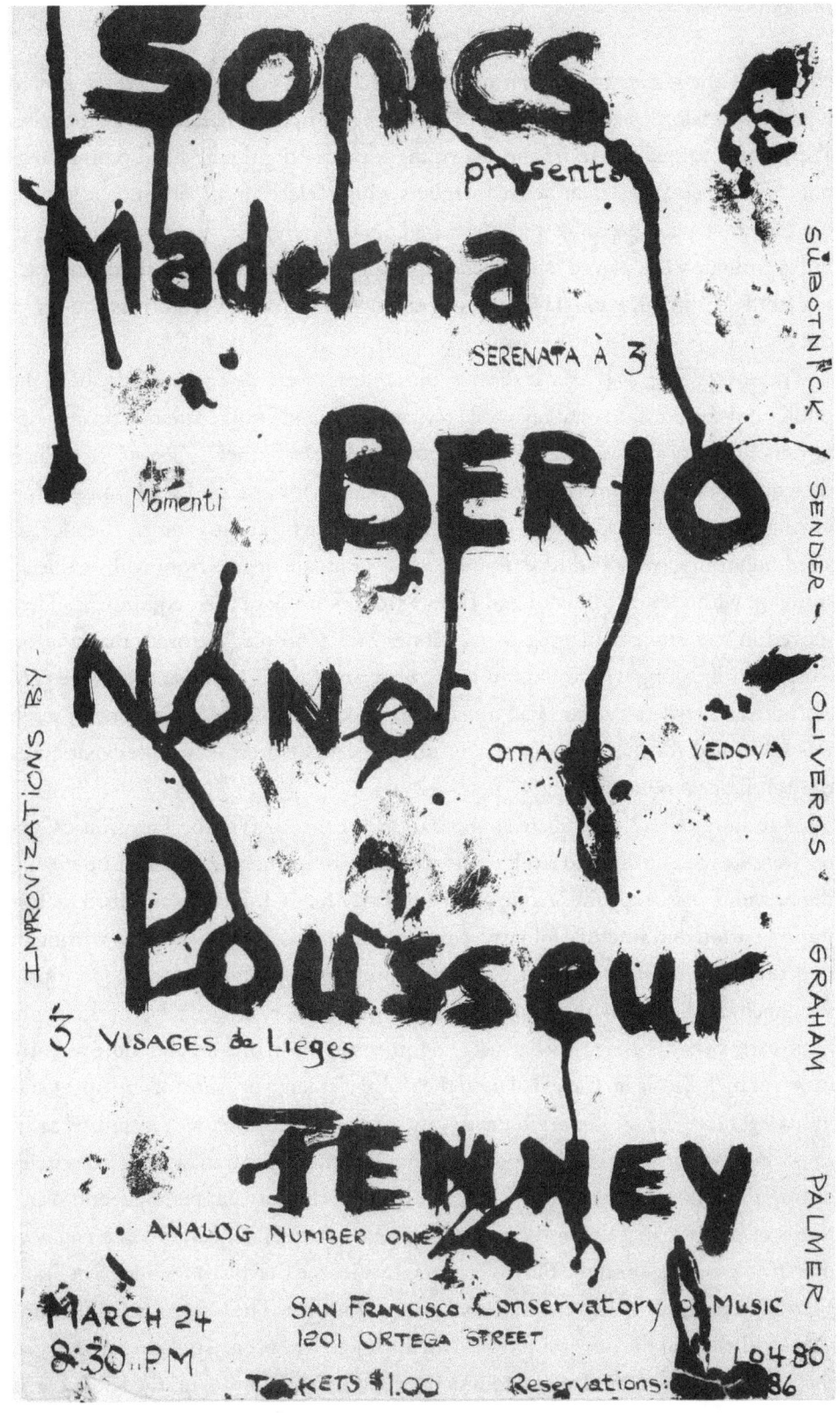

4 SONICS II PROGRAM (MARCH 24, 1962).

concert of the series, on June 11, 1962, also included a collaborative work entitled *Smell Opera with Found Tape* (1962). One of the composers had found a tape in an alley, which turned out to be about a young unmarried girl who had become pregnant.[22] Dancers sprayed audience members with a selection of perfumes accompanied by the tape. The concert also featured Sender's *Tropical Fish Opera* (1962), an indeterminate work played by Sender, Oliveros, Rush, and Morton Subtonick reading from a fish tank with staves on four sides. As the fish moved across the staves the performers sounded the appropriate notes.

The Sonics series was a great success; the concerts were well attended by both the public and the press. Several favorable reviews by Alfred Frankenstein, a strong supporter of the city's new music scene, appeared in the *San Francisco Chronicle*.[23] When the conservatory was unwilling to provide a budget for a second season in the following year (Sender had absorbed all the costs for the first Sonics series), Sender invited Subotnick (who had recently received a graduate degree from Mills College, studying with Darius Milhaud and Leon Kirchner) to pool their equipment. They moved in the summer of 1962 to 1537 Jones Street, an old Victorian mansion on Russian Hill. Along with them (on loan) went one square- and two sine-wave generators that Hewlett-Packard had donated to the conservatory. A new concert series was scheduled for the 1962–63 season, now under the group's new designation as the San Francisco Tape Music Center.

As an autonomous, unaffiliated organization, the members of the Tape Music Center were free to continue to explore the new directions they had opened up during the previous year. Tape music remained a primary focus, but this was joined by free improvisation and interdisciplinary experiments in what Michael Kirby, writing at that time, called the "new theatre" in describing an important trend in 1960s performance art.[24] A hallmark of the 1960s avant-garde, the historical roots of this genre lay in early twentieth-century dadaist and futurist performance art and more recently in works by John Cage. Cage had used theatrical elements in *Water Music* (1952) and in his legendary *Black Mountain Piece* (1952), a staged performance recognized as an important precursor of the "happenings" that became popular in avant-garde circles during the following decade. There was a proliferation of "happenings" and other forms of performance art in the 1960s, beginning with Allan Kaprow's *18 Happenings in 6 Parts* (1959) and the Fluxus "events" by George Brecht and others. San Francisco had a particularly rich experimental scene at the time. The Committee, an improvisational satirical theater group from North Beach, had been active since the 1950s; the San Francisco Mime Troupe, founded by R. G. Davis in 1959 (as the R. G. Davis Mime Troupe), incorporated diverse elements ranging from commedia dell'arte to

Antonin Artaud's "Theatre of Cruelty" and Bertolt Brecht's "Epic Theater" in order to advance a radical political agenda. The Actor's Workshop, a community-based organization like the Tape Music Center, was known for its performances of Beckett and Genet. Across the Bay, Ben Jacopetti, a former member of the Berkeley Drama Department, and his wife, Rain, founded the "Open Theater," a group known for their light projections on nude bodies, which they called "Revelations."

The above community of artists interested in exploring new theatrical forms inspired members of the Tape Music Center to do the same. The 1962–63 Tape Music Center season included Lee Breuer's theater piece *Composition for Actors.* Breuer was a writer and director who with Ken Dewey, R. G. Davis, and Ann Halprin founded the American Cooperative Theater. Members of the R. G. Davis Mime Troupe presented *Event II,* which pushed the limits of the avant-garde, beginning with two nude dancers sitting on toilets in a mirrored closet pondering the process of producing stool. Audience members sat on boxes of different heights and were covered with a black cloth, which had head holes cut out of it.[25] Other evenings featured poetry readings by Robin Blaser and the beat poet Michael McClure and a play by Robert Duncan, all of which were joined by improvisations and tape music. Robert LaVigne constructed an "environment" for another concert during which the audience participated in the creation of a tape piece.

When Performance Art Was Performance Poetry
LEE BREUER

Composition for Actors, a "one nite stand" presented in 1962 at the San Francisco Tape Music Center's first home at 1537 Jones Street, and *The Run,* staged in 1964 at its second home at 321 Divisadero Street, seeded my later work with the experimental theater collective Mabou Mines in New York through 2005. We asked ourselves a Cartesian question—in what does pure theater exist that is not dance (as in stage movement), not oratorical literature (as in script), not art (as in set and lighting), not media (as in projections, amplified speech, and music), and so on down the list of the so-called theater arts. We decided pure theater exists in a formal sequence of emotions akin to a series of musical figures performed in "characterizations"—personality presentations that were to some extent archetypical.

In *Composition for Actors,* Bill Raymond, Ruth Maleczech, myself, JoAnne Akalaitis—all founding members of Mabou Mines in the 1970s—and Susan Darby formed a choral ensemble that, sitting in chairs, simultaneously performed a series of emotions without words. All burst out crying at the same instant, segued to laughter, then on to rage, and so forth. It all seemed quaintly miraculous—there was no story, no psychological scenario, emotions were formal—like colors that could be mixed or sound that could be harmonized. This idea led us to a post-Brechtian dialectical methodology.

Bertold Brecht constructed his dialectic by synthesizing opposite messages in theater forms. Music opposed text; a mimetic acting style opposed a visual composition. Brecht didn't deal with emotion in the motivational tradition of Stanislavski or the Actor's Studio. Perceiving the "real" formally allowed us to use "real" feeling in the dialectical mix, to play counter to a typical psychological scenario, which, if "understood logically," appeared crazy, but if "understood aesthetically," was often beautiful, original, and radically deconstructive.

The Run was the second proto–Mabou Mines production. Here, for the first time I wrote and directed, and, also for the first time we, the ensemble, experimented with a total theater approach that was a clear harbinger of things to come in my "animation series."[1] The following is an excerpt from "You," a ca. 1967 rewrite of the original script performed at the Tape Music Center:

> *City dogs. never get their roles straight. never a clue how to play it from one minute to the next, you're cast as an animus switched to an incubus suddenly you're something out of the Sunday comics and now the dumb bitch wants you to be just plain pooch. it gets up stiff legged and trots toward Alice. it stops before it gets to her. it thinks some things are sacrosanct. it runs back and lowers its ass again. what happens to life's necessities. Alice goes PREEEOOOOEEEPP. the dog jumps. that's what happens. somebody blows the whistle. it trots toward Alice. no. this is ridiculous this is Pavlovian. it turns around. on the one hand life's necessities and on the other. it turns back to Alice. life's necessities. it starts chasing its tail in a blur without a sound. then it stops and just stands there and shakes. Alice picks it up and puts it in place. she gets her back up against the tree. cues the atmosphere. Frank takes his hand out of his pocket.*

In *The Run,* Bill Spencer accompanied the actors on the harp of an altered piano, Elias Romero projected a liquid light dialogue with Ruth Maleczech. Bill Ham sculptured a dog that flew. Ann Halprin dancers Norma Leistiko and Fumi Spencer, the runaway movie star Diane Varsi, the mime troupe, and Bill Raymond welded together a performing ensemble that was decades ahead of its time. Elaborating the ideas that first surfaced in these pieces has been my work for forty years.

The cultural climate in the 1960s in San Francisco was similar to that of the first decades of the century in Paris. The differences were minimal—more artists died of drugs than of alcohol, art took off commercially with rock 'n' roll, thanks to Bill Graham, rather than the likes of Gertrude Stein (whose book *The Autobiography of Alice B. Toklas* became a best seller). In Paris, Alfred Jarry and Antonin Artaud captured the avant-garde imagination, rather than R. G. Davis and the composers at the San Francisco Tape Music Center. Gérard de Nerval and Jacques Prévert were the poets one read, rather than Allen Ginsberg and Lawrence Ferlinghetti. Anarchists influenced radical politics, rather than hippies and Yippies. But the ethos in 1960s San Francisco, perhaps less intellectually "Old World" than that of Paris, and as a consequence, perhaps less classist, was essentially the same. Since then, to evoke the ghost of Hunter S. Thompson, one could say that it's been all downhill.

---

1. See Arthur J. Sabatini, "From Dog to Ant: The Evolution of Lee Breuer's Animations," *PAJ: A Journal of Performance and Art* 26, no. 2 (2004): 52–60. The first work in the series, Breuer's "Red Horse Animation" (1970), can be found in *The Theatre of Images,* ed. Bonnie Marranca (Baltimore: John Hopkins University Press, 1977, 1996), 113–56.

The culminating event of the season was *City Scale* (1963), a happening created by Sender, Dewey, and Anthony Martin (a visual artist who later became the Tape Music Center's visual director), which further explored audience-performer relationships, but on a much grander scale. Dewey was a playwright who had begun to challenge various aspects of traditional theater. In his 1961 production of Albert Camus's *The Misunderstanding*, for example, he moved away from the text by eliminating all but one character, changed the set, and added music by Varèse (*Poème electronique, Density 21.5,* and *Hyperprism*). In a short play entitled *The Gift*, presented at the Mission Neighborhood Playhouse in March 1962, two dancers from the Dancers' Workshop approached Dewey's text kinesthetically, creating movement inspired by the sound of the words. (A later performance of *The Gift* at the Sarah Bernhardt Theater in Paris employed Terry Riley's masterful use of tape delay effects applied to a recording of the jazz trumpet player Chet Baker.)

City Scale moved completely beyond the traditional venue for theatrical presentations; the entire city of San Francisco was the "stage" for a series of events, both planned and unplanned. During a North Beach sequence, Martin created light projections on the blank wall of the Wells Fargo building. He also drew the score,[26] which served as a blueprint, plotting "time and space throughout the evening."[27] Audience members were shuttled around to various locations in San Francisco; there was a "book-returning" ceremony at the City Lights Bookstore in North Beach, a trombone player (Stuart Dempster) in the Broadway Tunnel, and a woman in a bathrobe singing Debussy in a storefront window. In many cases, the audience was unsure whether the action around them was "real" or part of the piece. This was precisely the objective of *City Scale:* to blur the boundaries between art and life. As Sender explains, the most successful events in the evening

> were those which impinged upon the life of the city, interacted with it, transformed it or absorbed it into the structure of the work. The arrival of the audience in two trucks at a small park perched high on a hill overlooking the Mission coincided with a collision between two teenage gangs in the park. I had arrived early to inflate four seventeen-foot weather balloons, and noticed the kids collecting. Just as the two groups started toward each other, our trucks full of excited participants roared up. Sixty people started running across the park toward the balloons, and the teenagers scattered to the periphery. I don't know what went through their minds in the minutes that followed, as adults chased balloons and each other through the park.[28]

The Tape Music Center remained only a single season at 1537 Jones Street; a fire caused by a faulty electrical system destroyed the building. Sender and Subotnick had already found a new location at 321 Divisadero Street, however, on the eastern edge of Haight-Ashbury. The building contained two auditoriums, one of which they sublet to the Dancers' Workshop; the other, they shared with KPFA. The electronic music studio was on the third floor. During its three seasons at 321 Divisadero, the Tape Music Center evolved into the most prominent venue for experimental art in San Francisco, gaining a national reputation for musical innovation. It also continued to develop a unique artistic mission.

In the 1950s and 1960s, the equipment necessary for the creation of electronic music was expensive. As a result, most of the studios depended on the financial support of state-sponsored radio stations, research organizations, or academic institutions. Composers at the Tape Music Center, as members of an independent private organization, avoided the sorts of orthodoxies that characterized the larger, more affluent studios.[29] They rejected what they saw as the useless dichotomy between "pure" electronic music and musique concrète, simply referring to their work as "tape music," since tape was a medium used for both genres of electronic music.

The founders of the Tape Music Center defined themselves in terms of a new musical subculture, an alternative to what they saw as the artistic paralysis characteristic of musical institutions across the country:

> There is a growing awareness on the part of young composers all over the country that they are not going to find the answers they are looking for in analysis and composition seminars of the academies. Some retreat from the "avant-garde" music environment, live marginally on the fringe of the community, or attempt to work isolated from musicians and concert groups. They have insulated themselves by this isolation from the sickness of culture, but too often also from their own creative potential. Others have banded together and have produced concerts of their works outside of the usual organizations.[30]

Public access was at the core of the Tape Music Center's artistic mandate. Its organizers saw the center as

> a community-sponsored composer's guild, which would offer the young composer a place to work, to perform, to come into contact with others in his field, all away from an institutional environment. Each composer would, through his contact with the center, be encouraged to fulfill his own musical needs and develop his own personal language. He would have the advantage and support of all the facilities of the center, for rehearsals and performances of his music, for contact with other musicians and composers, [and] for work in the electronic music studios. He would be

6 THE SAN FRANCISCO TAPE MUSIC CENTER LOCATION AT 321 DIVISADERO (BUILDING IN THE CENTER), CA. 1964. PHOTOGRAPH COURTESY OF THE SAN FRANCISCO HISTORY CENTER, SAN FRANCISCO PUBLIC LIBRARY.

encouraged to involve himself in the musical life of the community-at-large. The community in turn would be offered the services of the center as a music-producing agency for films, for plays, for churches, and [for] schools. Such a program, carried through in detail, could produce a revolution. It would, I believe, in five years time, create a new cultural environment in at least our local area. Working closely with musicians' organizations and cultural and civic groups, it could break up some of the stagnant areas of our own local cultural environment, such as the traditional repertory of symphony and opera, the pork-barrel city band, the entrenched conservatism of some of the chamber-music organizations.[31]

This social agenda distinguished the Tape Music Center from the many other electronic music studios established during the same period. Its members also continued to forge new creative paths involving improvisation and artistic collaborations with theatrical elements, dance, and light.

The itinerary for *City Scale* included a visit to a light show by Elias Romero in the Mission district that piqued Sender's interest. Experiments with light and sound were part of the growing interest during the late 1950s and 1960s in collaborative work breaking down disciplinary barriers. An early example was the "Vortex" concerts held at San Francisco's Morrison Planetarium in the late 1950s.[32] Created by Jordan Belson, a painter and filmmaker, and Henry Jacobs, a radio engineer and a composer of musique concrète, these concerts featured light projected up onto the planetarium's dome, accompanied by tape music disseminated spatially through more than three dozen speakers. The objective was to immerse the audience in a virtual whirlwind, a "vortex" of sound and light.

During the 1960s, light shows, an outgrowth of the "polysensorial" environments associated with the "Acid Tests," became a major component of the psychedelic rock scene and were regularly featured at many dance and concert venues such as the Fillmore Auditorium, the Matrix, and the Avalon Ballroom. Seymour Locks, an art professor at San Francisco State, was a major influence on the development of this medium.[33] Locks had studied experiments with light projection in the early twentieth century. (For example, in the 1920s, László Moholy-Nagy, a member of the Bauhaus school, worked on plans for a "theater of totality" based on a synthesis of various art forms, including lighting.) In the 1950s, Locks devised a method for creating light shows by using an overhead projector with hollow slides and plastic dishes filled with pigments that could be stirred and swirled, thus creating moving patterns of light. Romero, a painter and a poet, learned the technique and began to present light shows at parties and other venues. Romero also collaborated with Bill Ham, another painter, who became a light show specialist. The two artists worked with floating colored emulsions, rotating color discs, and slide projections, all having the effect of a new form of kinetic art.

Several pieces in the Tape Music Center's 1963–64 program included light projections. *Improvisation No. 1,* a collaborative work with a tape by Subotnick accompanied by improvisations performed by Sender and Oliveros on two pianos, featured visual images by Romero. Subotnick's *A Theater Piece after Sonnet No. 47 of Petrarch* (1963)[34] included a set by Judith Davis, dancers (John Graham and Sarah Harvey), and light projections by Romero. Romero was subsequently replaced by Anthony Martin, who had worked with Tape Music Center composers during the Sonics series. A painter and former student at the Art Institute of Chicago, Martin (who now uses the first name "Tony") developed a beautiful repertory of visual imagery created with hand-painted slides, liquid projections, film footage, and other techniques. He was in essence a "visual composer" working in real time using film, prepared slides, overhead projectors with various images and found objects, and liquids on plates to create a changing visual presentation.

Along with Sender, Subotnick, Oliveros (who had rejoined the group after completing a residency in Europe), and the studio technician William Maginnis (who

Liquid to Light
The Evolution of the Projected Image Light Show in San Francisco
ROBERT R. RILEY

The Vortex Concerts (1957 to 1960) at San Francisco's Morrison Planetarium were among the earliest examples of electronic sound and projected light environments. Conceived for the acoustical properties and colossal scale of the Planetarium's domed ceiling, a vortex of light and sound was created by the painter and filmmaker Jordan Belson and the composer, radio engineer, and programmer Henry Jacobs. The Vortex Concerts broadened conventional cinema from a single projected image to the expansive curve of the dome as a screen for Belson's film projections accompanied by a live mix of amplified, multichannel sound. His multi-image film projections immersed the audience in an environment of luminous imagery overhead, bathed in tinted film imagery and color washes. A bank of prepared projectors freed the image from its frame, while spatially composed sound by Jacobs (and others), amplified through a circular arrangement of more than three dozen speakers, saturated the audience with multidimensional sounds and images. The series helped influence an emerging generation of artists to develop the time-based, euphoric correlation of image and sound that later flourished in experimental arts and music in San Francisco throughout the 1960s.

A leader in nonobjective, experimental filmmaking since the 1940s, Belson is artistically linked to the proto-psychedelic, avant-garde films of John and James Whitney. Like Belson, the Whitneys engaged direct cinema techniques—methods of working directly with celluloid, pigments, and perforations on the film surface and in its emulsion—to form explorations of metaphysical subjects related to themes in abstract art and aspects of spirituality. Known for hypnotic visual effects, early computer-assisted animation techniques, and the handcrafted appeal of direct cinema, the Whitneys' award-winning *Abstract Film Exercises* (1940–45) were landmark achievements in the representation of subjective states of consciousness as symbolized by the mandala and concentric form of dot-and-line animation.

The expansion of materials for the visual artist manufactured by postwar industry, such as Day-Glo and synthetic paints, soluble acrylics, colorful aniline dyes and gelatin, and the salvageable instruments and lighting equipment found in military surplus around the Bay Area created an environment of excess and experimentation. New materials for art were applied as relevant forms to the search for a meaningful articulation of place and time, and a refreshed definition of space. Seymour Locks, a professor at San Francisco State College, was invited to make a series of projections in 1952 at a conference for art educators to reanimate the European tradition of projected image sets in the 1920s and 1930s theater. Locks experimented with empty slide cartridges filled with pigment and the Viewgraph overhead projector, ordinarily used to enlarge and project book illustrations from a horizontal position to a vertical screen in classroom lectures. The use of the overhead projector revealed to him an ingenious application: Locks found this familiar instructional machinery could be used to project live imagery of paint stirred and swirled on its translucent base. The addition of single or layered glass plates in combination with hand-made slide transparencies made of fluids and solids simultaneously projected created patterns and motion.

Locks developed a studio art course titled "Light and Art." His new methods liberated painting from its flat two-dimensional surface into a vital new form of motion and plasticity. Projected light artworks introduced freedom from the material object, a tangible relationship to time, and the powerful effect of color in motion that interested Elias Romero. Romero had attended a performance in Los Angeles by two of Locks's students in the 1950s.[1] As did other visual artists trained in abstraction, color field, and gesture painting on canvas, such as Bill Ham, Tony Martin, and Glenn McKay, Romero embraced the unique aesthetic language of optical instruments and image-projection devices in combination with experimental filmmaking to experience in their aggregate a greater freedom for painting in light. Painters by training and innovators in spirit, these artists adapted the audiovisual hardware of postwar industrial display, such as the overhead projector and automated slide projector, to reorient the operation of data-projection machinery that is systematic in its function, but infinitely flexible in its adaptation to a new purpose.

Independently produced experiments in film, synonymous with the new forms of theater, psychedelic music, and expressive arts of the emergent counterculture in the Bay Area fostered a climate for moving-image art in which elaborate, innovative multiscreen projected-light shows were based. Artists, many of whom were members of Canyon Cinema filmmakers' collective (a group that included the light show artists Jerry Abrams, Kenneth Anger, Bruce Conner, and Ben Van Meter), rigorously experimented with the material properties of film, such as the medium's liquid emulsion and gelatin, its chemical process in development, and the percussive effect of film frames in rapid sequence combined with other mechanical properties of cinema. Their work emphasized the material qualities of film, subjective free-wheeling content, and the medium's flexibility in large-scale, multi-image projections.

Canyon Cinema added a screening venue to its roster of locations in the early 1960s, the San Francisco Tape Music Center. The Tape Music Center was founded by composers interested in electronic music, improvisation, and multimedia theater pieces. The center focused on the possibilities for musical composition with magnetic recording media and audiotape, electronic instruments, and any variation of nontraditional methods and disciplines. Tony Martin, the center's visual composer-director, created projected light imagery in collaboration with the composers Ramon Sender, Pauline Oliveros, and Morton Subotnick. Martin's synchronic projections in partnership with the performance of new musical forms catalyzed the potent affinities between them. The aural and visual perception of motion were seen by Martin as "painting in time" and experienced by composers as parallel vital and vibrant forms. The intermedia collaborations between Martin and his colleagues resulted in a large body of works presented both in San Francisco and at venues around the country during the period from 1961 to 1966.

The experience of art for the projected light artist and composer was not the distanced contemplation of a solid object but the immersion in moving image, color, light, and sound

1. Kerry Brougher, "Visual-Music Culture," in id., Jeremy Strick, Ari Weisman, and Judith Zicker, *Visual Music: Synaesthesia in Art and Music since 1900* (New York: Thames & Hudson, 2005), 159.

> as the means to fully appreciate synesthesia—the interaction of all sense perception simultaneously. Through a mechanomorphic vocabulary of forms drawn from image-generating instruments associated with instruction, illustration, and cinema, the artists who developed the projected-light environments came from different fine arts disciplines, worked collectively, and shared the inspiration of isolating light as an artist's medium in the tradition of László Moholy-Nagy, a pioneer in synthesis of the arts. The "theater of totality" Moholy-Nagy conceived of in 1924 has inspired generations of artists and has become a particularly significant touchstone in experiments with projected light. He introduced the notion of "direct light effects" in luminous projections and explored the perceptual complexities of light projections that defined space, form, and motion, advocating for a progressive, collective production process, inventive in its manual and mechanical realization, in step with developments in technology.
>
> In San Francisco, light shows originated in the context of painting, animated abstract film, visionary handcrafted instruments, and reconfigured machines and became not only a new art form but also a cultural force and phenomenon. The synthesis of forms is emblematic of the radical, freedom-seeking philosophy of broad social change, altered consciousness, and sensual pleasure associated with the drug culture. Projected live, the light show's fluid motion and perpetual change achieved through the artistic control of soluble or resistant liquids, transparent oils, and pigments applied to translucent materials over a source of light grew in complexity and vibrancy over a period of several years. The pulse-pounding effects of moving liquid and light were integrated into the production of psychedelic music and linked with the evolution of the dance-concert events in various theaters in San Francisco. In addition to its role within the counterculture, the poetic and determined operation of machinery and image-projection technologies of the multimedia movement formed a union of revolutionary artistic ambitions that inexorably corresponds with advances in sound amplification, magnetic tape recording, and electronic music composition.

had replaced Michael Callahan in the summer of 1964),[35] Martin became a core member of the Tape Music Center. His light projections, along with other theatrical elements and improvisations, became defining elements of their collaborative interdisciplinary approach to electronic music, an aesthetic exemplified by Sender's *Desert Ambulance* (1964), a composition for accordion, tape, and light projections. Composed for Pauline Oliveros, the "score" for *Desert Ambulance* consisted of instructions given to the performer through headphones. This made it possible for the work to be performed in the dark so that the audience could view Martin's light projections, made with hand-painted slides and painted 16 mm film, projected onto Oliveros playing the accordion. The title *Desert Ambulance,* according to Sender, refers to a photograph of an ambulance used by missionaries in the 1920s. He described the work as "a vehicle of mercy sent into the wasteland of (academic) modern music." After

7 SAN FRANCISCO TAPE MUSIC CENTER GROUP PHOTO. FROM LEFT TO RIGHT: TONY MARTIN, WILLIAM MAGINNIS, RAMON SENDER, MORTON SUBOTNICK, AND PAULINE OLIVEROS.

its first performance, Alfred Frankenstein noted the work's move away from the academic mainstream, calling *Desert Ambulance* an example of "aural pop art."[36] It also had a connection to the world of rock music. Sender created the tape part for *Desert Ambulance* on an instrument called the Chamberlin Music Master, a keyboard instrument that has a tape head under every key. A predecessor of the modern sampler, each key on the Chamberlin initiated a sound tuned to the appropriate pitch. The Chamberlin used three-track tape with recordings of conventional instruments, voices, and rhythm tracks. It was the precursor of the Mellotron, an instrument popular with such rock groups as the Beatles ("Strawberry Fields Forever") and the Moody Blues ("Nights of White Satin").

In the spring of 1964, Oliveros organized a festival celebrating the work of the pianist and composer David Tudor (1926–1996), which featured compositions by Tudor, Oliveros, George Brecht, Toshi Ichiyanagi, Alvin Lucier, and John Cage. The "Tudorfest," cosponsored by KPFA, was a significant event in the history of the San Francisco Bay Area new music scene, demonstrating the artistic diversity of the avant-garde, from the minimalistic explorations of barely audible piano sounds (played

KPFA
SAN FRANCISCO TAPE MUSIC CENTER
AND PERFORMER'S CHOICE
PRESENT

THREE CONCERTS WITH DAVID TUDOR

Monday, March 30 and Monday, April 6, 1964 at 8:30 p.m.

JOHN CAGE	34'46.776" for two pianists
	(intermission)
PAULINE OLIVEROS	Duo for Accordion and Bandoneon with Possible Mynah Bird Obligato, See Saw Version / Staging conceived and directed by Elizabeth Harris
	(intermission)
TOSHI ICHIYANAGI	Music for Piano # 4
ALVIN LUCIER	Action Music for Piano, Book I, 1962

Ahmed, Pauline Oliveros, Dwight Peltzer and David Tudor
Lighting by Anthony Martin – Ahmed loaned by Laurel Johnson

Wednesday, April 1 and Wednesday, April 8, 1964 at 8:30 p.m.

TOSHI ICHIYANAGI	Music for Piano # 4, Electronic Version
JOHN CAGE	Music for Amplified Toy Pianos
	(intermission)
TOSHI ICHIYANAGI	Sapporo
	(intermission)
GEORGE BRECHT	Card-Piece for Voice
JOHN CAGE	Variations II

Stuart Dempster, Pauline Oliveros, Dwight Peltzer, Loren Rush,
Ramon Sender, Morton Subotnick, David Tudor and Milton Williams

Friday, April 3, 1964 at 6:00 p.m. and 8:30 p.m.

	Atlas Eclipticalis with Winter Music, Electronic Version
	(intermission)
MUSIC OF	Concert for Piano and Orchestra
JOHN CAGE	(intermission)
	Cartridge Music
	Music Walk

Michael Callahan (electronics), John Chowning (percussion), Stuart Dempster (trombone), Warner Jepson (piano), Douglas Leedy (horn), Robert Mackler (viola & viola d'amore), Pauline Oliveros (horn & tuba), Dwight Peltzer (piano), Ann Riley (piano), Loren Rush (double bass), Ramon Sender (conductor), Stanley Shaff (trumpet), Linn Subotnick (viola), Morton Subotnick (clarinet), David Tudor (piano), Ian Underwood (flute & piccolo) and Jack Van der Wyk (timpani)

at KPFA's SAN FRANCISCO STUDIO
321 DIVISADERO STREET

by Oliveros and Tudor) in Ichiyanagi's *Music for Piano No. 4* to the instrumental chaos of Cage's *Concert for Piano and Orchestra* (1958) and *Atlas Eclipticalis* (1961–62).[37] Tudor performed as soloist in Cage's *Cartridge Music* (1960) and *Variations II* (1961). Two of the works, Brecht's *Card Piece* and Lucier's *Action Music for Piano, Book I* (1962), a performance emphasizing the act of piano playing more than its actual sound, crossed the boundary between music and conceptual art. Oliveros's collaboration with Tudor, *Duo for Accordion and Bandoneon and Possible Mynah Bird Obbligato* (1964), combined theatrical elements and music. The work was initially a duo for accordion and bandoneon, but Oliveros later added a part for Laurel Johnson's mynah bird Ahmed after the two musicians saw how excited the bird became by the focused sounds produced by the two instruments. The final version was staged by Elizabeth Harris, who created a revolving seesaw, which, in addition to its visual impact, allowed for a changing spatialization of the sounds. Originally, the plan was to work from a score, but this had to be abandoned in favor of improvisation because of the difficulty of reading from a score while suspended and spinning around.

The success of the Tudorfest and the other concerts in the 1963–64 season placed the Tape Music Center at the forefront of developments in new music around the country. In the summer of 1964, Oliveros, Sender, Subotnick, and Martin went on tour, playing concerts on the East Coast and in the Midwest. After returning to San Francisco, they decided to program new works by local composers during the 1964–65 season. A concert on November 4, 1964, devoted to music by Terry Riley included *Music for "The Gift"* (1963), *I* (1964), a tape piece in which John Graham inflected the word "I" in a variety of emotional tones, *Shoeshine* (1964), another tape piece based on a song entitled "Shotgun" by Junior Walker, *In B♭ or Is It A♭?* (1964), a tape piece featuring a recording using tape delay of Sonny Lewis playing the tenor sax, *Coule,* a modal piano improvisation, and the world premiere of *In C*. The latter, a seminal work in the development of minimalism, was performed by a stellar cast of musicians: Riley, Steve Reich, Werner Jepson, Jeannie Brechan, James Lowe (keyboards), Jon Gibson and Sonny Lewis (saxophones), Stan Shaff and Phil Winsor (trumpets), Mel Weitsman (recorder and trumpet), Subotnick (clarinet), Sender (Chamberlin), and Oliveros (accordion).[38] Martin provided a visual environment by projecting shapes from within the group of performers out into the audience using a prism, a few lenses, and three or four projectors.[39]

The performance of *In C* was enthusiastically received by the San Francisco press.[40] Another important concert devoted to the music of Steve Reich followed several months later. In 1963, Reich earned a master's degree from Mills College, where he studied with Darius Milhaud and Luciano Berio. His interest in tape composition dates back

```
SAN FRANCISCO TAPE MUSIC CENTER    321 DIVISADERO STREET   SAN FRANCISCO 17
                             presents
                   AN EVENING OF MUSIC BY TERRY RILEY
    8:30 P.M.                                              November 4 & 6
                              Program

    MUSIC FROM THE GIFT (July 1963).............................Terry Riley

    Composed in the Radiodiffusion - Television Francais studio at the Sarah
    Bernhardt Theatre, the tape was made in collaboration with the Chet Baker
    Ensemble for playback with The Gift, a piece for theatre by Ken Dewey.

    * I (July 1964)............................................... Terry Riley
                     John Graham, Voice

    * Shoeshine (June 1964)........................................Terry Riley

    * In B♭ Or Is It A♭ (October 1964) ............................Terry Riley
                     Sonny Lewis, Tenor Sax

    COULE (continuously being composed) .........................Terry Riley
                A piano improvisation upon a mode.

                     Terry Riley, Piano

    In C (October 1964)...........................................Terry Riley

    A piece for any combination of instruments, singers, or both, it consists of
    a series of motives built on a mode in C. The piece utilizes a type of very
    strict improvisation in that the performer is continuously choosing how long
    he remains on a certain given motive.

    Performers include: Pauline Oliveros, Morton Subotnick, Ramon Sender, Steve
    Reich, John Gibson, Jeannie Brechan, James Lowe, Sonny Lewis, Mel Weitsman,
    Warner Jepson, Stan Shaff, Phil Winsor, Anthony Martin, and Terry Riley.

    * These pieces were composed on equipment in the composer's home.

    TERRY RILEY studied in San Francisco with Robert Erickson, and then went to
    UC where he received his Master's degree in 1961. He left for Europe shortly
    thereafter for reasons of health, and spent two years in Paris, toured Russia
    and Scandanavia, working in Leningrad with the Leningrad Jazz Quartet, and in
    Helsinki at the Television Studios. He's now living on Potrero Hill and gen-
    erally enjoying himself.
```

9 **PROGRAM FOR TERRY RILEY CONCERT AT THE SAN FRANCISCO TAPE MUSIC CENTER (NOVEMBER 4 AND 6, 1964).**

to 1962, partially as a result of the influence of composers working at the Tape Music Center.[41] In 1963, he composed a tape collage for a film by Robert Nelson entitled *The Plastic Haircut*. The tape, produced in part through looping techniques and overdubbing, consists of sounds recorded from an LP entitled *The Greatest Moments in Sports*. In 1964, Reich obtained a small portable tape recorder (which he shared with

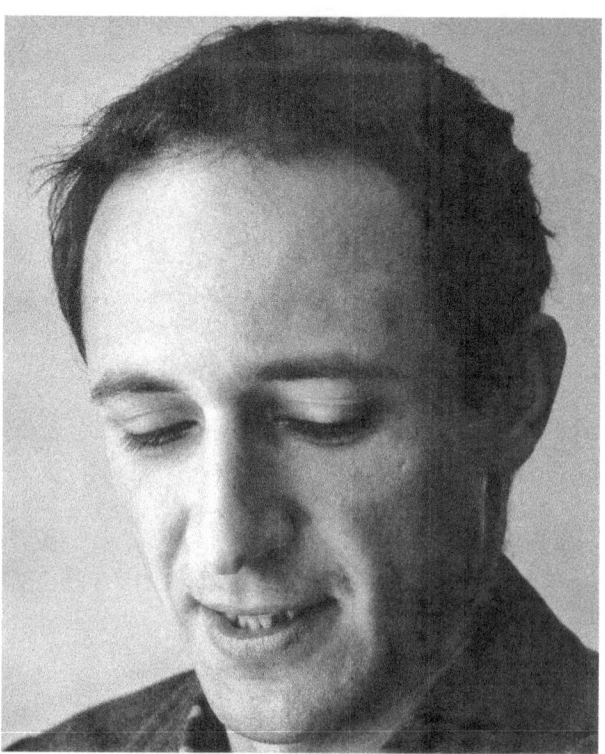

10 STEVE REICH (CA. 1965).
PHOTOGRAPH © WARNER JEPSON.

the Grateful Dead bassist Phil Lesh, also a former student at Mills) to record conversations in the back of a taxicab he drove after graduating from Mills. The resultant piece, entitled *Livelihood* (1964), is a collage of phrases, some of which repeat several times in succession. This technique, also present in *The Plastic Haircut,* anticipates the more extensive and complex use of phrase and word repetitions in another tape composition, *It's Gonna Rain* (1965). The later work, Reich's first piece employing his phasing technique, uses a recording of Brother Walter, an African American Pentecostal street preacher, delivering a sermon in San Francisco's Union Square. Both *Livelihood* and *It's Gonna Rain* were performed at the Tape Music Center on January 27, 1965.

During the 1964–65 season, composers working in the Tape Music Center continued to create works fusing sound, light, and theater, and to develop their ties to the 1960s avant-garde. Subotnick's *Play! no. 1* (1964), for a woodwind quintet, tape, and Martin's visual projections, combines a vast repertoire of instrumental gestures with precise indications for extramusical movements by the performers. Its theatrical component presented a humorous look at performing, the players shouting, counting, and exchanging accusatory glances amid virtuoso flurries of instrumental lines. Sender's *In the Garden* (1965), for clarinet, viola, tape film, and slides, took a novel approach to notation, which facilitated the combination of live performance and

11 PERFORMANCE AT 321 DIVISADERO OF MORTON SUBOTNICK'S *PLAY! NO. 1* (1964) FOR WOODWIND QUINTET, PIANO, AND TAPE, WITH FILM BY TONY MARTIN. WEST COAST WOODWIND QUINTET, FROM LEFT TO RIGHT: ROBERT HUGHES, EARL SAXTON, DONALD O'BRIEN, JEAN LOUIS LEROUX, AND GARY GRAY.

recorded electronic sounds. The instrumental parts were made by fitting a pen to an EKG machine connected to the audio output of an Ampex tape recorder. The performers were instructed to synchronize the resultant parts, which functioned as "rhythm tracks," to the tape. The work had a theatrical component, based on the story of the expulsion of Adam and Eve from the Garden of Eden.

Oliveros's *Pieces of Eight* (1964) is an elaborate theater piece written in prose notation, a practice that the composer frequently used in later works, such as her well-known *Sonic Meditations* (1971–73). The instructions carefully describe virtually every aspect of the piece, from the costumes, props, and staging to the performers' actions, including their emotional attitudes and breathing. The score calls for wind octet and a large selection of props, including a cuckoo clock, eight alarm clocks, a papier-mâché bust of Beethoven with blinking red eyes, a cash register, a tape of bird sounds, ticking clocks, telephones, and an organ. The performers dress as plumbers, pirates, priests, and other bizarre characters. Based loosely on Robert Louis Stevenson's *Treasure Island*, *Pieces of Eight* resembles early twentieth-century performance art such as the futurist "variety theater" or, as one critic observed, the theater of the absurd.[42] Its effect is, in part, a poignant criticism of traditional concert music.[43]

The 1965–66 season included compositions for acoustical instruments and tape by Mario Davidovsky and Robert Erickson.[44] It also featured Subotnick's *Serenade No. 3* (1965), for flute, viola, clarinet, piano, and tape, one of a group of works the composer wrote for live acoustical instruments and tape during the 1960s. Performed during the Tape Music Center's 1965–66 season by the Mills Performing Group, an ensemble established at Mills College by Subotnick, Berio, and Milhaud, *Serenade No. 3* is an interactive work interweaving pointillistic instrumental lines with elegant recorded electronic sounds.

Oliveros composed *Bye Bye Butterfly*, perhaps her best-known early work, at the Tape Music Center in 1965. Working in the studio at the Tape Music Center one night with two Hewlett-Packard oscillators, she discovered that a beautiful low difference tone would sound when the oscillators, connected to several line amplifiers, generated supersonic frequencies. Sweeping the entire audio range simultaneously on both oscillators produced a variety of sounds as the differences between the frequencies changed. Oliveros then combined this new setup with a tape delay system and quickly began composing with her new electronic instrument, improvising and recording the results in real time. The first of these compositions were five pieces called *Mneumonics*.

A tape composition made with two Hewlett-Packard oscillators, two line amplifiers, and two tape recorders, *Bye Bye Butterfly* incorporated an excerpt from a recording of Puccini's *Madame Butterfly* with electronic sounds. Oliveros created *Bye Bye Butterfly* in real time, using the technique described above, and improvising with the LP recording. Both the title and the appropriation of an operatic excerpt combine to make a powerful statement about nineteenth-century musical culture and specifically women's role in society.[45] Although the composer has devoted her entire career to similar critiques, it is interesting that she has explained that the selection of the Puccini excerpt was fortuitous, the record selected by chance from a table in the Tape Music Center studio.

Bye Bye Butterfly, like many of the works composed at the Tape Music Center, was created using limited technical means. Although the studios were more sophisticated than those at Jones Street or at the San Francisco Conservatory, the facilities at 321 Divisadero were certainly not comparable to European and American electronic music studios with institutional support. In addition to tape recorders (including an Ampex three-track recorder), the resources available to composers working at the Tape Music Center consisted of equipment obtained from military surplus, scientific laboratories, and telephone companies. But Subotnick and Sender did participate in the development of a new instrument that would revolutionize electronic music composition. Seeking a means to streamline studio time by eliminating the laborious task of tape splicing, they enlisted the help of Don Buchla, a gifted engineer who also had a background in music. Buchla had been working on a voltage-controlled modular synthesizer since 1963, and most likely by late 1964 or early 1965, he delivered an early model to the Tape Music Center. The new instrument, which he called "The Modular Electronic Music System," also known as the "Buchla Box," featured voltage-controlled synthesis, in which an oscillator's frequencies, timbres, and amplitudes could be controlled by other oscillators or by control voltages generated by a sixteen- or eight-stage sequencer or other control voltage sources. Additionally, the Buchla's "touch controlled voltage source" was unique in that it was not a traditional keyboard interface, but instead a copper plate with sixteen (twelve on the prototype) pressure-sensitive "keys" in addition to two independent voltage outputs per key, plus a trigger. It significantly reduced the need for tape splicing and created new possibilities for the generation of electronic music in real time. The Buchla's compact, portable design freed electronic music from the constraints of the classical electronic music studio, allowing composers to work at home and perform in concert halls and on tour. This emphasis on accessibility, consistent with the Tape Music Center's aesthetic mission, also responded to the growing impact of electronic music on contemporary culture. Buchla, Sender, and Subotnick were visionaries; they recognized that electronic music had "developed into a form that assumes all the roles of music in our culture, from concert pieces to film music and rock-and-roll,"[46] a situation that has evolved exponentially.

As with *Bye Bye Butterfly,* problematizing traditional concert music culture was also the focus of two other works by Oliveros, with similar titles, *George Washington Slept Here* (1965) and *George Washington Slept Here Too* (1965), both performed during the Tape Music Center's 1965–66 season. The former work featured Oliveros playing an amplified violin that glowed in the dark, accompanied by film and light projections by Anthony Martin and a tape that included the song "Roll over Beethoven." *George Washington Slept Here Too* calls for four performers, a grand piano, slides, and either a toy "sonic blaster" or a real pistol with blanks. The score consists of the following instructions:

> Performers one and two roll grand piano on stage. When piano is center stage, retreat a few steps and stand like guards. Then performer three walks to piano, raises lid, stands at keyboard and holds down sustaining-pedal. Then performer four walks on to stage from audience, aims gun into bass strings of piano and fires. When shot is fired all lights go out (all performers freeze) and slide projection shows. When sound has decayed, lights come on and performers exit in reverse order from the direction they came. No Bows.[47]

THE SAN FRANCISCO TAPE MUSIC CENTER, INC.

November 8 & 10   8:30 P.M.

Mario Davidovsky   Synchronisms No. 3
ELECTRONIC SOUNDS AND CELLO
Columbia-Princeton Electronic Music Center
Bonnie Hampton, Cellist

Elliott Carter   Sonata for Cello & Piano
Bonnie Hampton, Cellist
Nathan Schwartz, Pianist

Mario Davidovsky   Synchronisms No. 3
Repeat performance

INTERMISSION

Pauline Oliveros   George Washington
Anthony Martin, Projections   Slept Here Too

Pauline Oliveros   George Washington
Anthony Martin, Projections   Slept Here

Pauline Oliveros   Light piece
Anthony Martin, Projections   for David Tudor
David Tudor, Acoustologist

Speakers courtesy of James B. Lansing
Printed by Andrew Hoyem, San Francisco

The reductionist character of *George Washington Slept Here Too* resembles the "events" developed by the Fluxus movement. These pieces consisted of an action initiated by a concise instruction given to a performer. Because "events" usually involve only a single simple action, they differ from "happenings," which are more complex, often involving several simultaneous layers of activity.

Although a staged performance and therefore not a happening, Oliveros's *A Theater Piece* (1965) had many of the genre's attributes. Perhaps the composer's most ambitious theatrical presentation during this period, *A Theater Piece* was a joint effort with Elizabeth Harris, Ronald Chase, and the San Francisco Mime Troupe. It incorporated lights, slides, tape music, live performance, and a huge selection of props (including a three-foot-high hourglass, a model train, and a coffin). In the spirit of early twentieth-century avant-garde performance art, it featured a wide variety of disparate actions, such as jumping rope and other athletic activities, a "checkerboard duet," and a cameo appearance featuring Ronnie Davis in the nude playing the violin. The staged action was carefully planned, but the result was chaos and pandemonium.[48] *A Theater Piece* also involved the audience; a member of the cast walked among the audience with a tape recorder, asking for responses to the action onstage. The remarks—which in one performance ranged from complete bewilderment to an astute realization that the work attempted to bridge the gap between art and life—were subsequently played back during the performance. *A Theater Piece* included a section entitled the "bows," which was another spoof on traditional performance practices. It also made a strong political statement with a tape piece by Oliveros entitled *Rock Symphony (The SSSSSSSSSSSSSS)*. A collage using tape delay consisting of a series of rock 'n' roll hits such as "Norwegian Wood," "One Way Ticket," "I Can't Believe You Love Me," "I Fought the Law," and "It's My Life," it also included an excerpt from a speech delivered in 1964 by Mario Savio, founder of the Berkeley Free Speech movement: "At a time when the operation of the machine becomes so odious, making you so sick at heart, that you can't take part, you can't even passively take part, and you've got to put your bodies upon the gears, upon the wheels, upon the levers, upon all the apparatus, and you've got to make it stop, and you've got to indicate to the people that run it, to the people that own it, that unless you're free the machines will be prevented from working at all." Although Savio was specifically chastising the administration of the University of California for violating students' freedom of speech by declaring the area outside the main gates of the university's Berkeley campus closed to organized political activities, his exhortation is obviously leveled, in a more general sense, at the U.S. government and adds a poignant political edge to *A Theater Piece*.

A Theater Piece was performed several times at the Encore Theater during January 1966;[49] the final performance on January 23 was billed as a "Side Trip" at the close of the Trips Festival. Sender, Stewart Brand, and Ken Kesey played leading roles in organizing the festival, in which, in addition to Oliveros and Sender, Martin and Maginnis also participated. Sender was on leave from the Tape Music Center so as not to jeopardize negotiations Subotnick had arranged with Boyd Compton, an official from the Rockefeller Foundation interested in providing funding for the center. These negotiations resulted in a preliminary grant of $15,000 in 1965. The following year the foundation offered the Tape Music Center a grant of $200,000, with the provision that it affiliate itself with an academic institution.

The Tape Music Center had achieved national recognition and had finally secured substantial financial support. But, ironically, this success ultimately heralded the end of its activities: 1965–66 was its final season; in the summer of 1966, it moved to Mills College in Oakland, becoming the Mills Tape Music Center (later renamed the Center for Contemporary Music). Oliveros became the new center's first musical director, along with Martin and Maginnis as its visual and technical directors. Both Sender and Subotnick declined the offer to move to Mills. Sender joined the Morning Star Ranch commune founded by Lou Gottlieb, bass player for the Limeliters folksinging trio, in Sonoma County; Subotnick accepted a position working for the Actor's Workshop, which had moved to New York City and become the Repertory Theater of Lincoln Center. He also began working as an artist in residence at New York University's Tisch School for the Arts. Oliveros's arrangement at Mills lasted only a year; in 1967, she accepted a teaching position at the University of California, San Diego; Martin moved to New York, joining Subotnick at New York University. Maginnis left Mills in 1968 for a job running and maintaining a studio in San Francisco's Avalon Ballroom.

In the end, it is not surprising that members of the Tape Music Center resisted institutionalization. From its very beginnings, they had enjoyed a high degree of independence and self-sufficiency. Its commitment to community access and rejection of traditional concert music culture distinguished the Tape Music Center from institutionally supported electronic music studios in the United States and in Europe. Given the modest facilities at 321 Divisadero, the Tape Music Center had more in common with the small presses, underground newspapers, and filmmaker's collectives (such as Canyon Cinema, a Bay Area group of filmmakers that included Stan Brakhage, Bruce Conner, Robert Nelson, and Bruce Baillie, who presented their work at the Tape Music Center) that had increasingly emerged during the 1950s and 1960s as alternatives to corporate control and commercialization of the arts.

Canyon Cinema

SCOTT MACDONALD

During the Italian Renaissance, particular cities became known for particular styles of painting. For the past two generations, much the same has been true of American independent filmmaking: that is, specific cities have become identified with specific approaches to cinema. Boston, for example, has become known as a center for documentaries, especially for cinema verité/direct cinema, and in more recent years, personal documentaries. During the 1960s and early 1970s, New York City was identified first with what the cinema historian P. Adams Sitney has called "structural film" and later with "punk" or "No Wave" filmmaking. No American city, however, has been more identified as a center for independent filmmaking, and especially avant-garde and experimental filmmaking, than San Francisco. At least since the 1940s, the Bay Area has been home to generations of filmmakers identified with psychodrama, with recycled cinema, with spiritual aspiration, and with Queer cinema, as well as to a wide variety of accomplished film and video artists difficult to categorize.

Filmmakers have been drawn to San Francisco and its environs, or have chosen to remain in the area, not only because they have found interesting colleagues, but also because the institutions they found or created have in some cases become national and international models for the exhibition and distribution of alternative media. The original Canyon Cinema, established by the filmmaker Bruce Baillie in the tiny town of Canyon, California, behind the Berkeley hills during the early 1960s, instigated two of them: the San Francisco Cinematheque and Canyon Cinema distribution.

Baillie conceived of Canyon Cinema as a small, community-oriented organization that would sponsor informal screenings of a wide range of films, including both family fare and radical avant-garde work. Having begun making films himself, Baillie realized "that making films and showing films must go hand in hand, so I got a job at Safeway, took out a loan, and bought a projector. We got an army surplus screen and hung it up real nice in the backyard of this house we were renting."[1] Soon, Canyon was having weekly screenings: "the kids in the neighborhood gathered the community benches and chairs, and we'd sit under the trees in the summer with all the dogs and watch French or Canadian Embassy films and National Film Board of Canada stuff, along with our own."[2]

By 1962, Baillie had made contact with a good many independent filmmakers, including Bay Area locals Larry Jordan and Jordan Belson, and filmmakers from across the country: Jonas Mekas, for example, and Stan Brakhage. And Canyon had moved into Berkeley. There, Baillie worked to stay one step ahead of the authorities, who were unhappy with Canyon Cinema's embrace of nudity and various forms of political defiance and found various ways of shutting down scheduled screenings. Undaunted, Baillie—joined by the filmmaker Chick Strand, Ernest Callenbach (longtime editor of *Film Quarterly* and film book editor for the University of California Press), and others—presented films and hosted

---

1. Bruce Baillie in Scott MacDonald, *A Critical Cinema 2: Interviews with Independent Filmmakers* (Berkeley: University of California Press, 1992), 113.

2. Ibid., 113–14.

visiting filmmakers at various locations around Berkeley and San Francisco, including the anarchist café Bistro San Martin and Callenbach's backyard.[3] Decades later, when the San Franciscans Rebecca Baron and David Sherman established Total Mobile Home, widely considered the instigator for what has become a national network of microcinemas, they had Baillie's Canyon Cinema in mind.[4]

In December 1962, Canyon published the first issue of *The News,* an informal newsletter providing practical information to the local film community, which of course overlapped with communities that had developed for the other arts; Baillie was its first editor. *The News* would evolve into *The Canyon Cinemanews,* which by the end of the 1960s had become a fascinating, engaging monthly and a crucial source of both practical and theoretical insights, as well as gossip, recipes, and the occasional brouhaha, not only for the Bay Area film community, but for cineastes across the country. During its twenty-year run, *The News* was in a constant state of evolution; new volunteer editors came and went, including Chick Strand, Emory Menefee, Robert Nelson, Bruce Conner, Diane Kitchen, Henry Hills, Abigail Child, and Terry Cannon. Each new editor tended to redefine the journal's mix of columns, letters, how-to essays, polemics, experimental writing, drawings, and photographs.

By the mid-1960s Baillie had backed away from the everyday operations of Canyon, which had evolved into a dedicated group of volunteers providing three services to the community of independent filmmakers and cineastes: information *(The News),* exhibition, and distribution. The regular exhibition, now focusing on new avant-garde work, was overseen by Emory Menefee, a research chemist working for the Department of Agriculture. Canyon presented film events at various San Francisco venues, most notably at The Intersection (then housed at Glide Church Fellowship Hall in North Beach). In time, the Canyon exhibition program would be housed at the San Francisco Art Institute and would evolve into the San Francisco Cinematheque, which, under the directorship of Vincent Grenier, then Carmen Vigil and Charles Wright, then Vigil alone, and later, David Gerstein and Steve Anker, became, and has remained, one of the nation's premiere showcases for alternative cinema. The Cinematheque is currently under the directorship of Steve Polta.

During Canyon's early days, film artists who were involved with the organization often worked with artists involved with other developing arts groups, including the San Francisco Tape Music Center. Of course, many of these interrelations were informal and difficult to document. Baillie remembers that for a brief period Canyon shared the 321 Divisadero Street address with the Tape Music Center and that he and Ramon Sender "were quite close"; Baillie used tape outtakes by Sender in a film of his, and Sender composed a track for another—possibly *Here I Am* (1962).[5] In two instances, Steve Reich collaborated with Robert Nelson, who was one of the guiding spirits of Canyon Cinema during the mid-1960s. Nelson and Reich worked together, first on one of Nelson's first films, *Plastic Haircut* (1963), for which Reich supplied a tape collage. Later, the two artists col-

---

3. Baillie and Callenbach also established a small studio that they considered an "anarchists' cutting room," where anyone could come in and use the editing facilities and exchange equipment. Baillie edited his *To Parsifal* (1963) there.

4. Both Barton and Sherman mentioned this connection in an unpublished phone interview on April 24, 2004.

5. From an e-mail from Bruce Baillie to Thomas M. Welsh, February 27, 2005.

> laborated with the San Francisco Mime Troupe on *Oh Dem Watermelons* (1965), an entr'acte for the Mime Troupe's *A Minstrel Show*. Reich supplied a funny, memorable send-up of Stephen Foster that began as a follow-the-bouncing-watermelon sing-along and evolved into a looping of the word "watermelon." A satire of the then-pervasive stereotype of African Americans and watermelons, *Oh Dem Watermelons* became one of the most popular avant-garde films of the era.
>
> At the end of 1966, Canyon formalized its film distribution work by announcing the incorporation of a film distribution organization to be run by local filmmakers (Baillie, Larry Jordan, Ben Van Meter, and Robert Nelson were the original board of directors). Canyon Cinema Inc. was modeled on the New York Film-makers' Cooperative and, early on, received various forms of assistance from the New York Coop. Under the leadership of Edith Kramer (the director of the Pacific Film Archive from 1983 to 2005) and with the help of Larry Jordan, Robert Nelson, and others, Canyon organized itself so that it could remain open and flexible, but also solvent. Over the years, dozens of volunteers and poorly paid but dedicated directors allowed Canyon Cinema to become what it remains today, the most dependable distributor of 16 mm avant-garde films in this country and perhaps anywhere in the world. Dominic Angerame has been Canyon Cinema's indefatigable director since 1985.

In purely aesthetic terms, composers at the Tape Music Center also diverged from the mainstream. As Ramon Sender suggests in his description of *Desert Ambulance* as "a vehicle of mercy sent into the wasteland of (academic) modern music," they saw themselves as pursuing an alternative path away from academic high modernism and its obsession with technology, total serialism, and other theoretical approaches to electronic music. Their interest in "happenings" and other theatrical forms placed the composers at the Tape Music Center within the resurgence of avant-gardism that began after World War II and had gained momentum in the early 1960s. They also developed an antiestablishment stance that went beyond the arts scene, reaching into sociopolitical developments. The center's involvement in the Trips Festival was symptomatic of its place within this broader cultural landscape.

Creative activity at the Tape Music Center paralleled and in some cases foreshadowed the political and social upheaval of the 1960s. For example, the Tape Music Center's emphasis on breaking down disciplinary boundaries in the arts heralded the counterculture's advocacy of removing barriers on a much larger social scale. Similarly, the Tape Music Center's antiestablishment stance against traditional concert music and the academic mainstream anticipated the oppositional politics that became more and more widespread during the 1960s and 1970s. Of course, this connection between art and politics occurred in many forms in other venues around the country and the world. But the dynamic interplay between avant-garde art and the counterculture that emerged in the freethinking cultural environment of San Francisco resulted in a radical aesthetic applied to electronic music that inspired unique works of enduring quality, which are at the same time a reflection of a turbulent period in American history.

NOTES

1. This plan remained unrealized, but Buchla did add the synthesizer to the general "mix" on the final day of the festival.

2. Theodore Roszak, "Youth and the Great Refusal," *The Nation* 25 (March 25, 1968): 406, and id., *The Making of a Counter Culture: Reflections on the Technocratic Society and Its Youthful Opposition* (1969; reprint, Berkeley: University of California Press, 1995).

3. See, e.g., Arthur Marwick, *The Sixties* (New York: Oxford University Press, 1998), which examines cultural revolutions in France, Britain, and Italy, as well as in the United States.

4. Michael Davidson, *The San Francisco Renaissance* (Cambridge: Cambridge University Press, 1989), 11. See also Kenneth Rexroth, "Thar's Culture in Them Thar Hills," *New York Times Sunday Magazine,* February 7, 1965.

5. Frank Norris, "An Opening for Novelists: Great Opportunities for Fiction Writers in San Francisco," *The San Francisco Wave* 16 (May 22, 1897): 7, quoted in Davidson, *San Francisco Renaissance,* 11.

6. Michael Hicks, *Henry Cowell: Bohemian* (Urbana: University of Illinois Press, 2002), 3.

7. Rexroth, "Thar's Culture in Them Thar Hills," 78.

8. Richard Cándida Smith, *Utopia and Dissent: Art, Poetry, and Politics in California* (Berkeley: University of California Press, 1995), xx.

9. For a survey of electronic studios around the world, see Hugh Davies, *Répertoire internationale des musiques électroacoustiques / International electronic music catalog* (Paris: Groupe de recherches musicales de l'O.R.T.F.; Trumansburg, N.Y.: Independent Electronic Music Center; Cambridge, Mass.: MIT Press, 1968).

10. See p. 45 below.

11. Ramon Sender and William Maginnis, interviewed by David W. Bernstein and Maggi Payne, in the present volume.

12. A list of events at the workshop from June 20 through August 27, 1960, can be found in the Pauline Oliveros Papers, MSS 102, box 6, Mandeville Special Collections Library, University of California, San Diego.

13. Alfred Frankenstein, "New Music—Wacky and Interesting," *San Francisco Chronicle,* June 15, 1961, 36.

14. Heidi von Gunden, *The Music of Pauline Oliveros* (Metuchen, N.J.: Scarecrow Press, 1983), 9.

15. The score for Riley's *Concert* was published in *An Anthology* (New York: La Monte Young and Jackson Mac Low, 1963), a collection of works by avant-garde writers, artists, and musicians, which Young edited with Jackson Mac Low.

16. For the composer's description of *M . . . Mix,* see his liner notes accompanying the compact disk entitled *Music for "The Gift"* (Organ of Corti 1, 1998).

17. According to Heidi von Gunden, the KPFA improvisation sessions occurred in 1957 (von Gunden, *Music of Pauline Oliveros,* 32–33). However, the initial improvisations were done expressly for Claire Falkenstein's film *Polyester Moon* when Falkenstein was teaching at the California School of Fine Arts (now known as the San Francisco Art Institute). Thomas M. Welsh's archival research has revealed that Falkenstein was a visiting professor there only in the summer of 1958. Thus, the improvisations more likely took place that year.

18. See Oliveros's essay, "Memoir of a Community Enterprise," in the present volume.

19. Terry Riley, interviewed by David W. Bernstein and Maggi Payne, in the present volume.

20. Von Gunden notes that Lukas Foss's Improvisation Group was created in 1957 at the University of California, Los Angeles, around the same time as the KPFA improvisations. These developments occurred independently, and as Oliveros points out, there were aesthetic differences between the two groups (von Gunden, *Music of Pauline Oliveros,* 33).

21. Press release dated December 14, 1961, Pauline Oliveros Papers, MSS 102, box 6, Mandeville Special Collections Library, University of California, San Diego. Neither Sender nor Oliveros recalls whether Cohen's lighting was actually used in the December 18 concert. It is unlikely that it was since Cohen's participation is not noted in Alfred Frankenstein's review of the event (see n. 23 below). The plans, however, are noteworthy given the later interest in light projection documented below.

22. Morton Subotnick, interviewed by David W. Bernstein and Maggi Payne, in the present volume.

23. Alfred Frankenstein, "Conservatory Test: 'Romantic' Side of Electronics," *San Francisco Chronicle,* December 20, 1961, 40; id., "Stimulating Sounds Too New to Be Named," *San Francisco Chronicle,* March 26, 1962, 40.

24. Michael Kirby, "The New Theatre," *Tulane Drama Review* 10 (Winter 1965): 23–43.

25. R. G. Davis, *The San Francisco Mime Troupe: The First Ten Years* (Palo Alto, Calif.: Ramparts Press, 1975), 25.

26. Score to *City Scale, Tulane Drama Review* 10 (Winter 1965): inserted after p. 186.

27. Richard Kostelanetz, *The Theatre of Mixed Means* (New York: Dial Press, 1968), 172.

28. Ramon Sender, notes for score to *City Scale, Tulane Drama Review* 10 (1965): inserted after p. 186.

29. For a description of a similar independent electronic music studio established in the late 1950s in Ann Arbor, Michigan, see Gordon Mumma, "An Electronic Music Studio for the Independent Composer," *Journal of the Audio Engineering Society* 12 (July 1964): 240–44.

30. See p. 43 below.

31. See pp. 43–44 below.

32. In the late 1950s, Milton Cohen, working in Ann Arbor, also developed a light show, which he called the "Space Theater," featuring music by Robert Ashley and Gordon Mumma. These

activities anticipated the creation of the "Once Festival." See Leta Miller's extensive liner notes entitled "Once and Again: The Evolution of a Legendary Festival," in *Music from the Once Festival, 1961–1966,* New World Records Box Set 80567 (2003).

33. Charles Perry, *The Haight Ashbury: A History* (New York: Random House, 1984, 2005), 66ff. See also Kerry Brougher, "Visual-Music Culture," in Kerry Brougher, Jeremy Strick, Ari Weisman, and Judith Zicker, *Visual Music: Synaesthesia in Art and Music since 1900* (New York: Thames & Hudson, 2005), 159.

34. In its concert form, *A Theater Piece after Sonnet No. 47 of Petrarch* (1963) was called *Mandolin* (1963), which existed in several versions without the sets, dancers, and sometimes the violist. Portions of the electronic music in *Mandolin* date back to two of Subotnick's earlier works: *Sound Blocks: An Heroic Vision* (1961) and *Yod* (1962). He also used these materials and the title *Mandolin* for a tape piece played at Sonics IV on April 20, 1962. A program for a Composers' Forum concert on April 22, 1964, lists the date for *Mandolin* as 1961–63, reflecting the complex genesis of this work. (See Thomas M. Welsh's chronology in the present volume.)

35. Callahan, a talented engineer, left the Tape Music Center to form (with Gerd Stern) USCO, an artists' collective specializing in intermedia productions and installations.

36. Frankenstein, "Electronic Music—Mysterious, Romantic," *San Francisco Chronicle,* February 5, 1964, 43.

37. A cassette recording of an excerpt from the "Tudorfest" version of *Atlas Eclipticalis* accompanies the Canadian new music periodical *Musicworks 52* (1992). The beautiful Tape Music Center interpretation is especially noteworthy, given the earlier well-known "sabotage" of the work by the New York Philharmonic. Recordings of the entire Tudorfest are preserved in the Mills College archives. See listings in the "Archival Recordings" section in the present volume.

38. Edward Strickland, *Minimalism: Origins* (Bloomington: Indiana University Press, 1993), 174.

39. Tony Martin, interviewed by David W. Bernstein and Maggi Payne, in the present volume.

40. Frankenstein, "Music Like None Other on Earth," *San Francisco Chronicle,* November 8, 1964, 28.

41. Strickland, *Minimalism,* 184.

42. Dean Wallace, "Musical Peanuts, and Eden Too," *San Francisco Chronicle,* May 4, 1965.

43. For a detailed description and analysis of *Pieces of Eight,* see von Gunden, *Music of Pauline Oliveros,* 71–78.

44. Mario Davidovsky, *Synchronism No. 3* (1965) for cello and magnetic tape; Robert Erickson, *Ricecar à 5* (1966) for trombone and taped trombone sounds.

45. For a feminist interpretation of *Bye Bye Butterfly,* see Martha Mockus, "Sounding Out: Lesbian Feminism and the Music of Pauline Oliveros" (Ph.D. diss., University of Minnesota, 1999), 13–48.

46. *User's Manual for The Modular Electronic Music System* published by Buchla Associates, 1966.

47. Pauline Oliveros Papers, MSS 102, box 6, Mandeville Special Collections Library, University of California, San Diego. The score was also published in *Soundings* 1 (1972): 9.

48. Oliveros's plan for *Theater Piece* is in the Pauline Oliveros Papers, MSS 102, box 6, Mandeville Special Collections Library, University of California, San Diego.

49. As indicated on a sheet entitled "Income and expenses—Encore, Mime-Dance-Sound," Pauline Oliveros Papers, MSS 102, box 6, Mandeville Special Collections Library, University of California, San Diego.

The San Francisco Tape Music Center—
A Report, 1964

RAMON SENDER

When the San Francisco Tape Music Center was founded in 1961, neither of the two composers who founded it had thought much beyond the immediate need for a studio for the production of sounds by electronic means and for a concert hall in which to present programs of an experimental nature, the sort that might not readily fit into the concerts of already existing musical organizations. Looking back over the past three years, it now seems possible to see the emergence of a specific direction that has come out of the experiences of these years rather than out of any predetermined concept of where the center was ultimately heading.

Throughout this period we have remained independent of any university or college connection, and retained a balance in our relation to the community between our activities as a cultural agency on the one hand and a sound-recording studio on the other. Behind this balance has been the feeling that it should be possible for the composer to live from his work; that the solution to the composer's place in our society does not lie in having to choose between writing within the accepted "avant-garde" traditions for performances aimed at some sort of musical in-group, or "going commercial."

We have felt that somewhere there should be a place where the composer can find brought together all the necessities of his art in an atmosphere conducive to his developing his own personal utterance free from the pull and the tug of stylistic schools and from the competitive scramble that typifies much of the musical activity of today. In the race to make a "name," to win the right fellowships and awards, the young artist is drawn into a way of living that is completely opposed to the basic values of the art itself. We have often thought that this personality-centering syndrome (as much the fault of the public as the artist) might be countered by presenting works anonymously, as contributions to the field of music, thus focusing attention on the work itself and not on who produced it.

Somewhere there should be a place where the fragmented elements of our musical life could be melted together and recast through the reestablishment of the artist's dialogue with his community in a new and vital way. A place where a new music would find a dynamic and vital expression for our own era, and by its own vitality not countenancing the isolative practices of the cliques and factions that sicken the musical life of today.

There is growing awareness on the part of the young composers all over the country that they are not going to find the answers they are looking for in the analysis and composition seminars of the academies. Some retreat from the "avant-garde" music environment, live marginally on the fringe of the community, or attempt to work isolated from the musicians and concert groups. They have insulated themselves by this isolation from the sickness of the culture, but too often also from their own creative potential. Others have banded together and have produced concerts of their own works outside the usual organizations. The struggle of these groups for survival, and their high mortality rate, creates a situation in which it can be regarded as miraculous if the participants manage to avoid the pitfalls of destructive reactionism or sensationalism. On our 1964 summer tour in the Midwest, I often felt we were expected to perform amusing antics during concerts, and that some in the audience were disappointed in not witnessing some sort of scandalous behavior on our part. "Avant-garde" is coming to mean a comedy act, and unfortunately, composers are so eager for some sort of real contact with an audience that many set out to provoke at least the response of laughter.

To find the answer to these problems will require more than just demanding that composers turn to satisfying the needs of their audience. Nothing will be solved by turning out proletarian music in the fashion of the Soviets. First of all there must come about the recognition that until the composers' needs are met there can be no hope of somehow breaking through the encysted layer of action-reaction-action, the oscillation of meaningless trends away from meaningless established practices.

Society must recognize its dependence upon, and need for, a truly communicative experience. It must be willing to do more than wait for the talented individual who somehow has survived the struggle and remained intact enough as a person to produce some valuable work. The "cream-skimming" theory—that the talented few always float to the top—just is not true.

I would like to see the center become a community-sponsored composers' guild, which would offer the young composer a place to work, to perform, to come into contact with others in his field, all away from the institutional environment. Each composer would, through his contact with the center, be encouraged to fulfill his own musical needs and to develop his own personal language. He would have the advantage and support of all facilities of the center, for rehearsals and performances of his music, for contact with other composers and musicians, for work in the electronic music studios. He would be encouraged to involve himself in the musical life of the community-at-large. The community in turn would be offered the services of the center as a music-producing agency for films, for plays, for churches, and for schools. Such a program, carried through in detail, could produce a revolution. It would, I believe, in five years' time, create a new cultural environment in at least our local area. Working closely with musicians' organizations and cultural civil groups, it could begin to break up some of the stagnation of our own local cultural environment, such as the traditional repertory of the symphony and opera, the pork-barrel city band, the entrenched conservatism of some of the chamber music organizations.

None of this can happen unless others want it to happen aside from those directly involved in living these problems. And ideally, this support should come primarily from the local community, and secondarily from either the federal government or foundations.

We are all aware of the power of communications over the lives of a people. Direct control of communications media is a necessity for the dictator. The arts are communicative mediums also, and in totalitarian systems they too are subject to rigorous controls. The totalitarian governments are in actual fact much more realistic than ours, in that they recognize the power inherent in communication through an art form and control it accordingly. In the United States we are slowly beginning to move away from the notion of art as amusement, and to realize that a painting or a piece of music is much more than a "mood-setter"—that it contains the potential for a deep and moving human experience.

The San Francisco Tape Music Center up until now has served basically the two functions outlined in the first paragraph. But in fulfilling these functions it has become the focal point in the city for experimental events in the arts, with the primary emphasis on music, film, and dance. This coming together of artists has been an important part of the experience here. Out of this coming together there have been many important discoveries in performance procedures. A concert at the center often contains a multiplicity of elements, both visual and aural, and can be guaranteed to be a very different experience from a concert in the usual sense of the word.

The other important function of the center has been in its making available sound-producing and recording equipment to composers. This year the participating composers will number more than twelve, with the majority of them coming from universities and colleges in the Bay Area. The experience of working with electronically produced sounds and tape recorders is a very meaningful one for the composer. It used to be said that every composer must confront Arnold Schoenberg's "Method of Composing with Twelve Tones" and come to some sort of working agreement with it. Today the composer cannot afford to ignore the experience of working with tape. It is apt to deal many of his preconceptions a serious blow. I know of no composer whose music has ever been the same after he has once worked with tape, and in all cases the effect has been a freeing one. Suddenly he has the choice of writing the piece for live performers or for tape, a choice not available to him before, and he finds himself viewing the whole concept of performance from a new vantage point.

One of the most exciting aspects of the work at the center has been the combining of visual effects with both live performance and tape. A work such as Morton Subotnick's *Mandolin: A Theater Piece* combines live viola, recorded voice, and piano, recorded electronic and concrete sounds, slide projections, and View-graph projections into a total experience of overwhelming beauty. Improvised pieces using live performers, tape, and light projections also have proved to be a moving experience both for the participants and for the audience. *Desert Ambulance,* a work of my own, combines recorded instrumental sounds, live accordion, slides, and film. It also showed the efficacy of combining new visual elements with more traditional concert procedures. As one of the local critics said after the performance of *Mandolin* and *Desert Ambulance,* just before we took them on tour, there seems to be a new art form in the process of being born.

This year, in cooperation with another contemporary music group, we will begin the bringing together of a library of scores and tapes of Bay Area composers to serve as an information service for persons interested in knowing about what is going on in the area musically. We also hope to expand the library into one which will contain new music from all over the world, so that local composers and musicians can keep informed about what is happening elsewhere. Later we will acquire equipment for the reproduction of scores, so that new works can be copied and mailed to performing groups all over the world. Copyrighting and royalties will be handled for member composers, as well as other services of a similar nature. Thus, little by little, we hope to encompass the whole area of services necessary for the dissemination of new music, the protection and encouragement of the composer, and the creation of an atmosphere conducive to the production of original and valuable work.

About the electronic music studio: the studio seems to be evolving into three distinct production areas. The first, for the production of the sound material of the piece and the "shaping" of it by the use of attack and decay control devices. The final sounds produced in this area are then recorded and the tapes are loaded on the sixty tape carriages of the playback control unit. By means of multiple-channel recording and automatic selection of different segments of tape, up to 720 separate sounds can be stored in the unit. Once loaded, the unit can then be "played" by the composer, thus combining the sounds in any order he desires. From this stage he takes his completed material to the third area, where the final editing and mixing is done. By separating the composing process into three distinct areas we will be able to accommodate up to three composers working at the same time.

A question we are often asked is: "Where did you get the money for all this equipment?" What we have been able to build up until this point has been made possible through the careful use of whatever income was earned by the studio, through the donation of equipment by interested companies, or, in some cases, by the long-term loan of certain items. The rest we have been able to buy reasonably or have built for us by one of the three or four electronic engineers and technicians who have worked with us over the past three years. There are still many pieces of equipment, which would be very useful, but that we cannot afford at the present time. However, we feel confident that before long we will be able to acquire what is necessary for the smooth operation of the studio. We also feel confident that many of the long-term goals set out in the preceding pages can be met, and that these coming years should prove an exciting adventure both for ourselves and for the community in which we live.

An Overview of the Tape Music Center's Goals, Autumn 1964

RAMON SENDER

The San Francisco Tape Music Center is a nonprofit corporation developed and maintained by a group of composers and creatively oriented around engineers. The group is dedicated to the concept of promoting creative experiments in sound as music. It is founded on the firm belief that artists can and must extend their expressive vocabularies to include imaginative use of the materials of today. Furthermore, there must be an outlet for a healthy relationship between the products of these efforts and the ever-growing audience interested and involved in new modes of artistic expression. It is to these ends that the Tape Music Center was founded, exists, and is determined to continue.

The use of electronic devices as a tool for musical composition has become increasingly challenging to composers in all parts of the world. In response to the growing interest, electronic music studios have been established in many cities. Some European studios are under the auspices of electronics manufacturers such as Philips of the Netherlands and Siemans Verlag of Munich; others are operated by the European radio systems such as Radio Milan and Radio Cologne.

The largest and best-equipped studio in the United States is the Columbia-Princeton Electronic Music Center, which was founded under a Rockefeller Foundation grant. Other studios exist in this country, whether privately operated or under the auspices of a university.

The San Francisco Tape Music Center was founded in 1961 by composers Ramon Sender and Morton Subotnick in order to provide a studio for the production of electronic music in the Bay Area. At that time, the San Francisco Conservatory of Music provided the space and opportunity to gather together equipment in a temporary studio, thus centralizing the activities, which had previously gone on in the individual composers' homes.

The center gave a series of concerts under the title SONICS, at which not only local electronic tape works were performed, but also those from the already established studios in Europe and North America. Composers included Milton Babbitt, Luciano Berio, Luigi Nono, Pauline Oliveros, Henri Pousseur, Terry Riley, Ramon Sender, Morton Subotnick, James Tenney, Phil Winsor, and many others. The studio was modest; a lack of sound-generating equipment forced the group to search for new sound possibilities within everyday objects, somewhat similar to the methods and techniques used at the musique concrète studio in Paris. The use of the contact microphones on metal and other objects, and a piano soundboard for reverberation were the basic simple tools. The new sounds found their way into the improvisational compositions performed by composers on the same programs as the tape works.

The public and the press response to the SONICS series was encouraging, and those involved found themselves in a new relationship to the audience rather than the traditional concert hall situation. This stimulated new concepts in the performance procedures, and, by the end of the season, the improvisational compositions had become large collaborations between composers, painters, and dancers. Participants included members of the Dancers' Workshop company, painters Laurel Johnson and Anthony Martin, and composers Pauline Oliveros, Loren Rush, Philip Winsor, Morton Subotnick, and Ramon Sender.

In June of 1962 an offer from a friend of a large Victorian house was gratefully accepted as a temporary location. We also began to acquire equipment of a more sophisticated nature, including a six-speed, three-channel tape recorder, sine- and square- wave generators, and more adequate patching and mixing facilities. In September of the same year another series of concerts was initiated and continued throughout the winter. A number of local groups were invited to participate in the programs and to present events of an experimental nature. The intention was to further explore the potentials inherent in the newly formed concepts of production and performance techniques made evident by the previous season's experiences. Emphasis was placed upon the freedom of each group to realize these concepts within its own medium. The participants included the poets Robert Duncan and Robin Blaser, director Lee Breuer and company, painters Jess Collins and Robert LaVigne, and the R. G. Davis Mime Troupe.

The new series acquired a critical and enthusiastic audience whose active participation in the programs contributed greatly to the success of the series. The performances were more polished than those of the previous season, each group bringing to itself and the audience a fuller realization of the potentials and limitations of what can now be called "theater compositions."

The interest was not only local. The Tape Music Center was invited to produce a program at the Vancouver Festival in February 1963. For this program Ramon Sender, Morton Subotnick, and Robert LaVigne produced a theater composition entitled *Transformation.*

In March of 1963 the San Francisco Tape Music Center found a building that was ideally suited to its needs. Located at 321 Divisadero Street, near the geographical center of the city, the building contains two small halls downstairs, one seating about 100, the other about 50 persons, plus a soundproof control room and three other rooms. Upstairs there is large room sufficiently isolated from the rest to afford a good environment for the production studio proper. A three-year lease was signed in May, with a three-year option. The Tape Music Center in turn was interested in KPFA-FM and the Dancers' Workshop subleasing space and sharing in the joint venture of creating a place where a number of groups with common interests can come together.

For the 1963–1964 season, the center scheduled two series of four concerts each. Works presented on the first series (final concert February 1964) included *Synchronisms* for flute and tape by Mario Davidovsky, *Visages* by Luciano Berio, songs by John Cage and *Fontana Mix with Aria,* both sung by Cathy Berberian, *A Theater Piece after Sonnet No. 47 of Petrarch* by Morton Subotnick, and some electronic compositions from both this country and abroad. The second series will include performances by pianists Leonard Stein and David Tudor, and theater pieces by Pauline Oliveros and Ramon Sender as well as light and sound events by other local artists, and tapes from France and Poland. The second series will end in June, to be followed by a summer series.

Ramon Sender and William Maginnis

INTERVIEWED BY DAVID W. BERNSTEIN AND MAGGI PAYNE

The history of the San Francisco Tape Music Center begins with the first strikes with hammer and cold chisel by Ramon Sender into the cement floor of the San Francisco Conservatory of Music's attic when he started to build the electronic music studio later used to create many of the works featured during the Sonics concerts. Sender, born in Madrid, Spain, in 1934, arrived in America in 1939. The son of a Spanish Republican freedom fighter and novelist, he is as much a revolutionary as was his father. As a cofounder of the San Francisco Tape Music Center, he cultivated a radically individualistic musical voice. And, as a prominent member of the San Francisco counterculture, he coproduced the Trips Festival with Stewart Brand and cofounded the Morning Star Ranch commune in Sonoma County with the Limeliter Lou Gottlieb. In the following interview, Sender talks about his extensive traditional training as a young composer and his interests in electronic music, indeterminacy, and improvisation.

The composer and percussionist William Maginnis began working at the Tape Music Center in the summer of 1964 as a studio technician, replacing Michael Callahan. Maginnis was responsible for maintaining the studio at 321 Divisadero Street. He was also the first to create a piece on the center's newly acquired Buchla 100 Series Modular Electronic Music System (the "Buchla Box"). Maginnis and Sender participate here in a lively discussion of the Tape Music Center's rich history. The interview ranges from the first concerts in the Sonics series to the fire at 1537 Jones Street, and then from what is arguably the Tape Music Center's most exciting period at 321 Divisadero to the difficult decision to move the facility to Mills College in Oakland.

BERNSTEIN: Could you say something about your composition studies with [Robert] Erickson and [Darius] Milhaud? I also noticed that you studied harmony with Elliot Carter.

SENDER: I began studying harmony with Elliot Carter privately during the spring of my sophomore year off between high school and my next classroom experience.

13 **RAMON SENDER.**

BERNSTEIN: Where was that?

SENDER: That was in New York. We just basically did the Walter Piston harmony book. He tried to persuade me to listen [to more] modern music than I was listening to. So we had some discussions about [Alban] Berg's *Violin Concerto* and things like that. He was a very gentle soul and was probably just about right for what I needed. That next year I just studied with him and had counterpoint lessons with Ferdinand Davis at Hunter College, species counterpoint of all things, good God!

[I also studied] piano with George Copeland, who was my main music teacher at the time. He had been the first person to play Debussy's piano music in this country—one of the specialists in the French and Spanish impressionists. Our piano lessons usually lasted from ten in the morning until four o'clock in the afternoon.

[My lessons included] a homemade Italian lunch, and I learned how to cook Italian style. He was quite an influence on me. He was kind of a father surrogate in many ways. He convinced my American mother, Julia, that any musician had to be finished in Europe. It turned out that the Italian conservatories would let you in tuition free if you passed the entrance exam, so we figured it was actually cheaper for me to go to the Conservatorio di Santa Cecilia in Rome than to continue studying privately. [My composition] teacher there was very nice, but he kept patting me on the head saying, "My boy. The composition course is ten years here. You don't have to start writing like this for another four!"

BERNSTEIN: [Laughs]

SENDER: I found this discouraging because I was into discovering Schoenberg and Bartók. I was having a marvelous time listening to new music at the RAI orchestra concerts next to the foreign students' dormitory. And so I finally started taking my music to an American composer at the American Academy—Alexei Haieff.

Alexei was one of the neoclassical students in the Boulanger school and despite this, although I showed him some piano pieces that were serial and very derivative of Schoenberg's piano pieces, he was very charmed and said, "You really should show these to Boulanger." I said, "Well, all right, I am going to Paris to meet my mother and sister later, so maybe I will." He was very encouraging and I kept showing him stuff. That next spring I went to Vienna and from there to Paris, and indeed I did take my material over to Boulanger. She had actually a full classroom set up in her apartment, and a bunch of students were laboring over some sort of exam. I explained to her that I brought some pieces in the twelve-tone style, and she gave me her "what's wrong with twelve-tone music" lecture.

I didn't even open my briefcase. I just thanked her very politely and left. Alexei later told me he was disappointed because he thought I should have forged ahead. Anyway, I'm very glad I did not, because I would have been just another one of [laughs] nearly one hundred and fifty American composers whose minds were dented by Nadia.

BERNSTEIN: Milhaud wasn't enamored with the twelve-tone system either, but he was more open-minded.

SENDER: Well, yes. After that I came back to the States. I went to Brandeis and took graduate courses and some other classes. I remember that I received an "F" on my social science final because I refused to answer questions such as "Give three reasons for the downfall of the Roman empire" in the expected manner. Instead, I filled three exam booklets with paraphrases from Bergson about how there was no such thing as causality. Well, in truth I was in love, so I dropped out to get married and we moved to New York. There, after some months thrashing about trying to earn a living, I finally took a class with Henry Cowell at Columbia's School of General Studies. Cowell was a very affable, gentle soul who had been thoroughly traumatized by his jail time for being gay—the details escape me. And then, let's see, there were some intervening years. First, I got caught up in Zen Buddhism during a summer in North Beach on the edge of the beat scene in 1957. When I returned east glowing from a two-week solitary retreat on Mount Tamalpais, I landed in a very cultish coeducational Christian family monastery. Other than some minor events there, nothing else musical really happened until I returned to San Francisco.

During the summer of 1957, I had looked up Alan Rich, who then was music director for KPFA-FM in Berkeley. He introduced me to Loren Rush, and I asked Loren, "Who do you think is the best teacher in composition out here?" And he said, "Robert Erickson." So I filed the name away, and two years later, when I came back, I looked Bob up, and he talked me into taking a full course load at the San Francisco Conservatory, and that was the beginning of my three years with Bob, which were wonderful. He was just a terrific teacher.

After graduating from the conservatory, I was so surprised that I'd gotten a degree, I just had the momentum up, so I went to Mills and did a year with Milhaud and then ran out of money and took a year off and then came back and did the second year with Milhaud. So that's the story.

BERNSTEIN: When did you first become interested in electronic music?

SENDER: I first became interested in electronic music while I was in New York.

BERNSTEIN: Before you studied with Erickson?

SENDER: Oh, way before! I was living in New York, working odd jobs, and I hung out a little with the Elliot Carter and Milton Babbitt group. They had this concert demonstration where Louis and Bebe Barron showed their stuff. Louis got up there and demonstrated some of his little circuitries and networks. He received what I felt were a lot of very intolerant, kind of down-their-noses looks from the New York composers, who considered his approach very lowbrow. Then afterwards they played Stockhausen's *Gesang der Jünglinge* [1955–56], and I was just blown away. I'd never heard it before. And I think that really was the point where I got interested in using tape, although it took me a while to pull it all together. There weren't any real tape recorders at that time. I did do a dance piece for a young dancer and rented a wire recorder and then recorded it for her on that and then had a record made for her. That was my first experience in any kind of recording. Although that's not quite true—I used to go in every couple years and record a direct-to-disk for my dad so he could hear what pieces I was working on.

BERNSTEIN: What strikes me about your early musical training is that when you started composing *Four Sanskrit Hymns* [1961] and all those other works, you really had an individual voice. It seems you had broken away from academic music.

SENDER: Oh, exactly! I was way overtrained early on. [Laughs] If I were to put together a music education program for a young person, I would not have done it the way they did it for me. There came a point when I was so self-conscious about composition that I was all tied up in knots. The tape recorder was a great "freeing" device. It gave me, I felt, the same freedom a painter has to put a stroke on a canvas and stand back and [look at] it.

BERNSTEIN: Your works, starting in the early 1960s, reveal a unique voice. But there are, I think, some things that make me think of your earlier training. For instance, in the *Sanskrit Hymns,* you have simultaneous tempi working in the instrumental group. Did you get that from Cowell, or . . . ?

SENDER: No, I got that from Elliot [Carter]. I realized that if I wrote in three simultaneous tempi, the parts would look easy on the page and the conductor would have all the trouble. [Laughs] It's the way they come together that's a little complicated.

BERNSTEIN: Why did you use three tape recorders for that piece?

SENDER: I wanted the room full of sound, and I wanted some sound from the rear. I did left, right, and rear; it was great. I guess I could have gone quadraphonic. That word didn't exist in those days.

BERNSTEIN: What sorts of sounds are on those tapes?

SENDER: Well, mostly me banging on things. I used the piano as a source of a lot of sounds, making harmonics, and what have you. One of my favorite sounds, actually, I discovered at two in the morning. I had a very large Tibetan gong that I borrowed. I found if I scraped it with a very stiff piece of plastic and then dropped the pitch about three or four times, going from high speed to low, I finally got this sound that sounded like a whole bunch of monks chanting. And it just raised the hairs on my head. It was such a beautiful sound that I added it at the very end of the piece.

PAYNE: In 1961, you and Pauline Oliveros started the first Bay Area electronic music studio at the San Francisco Conservatory.

SENDER: Yes. I went there in 1959 to study with Robert Erickson, and Pauline was attending the composition classes, and we met in 1959 when we were both interested in improvisation—due to Bob's interest in improvisation—and tape recording. The conservatory had one home-style Ampex that was two-track playback, one-track record. And I remember how excited I was the day I realized I could record on one track, turn it over and then record a second track. That was my first experience with "sound-on-sound," as it was called.

MAGINNIS: But you had to do it backwards?

SENDER: Yes, but then I think I figured out a way to make the spindle pull it backwards.

MAGINNIS: You could loop it around.

PAYNE: Right. You could cast the tape around the pinch roller in the opposite direction.

SENDER: Anyway, all of those early tapes had wonderful 60-cycle hum, too. I think in 1961, Bob Erickson was presenting the Composers' Workshop. And for that, I decided to do *Four Sanskrit Hymns*.

I basically ruined Bob Erickson's classroom for three months by collecting every conceivable sound-making device I could find and every old clunky tape recorder. I did finally bang together three mono tapes that could be cued in and out of the ensemble. Then, by that time, I was hooked. I got some money together of my own and I started with a cold chisel and a hammer on the cement floor attic of the conservatory banging holes into the cement so that I could lay down a floor plate, a two-by-four, and start constructing a wall to wall off the back of the attic, which now is a library. I'm glad to say my wall stood for many years afterward. I built the room, and I had a friend, David Talbot, who was working for KPFA as a technician, build me a small board. Another friend, Richard Wahlberg, who had a small recording studio in his home, sold me an Ampex 601–2, was it?

MAGINNIS: Oh, that's right. Yes.

SENDER: You know, the ones in the tanned leather cases.

MAGINNIS: Yes, Samsonite cases.

SENDER: When they performed the *Sanskrit Hymns,* Morton Subotnick also had a piece on that program, a piano piece that Marvin Tartak played. And we got to know each other then. But it wasn't until we started the Sonics series in the fall of 1961 that Mort became really interested in participating. And by then for the first concert I had asked Terry Riley, Pauline, and Phil Winsor all to create new pieces in the new studio. And they all did. I remember Terry's involved a loop that was so long it went all the way around the room. It was called *M . . . Mix* [1960–61].

It was a "bring your own speaker concert." We had a dummy keyboard, a practice keyboard, that a friend of mine had put microswitches under a number of the keys, and we wired up a speaker to each key so the composer could sit at the keyboard and play his piece around the room.

PAYNE: Wonderful.

SENDER: Of course, every speaker was mismatched. We had about twelve speakers

14 **MORTON SUBOTNICK AND RAMON SENDER.**

up. Then we had our live improvisation, which I think was Pauline, Phil Winsor, me, and perhaps Laurel Johnson. And then Mort came along and said, "Wow, that's great. Can I be in the next one?"

Mort had a small studio in his garage, which had also an Ampex 601–2, and we were both trying to get ours fixed so that you could turn off the erase head. I remember, to do it correctly, you had to load the voltage onto some other little capacitor, or something.

MAGINNIS: No, you just had to put a resistor across it.

SENDER: Was that what it was? Anyway, the Sonics series was really the start of our collaboration. We went on to have four or five concerts, with the series ending with a "happening." We had a wonderful time, I must say, with that. We had a washing machine full of rocks that was on a long extension cord going down that main conservatory corridor. It really was a wonderful sound. It was unforgettable.

BERNSTEIN: *Traversals* [1961] was your piece on the first Sonics concert.

SENDER: Yes.

BERNSTEIN: And I know about the sounds that you used for that, but I also noted that you used an Echoplex.

SENDER: Oh God, yes, I fell in love with the Echoplex. That's sort of an embarrassment at this point.

BERNSTEIN: Why?

SENDER: Well, I don't know. The piece is just nothing but long echoes and I . . .

BERNSTEIN: I think it's a good piece. And, as you mentioned earlier, for that same concert you had a setup with multiple speakers and a keyboard with the microswitches. I know that all the other composers had the opportunity to use that setup. But were you thinking about it with *Traversals* in mind, specifically?

SENDER: I was thinking of *Traversals,* yes. I created *Traversals* to be able to play it around the room.

BERNSTEIN: And it seems that a lot of your other pieces also involve some form of spatialization. It seems to me that was an interest of yours. Of course, electronic music composers are interested in that in general. But, for example, *Parade* [1962] . . .

SENDER: *Parade* was a disaster . . .

BERNSTEIN: Really?

SENDER: . . . but it was definitely going to be very spatial. I added some loops of faint sounds that kind of sounded like they might be a parade, but they might not be. But what I learned in that concert was never, never replug your audio cables in the middle of a concert.

BERNSTEIN: Why, because the setup didn't work?

SENDER: I didn't get it right. I wanted the speakers in the hall and I wanted the parade to sound as if it would come closer down the hall as the people were marching into the concert hall.

BERNSTEIN: *Kronos* [1962] is another work from that same year.

SENDER: Right.

BERNSTEIN: What type of sounds did it use?

SENDER: Well, let's see. There's a white noise sound at the beginning, which is me running a pair of scissors over a large sheet of metal and using the men's room as an echo [chamber]. That was one thing I used. I also gathered a bunch of the [conservatory] students after the chorus practice and pulled them up to the attic and just told them to improvise and I'd record them, which I did. Then I used some of the sounds from their improvisations by standing a speaker against the soundboard of an upright piano on one end and poking a microphone in it at the other end of the soundboard and then wedging the sustaining pedal down. I was able to get a kind of a burst of vocal sound that would echo for a long time.

BERNSTEIN: Did you use any oscillators?

SENDER: Yes, I used an oscillator as a melodic instrument, again echoed into the piano in that same way.

BERNSTEIN: The Sonics concerts often included improvisations with dancers from the Ann Halprin Dancers' Workshop: Lynne Palmer, John Graham, and A. A. Leath. Could you say some more about what they contributed to those improvisations?

SENDER: Well, they were very skilled performers. They all were very good at working with words in different ways. And they would bounce words off each other and pick up phrases and repeat the phrases and sometimes this involved dance movements, and sometimes it didn't.

BERNSTEIN: I know that later on you did more theatrical work. Were they an early influence on your later theatrical pieces?

SENDER: Oh, yes.

BERNSTEIN: When did you first begin doing improvisations?

SENDER: Well, Bob Erickson, of course, was very interested in improvisation. I took his improvisation class, among other courses I took with him, and we talked a lot about it. I talked a lot about it with Pauline, who was also coming occasionally in to see Bob. Then Pauline and I began meeting up in the attic to just improvise. I think Terry was in on one or two of those sessions. I had made some recordings. So it was in our heads and I think it seemed quite natural to include improvisation in the [Sonics] series when we started out.

BERNSTEIN: *Tropical Fish Opera* (1962) involves improvisation, but it's also kind of an indeterminate score.

SENDER: Right.

BERNSTEIN: And looking through your list of works, I notice that there are a lot of pieces I might call indeterminate works, like, for instance *Time Fields* [1965]. Could you talk about that piece?

SENDER: OK. I decided I would cover the floor of my room with sheets of card stock of a certain size and that I would dribble ink on them. These ink spots became events, which I would offer to the performer as either the ink spot side or the realization of the ink spots [which I provided on the other side of each sheet]. The sheets were set up on a music rack in a way that, in theory at least, they would be circular.

You could start performing on any card and just go around the whole set. And then as part of this setup, I did offer a realization of the cards as a full score, as one possible outcome of performing it. And each card, each move from one card to another, involved a change in tempo, which was shown in, you know, old quarter note equals new quarter note and at a certain multiple of the old. And I wanted the instrumentalists spaced out as far as possible from each other within the hall.

So basically it sounded like six people all playing their own individual piece. I think the piece evolved from walking down the halls of the conservatory and hearing a jumble of music coming from all the different classrooms. I often was intrigued and amused just by the "Charles Ives" aspect of it all.

BERNSTEIN: Did you measure the distances between the dots?

SENDER: Yes, I did. I did it very carefully.

BERNSTEIN: That sounds like how David Tudor worked realizing Cage's indeterminate scores.

SENDER: Yes, I guess it does. [Laughs]

BERNSTEIN: And another piece that is also what I would call an indeterminate score, and I think a really ingenious one, was composed a year earlier, your *Star Charts for Piano and Tape* [1964].

SENDER: Oh, yes, that was kind of an interesting idea. First of all, I never saw it performed and never knew quite how well it came off.

BERNSTEIN: And it had a tape part?

SENDER: Yes.

BERNSTEIN: The score had phosphorescent dots on it?

SENDER: It was, as I recall, an opened umbrella attached to a rotating motor. Black cards were taped to the umbrella, and they had the phosphorescent dots. I had hoped originally that the phosphorescence would just be enough to stay on during the whole length of the piece, but it turns out it died out pretty quickly, so we had to keep activating it with a flashbulb.

BERNSTEIN: Another piece that I couldn't quite figure out how it worked is *Information* [1962].

SENDER: *Information* was an interesting piece performed in the Mills Concert Hall using the two standing candelabra there. I put a six-foot-long, two-foot-diameter drum between the candelabra and then ran a huge sheet of acetate, approximately forty-eight inches wide and twenty feet long, as a loop on it, with loops in front of two pianists, and then somebody cranked that main roller by hand that moved the acetate very slowly. I found a way to let it roll across the keyboard music racks on the pianos. It was a bit of a mechanical monstrosity, but it was fun. Both performers would be playing the same material, the same score actually, as it moved in front of them.

And then there was this little information booth also in the Music Building that kept intriguing me, so I set up another drum. This time a clear plastic drum, that was just the width of the information window and filled it with words, cut out of newspapers. I found if you rubbed it with a piece of wool, the static electricity made all the words jump around in a pattern. That became a vocal score. So I had two pianists and a vocalist. I liked what came out of it. I sent it off to Bob Ashley at the Once Festival. I gather on the way some parts of it disappeared and so they kind of made it up at the other end. They had to restuff the word cylinder and it became a lot more political piece when they did it as I recall. [Laughs]

BERNSTEIN: What did they choose? Newspaper headings . . . ?

SENDER: Yes, something like that.

BERNSTEIN: What sort of music was on the acetate?

SENDER: I used black acetate ink, and it showed a mark over the key that I wanted played. It was like a piano roll, in a sense, in that if the black mark came above, and it was over the C above middle C, you played the C above middle C and held it down as long as the mark went by, and then when the mark was no longer there, you could let the key up—that kind of thing.

BERNSTEIN: What about the vocal parts?

SENDER: That had all to do with the words and the way they placed themselves within the tube. You read them from left to right, and once you read all the way across, you could rub the wool cloth on the cylinder again and the words would arrange themselves in a new pattern. I forget if high was high and low was low—it probably was—in terms of pitch.

BERNSTEIN: That's interesting. What about *Balances* for amplified prepared string trio and double bass? I don't have a date for that.

SENDER: That was later, let's see, 1964, I think. I got intrigued with the sound of stringed instruments that had prepared strings. I had these little alligator clips and put rubber tips on them to keep the clips from ruining the strings. The clips had to be clamped to the strings of the instruments and in a certain way that produced certain pitches. I got a lot of very gong-like sounds and the instruments all were miked and I had a little mixer. There was a score for the mixer to move the sounds around the four speakers.

BERNSTEIN: So all of these pieces involve elements of indeterminacy?

SENDER: Yes.

BERNSTEIN: *Desert Ambulance* [1964] as well . . .

SENDER: True.

BERNSTEIN: . . . because the part for Pauline was the result of your instructions through her headphones?

SENDER: That's correct.

BERNSTEIN: So you were interested in a kind of, well, I don't know if you want to call it, spontaneity or . . . ?

SENDER: Yes, I wanted to give some type of impulse to the performer, but I did want to tie them down in a certain point.

BERNSTEIN: You wanted improvisation, but you wanted to have some compositional control as well.

SENDER: Yes, that's right.

BERNSTEIN: I also interviewed Anna Halprin and she mentioned that as well. She wanted to harness the energy from improvisation by adding elements of control.

SENDER: Right.

BERNSTEIN: Getting back to the end of the Sonics series, what was the reason that you moved from the conservatory to 1537 Jones Street?

SENDER: We had a great season at the conservatory. Dr. Robin Laufer was the director, whom most people did not like, but he was very nice to me. At the end of the year, I went to him and said, "Well, we've had a great season." (We had turned the conservatory a little bit on its ear.) And I said, "I'd love to have a budget for next year to go on and get some equipment and stuff." I put the conservatory on the penny-a-pound surplus program. Do you know about that? I think they still have a version of it. U.S. government surplus for schools, where you sign up and they sell you old equipment for pennies.

Well, anyway, Laufer said, "I'm sorry, we can't." He said it very charmingly. He also sort of had promised me that I'd get hired after I graduated. But he tempered his offer at that point, saying, "You'd better go get an MA and then come back and we'll hire you." So at that point—I was so amazed I had a bachelor's of music—I tried to get into UC Berkeley. I didn't have a bachelor's of art, and it would have required taking more undergraduate courses, so I went over to Mills.

With Laufer's refusal to fund the studio, I went to Mort and I said, "Well, look, the conservatory's not going to give me any money. Why don't we pool our equipment?" Mort said, "Yes." This young techie-type guy had showed up at the conservatory, and it turned out he worked for a contractor who had a building on Russian Hill they were going to demolish, an old Victorian. He made a deal with his boss that we could rent it for the amount of money the insurance would run, and use it as the center. So we did, and we moved into 1537 Jones Street, at Jones and Pacific. It was a great old Victorian. We had a season there before I burned the place down by mistake.

MAGINNIS: Are you finally admitting that you burned it down?

SENDER: I changed the fuse in the fuse box that short-circuited the attic wiring. Well, you know, we had a series of happenings there and everybody kept joking saying, "Well, for the last one, we'd burn the place down, ho-ho-ho, because they're going to demolish it anyway." And actually, we already had rented 321 Divisadero, and moved our best equipment over, but we were still subletting to various artist types upstairs, including the attic. The guy in the attic never had any electricity. He was running off a long extension chord. One day I went to collect the rent for the last time and say "Good-bye" and turn them over to whoever else was going to have the building. I took one last look for the fuse box and I found it and put a fuse in, and then glanced up the stairs and saw that his lights were on. We cheered. Then he walked me downstairs and out the front door, and we looked up and saw a red glow coming from his bedroom window. He went running up, and the next thing I knew, he had punched his fist through the glass and shouted "Fire!" and came running out. I went across the street and called the fire department. The fire department came, and some of our subscribers who lived in the neighborhood had heard about it, I guess, over the radio—"Big fire on Russian Hill." One guy from North Beach came and said, "Wow, great event!"

BERNSTEIN: How did you all get interested in happenings?

SENDER: That was due to the Ann Halprin [Dancers' Workshop] connection, which was through—I don't think Mort had started working with her—Terry Riley and La Monte Young, who had been her composers. I think they did one concert that got very involved in the sound of empty beer cans scraping on concrete. I think La Monte is the only composer I know of who ever won the . . . what's that grant that UC Berkeley gives with specific instructions to go *elsewhere* with it?

MAGINNIS: They didn't like his *Poem for Chairs, Tables, and Benches, etc.* [1960]?

SENDER: Well, the music department there was so staid in those days.

MAGINNIS: I think in 1959 or 1960, somewhere during that period, Terry and I were on the same concert at UC, at Hertz Hall. They did my *Three Pieces* [1960] for piano and a piece of Terry's that was for some sort of ensemble. I think it was a string quartet.[1] It was like a note every minute and a half, something like that. And then long pauses. Terry got quite a reaction from the audience.

SENDER: That winter at Jones Street, we decided that every concert should be a collaboration with some other group in the city. We started with Robert Duncan doing his *Halloween Masque*,[2] which he wrote for his friends. It was really a kind of *entre nous*–type piece he had done. And his lover Jess [Collins] put his paintings up on the wall.

So that was the first concert at Jones Street. The second or third one was with Ronnie Davis's Mime Troupe. Ronnie did a piece, which was actually the most scatological piece that's ever been performed, in my experience. It had the two dancers sitting on toilets, and then in the back of the room was someone describing taking a long involved dump with great ponderings about it all. The audience was covered in a canvas cloth with holes for their heads, and at some point, a performer walked through the audience wearing a striped T-shirt and striped socks, but nothing in between. That was the event that we had invited a man from the Ampex Foundation to come to, to see how serious we were. He lasted up to the entry of that gentleman in the striped T-shirt, and then left. So that was the end of an Ampex grant, although we did make a valuable Ampex connection later.

Another concert was a real "happening." That was *City Scale* [1963] that we planned together; I did it with Tony Martin, who later became our visual director, and Ken Dewey. The score was published in the *Tulane Drama Review*. It maps out the evening.

BERNSTEIN: Could you tell us something about how it was made?

SENDER: Well, it came out of a couple of brainstorming sessions between the three of us, and at a certain point, we decided to score it. We rented two trucks to take the audience around town. We were nicely positioned on Jones Street, because it was only three short blocks to a little park over the Broadway Tunnel that gave a view down into North Beach. People would be able to see anything we wanted to do in the streets of North Beach.

It was basically: the audience signed in and then was walked up a hill overlooking North Beach; and then we had a car "ballet" in North Beach, various cars moving through the streets with colored gels on their headlights for distinctive markings so that you gradually would notice them until they lined up in front of Coit Tower facing the audience; and the cars blinked their headlights, with firecrackers going off in the bushes under them; and then there was a trombone player [Stuart Dempster] in the Broadway Tunnel; and one of the nicest things was that when the audience walked back to the Tape Music Center past the piano tuner workshop on the corner, we had a woman in her bathrobe singing Debussy in the window, with a piano accompanist in tails. I think we also had a broken-down vehicle with two of Ann Halprin's dancers; John Graham was pretending to teach Lynne Palmer to drive and they were having loud arguments.

The whole theme of the piece was how to mix controlled events within the city's environment in a way that would sensitize the viewers, the audience, to look more carefully at everything and try to figure out if a particular event was staged or just happening. We were playing with that sort of chaotic edge, that is between order and chaos. Isn't that where all the good stuff happens?

BERNSTEIN: Allan Kaprow calls it "blurring the boundaries between art and life."

SENDER: Yes, there you go.

PAYNE: I understand that it was a six-hour performance.

SENDER: Yes. It went on until two in the morning. I remember that Alfred Frankenstein hung in until we loaded everybody into two trucks, and then at that point, he just couldn't make it into the back of the truck. He decided to drop out.

We ended up at a city park, and actually ran into the beginning of a rumble, which was really interesting. There were these kids in two groups about to go at each other and suddenly this truckload of people showed up and ran screaming across the park toward these weather balloons that I had blown up. And the kids thought something really odd was going on.

We also did a "book-returning ceremony" at City Lights, giving people books to put back on the shelves, because we figured so many books had been stolen from the bookstore over the years. This was our little gesture. Then this drunken guy came up and said, "What are you guys doing?" and we said, "Oh, we run an underground bus service to North Beach, would you like to come along?" We picked this guy up and took him with us. He didn't really know where he was going. He got a little paranoid, actually, but we took him to a Lee [Elias] Romero light show at an abandoned church that the Mime Troupe was using in the Mission.

It was my first view of a light show with liquid projections, and when I saw that, I said, "*That's* what we need." Because the more we did electronic music, the more it was obvious that there was this visual aspect to a concert which was really missing—

I mean there is nobody to look at playing an instrument and it was a real lack of dimension.

MAGINNIS: Yes, you really can't ask an audience to sit in the dark and listen to a tape. They can do that at home.

PAYNE: That's where Tony Martin came in?

SENDER: Well, first we tried Lee.

BERNSTEIN: The concerts there often included tapes by you and Mort.

SENDER: That's right.

BERNSTEIN: And one of them was *Kore* [1961]. Could you describe that piece?

SENDER: I created *Kore* at the conservatory. And it also used source tapes from my friendly costudents, whom I dragged up to the attic so they could make silly and strange sounds for me. They thought the sounds were silly; I thought they were interesting. And in that case, we had an old Ampex left-hand-drive 403, that Bill Maginnis still has, and the nice thing about it was you could vary the speed by the amount of tension on the tension take-up arm on the right. So you could get a pretty steady off-speed, although there were times it did speed up. So anyway, *Kore* used that, and I also used piano sounds that I made with scraping noises on the strings, again changing the pitch in various ways by holding the take-up arm on the 403.

BERNSTEIN: What about the title?

SENDER: Well, to me it had a kind of underground feeling at times, of moving underground. I guess I am thinking of that whole Persephone myth. It seemed to evoke her presence for me somehow. Of course, Persephone was kidnapped by Pluto, who fell in love with her and held her underground in his kingdom and was only convinced, I guess, by her mother to let her return. And she was going to be allowed to return forever if she did not eat anything beforehand, and I guess she did eat something on her journey back and that condemned her to spend half the year with her husband underground.

BERNSTEIN: Another piece from the Jones Street time was *I Laid Mr. Clean for the FBI* [1963]. [Laughs]

SENDER: Oh! [Laughs]. You know that was Michael Callahan's title for it. He had access to a, I think a Nagra or something through his collaboration with Gerd Stern, a nice small portable machine. I was trying to think of things to do with it.

BERNSTEIN: Is it a tape recorder?

SENDER: Yes, it's a high-end, professional portable tape recorder that came out during that time—Swiss, I believe. I said, "Look, I love the sounds I get when I'm moving around in a bathtub—the squeaks and squeals of my body against the wet surface. Come over and record me." So he came over and we recorded me actually playing the bathtub as an instrument.

BERNSTEIN: [Laughs]

SENDER: And then he put that funny title on it: *Ramon Takes a Bath, or I Laid Mr. Clean for the FBI.* God knows why.

BERNSTEIN: Tony [Martin] told me there was a film by Stan Brakhage of you and Mort working at Jones Street that can't be found.

SENDER: Yes, we were actually doing a little improvisation and not talking because it was a silent film. We had a rack of car parts that we used as percussion instruments, and we were banging on those and playing.

BERNSTEIN: I noticed that you dedicated your [unpublished] book "Naked Close-Up" to Brakhage.

SENDER: Well, the main character in the book is actually based a lot on Stan, on the things that happened when he came out here. He started living in Mort's garage with his wife and two very small children, whom they refused, on principle, to diaper. They didn't believe in diapering. So Stan was the first, I guess, real hippie I had met. He amused me and impressed me at the same time. It turns out his great guru was a relative of mine, which is a very funny story. My American family cousin was Jimmy Davis, who created mobiles out of colored plastic. When he hung them, the heat of the sun would turn them, and he became fascinated by the reflections they were throwing on the walls. So he started filming the reflections and out of this came a series of abstract movies, basically just light patterns. They now belong to the Museum of Modern Art. Some of the films are just extraordinary.

Anyway, so Brakhage had seen some of the films and got all excited and packed up his family one day and appeared at Jimmy's doorstep in Princeton. Here's this hermit—Jimmy was so reclusive that he would order his groceries over the phone and then lower a basket from his window and haul the groceries up. He was also very much not into children. He was a gay artist, by then probably in his sixties. So here at his door is Stan, his wife, and two little undiapered kids. "O master, we have come to study with you," Stan intoned. So they actually moved in with him for a while, probably drove him completely crazy and then came out here. It was while they were here in town that Stan had all of his 16 mm equipment stolen from his car and fell back to using Super 8. I'm not sure if the film [shot at 1537 Jones Street], which we can't locate, was shot in Super 8 or whether it was before he lost all of his equipment.

It was a little short film, which we used at KQED. Mort or somebody told me how angry Stan's wife was that we actually had the disrespect to talk over the film, which was a silent film. So, anyway, somehow, that original film has been lost and the hopes are, perhaps, that KQED took a dub of it.

BERNSTEIN: Did Brakhage live at Jones Street?

SENDER: No, I don't think they ever moved in. I'm trying to remember. I think it came up as a possibility at one point and we knew with the kids there we'd never be able to record. So I think we never offered him the possibility, unless I'm mistaken.

BERNSTEIN: How did you meet him? Did he influence you in some way?

SENDER: I didn't hang out with him that much. I guess his example interested me. He was a guy who was living in a very hippie-like fashion—I'd never seen that before. I was pretty straight. I guess in a way he did introduce me to that sort of lifestyle. By a kind of a setting a role model, a kind of image.

BERNSTEIN: How did you meet Ken Dewey?

SENDER: Ken was working with Ann Halprin. They did a double bill; he directed a double bill with two of her dancers, I believe Lynne Palmer and John Graham did—well I think Lynne did Genet's [*The Maids*], with another woman—and the second on the bill was Dewey's play *The Gift*. I was very impressed with Ken's play, to the point where I actually thought of turning it into an opera at one point. I understand that Terry Riley did write some music for it. I liked Dewey's work a lot. I liked him, he was a very personable guy, nice to work with. So the idea came along to do *City Scale* as a collaboration after that play.

BERNSTEIN: How did you find the new location at 321 Divisadero Street?

SENDER: We were looking for a new place, and Ronnie Davis said, "Well, there's this place at 321 Divisadero, and it's too much for us, but maybe we can share it. It's $175 a month." So Mort and I talked about it, and we both agreed that although we loved Ronnie, we were both kind of freaked out by that toilet happening and we thought we better take it by ourselves. So we did. I don't think Ronnie was really all that serious about it anyway. So we saw the building, loved it, and rented it. I signed the lease. Then I contacted Will Ogden, then music director at KPFA, and offered to share it. Will liked the idea of a city venue for concerts, so they rented it for $100 a month. The main auditorium needed work, and KPFA put together a volunteer day with their listeners. They came in and mounted large acoustic baffles on the walls and extended the stage. We invited Ann Halprin to move in and she took the smaller room, which was still a nice room for a dance studio, and we moved in upstairs on the third floor where there was a room adequate for the equipment.

PAYNE: So KPFA actually did live broadcasts from there?

SENDER: Yes, it was very nice. The main auditorium was across the back of the building—Ann's space was like a foyer, creating an L. Between the two, there was a control room booth with glass windows . . .

MAGINNIS: . . . to both auditoriums.

SENDER: The place used to be an old California Labor School. Before that it must have been a Masonic temple . . .

MAGINNIS: . . . or a lodge hall.

SENDER: So by now we were at 321 Divisadero. Gerald Hill, an attorney friend, incorporated us, which in those days I think was a lot easier than it is today. We got our studio started. I think it was my idea that Mort would be concert director and I would be studio director, but it really didn't matter. Pauline came back to town and started doing large theater pieces, which we performed. So that was neat.

BERNSTEIN: The first pieces with light projections at the Tape Music Center in the first season at Divisadero were with Elias Romero.

SENDER: Yes.

BERNSTEIN: You did a version of *Kronos* [1962] with him?

SENDER: Seems like we did, and another . . . ?

BERNSTEIN: The first time was in November 1963; there was a piece that was called *Improvisation No. 1*. And it featured Romero, you, Mort, and Pauline. So apparently Romero did some improvisations with his liquid projections.

SENDER: Yes, right.

BERNSTEIN: And I guess he also worked with Mort on his *A Theater Piece after Sonnet No. 47 of Petrarch* [1963].

SENDER: I don't remember why Lee stopped working with us. There must've been some reason, but I don't know why. Maybe he left town for a while. Then we got Tony. By that time, I really wanted projections. Here we were doing what Alfred Frankenstein called "inventing a new form." He said maybe it's called "theater music." We didn't know what it was. Tony was my friend, a painter, who had been a classical guitarist as a teenager. I thought, well, he's musical and he paints, maybe we can convince him. And we did, we finally did. And Maginnis came along, and we said, "Oh, you know technical stuff. Good, you're hired."

MAGINNIS: The day we met, he handed me a key to the front door. I said, "Are you kidding?" He said, "Come in anytime you want; work so many hours."

PAYNE: And he actually offered you pay for this?

MAGINNIS: Yes. I think you said work two hours a day for equipment maintenance, that sort of thing. Michael Callahan had started building this keyboard, and it wasn't finished. It was a Kimball organ keyboard. It was just contacts and was wired up to a bunch of relays so we could switch from loop deck to loop deck and have oscillator to oscillator and patch it in.

SENDER: Did we have our loop decks up and running?

MAGINNIS: No, we didn't, but eventually they were to be up and running.

SENDER: We should mention Michael Callahan. I think he showed up shortly after our move from the Jones Street address. He's gone on I think to a big career building museum audio equipment. Someday Michael's going to have to write his autobiography, because he hung out at Millbrook, he knew Leary and Alpert, that whole crowd. And his time and travels with Gerd Stern and the USCO family are another tall tale that needs to be chronicled.

The chronology now begins to get a little dizzy. One adventure that seems quite funny in retrospect, although at the time it caused us near nervous breakdowns, was the fire department's shutting of our auditorium the night before *In C*'s first performance on November 4, 1964. This occurred because of documentary filmmaker Sol Landau's screening of the supposedly obscene Jean Genet film *Un chant d'amour* [1950]. I say "supposedly" because I've never seen it, and also enough time has passed by now so that what was once deemed beyond the pale is now considered run-of-the-mill. Landau had phoned me to ask to rent the hall to show the film, and I passed him on to KPFA, via whom Canyon Cinema and others had rented our shared venue.

Mort arrived the following morning to set up for that evening's concert and found a fire department CLOSED UNTIL FURTHER NOTICE sign stuck on the front door for "non-compliance with fire regulations." Mort called our attorney, Gerald Hill, who was home trying to avoid being served a subpoena by hiding behind the sofa, which made their conversation a bit odd.

"Is the CLOSED sticker visible when the front door is propped open?" Hill asked.

"No," Mort replied.

"So prop the front door open," he replied.

15 LECTURE-DEMONSTRATION AT 321 DIVISADERO. FROM LEFT TO RIGHT: RAMON SENDER (SEATED AT THE CHAMBERLIN), TONY MARTIN, AND PAULINE OLIVEROS.

Which is what we did. Only after the fact did we learn that the fire department had closed down at least two other venues because of Landau's attempt to show the movie. I felt annoyed that he had not warned us this might occur, but of course then we would not have gone ahead and allowed him the use of the hall.

The technicality that the fire department had jumped on was that the passageway gate to the street from the rear emergency exit was barely under the width limit. A subsequent measurement showed that it was close enough to allow us a variance if we left the gate unlocked during concerts.

Mort also claimed that we were on the House Un-American Activities list because the California Labor School had previously rented the building.[3]

Desert Ambulance was I guess in the spring of 1964.[4] We heard about this machine that had a tape head under every key, the Chamberlin. I saw it in the paper; somebody was selling one. It turned out it was Dr. Gerbode, a well-known figure about the city. He was a tinkerer and organ enthusiast, and kept it in his basement rumpus room. So, Mort and I went out there, and it was an absolute gas.

While we were looking for the money to buy it, I went over one day with a portable recorder and recorded a bunch of source tapes for a piece for Pauline. So even before we had it, I was working on *Desert Ambulance*. We had one patron, God bless her, who we would go to in certain dire situations and she would donate the money. Mort was doing music for the Actor's Workshop productions. Their managing director was a man named Allen Mandel. He introduced us to Liz Heller, who ultimately married Allen. Liz Heller was one of their major patrons and a couple of times we went over to her house with projects and she helped us out. I think she bought the Chamberlin for us.

BERNSTEIN: *Desert Ambulance* is really a classic piece. It definitely has a unique sound. How did you arrive at that? I know that Frankenstein called it a kind of "aural pop art." I suppose that's correct.

SENDER: I suppose, yes.

BERNSTEIN: And how did you get to that sound? Was it the Chamberlin that inspired you?

SENDER: Yes. Our other patron was Eldon Corl, who worked for Ampex in their international department. Why he liked us I have no idea.

MAGINNIS: He truly believed we were all a bunch of communists.

SENDER: He was a crazed Republican. But for some reason he got a kick out of us. So he loaned us a 351–2, which was really his demo machine, state of the art, we had it for two years.

MAGINNIS: He had taken the 351–2 motors out of the transport and put 300 motors in. All the motors were much beefier than the standard. And it was in a case made of ¾-inch ply board. It weighed a ton and a half.

SENDER: We used to bring it downstairs to record with it.

MAGINNIS: But we quit that real early.

SENDER: Eldon every once in a while would show up with a new gadget, or he'd call up and say, "So-and-so is selling something, here's your chance." There was some high school teenager who had spent his summer in the Ampex lab building his own three-track tape recorder, and he decided to sell it because he'd made another model of it with transistors. Instead of it being in a cabinet six feet high, now it fit into a briefcase. So he wanted to sell us the old six-foot cabinets. We went down there to look at the thing and we bought it. That machine was a monster, but we desperately needed multitracking. You never saw it when the Tape Music Center moved to Mills because Bill Maginnis holds up part of his house with it.

MAGINNIS: I'm using it as part of the foundation. The guy didn't laminate, he just stacked the heads. That's why it doesn't work anymore. There's a piece of cellophane in the gap to keep them lined up. The center track was pulled back. So it wasn't recording or playing back. I figured, well, I could take it apart and take the head off the machine and see if I could tap it back out, screw it down, maybe lap it. I took it apart and the thing went "Bloing!" and fell into pieces. It wasn't laminated; it wasn't glued. It was just compressed.

SENDER: He promised us the specs on it.

MAGINNIS: I've got the paper on it.

PAYNE: So he literally made three-track erase, record, and play heads? Selective synch?

SENDER: If you wanted to replug the heads. The heads were "unpluggable." It was kind of neat. I discovered that there was a tension adjustment on the reels. You could actually put it in "record" mode, not turn on the track to travel, but just put on the tension adjustment, and the tape would creep very slowly. That was when I started doing things like putting all of a Wagner opera on an eighth of an inch of tape. I thought, wow I could sell this to conservatory students to help them do their assignments. You want to listen to the *Ring of the Nibelungen?* Here, you can do it in a quarter of a second.

PAYNE: Actually, I often do that to analyze the dynamics of the piece. It's quite interesting.

SENDER: Yes, it is. Well, one day Eldon came by with a computer-test direct-record amplifier (I don't know if that went to Mills or not), a testing unit, DC. We all got some great sounds out of that one.

MAGINNIS: It was a data recorder. It was a direct-record process. It would magnetize the tape one way or the other way, so it didn't matter.

SENDER: One of my favorite pieces came from that machine by doing a warble on it; it sounded like a jungle of birds. I named it Worldfood XII (1964). It was part of a series of drone pieces, most of them done with stacked loops on our loop machines.

MAGINNIS: I don't know if there's specs on the machine. There's all these schematics.

SENDER: My favorite piece of Bill's from that era was done on the 401 by beating against the bias, 50 k against the 100 k, and then you slowed it down umpteen times. I combined that tape of yours, Bill, with readings from the *Tibetan Book of the Dead* and I took acid trips with it. It was great.

PAYNE: So essentially you had aliasing early on.

MAGINNIS: Yes, I had aliasing. When you do that it turns out to be "just intonation," because all you are doing is playing the harmonics series. So you run the oscillators up and down.

SENDER: It was very Tibetan-sounding to me, I don't know why.

PAYNE: We had a very early Ampex 8-track for a while, and at that point they hadn't yet dealt with the concept of a master bias oscillator. Each head had its own bias frequency applied to it, so of course it would get off. It was all around 100 kHz, so one head would be at 101, one would be at 103. It was so far off that if you just hit the machine "record" with all the channels on, it would *sing*, because of all the beat frequencies. It was wonderful.

MAGINNIS: Great. I tried to record a woman who had been a close associate of Theremin. She brought one of his original Theremins to Mills and I tried to record it. Unfortunately, the frequency he chose for the Theremin was right around the bias of the Ampex 351–2. So you got this mirror-image effect, so that when the pitch would go up on the Theremin, the pitch would go down on the bias, and when it would get loud for the Theremin, it would go soft, and when it was supposed to be silent, you had everything running wide open.

SENDER: We were getting good reviews and everything was fine. Then, along comes the Rockefeller Foundation. The guy's name from Rockefeller was Boyd Compton who said, "Well, look, we can give you $15,000 to get through the 1965–66 season, but then if you want a larger grant you are going to have to affiliate with some kind of institution of higher learning."

MAGINNIS: The grant we split with the Mills Performing Group.

SENDER: Yes.

PAYNE: Not the initial $15,000?

SENDER: No. Boyd didn't have to go to the board for the $15,000.

PAYNE: Who made this connection?

MAGINNIS: It was Mort's connection.

SENDER: I don't know if they fired Compton because of our grant, but he left the foundation shortly thereafter. I guess Mort and I did a "reality check" that fall. The Actor's Workshop had moved to the Beaumont Theater in New York and were going on to big time. Mort was sort of thinking that the Actor's Workshop had been a big connection for him and could continue to be. At that point, he had also been approached by NYU, and they offered him a very good deal.

I was getting a little burned out. We were struggling, struggling, struggling, and there was always money trouble. I had been refinancing my house to keep a little money coming in. Then, one day, in 1964, Steve Reich came over to my house with a paper bag full of these odd-looking little green dried-up buttons. He asked, "Where's your Waring blender?" I said, "Why?" And he said, "I got some of these 'double O caps' we're going to fill up and we're going to try this." I guess he'd already had peyote.

We each downed sixteen. I went through a little bit of the nausea thing, but then I was having a great time noodling around at the piano, but finally he said he thought it was time for him to go home. I said, "You're going to go home? But why? We're having a wonderful time." He left and I lay down and began an absolutely Jungian, back-to-the-womb recap of my life, finally through the moment of conception, out into the universe type of experience. It was fantastic. I had never smoked pot, so this type of experience was something totally new to me. This whole new universe opened. Then I started smoking pot regularly.

MAGINNIS: That's why you got so upset at me and Bob Moran for lying under the piano playing with the nuts, bolts, screws, and threads. While you were sleeping upstairs or something like that, Bob and I were down in the auditorium deliberately trying to make the quietest sounds we could make. It still had some resonance—both of us stoned out of our tree. And we were lying underneath this grand piano. Like this, you could take your finger and make these little clicks on the exposed bolts and threads. And he was hearing them upstairs saying, "Keep it down! What the hell is all that? You guys stop that!"

SENDER: God, I don't remember that at all. . . . All I know is that peyote opened some amazing vistas for me. Unfortunately, it also put my wife, Marina, and me on diverging paths that ended in my leaving her and our son, Andres—and subsequently moving out of the city to a hippie commune. I've always regretted the way the separation came about and wish I could have caused them less pain. Marina offered important support during our struggle to keep the Tape Music Center financially afloat. She actually opened a custom dress design studio a half-block away from the Tape Music Center behind a Victorian house on Divisadero Street during 1964–65. I should also mention that Ruth Maginnis, Dinah Martin, and Linn Subotnick also contributed to the activities in the center in various capacities, including helping and performing at concerts.

About this time I decided I was tired of the concert format and I wanted to do Sunday morning church services, but in a kind of "new age" way. I thought we might do one each for all the ancient rites. We'd have one for the Mithraic rite—we'd sacrifice a cow on stage so that people would understand where their hamburgers came from.

MAGINNIS: And I didn't want to do that, because I would have had to clean it up.

SENDER: I wasn't sure, but I was reaching out for something new to do. I thought we could have people in to do guest sermons. I talked to Tony [Martin] and he said talk to Stewart Brand, he's doing these multimedia multiple slide things. So I met Stewart, he was living in North Beach, and he said, "Let's go down to Esalen because you might want to have your first sermon from old mister daddy gestalt himself, Fritz Perls."

So we went down there, and I dropped some acid and wandered off up the canyon. (I now had taken LSD a couple of times.) When I came down to meet Fritz, I told him our idea, and asked him if he'd like to do the first sermon. He said, "What kind of a stupid idea is that? I'm not interested in all this bullshit about church!" So that was the end of that.

Then, about a month later, Stewart called me again and he said, "Ken Kesey's in town with the Pranksters and would you like to go to an acid test?" I went to a Fillmore acid test. Kesey had already decided to do the Trips Festival, and Stewart said, "Do you want in?" and I said, "Sure." I wanted to do the Trips Festival, but when I talked it over with Mort, he wasn't sure. He didn't say it, but I think his thought was, "This doesn't sound too dignified." It wasn't going to help us get the bigger Rockefeller grant, but we were already on the $15,000 grant. So I decided that I'd take a month off and do the Trips Festival myself, and my new small salary (about $200 a month at that point) could go toward equipment.

Everybody had gotten involved with the Trips Festival except Mort. It was a little too druggy for him. But for everyone else, the vibes were building in the Haight. And we even had the first rock band in the city, the Charlatans, rehearsing at 321 Divisadero. I had met Big Brother before they got named; they were right around the corner. Stewart had asked if I knew any other groups who should be invited, and I suggested the Open Theater from Berkeley. They came in with "A Congress of Wonders," which was like a more-turned-on Committee, who were performing regularly in North Beach. Five guys who did a comedy act. We had the Open Theater, and Stewart's "America Needs Indians," the Merry Pranksters, the Grateful Dead, a rock band called Loading Zone, Big Brother [pre–Janis Joplin], and the Tape Music Center.

By now, 1966, Buchla had developed and delivered his box. He had drifted into one concert upstairs at 321 Divisadero and said he would build us a box. My dream was to run Big Brother through the Buchla box, very slowly, but gradually, turn up all the ring modulators until the whole thing would be way out in space. But that never happened for a number of reasons. We got Don [Buchla] involved in building the PA system and Stewart Brand and the Pranksters involved in nailing it to the ceiling of the Longshoremen's Auditorium.

PAYNE: So that was Big Brother and the Holding Company? Was Peter Albin a member of the group then?

MAGINNIS: Yes, and Sam Andrew was playing guitar.

SENDER: They had just named themselves a month before.

MAGINNIS: Janis was going out with Peter de Blanque at the time. They used to come to the Tape Music Center all the time. Should I explain Peter?

SENDER: Well, Peter was our briefly resident engineer, who said he could balance the studio 600 ohm, and who came in one night and cut every wire in the place and then disappeared. We had a concert coming up in five days.

MAGINNIS: I just put it back together enough to get the concert on the air. He and Janis would show up at our concerts.

SENDER: He was working at the Stanford University radio telescope . . .

MAGINNIS: Later on he asked for my recommendation, and I didn't send it.

SENDER: . . . and then they discovered all this pot growing up around the telescope.

MAGINNIS: He thought he was an engineer and had me convinced until he gave me this circuitry. He said, "We can get gain without a power supply. We don't need to build amplifiers." So, we went out and raided the telephone company dump for all these old repeat coils, and he showed me with geometric logic how all this would work. I said, "God, I can't believe it, it does work." And it did, there was voltage gain. He said, "Now don't worry about current, all we need is the voltage." Here was this graduate engineer telling me we didn't need current, and I'm not a graduate engineer so I thought, wait a minute, I know another graduate engineer. So I had him look at it and he said, "My God, I can't believe it." So, I wired it up, but of course it was a complete loss.

SENDER: Was he the one who built that dark red board?

MAGINNIS: I painted it red at his suggestion. I had originally painted it RCA gray, and it had all these RCA knobs on it. He said it can't be RCA gray. Mort came in and said, "Aaaaaah! It's red. I can't stand red things."

SENDER: Anyway, we had a few other people drifting through.

MAGINNIS: When Don came in it began to get fairly sane before the [Trips] Festival.

SENDER: We'd had some seminars on electronic music, which brought in some new young people. Alden Jenks and Shep [Gerald Shapiro] came in from Mills and then went to Paris.

After the Trips Festival, the energies kept building. Kesey had been busted on Stewart's roof smoking pot with Mountain Girl. He was already on probation awaiting sentencing, out on his own recognizance. The cops came up, and he grabbed the baggie from the cop and threw it off the side of the roof. This was all over the front pages, great publicity. We had a couple of other events around town, a parade through the financial district.

The *San Francisco Chronicle* sent a reporter to interview us. It was Lou Gottlieb, who had been in a small plane accident with the Limeliters, totally stressed out from travel, and had picked up a job reviewing concerts. I remember he reviewed a piano recital, comparing it to the *Tibetan Book of the Dead*. It definitely was the first time I had smoked a pot pipe with a reporter. And it was his pot. That impressed me. We started talking about communities, and he told me he had thirty acres in Sonoma County, and he said, "In case you ever want to try a communal experiment..."

We had needed an organizer for the Trips Festival, so I said I had heard about this guy Bill Graham who had just done a great benefit for the Mime Troupe, and so we called him up, and he said, "Yes, I'll do it," and we said how much, and he said, "Well, pay me what you think I am worth afterwards." I was taking $200 in lieu of my $200 from the Tape Music Center, and so was Stewart, so Bill also got $200. But we had made about $14,000, and were sitting on this pile of money. None of us had seen that kind of money before in our lives. I think we ended up giving all the rest of it to the Merry Pranksters, because they had done the bulk of the setup.

After that amazing weekend, I needed some time out. I went out and I bought fifty tabs of LSD and got in my car and said I was going to go to the Mojave Desert to cool out and think about things. We all scattered in different directions. The energy was centrifugal. I found a nice little cave in the Mojave Desert. Halfway there, I realized the little Fiat I was driving wasn't the right car, so I stopped at a used-car place in Monterey and traded it for a Tibetan-blue Chevy Carry-All with a blown engine. On the way south, the engine seized up right at the driveway into Esalen on Route 1 in Big Sur, so I coasted down into their parking lot to ponder auto mechanics for a few days. I realized that I would have to stop every hundred miles and fill it full of the heaviest oil available. After two weeks camping at the cave and by the Colorado River in Needles, I drove to a psychedelic church in Socorro, New Mexico, where an old couple would give people psilocybin mushrooms. A sweet, elderly, very staid couple, they ran this psychedelic church. I stayed there while I had the engine rebuilt. Then I visited Drop City, the only hippie commune I knew of. Then I came home after a while, but realized I could no longer live in a city environment.

When I came back I called Lou Gottlieb and asked to see his ranch in Sonoma County. Lou agreed, so my friend Joan Bransten, Lou, Stewart and his wife Lois, and I all drove up together to look over Lou's thirty acres. Lou brought along with him a pocket full of his musician friend Buck Wheat's famous hashish cookies for us to munch on. It was apple blossom time, beautiful, and nobody was living there. I said to my friend Joan, "I'm going to move up right away with the dog. I'm sorry, I know you are teaching school and you can't get away, but I'll come down weekends." I started living there then. Joan would drive up weekends or I'd go down. She found some old bills in the closet of what we called "The Lower House" (there were two houses on the property) made out to "Morning Star Ranch" so we realized the place had a mystical name. By summer we were both up there, and by the end of the summer there were about ten of us, including Bruce Baillie, the filmmaker, and Lou moved up, and Ben and Rain Jacopetti who ran the Open Theater, but would shortly thereafter change their names to Roland and Alexandra, given them by their Subud master.

MAGINNIS: By that time we were starting the move to Mills.

SENDER: That summer I went to Morning Star, Bill started the move to Mills, I think. I was out of there before the move to Mills and that was 1966. The Trips Festival was January 1966, and then I cut out for the desert. I just told Mort I had to get away and think, so the move occurred without me there. The move to Mills was in the summer of 1966.

We had a series of meetings that winter. I could see two paths. "Look, we have financial problems." Those of us, as I said to Mort, who owned houses could all sell our houses and buy a huge warehouse, move in together to form a commune, and run this thing communally.

Mort said that would never work. And he was right, because both his wife and mine would never have gone for it. As it was, my dropping out had wrecked my marriage, something that I know I managed very badly, I must admit.

Anyway, I went off to form my commune, and Mort went to New York, to the big time. Pauline wanted the directorship and wanted to go to Mills. For her, it was a great opportunity to prove herself within the musical community. I don't know how much you know about Pauline's struggles, but as a gay woman in the San Francisco music scene in the early 1960s, it was an absolute uphill battle for her. She had a very, very hard time, she was very impoverished, making ends meet by copying music and giving private lessons on the accordion and occasionally landing a performance. To get that kind of an option that Mills offered was very good for her—and very well deserved.

NOTES

1. The UC Berkeley noontime student concert on April 28, 1961, featured Maginnis's *Three Pieces* (1960) for piano and Terry Riley's *String Quartet* (1960). See Thomas M. Welsh's chronology in the present volume.

2. Although Robert Duncan's *Halloween Masque* is listed on the schedule for the season at Jones Street, his *Adam's Way* was performed instead. See Lewis Ellingham and Kevin Killian, *Poet Be Like God: Jack Spicer and the San Francisco Renaissance* (Hanover, N.H.: Wesleyan University Press, 1998), 239. I am grateful to Thomas M. Welsh for showing me this source—Ed.

3. Subotnick remembers that the *San Francisco Chronicle* art and music critic Alfred Frankenstein showed up for the repeat performance of *Un chant d'amour*. Subotnick stayed on the street in case the cops showed up, and one did show up. "He thought we were into drugs and nude dancing, so I invited him inside to listen to the music," Subotnick recalls. "I also showed him some of Frankenstein's reviews of previous concerts. Alfred, the cop, and I were standing in the hall, and the cop said, 'Franken-steen? You've got to be kidding!' 'No, he's a very famous critic,' I replied." Subotnick also remembers that "Terry [Riley] wore a floppy purple bow tie and orange pants. The audience was also dressed very colorfully. It was sort of the beginning of the psychedelic dress-up era." E-mail correspondence, Ramon Sender and Morton Subotnick, December 31, 2006.

4. The first performance of *Desert Ambulance* took place on February 3, 1964.

Memoir of a Community Enterprise

PAULINE OLIVEROS

Music is a guiding force and resource in my life. For me, music helps people to bond with one another and often plays an important role in communities and as a community focus. The San Francisco Tape Music Center in the 1960s was the basis of a community for me and helped to launch my career as a composer and improviser.

In 1958, I left the master's program in music at San Francisco State College (now California State University, San Francisco) to pursue my interest in composition. My college composer friends Loren Rush and Terry Riley were part of an informal composers' circle that included La Monte Young, John Gibson, Morton Subotnick, Ramon Sender, John Chowning, Steve Reich, Douglas Leedy, Bob Moran, Warner Jepson, William Maginnis, Alan Johnson, and others. I was marginally supporting myself by teaching privately, copying music, and playing musical jobs with my accordion and French horn. I enjoyed the freedom to organize my own schedule and to continue composing.

Around 1958, with encouragement from our mentor Robert (Bob) Erickson, I began to improvise together with the composers Loren Rush and Terry Riley, my former classmates. Loren was working at the Pacifica radio station KPFA in Berkeley as a program assistant and had access to the Ampex tape recorders at the station. Bob had been KPFA's music director.

Prompted by Terry's need to provide a sound track for a documentary film of the local sculptor Claire Falkenstein, we met for our first improvisation session at KPFA. Terry did not have time to write the music for the five-minute sound track, so we decided to improvise the track. Loren played bass and koto, Terry, piano, and I, French horn. We improvised several five-minute tracks, and Terry chose one to use for the film. I don't remember seeing the film, if we ever did see it. It might still exist in an archive somewhere. The recordings of the improvisations are in the archive of the Center for Contemporary Music in the F. W. Olin Library at Mills College in Oakland, California.

This first session piqued our interest in improvisation. We were amazed that we

16 **PAULINE OLIVEROS.**

could make music together this way. We decided to meet regularly for more sessions. We learned an all-important lesson in these early sessions: If we talked first and tried to impose guidelines or structure for the improvisation, the attempt would likely fall flat. If we played first without talking about it, then listened to the recording critically, our improvising would improve naturally. We liberated ourselves from unnecessary controls and developed trust in process through spontaneity. As far as we know, we were the first in avant-garde art music to engage in "free improvisation." Our process was new: play and record, listen to the recording, enjoy, talk, judge, criticize, analyze, and play again.[1]

After these early improvisation sessions, Terry formed a musical collaboration with La Monte Young, and Loren had other interests and compositions to write. I met the young composer Ramon Sender through Robert Erickson, who was now teaching at the San Francisco Conservatory of Music. Ramon and I started improvising together and talking about making tape music. We were listening to the European electronic music and musique concrète by Karlheinz Stockhausen, Pierre Schaeffer, Luciano Berio, Bruno Maderna, Luigi Nono, and others broadcast by KPFA in its morning concert. The morning concert consisted of four hours of new music presented daily by a succession of interested music directors: Alan Rich, Robert Erickson, Wilbur Ogden, Glenn Glasow, Charles Shere, and Charles Amirkhanian from circa 1954 to 1992. KPFA played a crucial role in my education and in the dissemination of new music and world music to the public. These broadcasts were an invaluable service to the local and national community and fostered tremendous interest in the Bay Area between 1957 and 1992.[2]

Ramon had created a tape music studio in the attic of the San Francisco Conservatory by 1961 and invited me to work with him. He and I launched "Sonics," the precursor of the San Francisco Tape Music Center at the Conservatory on December 18, 1961. Our first program of tape music included my *Time Perspectives,* a four-channel tape piece made from improvised sounds, Terry's *M . . . Mix (Mescalin Mix)* (1960–61), Ramon's *Traversals* (1961), Phil Winsor's *Sound Study I* (1961), and an improvisation for mixed instruments with Ramon (piano), Laurel Johnson (recorder), Phil Winsor (trumpet), and myself (French horn).

I created *Time Perspectives* (1961) at home with my Sears Silvertone tape recorder, mics, and improvised sounds with vibrating objects and voices. The Silvertone tape recorder had 7½ and 3¼ IPS speeds so that I could raise or lower recorded material by one octave. A special feature of this machine allowed me to use variable speed by hand winding the tape in record mode. I used cardboard tubes for filters by recording voices and sources through them, I amplified small sounds by clamping the source to the wall, and I used the bathtub for reverberation. The sections were improvised then spliced together. The quadraphonic sound for the concert was achieved by playing two tapes simultaneously on stereo tape machines into four amplifiers and speakers.

Morton Subotnick and the dancer-actors John Graham, A. A. Leath, Lynne Palmer, and Norma Leistiko from Ann Halprin's Dancers' Workshop also joined us in the 1961–62 season. When we welcomed Mort as a composer/improviser in our second Sonics concert, Ramon created a long tape loop between two tape machines that picked up our sounds and played them back much later and in altered forms. The headline for Alfred Frankenstein's review in the *San Francisco Chronicle* was "Stimulating Sounds Too New to Be Named."[3] Frankenstein thought that the tape loop in a live improvisation was "remarkable." Ramon seeded an idea that has continued in my work to this day in the Expanded Instrument System (EIS).[4]

Improvisation was an all-important tool for all of us in the development of much collaboration and of the community that was continuing to increase its numbers. Even though we improvised together often, each person retained individuality and a style that was specifically different. Even so we bounced off of each other's work with glee.

Ramon, Steve Reich, and Robert (Bob) Moran attended Mills College and received their master's degrees in composition during the San Francisco Tape Music Center era. Steve composed music for the San Francisco Mime Troupe; Bob Moran had many performances of his music at the San Francisco Tape Music Center and the San Francisco Conservatory. Mort was teaching at Mills and introduced us to the resident artists Luciano Berio and Cathy Berberian. We attended their concerts at Mills and played some of Berio's tape music at our concerts. Ann Halprin was another major force in the Bay Area in dance theater. Her inspiring work included music by Morton Subotnick, Terry Riley, La Monte Young, and Folke Rabe during the era of the San Francisco Tape Music Center. I worked with her on Divisadero Street and composed music for her work called *The Bath* in 1966.

Sonics became the San Francisco Tape Music Center in 1962–63 and found a new home in a three-story Victorian mansion at 1537 Jones Street in San Francisco. Mort and Ramon established the new studio and scheduled activities that always included live acoustic, electroacoustic, and theatrical improvisation along with tape music. They applied for nonprofit status with the IRS.

As Sonics continued, I was busy composing *Trio for Flute, Piano, and Page Turner* (1961) and *Sound Patterns for Mixed Chorus* (1961). I did not return to making tape music until 1963, although I was involved in improvisations on all the Sonics concerts for the rest of the season. After the premiere of *Trio for Flute, Piano, and Page Turner* on the Performer's Choice series (created by Loren Rush in conjunction with KPFA), I launched into composing *Sound Patterns for Mixed Chorus.* Fresh from my first tape piece and my experience of listening to electronic music, I decided to treat the voices as "instruments." I wanted the chorus to sound *electronic.*

Instead of text I explored vocal sounds or mouth noises and invented a notation for the sounds. I sent the four-minute piece to a competition sponsored by the Stichting Gaudeamus in Bilthoven, Holland. In 1962, I received an invitation to come to Bilthoven for the Guadeamus Festival. Györgi Ligeti was the judge for the competition. To my surprise and delight, I was awarded the Gaudeamus Prize (250 Dutch guilders) for the best foreign work for *Sound Patterns.* The prize and performance gave me international recognition that launched my career. *Sound Patterns* had its premiere performance in 1962 by the Hilversum Chorus conducted by Fred Barthe of Zurich, Switzerland. Two recordings were made—one by the Brandeis University Chorus under the direction of Alvin Lucier for Odyssey and another by the NME (New Music Ensemble) under the direction of Kenneth Gaburo. Many people thought that *Sound Patterns* was electronic.

At Gaudeamus I met the young Swedish composers Folke Rabe and Jan Bark, who later visited the San Francisco Tape Music Center and took part in our concerts and community. I am still in touch with Folke and Jan. The circle of our community of composers interested in electronic music widened. I traveled from the Netherlands through Germany, Scandinavia, Switzerland, and France in a VW bug rented with my prize money. I visited Folke and Jan in Stockholm and met many Swedish composers. They told me how they would love to work with electronic music but had no studio as yet. Later, many of these composers came to work at the San Francisco Tape Music Center. I visited Terry in Paris then returned to New York, met Varèse, and heard a concert of his music that included *Density 21.5, Octandre,* and other pieces at Carnegie Recital Hall.

When I returned from Europe and New York in 1963, the San Francisco Tape Music Center at 1537 Jones Street was thriving and busy. I attended some events, but never worked in the studio. 1537 Jones Street burned down and a new home was found for the San Francisco Tape Music Center at a former labor hall at 321 Divisadero Street in San Francisco. Jones Street was not for me, though Ramon kept after me to come on over and do something. I was still processing my European journey, scrambling to make a living again, and busy composing acoustic music. I was working on the *Duo for Accordion and Bandoneon.* Jones Street felt like a messy "boy's club" with a lot of transients sleeping over and working in the studio. Even though Ramon was very welcoming to me, the place did not feel very comfortable or safe for a young woman in those days. Nothing was familiar about the situation except for Ramon and Mort. I had been away and felt a bit removed from the ongoing activities.

The new San Francisco Tape Music Center location on Divisadero Street was a haven for me. Otherwise, there was no welcoming institution for me as a young independent avant-garde composer (only recently out of school) with an intensely growing interest in new media, electronic music, theater pieces, and improvisation. Mort and Ramon welcomed my participation, and we proceeded to work and perform together. I remember this period as a lot of fun, as well as very important in my development as a composer. Our collaborations included performing in each other's pieces, improvising together, sharing in the production of events, and giving each other feedback after performances.

Divisadero Street accommodated the studio on the second level. The studio now sported oscillators, professional Ampex tape machines, a patch bay, ring modulators, amplifiers, mics, an array of tape recorders and loop machines, as well as other gear that formed the so-called classical electronic music studio. Downstairs there was a room large enough to seat 100–150 people, with a small stage, that we used as our concert hall. Ann Halprin and her Dancers' Workshop occupied an adjacent room for her studio. A control room between these two rooms was used by KPFA as a remote studio location for a time. There was also a relationship with Canyon Cinema. Thus a prototype artist's co-op was born in San Francisco and became the hub of some significant events and a facility for a thriving artists' community interested in new media.

I performed the premiere of Ramon's *Desert Ambulance* for accordion, tape, and light projections on February 3, 1964. The piece was played in the dark, with Tony Martin projecting background behind me as well as foreground onto my white lab coat and white accordion. He used a cutout cardboard frame in front of the lens for the foreground. Ramon's instructions for me were semi-improvisational. Our experience of improvising together helped. Ramon recorded the instructions (half sung, half spoken) on one channel of the tape that came to me through earphones. The other channel of the tape that the audience hears was made from sounds played on the Chamberlin Music Master and then edited. The Chamberlin was an earlier version of a sampler. A keyboard instrument similar to an electronic organ in appearance, it had multiple tape loops containing prerecorded material of all kinds of instrumental and vocal sounds, as well as sound effects. Ramon's piece was a new concept, with its pop-like flavor derived from the Chamberlin's instrumental and vocal sounds. I performed *Desert Ambulance* at least twenty-five times. One of those times, the instructions were mistakenly sent to the audience and the sounds intended for the audience were sent to my earphones! Once when I had to perform *Desert Ambulance* without the projections, I almost could not do it, so integral was the feeling created by Tony with the projections. I never performed without the projections again. *Desert Ambulance* is a delight to perform and is a signature media piece from the San Francisco Tape Music Center.

Desert Ambulance and Mort's *Mandolin* with Tony's projections were key pieces on our national tour in the summer of 1964. I also had a performance role in *Mandolin*. Mainly, I was still, while projections played over my back. Also included on the tour were my *Mnemonics III* and a group improvisation with Mort on clarinet, Ramon on piano, and me on horn. Mort and I had discovered an outrageous method of acoustic frequency modulation that we used in our improvisations. Mort would stick his clarinet into the bell of my horn and our sounds would modulate.

The 1964 tour was most important for connecting us directly with the members of the Once Group in Ann Arbor including Robert Ashley, Gordon Mumma, Anne Wehrer, and George Manupelli.[5] *Tape Music* by Ashley and Mumma had been included in our San Francisco Tape Music Center concerts, and there was much correspondence with the only other group that we knew that was a cooperative venture in new media.

In 1963, I was invited to the home of Olive Cowell, aunt of Henry Cowell, in San Francisco, at the request of David Tudor. David had learned of my music from Tom Nee, a conductor friend. Meeting David was the beginning of a delightful friendship and professional relationship. We decided to put on a festival at the San Francisco Tape Music Center. I wanted to call it the "Tudorfest" to honor David for all his support of composers with his outstanding interpretations of contemporary music. David curated the Tudorfest in 1964. He included pieces by George Brecht, John Cage, Toshi Ichiyanagi, Alvin Lucier, and me. The festival consisted of three days and nights of programming, with repeat performances for a total of six days. This was the largest undertaking to date for the San Francisco Tape Music Center. Staff and technical resources were strained by this effort, but our community rallied, and the Tudorfest was successfully produced for appreciative audiences. Reviews by Alfred Frankenstein and Alexander Fried appeared in the newspapers. John Cage was in attendance, with the Japanese composers Toru Takemitsu and Toshi Ichiyanagi, and the journalist Kuniharu Akiyama. We performed Cage's *Atlas Eclipticalis* (1961–62) with *Winter Music* (1957) with our "community" orchestra conducted by Ramon, with David at the piano for *Winter Music*.

David was interested in my accordion playing, because he had been recently introduced to the bandoneon by Mauricio Kagel and was learning to play the instrument. I immediately began to compose a duo for accordion and bandoneon. (A provisional score is in my archive in special collections in the library at the University of California, San Diego.) David and I rehearsed at my home in Hunter's Point, which I shared with Laurel Johnson and her mynah bird, Ahmed. As David and I rehearsed the music, Ahmed got very excited. I tried covering Ahmed's cage to quiet him. Nothing worked. Ahmed insisted on joining our rehearsal. I realized that the bird was picking up on the sounds we were making. So I thought, "Why not include the bird?" The duo became a trio: *Duo for Accordion and Bandoneon with Possible Mynah Bird Obbligato* (1964).

We needed a way to stage this trio. I invited Elizabeth Harris to do the staging. Elizabeth asked, "How would you like to play the piece on a seesaw?" David and I innocently agreed. Elizabeth turned up at 321 Divisadero with a large, handsome seesaw mounted on a turntable. The seesaw went up and down and around and had swivel seats. She placed Ahmed's cage in a mobile suspended above the center of the seesaw. I swallowed hard and abandoned the written score that I had composed and decided on improvisational instructions. After experimenting with the possible motions of the seesaw, we needed some choreography. Elizabeth provided choreographic instructions. David and I both had to work very hard to integrate this new element of performance. I had to employ a safety belt to negotiate the swivel chair because of the imbalance of the motion of my accordion bellows. David could center on the seat with the bandoneon without a safety belt since the bellows were bidirectional. Slowly, we gained some control of the seesaw and began to enjoy it. The motions of the seesaw served to project and spatialize the sound of our instruments in all directions as we flew around on the seesaw and turned in the swivel seats.

Tony Martin provided lighting for the piece. Ahmed was turned on by the audience at the premiere performance during the Tudorfest and began chattering the minute he appeared on stage. Ahmed became quiet though when the lights went out at the beginning of the piece. It was dark and Tony's lighting was minimal at first. It took a while for Ahmed to make a sound in this new strange environment. The critics on the first night claimed that Ahmed was "mum," even though Ahmed had joined in the music. The second night, we decided to let Ahmed make the first sound. That strategy worked and the audience was delighted with the mynah bird obbligato! Our performance of *Atlas Eclipticalis* came shortly after the notorious and sophomoric performance given by the New York Philharmonic. The Philharmonic players behaved badly and reportedly tried to sabotage the piece by not taking it seriously.

The experience of working with David Tudor had a large and lasting impact on me and on all associated with the Tudorfest performances. David was a master musician. He taught patience, perseverance, and listening by his actions and preparation for the performances, and mostly without words.

The year 1964 was a dynamic one at the San Francisco Tape Music Center. In addition to the excitement of the Tudorfest, we did the premiere performances of *In C* by Terry Riley. We all knew that Terry had done something special with this piece. Alfred Frankenstein declared *In C* a twentieth-century masterpiece,[6] something hundreds of performances over the past forty years and more have verified. Performers of *In C* included myself on accordion, Steve Reich, clarinet, Morton Subotnick, clarinet, Terry, flute, and several others. Because we had difficulty keeping the pulse, the piano pulse was added to the score at that time.

I composed *Pieces of Eight for Wind Octet, Props, and Tape* in 1964. *Pieces of Eight* was my first real theater piece and had references to Robert Louis Stevenson's *Treasure Island*. There were puns like "Beware of piracy on the high C's." The clarinet player wore a black eye patch and a bandana on his head. Props for the piece included a weathercock on the conductor's stand; stand-up scales, a cash register with a bell, eight alarm clocks, a cuckoo clock, a wooden packing case, and a larger-than-life papier-mâché bust of Beethoven with flashing red eyes. Mort called *Pieces of Eight* "a theater piece of the absurd."[7] The analog tape part was integrated with the sounds of the acoustic players. The score provided instructions on what to play. There was an intricate cuing system that triggered musical and theatrical events. The conductor was busy for most of the piece opening the wooden packing case with a lot of squeaks behind the players, while the weathercock presided on the conductor's stand. In the end, the conductor got the bust of Beethoven out of the box and carried it with red eyes flashing through the audience while acolytes passed the plate, with tape music playing. At the right moment, the offertory ended with the conductor standing under the cuckoo clock with Beethoven. The cuckoo sounded 12 o'clock and the metaphor of twofold cuckold was well understood by the audience, since who was cuckolded by whom was part of the absurdity of the piece.

I worked most often in the studio from midnight to dawn when the daily hubbub was over and there was quiet and a peaceful space. I had no training in electronics, mathematics, or physics. I had to teach myself about the hardware in the analog studio. Though well meaning, the "boys" were not necessarily helpful. The tech-oriented attitude put me off more often than not—mostly because of lack of vocabulary and knowledge on my part. Men have a way of bonding around technology. There seemed to be an invisible barrier tied to a way of treating women as helpless or hapless beings. I wanted to learn and be in on the latest gadgets, but it was difficult to make my learning needs known. I also had my pride. I learned by drawing pictures of every piece of equipment, noting every term, then searching in references for their meanings. After this research, I asked questions and gradually learned how to operate the equipment that had accumulated in the studio. This was hands-on, trial-and-error learning. My procedure was to work from sound sources that were mostly found objects or unorthodox ways of playing instruments. For example, I clamped bronze rods to the bars on the piano soundboard, blocked the sustain pedal, and bowed the rods, eliciting reverberating high partials. I rubbed the wire-wound bass strings with a thin metal piece and struck the soundboard with mallets to get material for *Seven Passages* and other pieces in 1963. Mort had steered a commission for a dance piece with the choreographer Elizabeth Harris my way. I had not yet made any electronically generated music. I also made music for a couple of productions for the San Francisco Mime Troupe, *The Chronicles of Hell* by Michel de Ghelderode, and a Brecht play.

In 1965, I invented a process to make my first electronically generated music. My accordion teacher Dr. Willard (Bill) Palmer had taught me to listen for difference tones as I played my accordion. I was impressed that I could perceive ghostly tones resulting from the difference between two pitches, especially high pitches played at high volume. I was staring at the Hewlett-Packard oscillators in the studio one night and wondering how to use them to make music. I noticed that I could set the frequency range above the range of hearing. An *ah ha!* lightbulb flashed in my mind, and I remembered difference tones. I set the generators above hearing range around 30–40 khz and listened. Hearing nothing, I decided that the difference tones must need amplification to be perceived. I patched in a couple of line amplifiers, and boom there was a beautiful low difference tone!

What a moment for me. I began experimenting. The first discovery was that the dials on the generators became supersensitive with this technique. I could sweep the entire audio range with a very slight twist of the dial. A variety of sound qualities became audible as the relationship of the generating tones changed. I had invented an electronic performance instrument for myself. Soon I began to use two tape machines as a delay system by running the supply reel on one machine and the take-up reel on the other. The patch bay allowed me to configure the signal routing and delay paths. I patched the output of one machine back to the first machine and used the distances between record heads and playback heads in a variety of configurations.[8] With two oscillators, two tape machines, two line amplifiers, and a patch bay, I began to make my first electronic pieces *(Mnemonics I–V)* in a real-time improvised studio performance, with the result on tape.

In December 1965, Don Buchla demonstrated his 100 series modular synthesizer (the "Buchla Box") downstairs in the concert hall at 321 Divisadero. Mort and Ramon had advised Don on what they really wanted for the studio, so the demo was a great moment for the San Francisco Tape Music Center.[9] I went upstairs to the studio after I left the Buchla demo and made *Bye Bye Butterfly*. I was still pretty attached to the sounds of those tube oscillators, and the days of the classical electronic music studio were numbered. I wanted to use a record as a sound source in this new piece. I noticed an LP lying on a table in the studio. I patched the phonograph into my performance system and began playing. I dropped the needle on the record without knowing what it was. I wanted to be surprised. The record was an aria from *Madame Butterfly* by Giacomo Puccini. And I played with it, improvising as the music was processed by my delay configuration. *Bye Bye Butterfly* could be called an early "re-mix" without a mixer.[10] (The studio had no mixer.)

After the Tudorfest, David and I continued to perform together. We played my *Apple Box Double* at San Francisco State College in 1965. *Apple Box* took its name from the use of an apple box as a resonator for small vibrating objects that could be struck or bowed. The apple box had solid panels on all sides except the bottom. So the box was ideal as a resonator. I put contact mics on the apple box and fed them to Radio Shack battery-powered input splitters that could accept and amplify four sources to one output. These powered input splitters served many of us, including David, in the time before mixing boards became available for performances, which was only much later. The small sounds on the apple box became larger than life through amplification. There was no score for the piece; it was a just play and listen improvisation. When David joined me, the title became *Apple Box Double.*

In 1965, Ramon became involved in the psychedelic movement with Richard Alpert. Mort and I were alarmed by Ramon's involvement with LSD. Ramon wanted us to join him and tried to convince us of the beauty of an LSD trip and how it could inform our humanity and creative work. I did not trust involvement with drugs and resisted as the psychedelic movement revved up. Ramon resigned his position as director of the center and teamed up with Stewart Brand to produce the Trips Festival. We were sad to lose Ramon's participation in the San Francisco Tape Music Center. Ramon was and has always been one of the most creative friends in my life.

I produced what I called a "side trip" at the Encore Theater during the Trips Festival. *A Theater Piece* (1965) was an hour long, with direction and staging by Elizabeth Harris and Ronald Chase. Ronnie Davis, then director for the San Francisco Mime Troupe, made a cameo appearance with his violin. The music for *A Theater Piece* was performed live by me and other musicians and vocalists. I used amplified sound sources processed by tape delay and included *Mnemonics III* and *Rock Symphony* on tape. *A Theater Piece* was performed several times. After the run, we did a concert at the Encore Theater of *Apple Box Orchestra with Bottle Chorus.* There were ten apple box players, and Bob Moran led a group of volunteers blowing on tuned bottles. The composer Charles MacDermed shared this program with a piece of his, in which he handed out electronic devices he had made for the audience to play.

In 1966, the Rockefeller Foundation wanted to fund the San Francisco Tape Music Center, with the proviso that a responsible fiscal agent be involved. Mort negotiated a transfer of the San Francisco Tape Music Center nonprofit to Mills College, and 321 Divisadero, beloved by me, was finished. I insisted that there be public access to the studio at Mills. It seemed important to me that the community outside of Mills be involved as much as possible. The visitors who needed access to facilities to make their music always increased the excitement and stimulation at San Francisco Tape Music Center. Mort was leaving for New York University, Ramon had dropped out, and Tony and I were appointed codirectors of the new Mills Tape Music Center.

At the Mills Tape Music Center, I plunged into learning to use the Buchla 100

17 TONY MARTIN AND PAULINE OLIVEROS AT MILLS COLLEGE, OAKLAND, CALIFORNIA (CA. 1966).

series modular synthesizer. I felt the loss of the sound of the old tube oscillators, and it took some time for me to adapt to the coolness of transistor-generated sound. The oscillators also did not have the high-frequency range above hearing like the tube oscillators. By 1967, I had made some pieces with the Buchla Box, still using my tape delay system, which included *Beautiful Soop* and *Alien Bog*. I designed a four-channel mixer to be used for performance. Nothing was available for performance except the input splitters from Radio Shack. We still had no mixer in the studio. Carl Countryman, a young engineer, undertook the construction of this mixer, which had eight inputs, four outputs, and DC voltage-control outputs. I used the mixer in a few performances before I left my one-year position at Mills.

I composed *Circuitry for Percussion and Light* in 1967 as well, in collaboration with Tony. *Circuitry* was a benchmark piece and signaled some new directions. Five percussionists were reading a matrix of suspended lightbulbs as indications of what to play. Each section of the matrix had a different instruction tempo, dynamic, method, or quality. A desk indicator light for each player told them when to play. Audio signals from the players were picked up by microphones and filtered. Those signals turned the lights on and off. Thus the players were engaged in a feedback situation where what they played changed the score indications and who was playing when.

CIRCUITRY

	1	2	3	4
a	SLOW	PPP	SHORT (choke)	ROLL OFF
b	SPEED UP AND/OR SLOW DOWN	> AND/OR <	GLISSANDO	STREET BEAT
c	FAST	fff	INDUCTION OR SUSTAIN	SINGLE STROKE ROLL

Each of the above twelve boxes is represented by one light bulb. In addition to the twelve light bulbs representing the score, each percussionist has an indicator light. Light on means play, light off means don't play. If light bulbs 1a, 2c and 4a of the score are on, a slow, loud roll off is indicated. More than one light on in a vertical column indicates choice. No lights on in a vertical column indicates free choice. All score lights off means do not play.

Choice of metal, wood or skin instruments and mallets, sticks, metal beater, hands or bow is free. Do not change instrument or combination of instruments and maintain tempo a or c until indicator light goes off or score lights change.

The fifth percussionist does not read the score but plays either jazz, rock and roll or dixieland when his indicator light is on.

Pauline Oliveros
Feb. 1967

18 PAGE FROM SCORE FOR *CIRCUITRY*, BY PAULINE OLIVEROS.

The audio signals were also fed to lighting that Tony had composed for the piece. The premiere performance for *Circuitry* occurred at Mills in the concert hall, and it was subsequently performed at the University of Illinois. Otherwise, there were no performances until the San Francisco Tape Music Center Retrospective held at the Experimental Media and Performing Arts Center (EMPAC), Rensselaer Polytechnic University, in October 2004.

As the first year of Mills Tape Music Center came to a close in 1967, I was invited to take a job at the University of California, San Diego, in the music department established by Wilbur Ogden and Robert Erickson. Will and Bob wanted me to establish an electronic music program for the graduate students. It was uncertain whether my one-year position at Mills would be continued, and I decided to take the opportunity that was offered to me at UCSD.

My farewell to San Francisco was a "Tape-athon" at my artist friend Ronald Chase's loft on the Embarcadero. The Tape-athon ran from 6 P.M. to 6 A.M. and included all the tape music that I had made to date. Morton Feldman was one of the distinguished audience members. I left San Francisco with some regrets, because the San Francisco Tape Music Center and Mills had played a large part in my emergence as a composer. It thrills me that the spirit of the old center lives on at Mills today, and that hundreds of composers have benefited and contributed to the continuing development of electronic music and new media through our efforts in the 1960s. It also thrills me to be connected in a worldwide community of interest that includes Mort, Ramon, Tony, Bill, and so many of my old and new friends.

NOTES

1. Tape recorders had only recently become available at the time. Recording engineers were still learning this medium, which radio stations embraced in the 1950s for its new flexibility and fidelity for editing radio programs. See "John (Jack) T. Mullin (1913–99) Recalls the American Development of the Tape Recorder," http://mcckc.edu/~crosby/mullin.htm (accessed May 26, 2006).

2. An archive of these broadcasts is now available online at the Other Minds KPFA Music Archive: http://otherminds.org/shtml/KPFAarchives.shtml (accessed May 26, 2006).

3. *San Francisco Chronicle,* March 26, 1962, 40.

4. See www.pofinc.org/DLBhome.html (accessed May 26, 2006).

5. The tour included Ball State College in Muncie, Indiana, Central Michigan University in Mt. Pleasant, Michigan, and the College Conservatory of Music in Cincinnati, Ohio, and ended at the New Hampshire Music Festival, Lake Winnipesauke, New Hampshire.

6. Alfred Frankenstein, "Music Like None Other on Earth," *San Francisco Chronicle,* November 8, 1964, 28.

7. *Pieces of Eight,* reported Arthur Bloomfield in the *San Francisco Examiner* (May 4, 1965), "unwound amidst a concatenation of alarm clocks, cuckoo clock, cash register, and assorted glissandos, burps, and bellows from an ensemble of eight performers who looked rather more plausible than they sounded. As part of the overall whimsy, the oboist entered in a fur-lined parka which he removed, then unpacked his instrument, sounded an eight-second whirling cadenza, and put on his parka again and stalked off. There was a solo for a cash register. A bust of Beethoven was paraded up and down the aisles."

8. See Pauline Oliveros, "Tape Delay Techniques for Electronic Music Composers," in *Software for the People* (Baltimore: Smith Publications 1984), 36–46.

9. According to Morton Subotnick, the Buchla was delivered to the center in late 1964 or early 1965. See Morton Subotnick, Ramon Sender, and Maggi Payne, "The Genesis of the Buchla 100 Series Modular Electronic Music System" in the present volume. Oliveros is most likely describing the first public demonstration.

10. *Bye Bye Butterfly* was named one of the most significant pieces of electronic music of the 1960s by John Rockwell of the *New York Times* (July 27, 1980).

Pauline Oliveros

INTERVIEWED BY DAVID W. BERNSTEIN AND MAGGI PAYNE

Pauline Oliveros played a major role in the development of the San Francisco Tape Music Center as it evolved into the most prominent venue for experimental music in San Francisco. At the same time, the Tape Music Center provided Oliveros with an environment within which she could develop her continuing work in electronic music, mixed media, and improvisation. This opportunity was especially crucial for a woman composer in a technological field dominated by men.

On July 22, 1967, a twelve-hour concert devoted entirely to Oliveros's electronic music took place in a loft on the Embarcadero in San Francisco. The event, entitled "Tape-athon," featured thirty works written between 1961 and 1967, an impressive accomplishment in only six years, especially considering the fact that the program included works, such as *Bye Bye Butterfly* (1965), now considered "classics" in the history of electronic music. During that period, Oliveros, along with the composers Ramon Sender and Morton Subotnick, cofounded the San Francisco Tape Music Center. Oliveros later became the director of the center when it moved to Mills College in the summer of 1966. The Tape-athon was Oliveros's farewell to the Bay Area, for she had just accepted a new teaching position at the University of California, San Diego. It marked the end of a period during which she had established her compositional career. Although Oliveros was at Mills for only one year, the creative spirit she cultivated at the San Francisco Tape Music Center took root and continues today at the Mills Music Department and Center for Contemporary Music.

The following interview surveys Oliveros's activities in San Francisco in the 1950s and 1960s, including her early studies with Robert Erickson, her famous improvisation sessions with Terry Riley and Loren Rush, her work with dancers and the San Francisco Mime Troupe, her collaborations with David Tudor, and her pathbreaking work in electronic music and emerging forms of mixed media. Finally, it also reveals that Oliveros was very much attuned to developments outside of music. Many of her theater pieces created during the 1960s were both humorous and

19 PROGRAM FOR THE "TAPE-ATHON" OF PAULINE OLIVEROS'S MUSIC, HELD AT RONALD CHASE'S LOFT ON THE EMBARCADERO, SAN FRANCISCO (1967).

at the same time poignant critiques aimed at traditional concert music, as well as the American political and social scene.

BERNSTEIN: You were a student at San Francisco State, and, as I understand it, you didn't have a composition teacher there. Is that correct?

OLIVEROS: Well, no, there was Dr. Wendell Otey. He ran what was called the Composers' Workshop, which met once a week. He would look over students' scores and comment on them. But that was it.

BERNSTEIN: Was Stuart Dempster in your class?

OLIVEROS: He was not in the first Composers' Workshop I was in [1954]. I think he might have joined [the workshop] later on.

BERNSTEIN: Around 1954, you also started taking private lessons with Robert Erickson?

OLIVEROS: Yes, I did.

BERNSTEIN: And that continued for about six years?

OLIVEROS: Yes.

BERNSTEIN: Can you tell me about Erickson, about the classes, and how he influenced you?

OLIVEROS: Well, Erickson was a wonderful teacher. He really knew how to put his finger on why you were stuck in a composition. He could find that and help you to move it along. He was very good at putting materials in front of you that related to whatever it was you were doing. If I didn't have any new work to show him, we would do some analysis. He was interested in theory. So we did that. But he was mainly supportive and intelligent.

BERNSTEIN: It's interesting that Loren Rush, Terry Riley, Stuart Dempster, and Ramon Sender also studied with him.

OLIVEROS: Yes.

BERNSTEIN: It's clear that he was a very influential teacher in the Bay Area at that time.

OLIVEROS: Yes, he was. He also would invite us over together to his house. He had a "familial" style. It was nice.

BERNSTEIN: Did these get-togethers include Ramon and Loren Rush?

OLIVEROS: Later. Ramon came on the scene a little bit later in about 1959, when he showed up from New York. Bob started to teach at the San Francisco Conservatory. He had a composition seminar there. Sometimes I'd go and sit in on that. He also had a musicianship class that I sat in on at the conservatory. And so I learned quite a bit about his teaching of musicianship.

BERNSTEIN: So in about 1958 you started an improvisation group with Terry Riley and Loren Rush

OLIVEROS: Right.

BERNSTEIN: Was that the beginning of your interest in improvisation?

OLIVEROS: It wasn't the beginning, because I always improvised. But that was the first time I ever improvised with anybody else.

BERNSTEIN: I think I remember that you mentioned that when you were younger, you had a tape recorder and you used to improvise and record yourself.

OLIVEROS: Yes.

BERNSTEIN: So you started to improvise very early on?

OLIVEROS: Oh, yes.

BERNSTEIN: Around the same time, Lukas Foss came to the Bay Area with his Improvisation Group. Is that correct?

OLIVEROS: Yes. Terry, Loren, and I had been doing these improvisations, and we were kind of excited about it. And when Lukas Foss came to town, he was supposed to come and do improvisation. We were very excited to hear another group doing improvisation. So we went to the concert. But we were all kind of looking at each other and wondering, because they all had music stands. [Laughs] They were doing "guided" improvisation. And afterwards we asked the question, "What would happen if you didn't use music stands?" And Lukas Foss said, "It would be utter chaos." So what we understood was improvisation was not what he understood was improvisation.

BERNSTEIN: Did your improvisations have a direct relationship to the music you were composing?

OLIVEROS: Well, I always would improvise my way through whatever work I was composing.

BERNSTEIN: At that time you were writing *Three Songs for Soprano and Horn* [1957] and *Three Songs for Soprano and Piano* [1957] with poems by Robert Duncan and Charles Olson. How did you first get familiar with the work of those poets?

OLIVEROS: Well, I had decided I wanted to write some songs and I also thought I wanted to know the poet. And so I went to the Poetry Center at San Francisco State and Robert Duncan was the director. And I talked to him and I told him what I was interested in and he offered himself. I met with him and he pulled out some poems. And I wrote a song; he was really delighted with it. He introduced me to Charles Olson's and Robert Creeley's poetry. He was living with Jess Collins, the painter. I became friends with them and went to their house very often and went to events that were happening in the Bay Area with Robert and other poets. So I met a lot of them, such as Robin Blaser and Jack Spicer. So it was a very interesting time. Robert was a very important connection for me with the world of poetry.

BERNSTEIN: The songs are in an atonal style?

OLIVEROS: Yes. I guess you could say that.

BERNSTEIN: What sort of music were you interested in?

OLIVEROS: I was always interested in the most dissonant music that I heard. I was attracted to dissonance from the beginning.

BERNSTEIN: Were you interested in the twelve-tone system?

OLIVEROS: No, not really. I did write a twelve-tone piece, but I made it sound tonal.

BERNSTEIN: What piece was that?

OLIVEROS: I think that one was the *Serenade for Viola and Bassoon* [1956].

BERNSTEIN: It's interesting that following your early pieces you gradually began to break from traditional notation, write more graphic scores, and include improvisation in your work.

OLIVEROS: Right, exactly.

BERNSTEIN: Am I correct in saying that your *Variations for Sextet* [1960] was a work written just before this development took place?

OLIVEROS: Right.

BERNSTEIN: I understand that it has a long C drone?

OLIVEROS: Yes.

BERNSTEIN: It makes me think of La Monte Young's *Trio* [1958]. Did you know that piece?

OLIVEROS: Oh, yes. La Monte and Terry were students at UC Berkeley, as was Loren [Rush]. There was a seminar with Seymour Shifrin and I sat in on it with La Monte and Terry. La Monte was writing music more along the lines of Stockhausen at that time.[1] In [1959], he went to Darmstadt and met [David Tudor] and [learned more about the music of John Cage] and was converted to "John Cage." [Laughs] He started to write differently and talk quite differently. That's when he did the piece with the B-F# fifth "to be held for a long time" [*Composition 1960 #7* (July)]. Interest in drones was very much in the air. It was not only La Monte and Terry; I was also interested in that as well.

BERNSTEIN: In 1961, you wrote the *Trio for Flute, Piano, and Page Turner*.

OLIVEROS: Right.

BERNSTEIN: That had a theatrical element in it; the page turner was quite busy.

OLIVEROS: Yes.

BERNSTEIN: I think that putting in that theatrical element in way anticipated the importance of extramusical activities in your later work.

OLIVEROS: Yes. The page turner was necessary; I needed some extra things to happen. [Laughs] So the page turner was the one to do it. So then I decided to call it the *Trio for Flute, Piano, and Page Turner*.

BERNSTEIN: And it's kind of humorous.

OLIVEROS: Yes, right, it was intended to be.

BERNSTEIN: You are really good at that.

OLIVEROS: [Laughs]

BERNSTEIN: After that piece, that's when your music really started changing, with *Sound Patterns* for mixed chorus (1961) and your first tape piece, *Time Perspectives* (1961). The score for *Sound Patterns* is very original and was already moving away from traditional notation.

OLIVEROS: Right. *Time Perspectives* was really my first work for [what was to become] the San Francisco Tape Music Center. Ramon was going to the San Francisco Conservatory at the time, and there was an attic space that was used for the first studio. The operation was called "Sonics." And the idea was to gather equipment together and make tape music, because there was no other place to do that at the time.

I was interested in talking with Ramon, and then Mort came into the scene a little later. But Ramon wanted to start a studio and get stuff together, which he did. And I found that for me, it was better to work at home with my tape recorder, which is what I did. I didn't really work in the studio at all. I created that first tape piece with my Sears and Roebuck Silvertone tape recorder and a microphone. I used mechanical devices to simulate filters and reverberation.

BERNSTEIN: What mechanical devices?

OLIVEROS: Cardboard tubes. [Laughs] And a bathtub, and using the wall or a box for amplification.

It was interesting because I could hand wind the tape in "record" mode so I could do variable speed recordings with it. I did a lot of stuff with it. I was very ambitious—I did a four-channel tape piece for my first tape piece. What I did was use two stereo machines. The way we lined up the tapes was: Ramon and I rolled [the tape reels] out and down the long halls of the conservatory and we synched them up by hand. That piece was called *Time Perspectives*.

PAYNE: What were the sound sources for that piece?

OLIVEROS: I was very interested in small found objects that I would attach to apple boxes—you know those wooden apple crates made great resonators. I would use things like curb scrapers from cars, and little things that vibrated. The box would amplify the sounds and I would pick them up with microphones: air mics and contact mics as well. I think I used my voice, too. I used cardboard tubes to filter sounds, bathtub reverberation, and whatever. It was a kind of mechanical, analog way of putting sounds together. And then I would do variable speed and drop things an octave or push them up. Mostly it was dropping things.

PAYNE: Did you do a lot of editing?

OLIVEROS: No. Not at all.

PAYNE: No razor blades for you!

OLIVEROS: No. I didn't like that at all. I would experiment and then I would play the thing. That was my modus operandi all along. I wasn't interested in cutting and splicing. I was probably the complete opposite of Mario Davidovsky—the complete opposite. We were friends, but what I would do was to try to make the tape as long as possible.

BERNSTEIN: Did you study any other electronic works, Stockhausen and all the others?

OLIVEROS: Oh, well, I heard those things on KPFA. We did not have that much access in those days. We would get tapes sometimes, but they weren't as freely available as they were later. So hearing things on KPFA was how we got acquainted with things.

BERNSTEIN: So moving on to electronic music was a natural thing for you.

OLIVEROS: Yes.

BERNSTEIN: Erickson was very interested in tone color and the nature of sound a lot. And that could have been an influence as well.

OLIVEROS: Yes, of course.

BERNSTEIN: When I think about *Time Perspectives* and your use of a bathtub as a reverberation chamber—this might be true for many electronic music composers, but it certainly is true for you—it seems that you have always been especially interested in resonance.

OLIVEROS: Yes.

BERNSTEIN: And that interest in resonance is also reflected in other pieces using apple boxes: *Apple Box* [1964], *Apple Box Double* [1965], *Apple Box Orchestra* [1964], and much later, such as when you played in a cistern with Stuart Dempster.

OLIVEROS: Yes, all of those things.

BERNSTEIN: So that early work foreshadows directions that you took later.

OLIVEROS: Sure.

BERNSTEIN: It's amazing to me, thinking of this change in your musical style, that it begins a period of about six years, from 1961 to 1967, during which you wrote a lot of music. The period culminated with the "Tape-athon," a 1967 concert featuring thirty of your works played in twelve hours. It must have been a really exciting period in your life.

OLIVEROS: It was, definitely.

BERNSTEIN: The name Laurel Johnson often comes up. Could you say something about her? Was she a percussionist?

OLIVEROS: Well, Laurel was quite versatile. She was interested in visual art, and you know she designed the programs for the Sonics series. That was her artwork. She played the recorder and did improvisation. I had a little improvisation class in which she took part. She got very turned on by all the recording and things. She helped me a bit with *Time Perspectives*. I think some of the sounds came from her, with the cardboard tubes, for example.

BERNSTEIN: Where was your class?

OLIVEROS: At home. I had a small group, maybe three people. It was a little class. We did a year of programs at the conservatory, maybe four or five programs. Mort Subotnick joined us and A. A. Leath, John Graham, and Lynne Palmer from Ann Halprin's Dancers' Workshop. We started doing things we called "opera." And they were a lot of fun. They were improvisations that came out of the collaborative effort between the dancers and us, the composers.

After that first year, I went away for a while, because I had won a prize for a piece from the Gaudeamus Festival, and I went to Holland. I took the prize money and traveled around Europe. I was gone for about six months. When I got back, Ramon and Mort had cofounded the San Francisco Tape Music Center using a 501(c)(3) status. They had rented an old Victorian on Jones Street and set up a studio there. That's the one that burned down. There were a number of performances there, involving a lot of interesting creative artists, such as Lee Breuer and Robert Duncan. I wasn't too involved with Jones Street because I was very busy writing a piece. Then [the building] burned down, and the next venue was 321 Divisadero. And there the Tape Music Center really emerged as an interesting organization.

BERNSTEIN: What period was that?

OLIVEROS: 1963 through 1966. I believe, about three years. It was very lively all the time. I used to work from midnight to dawn because it was quiet and no one was there and I could figure out what I wanted to do without interference or preemption. That was my shift. I had a very good time there. The subscription audience was good. Up to about 100–150 people would show up, sometimes less, but it could seat up to 150 people.

BERNSTEIN: Were there any outside composers?

OLIVEROS: Absolutely. Mort would bring people over, like Luciano Berio. There was a group of Swedish composers [Folke Rabe, Jan Bark, and Arne Mellnäs] who came through. They were trying to build the perfect electronic music studio in Sweden.

BERNSTEIN: Ramon wrote a report, I believe it was after the end of the first season, and in that report he articulates some of the aesthetic principles behind the Tape Music Center. One of the principles was community access. Did you play a part in formulating that, because I know this idea has been very important to you.

OLIVEROS: Ramon wrote that report, because he was the director of the Tape Music Center. I think we all had discussions about all kinds of things. I know that when it came time to move the center to Mills College, I insisted on maintaining the idea of public access.

BERNSTEIN: Ramon's report is very precise. It sounds like everybody came to a consensus as to what direction the center would take. Do you remember how that came about, how you decided?

OLIVEROS: I think it just came about pretty organically, because it came about through what we were actually doing. So Ramon's report is a synthesis of what we were all doing. But I think that Ramon had a deep interest in community, and of course, the San Francisco Tape Music Center was a community; it definitely was. It certainly was a place that I connected to very deeply. There wasn't any other place for me.

The Swedish group came from my connection with [the] Gaudeamus [Foundation]. There were lots of locals like Terry Riley and Steve Reich, eventually, Janis Joplin and Big Brother and the Holding Company too, and Grace Slick. It was an amazing time. For me, I hesitate to think about what it would have been like not to have all that. It provided me with a platform for developing my work.

BERNSTEIN: 1963–64 was a great first season. You performed in *Desert Ambulance* (1964). And for the season opener, do you remember there was an improvisation with you, Mort, Ramon, and Elias Romero doing light projections?

OLIVEROS: Yes, well, it's a dim memory, but we felt very comfortable improvising together and having the lights was a new aspect, a new element. It was not too long after that that Tony [Martin] joined us.

BERNSTEIN: During that same season was the Tudorfest. Ramon and Mort were completely amazed by how far you took that whole idea, with all the press and the organizational talents that you had, let alone the creative aspects. It reminds me of what you do now; you are able to get so many things to happen. What inspired you to produce the Tudorfest?

OLIVEROS: Well, I think that having David [Tudor] take such an interest in what we were doing and his willingness to perform was a great moment for us, and [I felt that] we should take advantage of it to promote the work we were doing. So I just went at it with that attitude I guess.

It was a six-day festival, and it featured the music of John Cage, Alvin Lucier, Toshi Ichiyanagi, and myself. I had met David Tudor the year before, and we had performed together. So this festival was organized, and David selected the music. It turned out that John Cage came [as well].

I had an interview with John Cage on the radio, and he was really very happy because we were doing *Atlas Eclipticalis* [1961–62] with *Winter Music* [1957] and the *Concert for Piano and Orchestra* [1958]. The performers were Mort Subotnick (clarinet), David Tudor and Dwight Peltzer (piano), Stuart Dempster (trombone, bass trumpet, and garden hose), Linn Subotnick (viola), with Ramon Sender conducting. I was playing in it (French horn and tuba) and Stanley Shaff [played the] trumpet. It was a very interesting collection of local musicians. I think John Chowning (percussion) and Loren Rush (double bass) also played. There is a recording of it in my archive. You should definitely get copies of it, because it is part of the history of the Tape Music Center and it stretched the center at the time, pushing it into another domain. That was 1964.

The next year I think the first Rockefeller money came, a grant for $15,000. Ramon was the director of the center, and it was going to pay for his salary.

PAYNE: How did you all support yourselves during this time?

OLIVEROS: Mort was, of course, teaching at Mills, so he was covered. Ramon, well, I don't know how he did it. I was piecing it together like mad. In those days, I taught a string of students: accordion and French horn. I copied music. I played in a variety of situations. I played accordion and French horn. I have no idea how I did it in a way. And yes, I did do it. You know, you look back on it, and it wasn't easy. I had maybe $250 dollars a month to get by on.

BERNSTEIN: In 1964–65, you really started to work with theatrical elements. *Pieces of Eight* [1964] was your first major theater piece. I understand that it was premiered at the University of Arizona in 1965. Do you remember that?

OLIVEROS: Yes, I do. I wasn't there. I wrote the piece, and I sent it to Barney Childs, and they put it together. God knows how they did it; what it was like. [Laughs] I don't know.

BERNSTEIN: In November 1965, there were several theater pieces. You did *George Washington Slept Here* [1965]. Could you say something about that work?

OLIVEROS: It was a "patriotism-buster," a caricature of patriotism. It was a humorous idea for me to think of George Washington sleeping at the Tape Music Center. The title was some kind of a pun. I had this violin that was luminous. And Tony had the idea of dipping the violin into a bucket of lights, so it would phosphoresce. So we did that, and I would play that violin with it glowing like that. And I had made the tape, and I think the tape had a remix of [Chuck Berry's song] "Roll Over Beethoven" by the Beatles.

BERNSTEIN: Were there other instruments?

OLIVEROS: No, it was just me. It was a solo.

BERNSTEIN: Tony created projections for it as well?

OLIVEROS: Yes, he had a light show going with it.

BERNSTEIN: It's also interesting that it had a political edge.

OLIVEROS: Yes, it did.

BERNSTEIN: That was beginning to happen a lot in your work at that time. *Pieces of Eight* was a critique of traditional concert music.

OLIVEROS: That's true. It was a deconstruction of the conductor and the conducted ensemble.

BERNSTEIN: And *George Washington Slept Here* was a critique of patriotism. Obviously, you were you thinking of what was going on in the world at that time.

OLIVEROS: Absolutely, yes.

BERNSTEIN: And in *A Theater Piece* [1965] as well, with the famous Mario Savio speech about the destruction of "the machine."

OLIVEROS: Yes.

BERNSTEIN: *George Washington Slept Here Too* [1965] seems to me to be almost like a Fluxus event. The performers appear, shoot into the piano, and then the lights go out.

OLIVEROS: Right, and then you see a flag and a slide of Uncle Sam's arm pointing [to show that] "Uncle Sam wants you."

BERNSTEIN: There's the idea of critiquing patriotism again.

OLIVEROS: That's right; it was definitely that.

BERNSTEIN: I'm sure there were some horrendous things happening in Vietnam at that time.

OLIVEROS: There were.

BERNSTEIN: In the same month you did *Light Piece for David Tudor* [1965].

OLIVEROS: Right. There's where I really took an interest in drones. David's part was to play D♭ on the piano. He could play it any way he wanted to, but just play D♭ in a specific register. I made this tape. My idea was ideal; I mean I had an "ideal idea," which was I would record a piano D♭, and I wanted to reinforce the harmonics of that note with sine waves. I wanted to run loops of this D♭ that would have a continual change of harmonic structure while David was playing the D♭. We had these loop machines. There were twenty-four loop machines. I naively thought that they would run at the same speed, and that I could be able to have a kind of additive synthesis of these harmonics. Well, as it turns out, analog is just not that precise. Those machines didn't run at the same speed. And so I got microtonal differences instead of the harmonic reinforcement that I was looking for. So it was more accidental than it was what I had planned. [Laughs] But David played the D♭, and he played it amazingly. He used all kinds of ways of playing on the piano and on the keys, with a vibrator and all kinds of stuff. So that D♭ on the piano really got a workout. [Laughs] It sounded different after he was done with that piece. And Tony used a prism, which he had suspended on a long string, and he wound up the string and let the prism go and then he beamed light into the prism and sent rainbows out all over the place as the prism gradually wound down.

That piece was really controversial. We went to play it at Case Western University in Cleveland, Ohio. That was David [Tudor's] concert and he invited me, Alvin Lucier, and David Behrman to do pieces there. Well, both Alvin's piece and David [Behrman's] piece were very noisy. My piece was the drone piece for David [Tudor]. People almost started to riot and I remember some guy stood up in the audience and started shouting about something. So I just raised the volume and drowned him out. But it was interesting that my piece was the one that was controversial. [Laughs]

BERNSTEIN: Do you remember what year this was?

OLIVEROS: 1965.

BERNSTEIN: The summer of 1965?

OLIVEROS: It might have been.

BERNSTEIN: What do you remember about *A Theater Piece*, the piece that was performed as a "side-trip" for the Trips Festival, and before that as well?

OLIVEROS: Well, I had been working with Elizabeth Harris and Ronald Chase, and they invited me to work on this piece. I had some specific ideas, like the "bows," for example. The beginning of the piece had an electric train.

BERNSTEIN: It used a lot of props.

OLIVEROS: Yes, there were a lot of props in *A Theater Piece*.

BERNSTEIN: Did Elizabeth Harris make them?

OLIVEROS: Yes, she always used a lot of props. Ronnie Davis played violin; he made a cameo appearance.

BERNSTEIN: At that same time you were doing pieces outside of the Tape Music Center that involved theater. You did a lot of work with the San Francisco Mime Troupe.

OLIVEROS: Yes, I did do several pieces with the Mime Troupe.

BERNSTEIN: How did you make the connection with them?

OLIVEROS: I don't remember. I know that Steve Reich had worked with them. I did a Brecht piece and a work by Ghelderode . . .

BERNSTEIN: . . . *Exception and the Rule* and *Chronicles of Hell?*

OLIVEROS: Right.

BERNSTEIN: And *Candelaio* [by Giordano Bruno]. Do you remember the music for any of these works?

OLIVEROS: I used a tape for *Chronicles of Hell*. For the Brecht, I had the actors do the sound. For example, every time the Ruler appeared, he would crash the wind chimes together and let them go.

BERNSTEIN: What about *Covenant* [1965]? Was that music for a film?

OLIVEROS: Well, *Covenant* was actually a dance piece first with Elizabeth Harris and then it was filmed. I was bowing brass rods in the piano.

BERNSTEIN: At this point you are doing theater pieces, working in film, and doing work with the San Francisco Mime Troupe. So 1964 and 1965 were important years for you.

OLIVEROS: Yes, definitely.

BERNSTEIN: This was also an important period for your electronic music. Is it correct that in 1965 you first put together the setup with two Hewlett-Packard oscillators and line amplifiers that was eventually used in *Bye Bye Butterfly* [1965]?

OLIVEROS: Yes, that's right.

BERNSTEIN: You also were working with delay very beautifully.

OLIVEROS: Yes.

BERNSTEIN: Was that the first time using this technique?

OLIVEROS: No, I used delay in *Pieces of Eight*.

BERNSTEIN: Oh yes, and *Rock Symphony* [1965] uses delay as well. When did you first start to use delay?[2]

OLIVEROS: We did an improvisation at the San Francisco Conservatory in which Ramon set up a delay. And it was a very long delay, with the tape running from one machine quite a long distance to another machine. I know that Frankenstein wrote a review of that piece, thinking it was a very novel idea. What we played was picked up by the first machine and then it came back later in the piece. Sometime after that, I discovered the delay between the playback and the record heads on a tape machine and started to play with that, and one thing led to another. It was mainly [a matter of] having access to a studio that had two tape machines in it, which we had at Divisadero Street.

BERNSTEIN: Today it doesn't sound like so much, but then it was a really big deal. You were able to do so much with so little.

OLIVEROS: Well, that's what you do; you work with what you have.

BERNSTEIN: Prior to *Bye Bye Butterfly*, you started to write the *Mnemonics* pieces with your new "setup." There are five. They anticipate *Bye Bye Butterfly*, but I wouldn't call them "studies." They are beautiful pieces. You created *Bye Bye Butterfly* in 1965?

OLIVEROS: Yes.

BERNSTEIN: It's very interesting that you selected the Puccini excerpt by chance. Isn't it ironic that this piece has so many levels of critique, from the standpoint of nineteenth-century concert music traditions, and from feminist and orientalist perspectives? All of this was serendipitous? [Laughs]

OLIVEROS: Yes, absolutely all of that. You could say it's by "synchronicity." I was able to interact with that synchronicity instantaneously.

BERNSTEIN: It's a very powerful, moving piece.

PAYNE: Were you there during the genesis of the Buchla?

OLIVEROS: Yes, I was. It was Mort and Ramon who gave Don [Buchla] input about what they'd like—the concept of voltage control and all that. They gave him the input. They were trying, before Don showed up on the scene, to talk to other engineers. But it was Don who really caught fire, and did it.

When the first Buchla prototype was demonstrated down in the concert hall, I was upstairs in the studio, making *Bye Bye Butterfly*. I listened to the sound of the Buchla and I really didn't care for it much. I was used to those classical sine waves. Also, tubes and transistors were very different in their sound.

PAYNE: So you had those Hewlett-Packard oscillators and little Lafayettes?

OLIVEROS: I was really happy with the super heterodyne technique that I had developed. I set those oscillators to superaudio and then amplified the difference tones. And beat them against the bias of the tape recorders. And I was running a tape delay. So I had all these artifacts and instability that created those wonderful sounds. I had an ambivalent feeling about this new development, the Buchla. It was taking away my old toys. It didn't feel like an addition at the time, because I couldn't get the sounds that I could get with the oscillators.

BERNSTEIN: I like analog sounds.

OLIVEROS: I like acoustic sounds myself. All sounds. It's really all about how you make the music. You can use anything; you can use a kazoo. But you've got to make music. I eventually did end up using the Buchla. But it was never the same. It was a different instrument, that's all. So I had to learn what I could get from it. If you compare *I of IV* to *Alien Bog,* it's interesting to note the difference in the sounds. *I of IV* was produced in a classical studio in Toronto. It had twelve Lafayette oscillators, and a keyboard. It was a wonderful studio.

BERNSTEIN: Did you ever work at Columbia-Princeton [Electronic Music Center in New York City]?

OLIVEROS: Yes, [the Russian American composer] Vladimir Ussachevsky was there; he was a wonderful man. I did one piece there. It was really a tape-splicing job, a piece I did for Stuart Dempster, a [work for] trombone entitled *A Theater Piece for Trombone Player* [1966]. That was the year that I did the *Caucasian Chalk Circle* in New York.

BERNSTEIN: You also did music for dancers. We have been talking about Elizabeth Harris. Can you tell me more about her?

OLIVEROS: Mort connected me with her. She had wanted him to make music for her choreography, and he was busy with Ann Halprin and other things. So I started to work with her. She commissioned me to do *Seven Passages* [1963], and I worked with her on that first. And then I did *Covenant* [1965] and maybe *Before the Music Ends* [1965]. These were different things we worked on.

BERNSTEIN: What was her background?

OLIVEROS: Well, she trained with Louis Horst. But she was also very "handy"—she built things. So she used a lot of props in her work. As you know, she built the seesaw for my *Duo for Accordion and Bandoneon with Possible Mynah Bird Obbligato* [1964].

BERNSTEIN: What was the music for *Seven Passages* like?

OLIVEROS: That was a tape piece. I think I used sounds from the inside of the piano. I improvised using the inside of the piano.

BERNSTEIN: What was the title from?

OLIVEROS: Well, I think Elizabeth was looking for a title for the piece, and I suggested *Seven Passages* and she used it.

BERNSTEIN: Maybe it has seven sections?

OLIVEROS: It probably did.

BERNSTEIN: Do you remember the music for *Before the Music Ends?*

OLIVEROS: *Before the Music Ends* was really a collage of a lot of different sounds that Elizabeth wanted to have associated with the different things she was doing in the piece. So she really kind of directed it. I put it together, but it was not really my music. It was the sounds she wanted, and she directed me to put them in certain places.

BERNSTEIN: What about the title?

OLIVEROS: I don't know why she used it. I guess she was going through a sequence of movements with all of these props. It was something she had to get through "before the music ends." [Laughs]

BERNSTEIN: The other dance piece you did was entitled *The Bath* [1966], which you did with Ann Halprin.

OLIVEROS: The main idea for me was to record the sounds made by the dancers and then to elaborate that with the different processes including playback-record tape head delay, rewinding tape and playing it back. I used several tape recorders for that piece.

NOTES

1. La Monte Young's *String Trio* was composed in the summer of 1958. After beginning his studies at Berkeley in the fall of the same year, he was encouraged by Seymour Shifrin to write in another style, since Shifrin thought, after hearing his *Trio*, that "he was writing music like an eighty-year-old man." Young's solo piano works written in 1958–59, *Studies I, II,* and *III,* point to the influence of Stockhausen's serial music. See Keith Potter, *Four Musical Minimalists* (Cambridge: Cambridge University Press, 2000), 42–43.

2. For more on Oliveros's use of tape delay techniques, see Pauline Oliveros, "Tape Delay Techniques," in id., *Software for People: Collected Writings, 1963–80* (Baltimore: Smith Publications, 1984), 36–46.

Music as Studio Art

MORTON SUBOTNICK

After getting out of the army at the end of the Korean War, and after a summer of finishing my BA at Denver University, my wife at the time, my first son, and I ended up in San Francisco, where I attended Mills College as a graduate composition student. During those years (the end of the 1950s), I was a divided person. One side of me was playing regularly as an extra with the San Francisco Symphony and performing with the Mills College Chamber Players, a newly created chamber group, which consisted of Bonnie Hampton (cello), Nate Rubin (violin), Naomi Sparrow (piano), and myself (clarinet). The other side was continuing to compose for traditional instruments. During that time, I was commissioned by Herb Blau, who at that point was the director of Actor's Workshop, to write music for a production of *King Lear*. I accepted. It was while I was thinking about *King Lear* that I decided to create a musique concrète / electronic score for the production. It seemed that "music" for a play should come from the sounds of the stage and the demands of the content, rather than a musical background or what had become known as "incidental music." So, with an advance on my commission money, I bought my first tape recorder and began exploring a road that, almost fifty years later, I am still exploring. This road has literally created itself and has taken me through a landscape of technological change, which has come into being at every turn of my head.

The score for *Lear* was based largely on the storm scene. Because I saw the storm as the raging turmoil of Lear's mind, I created the storm from the actor's voice through, at first, hours of recording his reading and even more hours, days, and weeks of cutting, pasting, changing, and adding sounds until I had completed a landscape of sound that created the sonic rage that was the storm of Lear's view of a world out of control. When I finished, I felt that my life's work was before me. Here was a chance to be both performer and creator. I could get rid of the clarinet and the two sides of me would become one. I could create and perform in my studio, and it would come out as a sound piece, which was at once a musical creation and a performance. It needed no further intervention. It was music as studio art. I was ecstatic and clear

20 **MORTON SUBOTNICK.**

in my vision of my future. But I was also dejected at the thought of spending my life cutting and pasting together tiny bits of tape. I began to dream and research ways to create a kind of electronic music easel in keeping with the studio art metaphor. And, as it turned out, there were many out there thinking the same thing, one of whom was my new friend Ramon Sender, soon to be my colleague.

Ramon and I had common dreams, and we became close almost immediately. I had created a studio in a garage, made of automobile parts hung from the ceiling and the guts of an old piano. The objects were hung in a way that allowed me to turn the tape recorder on, run through the space playing my "instruments" and back to the tape recorder to turn it off. These would become "phrases" for a longer piece. Ramon had created a small "electronic" studio at the San Francisco Conservatory of Music. We decided to pool our resources, meager as they were, and create a single studio.

Later, we were "loaned" a Victorian mansion on Russian Hill, a building that was to be torn down at some point in the future. There we started the San Francisco Tape Music Center. Since I am trying to keep to a vision of my studio art dream, I shall reluctantly abstain from any description of that year and the events that caused us to leave Russian Hill. Leave, we did. We moved everything to a new space on Divisadero Street, where we were joined by the Ann Halprin Dancers' Workshop and a new San Francisco wing of the listener-sponsored Berkeley radio station KPFA 94.1 fm. Shortly after arriving, Ramon and I began to share our dreams of some sort of "black box" that would serve us better for creating tape music. We had begun to imagine this electronic music easel as a tool for any person who wanted to be creative with sound, to be able to afford it, and to have it in his or her home. The transistor had arrived, and most of us knew that the consequences of that foretold that electronics were now destined to be affordable by all. We put an ad in the *San Francisco Chronicle* to find an engineer who could build our music box. Although we had no background in electronics, we had outlined a possible approach to such a machine. After meeting several of these people, a young man named Donald Buchla arrived.

We explained our scheme to Don, which was based on a rotating a disc with holes in it passing light patterns over a photocell and translating that into sound. Don returned the next day with a prototype of our device. We were amazed that he had been able to produce it, and that it actually made sound. But Don explained that this was NOT the way to go. And, for the next few months, the three of us began a theoretical journey with pencils (Don is the only person I have ever known to use a no. 1 pencil regularly) and paper. We fed Don musical needs, and he returned with theoretical modules to meet those needs. We finally reached the point that we had a virtual electronic easel. I never thought that we were primarily creating a performance instrument. It was always a personal tool for creating music/art with sound, more of an analog computer than a musical instrument. I think Ramon felt as I did. Don perhaps had a slightly different view, because he has continued through his life to create wonderful alternative musical instruments.[1]

The point came when we felt we were ready to move from a virtual instrument to reality. The tough question was then asked, "Don, how much to build this?" The answer was "$500." Of course, this wasn't much, even by 1960s standards, but it was way beyond anything we could afford. A short time later, I was in New York for a performance and made an appointment with the Rockefeller Foundation. They were, and remain today, one of the few continuously visionary foundations in the country. Since they had helped to fund the Columbia-Princeton Studio, I presented our dream. We would like funding to do work with electronics and sound in San Francisco. Soon people would be able to create with sound in their living rooms. We had developed a notion, not of an electronic organ, but of a sound easel that was closer to an analog computer, with which people could create with sound in the same way that they have always been able to create with paint and paper. With $500 for parts and a little more for some other equipment, we could create a facility centered around this idea.

The response of the Rockefeller Foundation was that, though it appreciated what we were trying to do, its view was that there would never be enough interest in this kind of thing to warrant a second studio in the United States. As I recall, the foundation thought that there would be so few people interested that it would be cheaper to fly people to New York than to build a second studio in the United States. I had asked for too much, and the result was that we did not even get the $500.

Some time later a Rockefeller representative, Boyd Compton, came on a "hunting and gathering" expedition to the West Coast. He came to see us and had his own epiphany. He called New York, and we had our check for $500. Within a year or two of that, the Rockefeller Foundation awarded $200,000 to merge the Tape Music Center with the Mills College Chamber Players. We were not sufficiently "fiscally responsible," it seemed, so we had to unite with an institution that was, and Mills College in Oakland fitted the bill.

All the modules of the first Buchla synthesizer were labeled "San Francisco Tape Music Center, Inc.," but Ramon and I were a bit reluctant to be in business, so we declined to continue having the Tape Music Center be the name of a commercial object. The second generation was to become known as "The Buchla" and the modules were labeled "Buchla and Associates."

The Buchla became a centerpiece for the studio and a kind of underground hit. (Vladimir Ussachevsky immediately ordered a box for Columbia and another for Princeton.) Since we were using lights and images as well as sound, modules were developed to control lights and motors as well.

I left San Francisco in 1966 to join Herb [Blau] and the Actor's Workshop in New York to start the Repertory Theater of Lincoln Center (based in the Vivian Beaumont Theater). As part of the package, I was offered a position as artist-in-residence at the then new Tisch School of the Arts at New York University. NYU gave me a studio on Bleecker Street and, at my request, a "Buchla" with full sound and light capability.

Within my first year at the new studio on Bleecker Street, change, literally, kept knocking at my door. Two entrepreneurs visited me with the idea of creating a multimedia discothèque called the Electric Circus. I demonstrated what that might mean with my Buchla, and after months of working with them, I was hired to develop and be the artistic director of the new facility. At my request, Tony Martin was invited out, and Don Buchla was hired to develop the equipment. NYU expanded its artist-in-residence program and invited Tony to join the artist-in-residence faculty. An administrator was hired to try to create a new media program (Boyd Compton, who left the Rockefeller Foundation to join us). A young man named Serge Tcherepnin (creator of the "Serge" synthesizer) came to work with me. I was commissioned to create a work for Nonesuch Records *(Silver Apples of the Moon)*. By the end of 1967, two years after I left San Francisco and the Tape Music Center was transferred to Mills College, I was living in a world quite different from the one I had inhabited a few years earlier, in which it had been supposed that there would "be so little interest that it would be cheaper to fly people to New York from all over the world than to build a second studio."

Now, with the computer as the tool, I am still pursuing music as studio art (with a few major side trips along the way). That view of "my life's work" formulated in the late 1950s and intensely pursued through the Tape Music Center years has evolved, grown, and matured.

Over the past fifteen years, I have been developing ways for young children to be able to experience the empowerment of being composer, performer, and listener. Things have changed; the Rockefeller Foundation has generously offered to help me with the task of expanding a major series of CD-ROMS for children. For years, homes had been filled with electronic tools for creating music, but they were mostly standard instrumental devices (notably keyboards), rather than what Ramon and I had imagined. Now, however, there is a generation of young people creating soundscapes with electronics in the home studio (largely facilitated by Macintosh computers), as well as creating music in clubs and concert halls. Even though we knew it had to happen, there was no way to have anticipated the magnitude of the numbers of people and the social as well as aesthetic impact of what the studio art metaphor would become. The past, present, and future of this still thrills me as I write!

NOTE

1. For more on Buchla's instruments, see www.buchla.com (accessed September 2, 2007).

Morton Subotnick

INTERVIEWED BY DAVID W. BERNSTEIN AND MAGGI PAYNE

Reading through Morton Subotnick's interview, one quickly encounters the fact that Subotnick had an artistic vision from early on, which he has pursued throughout his compositional career. This agenda involves two key components. The first entails a commitment to combining music with other media. As a young composer, Subotnick quickly demonstrated a talent for working with artists from other disciplines. During his collaborations with the Ann Halprin Dancers' Workshop, for example, he had a certain natural affinity with the dance that allowed him to work, not merely as a composer providing music for a dance, but as a contributor to a unified artistic conception. Similarly, in his work with the San Francisco Actor's Workshop, he did not compose incidental music but rather sought to create music approaching the essence of the theatrical action. Subotnick also applied his integrated approach to media in his own compositions, beginning with *Sound Blocks* (1961), followed by his classic multimedia works created at the San Francisco Tape Music Center, such as *Mandolin* (1963) and *Play! no. 1* (1964), to his most recent works employing interactive computer music systems.

Subotnick began his musical career as a virtuoso performer, but he quickly sought to reconcile this aspect of his musical life with his work as a composer. He committed himself to a search for ways to combine the performative dimension of music with the compositional, a project that was the second component of his artistic vision, what he termed "music as studio art." Electronic music was clearly the means to this end, but Subotnick was not satisfied with the technical limitations of the classical electronic music studio, especially the laborious cutting and splicing of magnetic tape. His search ultimately led him to Don Buchla, with whom he created the Buchla 100 series Modular Electronic Music System. Composers could now compose and create electronic music alone in their own studios. Subotnick's dream of "music as studio art" had become a reality. This interview covers his efforts toward realizing the goals he set for himself, starting with the period before the official establishment of the Tape Music Center and ending with its move to Mills College and the beginning of Subotnick's career in New York City.

PAYNE: Could we start with the early days of the Tape Music Center?

SUBOTNICK: The very beginning of the Tape Music Center was Ramon [Sender] and myself.[1] And Pauline [Oliveros] came in the next year. Basically, [at first] it wasn't called the Tape Music Center, but what happened was that Ramon and I decided to pool our equipment and start a little co-op. Ramon was studying at the [San Francisco] Conservatory, working with [Robert] Erickson. I was working with Darius Milhaud and Leon Kirchner at Mills [College]. Ramon and Pauline started the series called "Sonics" at the conservatory, and I went to those concerts. We were all friends.

PAYNE: How did you first meet Ramon and Pauline?

SUBOTNICK: I met Pauline because I was playing concertos [and she was playing French horn in orchestras]. I had a group, which toured, and probably did one of the first performances on the West Coast of Olivier Messiaen's *Quartet for the End of Time* [1940–41]. We were touring and I was playing part-time with the San Francisco Symphony and conducting. I conducted a bunch of concerts: an early piece of La Monte Young's and a Terry Riley piece [entitled *Spectra* (1959)]. We were all graduate students at the same time. La Monte and Terry were graduate students at Berkeley; I was at Mills, and Pauline and Ramon were at the conservatory. We did a concert for the Composers' Forum that I conducted, which included a piece of mine, in a twelve-tone, Dallapiccola style,[2] a work by La Monte [Young], which was in the style of Boulez's Second Piano Sonata [1947–48], and Terry Riley's piece, which was modeled after *Zeitmasse* [1955–56] by Stockhausen.[3] I had to learn to conduct three different tempos: one with the left hand, one with the right hand, and one with my head. We only had two hours with the musicians, so I practiced at home in a mirror, and, of course, it was a mirror image. So the musicians over there had to follow this hand, and the musicians over here had to follow the other hand. After having practiced, I couldn't turn it around.

Steve Reich came to Mills around that time, to study with Berio, who had come to take Kirchner's place. Gerald Shapiro was also studying at Mills. When he [later] came to the Tape Music Center, I became his mentor in electronics. There were a couple of people at Stanford, John Chowning and Loren Rush. We were all playing together.

I had a little studio; I had been hired to do some movie scores for NET (National

Educational Television, the early KQED), a series called *The Computer and the Mind of Man*. There were to be six movies, and I think they gave me $300 a film, which was major money to me at that time. Then, I was also hired to do a score for an experimental production of *King Lear* for the Actor's Workshop.

I decided that I wanted to do electronics for that production of *Lear,* so with the money I got for the first movie score, I bought a tape recorder and made all the sounds from found objects. My studio was basically made of automobile parts and fenders and coil springs. (Berio got the coil springs from my studio for all his pieces later on. They were coil springs from trolley cars in San Francisco.) I had a hammer and had set up a path, and would go through the studio and make these sounds, with very little splicing; it was real time. I did the first three scores for *The Computer and the Mind of Man* using this technique. At the same time Ramon had started a little studio at the conservatory, with a couple of oscillators; it was up in the attic above the practice rooms. (We got kicked out later because we were making too much noise.) So then I went out and bought my first oscillators, and I made the fourth score using the oscillators, but they rejected it because they said it wasn't electronic sounding enough! All these sounds I had made acoustically sounded really far out to them, whereas square waves sounded just like a clarinet.

PAYNE: Oh, that's great. Were they Lafayette oscillators, or Hewlett-Packard?

SUBOTNICK: Hewlett-Packard. In 1961, I think it was in September or October, [there] was a series of about four or five concerts at a coffeehouse.[4] It wasn't the Spaghetti Factory. There were concerts at the Spaghetti Factory, but this was another place in town. [I wrote a piece entitled] *Sound Blocks* [1961], which used four musicians: Nate Rubin, Bonnie Hampton, and I think two xylophone players. Robert LaVigne made four lighting flats, which were the kind of things we used in *King Lear*. Depending on how you light them, you would see different shapes and objects and colors. It was like a light show, probably before they started, a theatrical device because you could get multiple things out of a single thing hanging in the auditorium. He designed those and they changed throughout the piece, according to some score, which I don't remember. The piece had two two-track tape recorders, not going at the same time. It was probably close to an hour long, so in order to get enough music, I dovetailed the two tape recorders. I was living in Haight-Ashbury, and I did not have a studio; I made all of the sounds in the apartment there. Later on I had a studio that was also in Haight-Ashbury in the garage of a house on Belvedere Street, right off the Panhandle. It was my decision just prior to that point not to make any more instrumental music. *Sound Blocks* was the piece that came out of that decision. What I really wanted to do was to develop a whole new form of media. This piece was my first attempt to do this.

BERNSTEIN: What inspired you to take that direction?

SUBOTNICK: A number of things. I can't tell you exactly. I was playing as an "extra" with the San Francisco Symphony and doing all this chamber music and I think I began teaching at Mills College around that time. I also had worked with the Actor's Workshop. It was really the work with *King Lear* that made me understand that I could combine my performing ability with my composing and put together a new concept, which I called "music as studio art," where one could be the composer and the audience all at the same time. I was working with Ann Halprin. I was working in the theater. I felt that I had a natural affinity immediately [with all of this]. I was directing in a way; I had a sense of the theater from day one and was not really writing music for the theater. I was creating sound. It's what became known as "sound design." Gerd Stern had introduced us to the early works of Marshall McLuhan right around that time. That was for most of us our first look at his work. The whole thing together, the new technology, the media, trying to break away from being a clarinetist, or being a composer of instrumental music and just adding more to what was already a great literature, felt like the right things to do for me. And I had this "studio art" notion, which led, of course, to looking for a Don Buchla. The whole idea preceded my meeting Don. It was not putting a tape recorder in an auditorium; it was to create a new medium. And the way we made electronic music was clearly not what I had in mind. [Laughs] It had to be something a lot better than that.

And I have to say that that *Sound Blocks* was very successful. It was done on a Sunday and we repeated it the next Sunday because so many people wanted to see it and it got such a good review. It was reviewed in the *Chronicle* and, I believe, in the *Examiner* as well. They called it a "new art form." It caught the public's eye. Of course, I didn't know that the entire world was about to change within two years, and I was actually playing right into that and I didn't even know it.

BERNSTEIN: Michael McClure was also there?

SUBOTNICK: Yes, at the end of the piece. The audience was surrounded by the lighting flats and loud speakers, and Michael McClure was in the middle at a table. Toward the end, he read from a poem entitled "Flowers of Politics." It was subtitled "An Heroic Vision." It may be a little pompous, but I had a certain concept of "hero" in mind. It comes from the notion that the heroic is doing something that no one recognizes; doing something for good when no one can really see that you are doing something good. It comes from Camus; I think it's in *The Plague,* where the doctor is being thanked at a dinner for having saved so many lives and being a hero, and he says: "I would have been a hero if I told you that your conditions were unsanitary and that a plague would come and you wouldn't have listened to me and would have ridiculed me. That would have made me a hero. I was not a hero for being a doctor and helping people who were sick."

It was the notion that the world was about to change, and that media and this music as studio art . . . all of this was about to enter the world and transform it. I had no idea I was probably about 85 percent right about everything I thought at the time. The main thing I was wrong about was the timing. I thought it would take about one hundred years, literally. The reason it felt heroic to me was that I felt I would spend my life [trying to realize this idea], and it would never happen during my lifetime. I never imagined for a day that I would see any of this.

BERNSTEIN: And how far it developed in the next forty years.

SUBOTNICK: Isn't that amazing? In fact, within ten years, we could see the whole thing absolutely. And it's now part of history; it's not as if it arrived in forty years. We are now talking history. It's totally amazing to me. There's so little documentation, at least, I can speak for myself, because there was no idea that we were playing a role. It was just being part of something that was happening. But that's what we all do in life.

The artistic community in San Francisco was really exciting at that time. [Do] you know [about] Ken Dewey? Well, he died very young. In the city at the time there was the Ann Halprin Dancers' Workshop, the Actor's Workshop, which was very avant-garde. They were the first people to do Beckett in this country and things like that. Lee Breuer was an assistant director there, and Ken Dewey was an assistant director as well. Herb Blau was the artistic director, and he brought in all these younger avant-garde people. Ken did the big *City Scale* [1963] event. Then Ken went to New York (he was independently wealthy) and became the first director of the New York State Arts Council. He developed the whole notion of funding in New York City with Mayor Lindsay. He was killed after the first year there in an airplane accident; he had a private plane. He was very influential at the time.

BERNSTEIN: Do you remember the music you wrote for the Actor's Workshop production of Brecht's *Galileo* in 1962?

SUBOTNICK: Yes, there was a sword fight somewhere in *Galileo;* I think it was a sword fight, or a battle or something. I don't remember what it was. Or I may have this mixed up with another play, but it's an idea of how I did the music. And I brought it in, and it constituted three or four swishing noises that moved across the proscenium, and that was it. It was about ten seconds long. The company went nuts; they thought I was totally out of my mind. But [Herb] immediately understood and developed this kind of a haiku of a battle. It was a "swoosh," a suggestion of metal touching metal, but not hitting it, but swishing across it. And so he created a kind of strange choreography for that. And then there was another scene in *Galileo* where there's one of the—I don't think it's the pope—but one of the priests comes through, a cardinal or somebody with a big gown. And he comes through and the [staging directions] had called for people playing chess. And so I imagined the entire gorgeous room with people playing chess and this guy with a beautiful gown coming through. They had a chandelier as part of the set, and so I made the score out of clinking and breaking glass that changed in speed. Herb really liked it, so I began to choreograph the chess playing so the music would start and stop. And I made some music that was almost like a waltz or a minuet, but you couldn't really hear that, but it was a very stylized kind of glass breaking. The actors' movements would freeze depending on where the score would have moments of silence or moments of some kind of a particular sound that would freeze everybody on the stage except for the cardinal walking across the stage. All the scores I did for the theater were of that sort; they were really—as I said of *King Lear*—integrated into the play. It was really sound design. It wasn't really music. I mean, there wasn't a thing called sound design as far as I know at that point, but that's what I was doing. I was working with the world they were in and trying to create some kind of sound environment that interacted with it.

BERNSTEIN: Are those the only two productions you worked on?

SUBOTNICK: No, I did lots of them. I did a score for the production of *Caucasian Chalk Circle* [in 1964], but that was more traditional. It was directed by Carl Weber, who had just come from East Germany at the time and had worked with Brecht. He wanted to use the [Hanns] Eisler score, but couldn't get it out of East Berlin, and so Herb said, "Well, Mort can probably do it." And Weber said, "But, he writes all this crazy music. He couldn't do this." So, anyway at the last minute, he was stuck, so he asked me to give it a shot. By then, we were almost ready for dress rehearsals. So I wrote the first song, and he absolutely loved it. I modeled it after Eisler, and I had—because the time was really short at that point—to write the songs [at the same time] I had a pianist working with the singers on another song that I had already finished. [Laughs] I finished the entire score that way, and then we went into dress rehearsals. Pauline Oliveros played the accordion, and it was done with automobile parts as the percussion.

BERNSTEIN: I remember that Blau faced a similar situation that you and other members of the Tape Music Center faced when the [Actor's] Workshop moved to an institutional setting in New York. Do you remember that?

SUBOTNICK: I think what you are referring to was when the company was brought to New York to start [the Repertory Theater of Lincoln Center in] the Vivian Beaumont Theater. That's how I got to New York, because he invited me to come with the company. He may have had misgivings about other things, but I know he had misgivings about the move to New York. And, in fact, he made the first season so uncompromisingly difficult from a social standpoint that he was fired after the first year.[5]

BERNSTEIN: Oh, I didn't know that.

SUBOTNICK: We started with *Danton's Death,* which is almost impossible to do anyway. We used it as a metaphor for tyranny and had all the leaders, the tyrannical leaders of the world, in pictures and photographs on the walls of the foyer, which included Lyndon Johnson and Richard Nixon. [Laughs] The "money" people behind the repertory theater insisted that Blau take them down, and he didn't. He also did Sartre's *No Exit* that season; he presented every possible thing that was both difficult and, [if] not always political, always really tough stuff. The entire season was a season out of heaven for most of us; but was just awful [for almost everyone else]. I stayed on for a second season and then I left. I couldn't deal with it either.

BERNSTEIN: That's very interesting. Bringing the antiestablishment attitude that he cultivated in San Francisco to New York didn't work out.

SUBOTNICK: Right.

BERNSTEIN: I would also like to ask you some questions about your work with Ann Halprin and *The Five-Legged Stool* [1962]. Was it composed in your studio with all of the found objects?

SUBOTNICK: Part of it. The way the piece started was that A. A. Leath would appear on the stage. He was there in the darkness, and you would [very] gradually become aware that he was looking [at the audience with a handheld] telescope. I had a couple of tape recorders and a lot of microphones. I had a booth—a little area—with tape recorders in the auditorium. I recorded people in the audience while they were waiting for something to happen on the stage and then rewound [the tapes], and played them back with some kind of very basic modification, probably feedback or something. I had speakers all over the place and I began to play with the audience's talking and coughing. They began to understand that they were being recorded so people would make noises, and some people didn't understand and they would just hear these things, and the more I did it, the louder the audience got. So I was actually playing the audience, and then gradually the lights came up on the stage so that you could see A. A. Leath looking at the audience. The idea of the opening was that the audience was the music, and A. A. Leath was the audience. And that went on for some time, until things began to happen on the stage.

There was another section where I had people in the audience who weren't audience members. They had what I called "Braille scores." This was a rectangular piece of cardboard with a series of evenly spaced notches on each of the long sides. Some of the notches were deep and the rest of them were shallow. There was a light—a little tiny flashlight—that was activated on the stage, that was almost imperceptible unless you knew it was there. It triggered a tempo, and then the people—there were about eight or nine of them spread in the audience—would keep a tempo going by tapping the little notches. When they came to a deep notch, they would whisper for a couple of beats and then move on. They would turn the scores over and forward and backward, so that you had four different scores. They were based on all sorts of prime numbers—the large notches—so that there tended to be no real repetition and you didn't hear a real rhythm going with it. It created a kind of snaking whisper through the audience during one of the sections.

BERNSTEIN: That the performers were all around the whole theater fits into Halprin's idea of breaking from the tradition of the proscenium arch.

SUBOTNICK: Right. But in *The Five-Legged Stool,* there wasn't much in the way of action around the theater. When we did *Parades and Changes* [1965–67], there was a little bit more, because we tended to do it in larger theaters, and we brought the dancers in through the audience. I don't remember it happening in *The Five-Legged Stool* so much.

BERNSTEIN: Could you talk a little bit about the music for *Parades and Changes?*

SUBOTNICK: Yes. That piece was fairly open ended; it had a score I created for it.

BERNSTEIN: Was this your "cell-block method"?[6]

SUBOTNICK: Yes, and it involved various parameters of both movement, blocking on the stage, and music. It called for certain "attitudes," so that you might have, for instance, very busy, very dense textures, but that could be a blocking on the stage and you had a block of music that you could pick that would be very empty. There were various values and attitudes and then ways to realize those things, tasks for dancers to do and certain values for the music.

BERNSTEIN: Could we discuss the Sonics series?

SUBOTNICK: Yes. Did [Ramon] tell you about the last concert in the Sonics series?

PAYNE: Oh, probably, but we'd like to hear what you have to say about it.

SUBOTNICK: At the time I was writing music for Ann Halprin, so we brought members of the Halprin company in for that last concert. One of us had found a tape—I don't remember who it was—but someone had found a tape in an alley and we sealed it and brought it to the concert. Ann Halprin was already into confrontation and everything, and there were these new perfume kits that were just on the market where you could make your own odors. So the dancers went through the audience and interviewed people and decided on an odor that belonged to that person and then would spray them. And while they did that we played that found tape for the first time.

PAYNE: That you had never heard, right? So what if it had been blank?

SUBOTNICK: Then there would have been silence. So we called the piece *Smell Opera with Found Tape* [1962]. The tape turned out to be a Sunday morning psychodrama about a young girl who had become pregnant out of wedlock. A church thing. It was stupendous; it was unbelievable!

On that same concert we did a piece that has become fairly well known now, the *Tropical Fish Opera* [1962]. We got a rectangular tank and some fish from a tropical fish store and we put staves on all four sides of the aquarium, and the fish became the notes, and Pauline and myself, Loren Rush, and Ramon played this quartet that the fish were composing. I was on clarinet, Ramon on accordion, Pauline on French horn, and Loren played acoustic bass.

That concert, because of the "smell opera," ended up notorious. The newspaper the next day said, "it literally stinks," and so the [San Francisco] Conservatory began to feel that because of the noise we were making and the kind of publicity we were getting they couldn't afford to keep us there any longer.

So we left the conservatory and had to find a new place, a house at 1537 Jones Street. By then Pauline had gone [to Holland], Terry had gone off to Paris, so it was basically Ramon and me. We pooled our stuff and moved into this house on Jones Street that we had been given because they were going to tear it down. And we decided to incorporate, because we had gone to see a woman who had a lot of money, and she said she would give us money, but we would have to form a nonprofit organization. So we paid $125 to become a nonprofit corporation and then she gave us a check for $25!

We decided to call it the Tape Music Center because Cologne and the Paris studio and Columbia-Princeton [Electronic Music Center in New York City] were involved in this big argument about musique concrète and pure electronics, and everyone hated everyone else. There were only ten people in the field, and all ten people hated the others. It seemed to us that we were really not interested in the academic dispute, and since everything ended up on tape, we called it the Tape Music Center, so that it could include everything.

BERNSTEIN: What do you remember about the piece entitled *Yod* [1962]?

SUBOTNICK: That was my first tape piece that was to be listened to just as a tape piece—not with anything else. It was done at the first Tape Music Center on Jones Street. *[Yod]* is a mystic name for God, I think. I'm not really sure where I got that from, but it had to do with the word, with the uniqueness of "the word"—of words in general—but also, you know, "the word." What attracted me wasn't the religious aspect, but the idea that in the Old Testament and throughout the Talmud and various writings, the word "God" couldn't be spoken.

The idea that the word was so powerful attracted me. In the piece there are hidden words underneath everything in addition to long tones and so forth. So you hear these little gated things that sound like—well, they are language being gated—the mystery of language.

BERNSTEIN: *Yod* was presented at 1537 Jones Street. What else do you remember about the performances there? The first event was a play by Robert Duncan and also featured tape music by you and Ramon Sender.

SUBOTNICK: Right. It wouldn't have been much in the way of tape music, because we didn't have much going at the time; we were just getting started at that point. Ramon and I did improvisations using a piano and processing, well, not really processing, but feedback and various kinds of things. The place was picketed, which brought the police; so it's very vivid in my memory.[7]

BERNSTEIN: Then the next concert featured poetry by Robert Blaser and tapes by Robert Ashley and improvisations by you and Ramon.

SUBOTNICK: I don't remember that particular evening too well. That wasn't one of the memorable ones for me.

BERNSTEIN: Do you remember the happening by Lee Breuer?

SUBOTNICK: That I remember very well; it was Lee Breuer's very first original piece. I don't remember the details, but it was quite wonderful.[8] This was his very first time to do something on his own. Ramon and I did an improvisation?

BERNSTEIN: Yes, apparently the concert featured tapes by Mario Davidovsky, Sender, and Subotnick.

SUBOTNICK: Yes, we probably did improvisations. That was probably Mario's *Electronic Study no. 1* (1961). I think he did two or three studies for just tape and it was all brand-new at the time.

BERNSTEIN: And then, on January 7, there was an event by the R. G. Davis Mime Troupe, which is well documented. The February 4 concert included a painting by Robert LaVigne?

SUBOTNICK: Oh yes, Bob, Robert LaVigne was a set designer at the time and a painter. He still is. He was with the Actor's Workshop and later went to New York. He became well known as a set designer for television and off-Broadway. And so what he did was he painted a painting in real time. That was his thing. I don't remember—I think it was huge, but I don't remember it.

BERNSTEIN: And you played tapes?

SUBOTNICK: We played tapes, yes. I think they were in response to the painting.

BERNSTEIN: And, of course, there was also *City Scale* . . .

SUBOTNICK: Yes, I think that ended the season, but I'm not sure. There were a couple of things from the technical standpoint. I don't know how much you got filled in on the studio at 1537 Jones Street itself.

BERNSTEIN: No, that would be good.

SUBOTNICK: The studio was originally made up of a combination of my garage and Ramon's studio we had at the conservatory, so it had a few oscillators, and all of my bumpers and all of that stuff. My broken piano was there. It was an upright and not in very good shape. It was used mostly as a sound source. We had very little real electronic equipment. Then Ramon and I met people at Ampex and they gave us a tape recorder that played in several speeds. I seem to remember that the power supply blew before one of the concerts, making a terrible odor. So we called Ampex, and spoke to someone we hadn't met—a man by the name of Eldon Corl—"L. Don" we called him. We borrowed another Ampex from him to do the concert. It was one of those classics, probably stereo, but I don't remember, could have been even mono or—but I think it was stereo. After the concert, instead of returning it, we called him and asked if we could hang on to it. It lasted all the way to Mills College.

And the other aspect of the studio, which I'm sure you must know, was Michael Callahan. He was a high school student, and I don't know how he got to us. There was a lot of publicity around what we did. It was really amazing because we were all just getting started and had a lot of stuff written about us. Anyway, Michael came to us and he was this whiz kid at his high school. He brought things from his lab, an oscilloscope and various things that became part of the studio. I assume they were borrowed, but in any case he did his work there. He really put our studio together. It was really amazing.

I should also mention that there was a film by Stan Brakhage that we can't locate. Brakhage was in San Francisco that year and was an old friend of mine from when I got out of high school and went to Denver in 1951. I guess it was to play in the symphony. I met Jim Tenney and Stan Brakhage at that point; we were just out of high school. I think Stan came to San Francisco the year we started Jones Street. He did a film of Ramon and me in the Jones Street place, and that film is now lost.

BERNSTEIN: That's too bad.

SUBOTNICK: Yes, we did it actually on television. Ramon and I did a live program on KQED [Public Television], and they showed the film.

[Did you know that] the Jones Street studio burned down after the first year?

PAYNE: Yes, Ramon told us that story about replacing a fuse.

SUBOTNICK: So he told you, huh? He wouldn't admit it for a long time.

PAYNE: Well, it was still not his fault, you know, [the house had] faulty circuitry.

SUBOTNICK: The thing that was funny about it was that we had already decided to leave, and we were in the process of moving out. Partly we were moving out because everybody who was living there—there were all these poets and painters—they were all on drugs, and we weren't getting any rent from them, and it was clear . . .

PAYNE: . . . you didn't want to get busted.

SUBOTNICK: It was clear we were going to get busted. So we were going to leave them there, and we had found this place that required first and last months' rent. We didn't have enough money, so we decided to go to these people who had been there at Jones Street for almost a year and had not paid any rent, and ask them for the rent.

I called Ramon and said, "You know, I can't do it," and he said, "Oh, no problem, I'll do it." So we went to the place together to get the rent, and we had both felt so sorry for them. (That's why we hadn't asked them for the rent before.) Ramon felt so sorry for this guy who was living without electricity in the attic, he tried to replace the fuse, and that's how the fire started. We had gone there to collect rent, but instead we burned the place down.

So we moved to Divisadero Street and we took the attic and rented out the two halls. It was a great building: there were two large spaces, they could each easily seat 100 people, each with a small stage, and so we rented one space out to [the listener-supported Berkeley fm radio station] KPFA, because they wanted a sound booth and there was a logical place for it there. They renovated the space into a concert hall and added in the sound booth and paid us $100 a month. Then we rented out the other space to the Ann Halprin company for $75 a month, and we all shared the utilities. The total rent was $175 a month, so we actually had enough money between the two rentals for upkeep and didn't have any rent to pay. We also had use of the KPFA space to do our concerts. It worked out really well. We ran the studio there for three years, and it became very well known. People came from Sweden on grants—you know, they had the choice of Columbia-Princeton or the Tape Music Center, and they chose us. There is a lot of documentation about the place.

PAYNE: Yes, Ramon has reams of it—reviews and programs.

BERNSTEIN: How did you get interested in improvisation?

SUBOTNICK: I was never interested in improvisation as such. Improvisation was just a part of the compositional process for me and still is, somewhere between performing and composing. I feel that it's all the same process. I don't really think of the end result for myself as improvisation, but as something I worked out and finally put down, but I get there through improvisatory means.

We did a lot of improvisations that weren't in public. We did a regular improvisational session, and that was sort of learning things among ourselves and exploring the instruments and trying things out. And then sometimes we'd do them in public. It was just like a process. I don't consider myself an improviser like other people [who view improvisation as their] main thing. I thought of it more as a process.

BERNSTEIN: When I look at all the work you were doing, it is striking that a lot of the pieces that you did—you mentioned the *Serenades*—were combinations of acoustic instruments and electronic tape.

SUBOTNICK: That was part of my life. It was a big part of my life—the performance part and writing for traditional instruments.

BERNSTEIN: I guess what you're saying is that because you were a performer and you also were writing with tape, it was a natural thing for you to start combining tape music with acoustical instruments.

SUBOTNICK: Yes, I moved back and forth between the two and then gradually— I made the decision to not do instrumental music. I made a conscious decision around the end of 1961, even though I did pieces with instruments after that. I had made a decision to—just to dedicate myself to the technology, and then right after that, I got a commission from a woodwind quintet and did the first *Play!* It became *Play! no. 1* [1964]. It was just *Play!* at the time, for woodwind quintet, piano, tape, and film. It was premiered at the Tape Music Center, and was one of the early theater pieces.

BERNSTEIN: Right, and you were poking fun at traditional performance practices.

SUBOTNICK: It was satire. It deals with all the rituals of performance. I have one for orchestra [*Play! no. 2* (1964)] also, which was done by the St. Louis Symphony and later the Oakland Symphony.

Play! no. 4 [1965] was for people from the audience who play a game that requires movement and voices and things. In *Play! no. 3* [1965], which was for Leonard Stein, the pianist never plays, he just bows. He gets ready to play and takes bows and literally disappears; he vanishes before the piece is over. There's a black curtain behind the back of the piano and there's a black spot of about four seconds that he has to time himself with and when the lights come on he's gone. He has actually disappeared.

BERNSTEIN: Do you remember the Tudorfest?

SUBOTNICK: I remember a couple of things. After Pauline had come back into the picture again, we decided to take turns running the place, and when it was Pauline's turn, she decided to do a Cage-Tudor festival [the "Tudorfest"] for two weeks. I guess that must have been 1963–64. We did two concerts a day that were all sold out. It was a major event. We had heard (I don't know if it was true) that the faculty at the University of California had told the students there that they were not allowed to use the words "John Cage," so that gave us the idea that it was time to present a major festival of his work.

I conducted a few things, and I remember Cage's *Concert for Piano and Orchestra* [1958] very well. I don't remember how many performers we had on the stage, but one of them was Stuart Dempster. There's a place in the trombone part where there's an instruction to gargle. It had to do with the things that you would ordinarily see people do and putting them into the score in some way. You know, the emptying of the valves in the trombone and the horn were always something we always saw a lot of, and he had a gargle at one point, and there's only one place you could do that. It's one line of the score and it made people laugh, and Stew really enjoyed that, so he kept gargling, and people really laughed. He made a sort of comedy out of it, and the piece got a bigger applause than almost anything had gotten up to that point. But Cage was really angry. He came up onto the stage to take his bow and went right to Stew with his face red and pointed to him and said, "Don't ever do that again." [Laughs]

BERNSTEIN: That's interesting. It probably reminded Cage of his earlier experiences with the New York Philharmonic.

SUBOTNICK: Yes. Then when my turn came, which was the following season, I decided to commission works (not with money) from all the local composers to do an evening of their music. So, instead of always doing Cage and Berio, we would do our own work. Each of us had a concert: Ramon, Pauline, me, Terry Riley, who had come back to town, and Steve Reich. He was working with the Mime Troupe at the time, and I was working for Ann Halprin and the Actor's Workshop, so all the groups were intertwined in a major way.

Evidently, according to Terry, I commissioned *In C*. I didn't call it that, of course, but I had commissioned him to do a new work for his concert and that is what he did. That was November of 1964. Steve Reich was in that concert, too. He was scheduled to do his concert in January 1965 in that same series.

[By the] very last season at Divisadero [1965–66], we had "done" everybody and we had created all these pieces with visuals and the first light shows. All of that stuff that became so popular within "pop" culture had been developed at the Tape Music Center. Tony Martin, who started those light shows with us, ended up doing the light shows for the Jefferson Airplane.

PAYNE: Bill Maginnis said that Janis Joplin came to your concerts?[9]

SUBOTNICK: Yes, it was all one big thing. A lot of jazz people as well.

I had approached the Rockefeller Foundation early on when we first got started. I was the most institutionally savvy, partly because I was teaching at that point and partly because I had played with a symphony orchestra since I was seventeen. I was out in the world early on. I was probably the most knowledgeable about that part of the world, and so I went to the Rockefeller Foundation in New York City.

At that time, I was quite well known as a clarinetist. I played a lot, and people would come into town to study with me. I wasn't known as a composer particularly, although in 1959, [I] attended the Princeton Seminars in Advanced Musical Studies. They invited fourteen or fifteen young composers who were all graduate students to try to establish a new elite, to "battle" the Berios and the things that were happening in Europe. I was one of the ones they invited. I was written up at that point in books about new music in the United States. So I was known by people in the Rockefeller Foundation, both as a clarinetist and as this mysterious young composer from this inner circle, [which included] Salvatore Martirano and [others]. Most of the composers did hang on and became fairly well known from that generation. People like Stravinsky were also there, and Elliot Carter, Varèse—I got to spend a week with Varèse. It was an incredible two summers.

You know they had built Columbia-Princeton at that time, and I [asked the Rockefeller Foundation], "Why don't you do one on the West Coast." And they said, "There will never be enough interest in electronic music in the United States for *two* studios."

Ramon and I already knew that it was possible to make a small synthesizer. We didn't know much, but we knew transistors and we could see the writing on the wall. I called it the electronic music "easel." You know a little black box. But the idea was that each person could have a little black box in their home to make music. I proposed this to the Rockefeller Foundation, and they said, "No way."

Consequently, we didn't get anything from them at that time. But then I went back a year later and by then [we had] more of a reputation, and so they sent this guy out, Boyd Compton, who was either the top person or next to the top, and he spent a week with us. He was totally "whacked out." His life literally changed. He said, "I now know what it is I have been looking for in life. This whole thing you have done here is what I really believe in." He said, "I'll get you the grant, but you should think about it carefully, because it could be the end of what you are doing."

PAYNE: You mean from being more institutionalized?

SUBOTNICK: I think he meant just getting that much money all at once. We were talking about hundreds of thousands of dollars, and we had nothing. Zero. This is a big shift, and you have to take this seriously. Then it turned out they couldn't give us the money unless we associated with an institution.

The two institutions that wanted us were, one, the [San Francisco] Conservatory, which had kicked us out, and, two, Mills [College]. And that was primarily because of Milhaud, because Milhaud desperately wanted to know everything about what was going on. He was a wonderful person in that regard. Berkeley couldn't have cared less. We never even approached Stanford; it was too far away. We wanted to be near San Francisco. (It never even occurred to us to appeal to Stanford, really, [although] we knew John Chowning back then, and he was really interested in the lively production side of things, in the scene.) So, since I was teaching at Mills (by then I might have been full-time, I don't know) and there were a lot of connections with Mills, we decided on it. Milhaud was really very special, and I think Berio was also around at that point.

The Tape Music Center made the move, and in the process of doing it, we realized that none of us wanted to make the move with it; we really liked what we were already doing. Ramon was ready to move to Morning Star [Ranch], and we had this meeting, about five or six of us, about what to do: whether we should take the grant, or not take the grant, whether we should move to Mills or not. Ramon's proposal was not to take the money, but to either split up the equipment and go our separate ways, or to all go to Morning Star together. I don't know that anybody wanted to keep it going. If we hadn't been offered the money, we probably could have kept on going as we were. Boyd was right.

I had been offered a job in New York City to teach two hours a week at the New York University School of the Arts and to work with the Actor's Workshop in Lincoln Center. The two jobs together gave me about ten thousand a year, which was an amazing amount of money for me at the time. I decided to move, and Pauline took the studio to Mills, as a transition. We wanted to somehow make it continue to flow in some way.

So Pauline stayed there a year or so, and she took Bill Maginnis and Tony Martin with her and she ran it for a year. I did the negotiations, because I was still at Mills then.

The equipment [at Mills] came from the Tape Music Center. We didn't keep our own equipment; the Tape Music Center owned it all. It didn't really amount to much. Most of it we had gotten over the years from junkyards and used-equipment places, or we borrowed equipment. The biggest amount of equipment we got was from an insurance company; Ramon and I were really "wheeler-dealers." We had inroads to insurance companies that insured hi-fi stores [and that] would call us and say that a hi-fi store had burned down say in Denver. They needed to get rid of the stuff, because it was in a warehouse in San Francisco, and if we gave them $500, they would give us the entire thing. But we didn't have $500. So we made out a check for $500 on a Friday and rented a U-haul truck, and picked up the equipment (so now we are $650 in debt). We thought we would just make a bunch of pieces over the weekend and then we'd give it all back. The check bounced, of course, but they didn't want the equipment back. They kept sending our check in again and again, saying there must be some mistake. And then we put an ad in the paper and we sold several of the intercoms. We sold seven hundred dollars worth of intercoms, so we actually made a few bucks on the deal. Most of the equipment at the early Tape Music Center was from that sale. They had loop machines.

PAYNE: We still have them. I wonder why they had them?

SUBOTNICK: Evidently, it was a store that catered to radio stations. Buchla's ten-key touch board, not the Buchla itself but earlier on, was made because we had these ten loop machines. People think it's because there are ten fingers, but it was actually because we had ten loop machines. David Tudor came in and used it. He was the first person to use that machine.

PAYNE: The Buchla that you used for *Silver Apples of the Moon* was not the same Buchla at Mills, right?

SUBOTNICK: No, it was a duplicate of that original one, which New York University bought from Buchla.

PAYNE: Anyway, I know the time is short. Thanks so much for this interview, Mort.

SUBOTNICK: You are welcome. I'd like to end by telling you a really touching story about Milhaud. He was really, really sweet. That first summer I went to the Princeton Seminars, that was the summer I graduated from Mills. I was very, very broke, amazingly broke at the time. And I was conducting a concert of Milhaud's music, and he was at a rehearsal, and he said, "You know, my dear, I got you a $500 grant to go to Aspen this summer." And I was really moved, I said, "That's great, but I have all these doctor's bills and my debts are outrageous, and I couldn't afford to go." I was practically in tears because I couldn't go. And he said, "How much do you need," and I said, "Oh, I don't know, at least another $500." The next rehearsal, I came back and asked him does everything sound okay, and he said, "My dear, it's just perfect," and he grabbed my hand, and when I pulled it away there was [another] check for $500. And he said, "I want you to understand you can't come to any of my classes, and don't show your music to any of the students." [Laughs]

I had written this piece for Milhaud for string quartet and clarinet, and he loved it. He programmed it, but then I wrote another piece, which was [entitled] *Piece for Four Hands,* and I took the quintet off and put my new piece on without telling him, and then just before the performance, I thought I better tell him. And he looked at the program, and he said, "Oh, no." And I said, "Milhaud, you don't know what this piece sounds like, it's beautiful and its fresh, it's a wonderful piece!" So he said, "Okay, okay."

So these two pianists played it in four movements. I thought the audience was going to rise up and cheer. At the end of the third movement, the audience was yelling, and the performers sort of stared them down, and by the end of the fourth movement, the audience did rise up, but they didn't cheer—they sort of ran up onto the stage and started pounding on the pianos. I left the auditorium sick to my stomach. I saw Milhaud in his wheelchair, and there really were tears coming down his cheeks, and he said, "Thank you my dear, it reminds me of the old days."

NOTES

1. Subotnick is referring to the official founding of the San Francisco Tape Music Center, when it became a nonprofit organization and had moved to 1537 Jones Street.

2. That is, in the style of Luigi Dallapiccola (1904–1975), an Italian composer known for his twelve-tone compositions.

3. It is not clear whether this program was presented as a single concert, since no record has been found. It is possible that it is a conflation of several events.

4. The venue was called "Opus Too." See Alfred Frankenstein, "Subotnick's 'New' Music: 'An Heroic Vision' Is All of That," *San Francisco Chronicle,* September 26, 1961.

5. For more on Blau's season at the Vivian Beaumont Theater, see Herbert Blau, *Take Up the Bodies: Theater at the Vanishing Point* (Urbana: University of Illinois Press, 1982), 29–77.

6. See Larry Halprin, *The RSVP Cycles: Creative Processes in the Human Environment* (New York: George Braziller, 1969), 36.

7. The event is described in Lewis Willingham and Kevin Killian, *Poet Be Like God: Jack Spicer and the San Francisco Renaissance* (Middletown, Conn.: Wesleyan University Press 1998), 239.

8. See Lee Breuer's essay, "When Performance Art Was Performance Poetry," in the present volume.

9. Maginnis also remembers that "The Great Society, Darby Slick's band, rehearsed in the apartment next to our performance space [at 321 Divisadero Street]. At some times the Great Society could be heard better than the performer on our stage." William Maginnis, e-mail to Ramon Sender and David W. Bernstein, December 28, 2006.

Composing with Light

TONY MARTIN

Clear and intimate, then mysterious with Asian fog, San Francisco's extreme diagonals were a different place for me and provided a new way of seeing and working. An "anything-is-possible" feeling pervaded the population. My musical instruments and the horse-headed sitar I built during my first year at the Art Institute of Chicago were with me in my warehouse studio at 136 Embarcadero. I was a musician turned painter. Rembrandt, Goya, and Soutine did that for me. The painting I still like best of my early work is *Shostakovich's Room,* inspired by his string quartets, which moved me intensely.

Gabo, Moholy-Nagy, and Schwitters sparked explorations, along with the imprint of a youth filled with blendings of visual images and sound. My father drew album covers of jazz musicians, my mother photographed Leadbelly. The serial images of Plastic Man comics and Rajput paintings were around. I knew I loved these things, and my instincts for making visual music flourished in the seven years from 1960 to 1967, mostly with the people and in the performing spaces of the San Francisco Tape Music Center. I gave vent to desires, indeed necessities, to make visual events that changed in time. It felt completely natural to make a translucent image roll shown behind glass of varying optical qualities. Put in motion with a variable-speed blender motor, it became my moving visual poem TV. I scratched, drew, and painted on glass and film slides for cross-dissolving with sequences painted on 16 mm film. I explored lens, mirror, and prism arrangements, creating confluences of light, dark, and color that evoked emotions, states of being, for me. One beam of sunlight through my geranium-vined windows could modulate with infinite variation. One beam from an old projector could generate a wall alive with imagery. Feeling a certain dislike for decorative art, I was wary of what could be made from this. I had seen the *Lumia* of [the Danish American artist] Thomas Wilfred, and found them pleasing, but lacking the emotional grit I found in Gorky's drawings or in the films of Keaton or Eisenstein. Through such influences, as well as my own inventive forays, I saw the potential of abstract visuals to convey every feeling and meaning that might be available when composing with nonillustrational abstract light in motion.

The occasion soon arose to put some of these explorations to use. It was suggested by mutual acquaintances that Ramon Sender and I meet; we had a robust get-together, and within a week, I had met Morton Subotnick as well. This coincided with the time they put together a series of performances at the San Francisco Conservatory and the beginnings of plans to make a Tape Music Center. Our events there were wide-ranging in how we made sound and light, using such things as rocks in a washing machine and beaming light through windows into a courtyard from film and altered projectors. Then, a bit later, out of the newfound Jones Street space, Ramon, Ken Dewey, and myself organized the citywide piece *City Scale* (1963). There were sounds through the Broadway Tunnel, a ballet of cars and their headlights on Telegraph Hill, my projections on the Rincon Annex Post Office. Nearly a hundred artists, performers, and friends participated in this evening of mutual creation.

Working with Morton on *Mandolin* (1963) fortunately coincided with a direction that was occurring in my work with dry ingredients and drawing, "collaging" on the 10" × 10" focal planes of overhead projectors. After talking with him and listening to the sequences of sound development he was working with (processing for tape, viola, and the poetry of Petrarch), I felt that a slow coming out of darkness was essential in the first section. I wanted bits of light in a large dark space to elicit feelings of questioning. These bits could move and warble, using liquid lensing over pinholes and apertures. In our first run-through, this created a planetarium-like first section. The musical shift to the poetry was a challenging juncture. Using the overheads and some wire drawings, sticks, and pieces of glass, the onstage scene of piano with or without live performers could become a somewhat otherworldly place, albeit grounded with earthly origins and inspirations: large and small visual forms rising up from the floor, sliding over the piano and into an invented "sky." The height of an auditorium or other space could be filled to develop some mythlike, Petrarch-inspired "temple of the sky," as I privately referred to it. The pieces of white light grew and shrank, altering continuously with the use of the dry and liquid ingredients. They were threaded through with saturated colors to create mysterious shapes within the prepared dry drawings on two 18" glass plates. Finally, the projected light darkened to a feeling of night.

For Ramon's *Desert Ambulance* (1964), both he and I felt that illuminating Pauline with film would be an effective way to begin. Both Pauline and the accordion could be substantially three-dimensional and also be filled with pulsing energy. I painted on 16 mm film, both clear and already exposed, encouraged from early on by the

21 TONY MARTIN'S COLLAGE-ASSEMBLAGE FOR THE SFTMC SEASON PROGRAM BROCHURE COVER (1964). © TONY MARTIN.

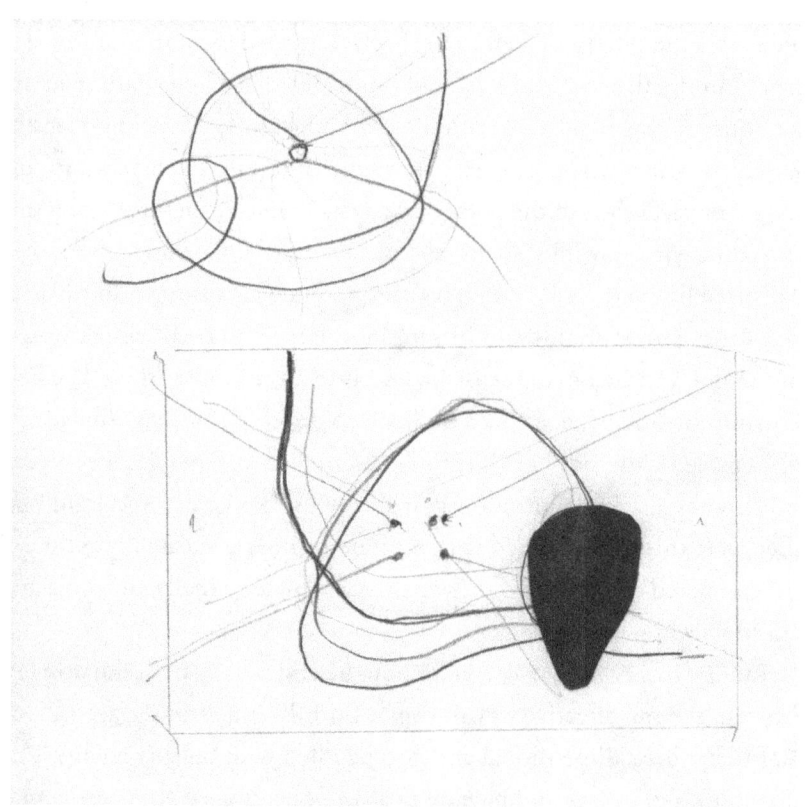

22 DRAWINGS BY TONY MARTIN FOR INWARD-OUTWARD MOTION FOR TWO PROJECTORS (1965). © TONY MARTIN.

23 **TONY MARTIN'S VISUAL SCORING SEQUENCE FOR A COMPOSITION FOR CROSS-DISSOLVED PROJECTED DRAWINGS AND LIQUIDS (1966). © TONY MARTIN.**

24 **DRAWINGS BY TONY MARTIN FOR MULTIPLE LIGHT PROJECTIONS COMBINING "MICROCOSMIC" AND "MACROCOSMIC" SCALE DIFFERENCES (1966). © TONY MARTIN.**

potential for meaningful dynamic rhythms, and for strong light coming through darkness and color. I experimented with various acetate inks, solvents, and various ingredients of my etching and painting supplies for the most satisfying result. I cut and spliced the film into lengths appropriate for making counterpoint to the sound, remaining vigilant against working "one to one" or in any way simply ornamenting sound meanings. Again, all that was available with these techniques allowed for dynamic differences of large and small, of dense and open, and of color oppositions or play of straight black and white. Adding film that I had photographed using an improvised animation stand provided the transitional sequence toward the opening up and enlarging of the visual experience beyond the performer/instrument. For this particular section, I spliced two- and five-frame sections with some longer ones of found footage, such as hands playing a piano. A negative print of these played over Pauline's hands and the accordion pleats was simultaneously mysterious and humorous, and often elicited laughter.

At a chosen moment, all of the preceding became immersed in a larger, more majestic environment through slide projectors with wide-angle lenses that generated images fifteen to twenty feet tall. This was in response to what I felt was Ramon's music reaching for limitless, uncontoured spaces. I matched it with increasingly landscape/skyscape-inspired abstractions, which, ironically, I had to paint on 2" × 2" glass slides. Key pieces of equipment made a very attenuated feeling of expansion. These were two old 1,000-watt rheostats, found on Mission Street, that I could dial very slowly to cross-dissolve my hand-painted images. Both Ramon and I were pleased with these almost imperceptible slow changes in the expanding, cathartic closing of the piece.

Late in 1965, I began in earnest to discover how I could employ electronic circuits for anything that might need to be interfaced or regulated in a sound-visual-tactile event of any sort. This was partially motivated by wanting to revisit my interactive-installation-sculptural works begun in 1961 while working with Ann Halprin. My *Theater for Watchers, Walkers, Touchers* (1962) provided a nonelectronic environment of interpersonal viewer participation, a twenty-foot-diameter spiral course of many viewer-influenced experiences. Ann commissioned this work by me for a festival of hers at the San Francisco Museum of Art in 1962. It remained in my thoughts for many years, culminating later on in the viewer-interactive sculptures shown at the Howard Wise Gallery in New York City in 1968 and 1969. (Three are now in the collections of the Everson Museum in Syracuse, New York, the Butler Institute of American Art in Youngstown, Ohio, and the Indiana Art Museum in Bloomington.)

The obvious answer to my desire for interconnection between media was to enable information to freely flow between visual and sound equipment. That there were a

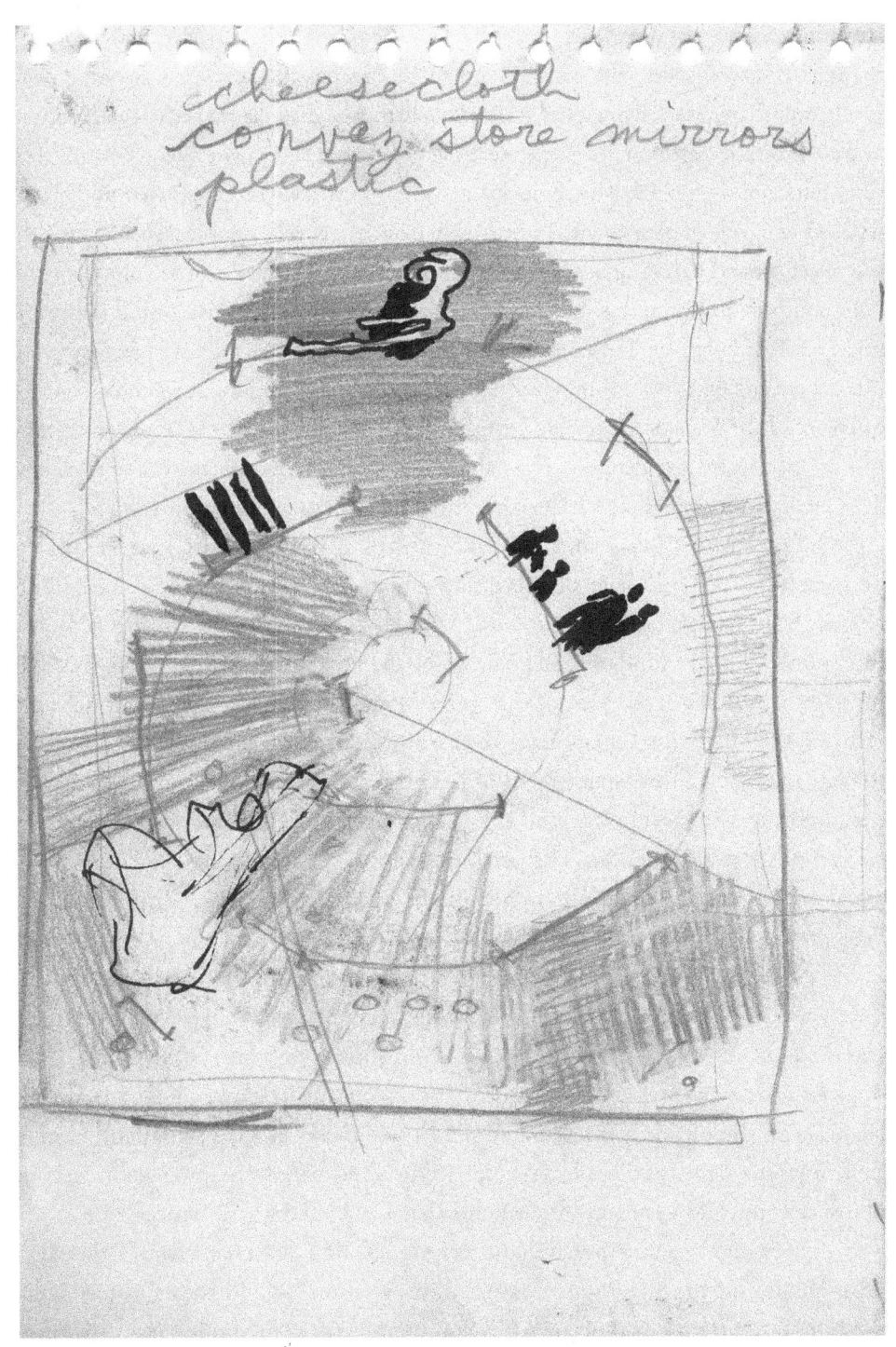

25 **DRAWING BY TONY MARTIN FOR** *THEATER FOR WATCHERS, WALKERS, TOUCHERS*, **A POLYSENSORY INSTALLATION COMMISSIONED BY ANN HALPRIN FOR THE SAN FRANCISCO MUSEUM OF ART (1962). © TONY MARTIN.**

few young electronic engineers in the Bay Area exploring these realms and applying the relatively new solid-state components made this possible. Carl Countryman was the answer to my wishes; my ideas worked easily in concert with his active imagination and electronic expertise. Ultimately, he built a filter, counter, and a silicon control rectifier unit that was portable, ingeniously made to fit into two briefcases. It could interface sound or other voltages with information from photo cells or other sensors, providing selection and patching of this information and distributing it to ten channels for light equipment. Using this, I created *Floorlamps* (1964–65), for five sound performers and five floor lamps. The lamps—one stationed by each performer—went on and off, depending on the combining of two sets of information: one set a choice of frequencies of the sounds produced, the other set determined by the counter. I patched a loop of the interdependent activity of the five performers, electric lamps, and speakers. This created a process that was at once structural and, at the same time, free.

Soon after this, Pauline and I collaborated on a work called *Circuitry* (1967), performed at the University of Illinois, in which Pauline configured microphone circuits from five percussionists to connect with light sources for scoring and illumination. We used a kind of scoreboard of small lights the performers read to determine the dynamics of the sounds they made. Each had a light near him or her that changed their individual character in the composite visual event and indicated when to play. I assembled this arrangement of light bulbs and additional spotlights that lit the performers in varying ways, all depending on the sounds produced and the on and off of these illuminators. The performers appeared and disappeared in front of a rear cyclorama that made a dramatic overlay of light through the drumheads, reflected off their figures and the casting of their shadows.

My pure light-projection setups resulted in such configurations as I used for the initial performance of Terry Riley's *In C* (1964), where I took the tops off overheads and used turning mirrors for imagery, and light shot straight up. For Pauline's *Light Piece for David Tudor* (1965), I put mirrors and scanning prisms into play. Ten years later, David Tudor and I collaborated on a piece for Merce Cunningham. Here I took those free light-motion ideas further, using elliptical reflectors and color-specific photo cells to collect dancers' movements that David and I both processed.

Every person who contributed to the techniques and visual character of light composition and the more spontaneous and improvisational "light shows"—few of us used this latter term—had his own development of those methods. As a basic mix, all used a projector combination, usually liquids, intermingling oil and water, solvents and color mediums, and dry substances in motion in large clock faces on overhead projectors, prepared slides, and 8 and 16 mm film. Film could originate as camera work, or be painted by hand, or recycled from any source. The way these elements were combined and handled made various amalgams with different feeling and meaning. This work was related to, but not directly influenced by, the historical lineage of kinetic art and experimental film work since the early 1900s, such as the films of Czech artist Zdenek Pesanek in the 1930s, and Len Lye's and Stan Brakhage's hand-painted 16 mm films from the 1950s. The highly articulated, somewhat mathematical and mechanically generated abstract film work of the Whitney brothers and the Morrison Planetarium concerts by the sound composer Henry Jacobs and the visual artist Jordan Belson were important influences in the Bay Area. These were often highly symmetrical, concentric, and applied a harder-edged geometry than the light-projection shows that would follow.

I first saw a full-scale liquid wall projection, accompanied by jazz, performed in a studio setting on Capp Street by Elias Romero. The experience was unique, and the techniques had potential for producing great beauty. I think almost anyone who has seen this painting in continuous motion feels its magical, sometimes powerful excitement. The degree of its power relies upon the performer having the sensitivity, know-how, and improvisational ability to mix and meld the visual instrumentation. The work is enjoyable, also hard and intense, especially with a full audience and loud music. Considerable energy must be given to the constant handling of plates, controlling of liquid mixes and their motion, changing of slides and film changes, and on/off of auxiliary lights. In the light shows of the 1960s era, within the high energy of the light show venues, a kind of subliminal ease was created in the fluid mix of people, sound, and light. A communal resonance of partaking and joining together occurred between individuals of many kinds: merchants, artists, bikers, office workers, and students.

The halls in which we presented our rock music–oriented light shows differed in character depending on their size, on when the shows took place, and on what groups were playing. The early Fillmore concerts for which I did multiprojector light shows, with such groups as Quicksilver Messenger Service, Them, and the Great Society, had a sort of innocent dancing and watching. Bill Hamm, Ben Van Meter, and Roger Hillyard would sustain the immersive psychedelic Avalon Ballroom projections in keeping with the feeling of the place. Glen McKay created well-hewn performances keyed more specifically to each band's songs, as did Josh White's group later on in New York City. In New York City, the Fillmore East shows made use of the added luminosity of rear projection screens. I varied my projection work considerably according to the music, and at times in counterpoint to it. A different "palette" was called for when I worked with Muddy Waters or Lightnin' Hopkins than with the Jefferson Airplane or with the Byrds in Los Angeles. I remember making shows

26 ELIAS ROMERO (CA. 1960). PHOTOGRAPH © WARNER JEPSON.

exclusively for blues and soul groups at the Fillmore Auditorium on Sunday afternoons. These swayed rather than rocked; I used a lot of purple and green, along with the acid yellow that was my staple for hard rock shows. A signature show was the Grateful Dead on New Year's Eve, an unceasing "midnight hour" that was hypnotic, pulsing, and left me sore-eyed and weary-handed, but happy.

Concurrent with light shows were theater and dance applications in the same spirit of multimedia. West Coast theater and dance offerings were rich and explorative. I composed a light score for the poet Michael McClure's play *The Beard*, which was hosted by Bill Graham. And I also recall the poignancy of an evening I lit with a single flat light: Lenny Bruce, alone on stage, late in his career. The inventive use of large-scale environments, such as the well-known cargo-net pieces and dance "journeys" on the land, evolved through works created by Ann Halprin and her dancers. Ronnie Davis's Mime Troupe, the rather loose and spontaneous Straight Theater on the Haight, the Committee, and other theater groups also contributed greatly to the energy and aesthetic spectrum of the times.

In the case of my own focus in the mid-1960s, I can point to my ongoing interest in organic asymmetry, kindled through the love and practice of painting, spurred on by my exposure to the emotional intensity of Soutine and Gorky. Another inspiration

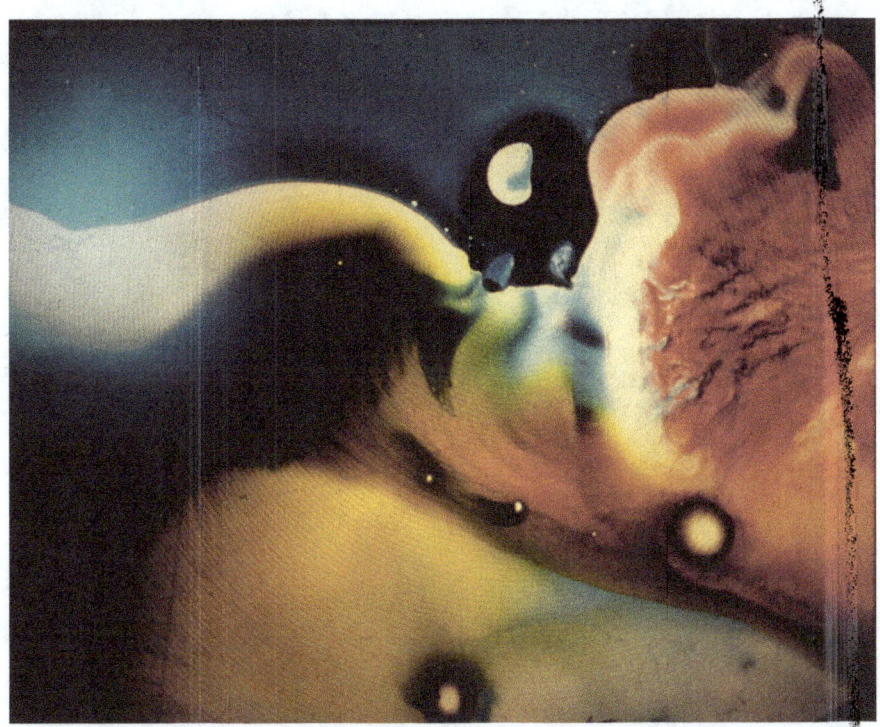

1 TONY MARTIN, MULTIPLE LIGHT PROJECTION, STILL FROM *IMPROVISATION 1967*. NONESUCH RECORD COVER FOR MORTON SUBOTNICK, *SILVER APPLES OF THE MOON*. © TONY MARTIN.

2 TONY MARTIN, MULTIPLE LIGHT PROJECTION, STILL FROM THE VISUAL COMPOSITION FOR *DESERT AMBULANCE* (1963) BY RAMON SENDER. © TONY MARTIN.

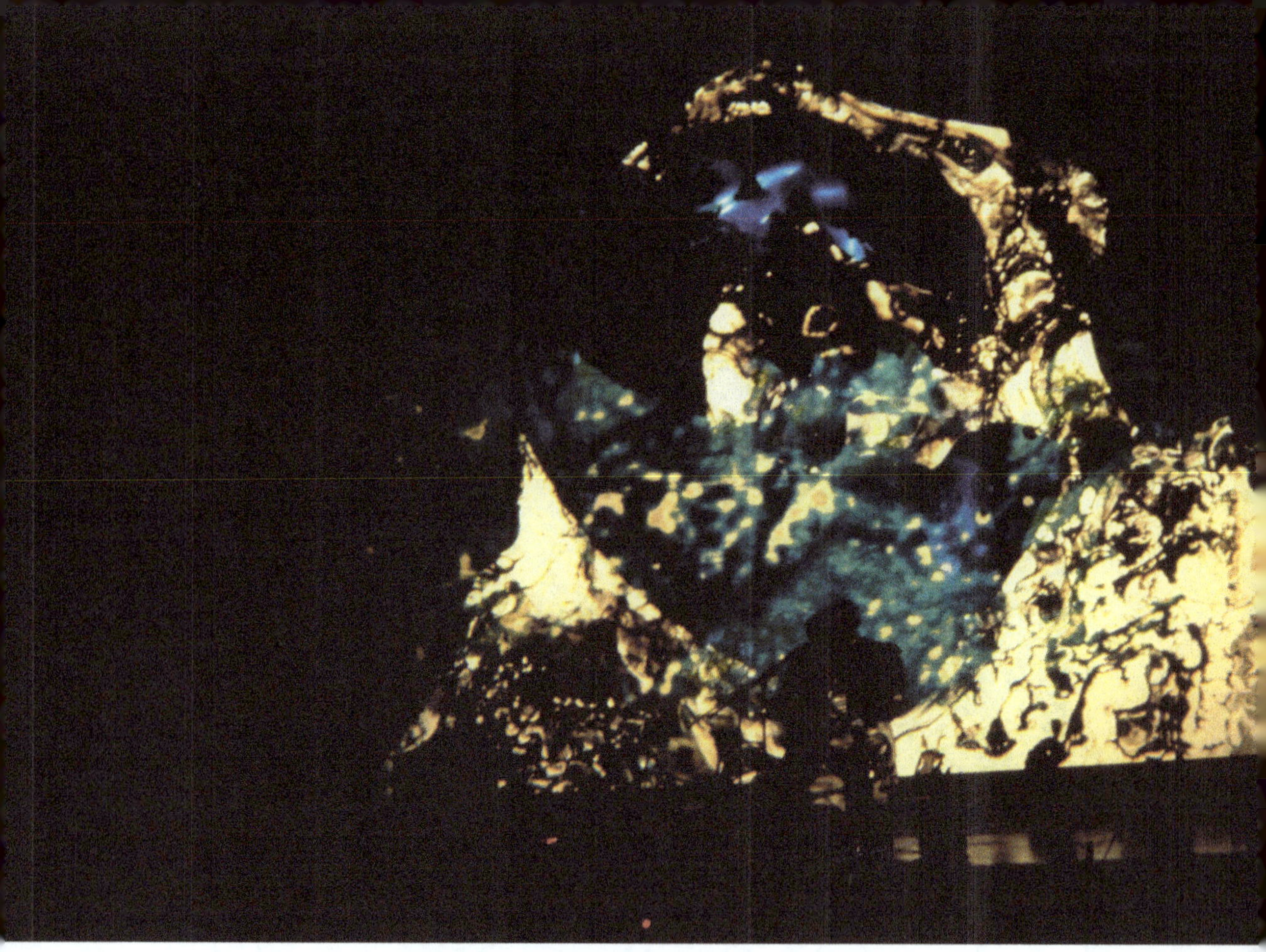

3 TONY MARTIN, STILL FROM THE VISUAL COMPOSITION FOR *DESERT AMBULANCE* (1963) BY RAMON SENDER. THE PERFORMER IS PAULINE OLIVEROS. SAN FRANCISCO TAPE MUSIC CENTER RETROSPECTIVE, VICTORIA THEATER, SAN FRANCISCO, 1988. © TONY MARTIN.

4 TONY MARTIN, STILL FROM *IMPROVISATION* (1963). © TONY MARTIN.

5 TONY MARTIN, IMAGE USED FOR *INTERIOR BLOOM* (1966). PAINTED SLIDE, DRAWING ON ACETATE, LIQUID/DRY PROJECTIONS. MILLS COLLEGE, OAKLAND, CONCERT HALL. © TONY MARTIN.

6 TONY MARTIN, STILL FROM THE VISUAL COMPOSITION FOR *MANDOLIN* (1963) BY MORTON SUBOTNICK. "WOW & FLUTTER: THE SAN FRANCISCO TAPE MUSIC CENTER, 1961–NOW," EXPERIMENTAL MEDIA AND PERFORMING ARTS CENTER (EMPAC), 2004. © TONY MARTIN.

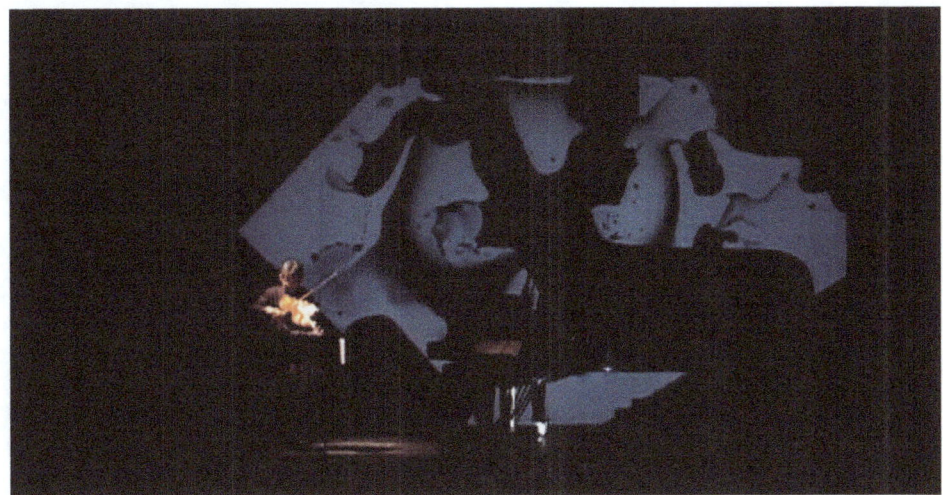

7 RAMON SENDER, *TROPICAL FISH OPERA* (1962), PERFORMED BY (FROM LEFT TO RIGHT) BILL MAGINNIS, RAMON SENDER, MORTON SUBOTNICK, AND PAULINE OLIVEROS. "WOW & FLUTTER," EMPAC, 2004.

8 TONY MARTIN, STILL FROM THE VISUAL COMPOSITION FOR *DESERT AMBULANCE* (1963) BY RAMON SENDER. "WOW & FLUTTER," EMPAC, 2004. © TONY MARTIN.

9 PAULINE OLIVEROS AND TONY MARTIN, STILL FROM *CIRCUITRY* (1967). "WOW & FLUTTER," EMPAC, 2004.

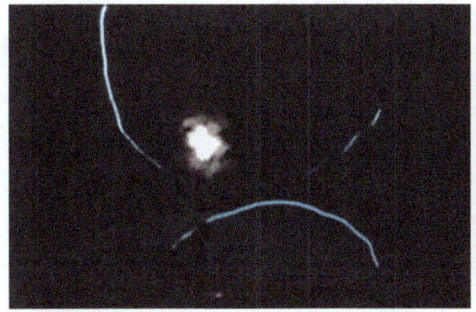 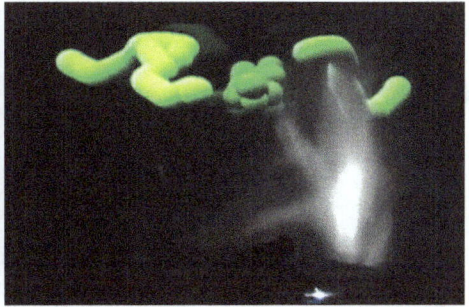

10 TONY MARTIN, STILLS FROM *SILENT LIGHT* (1967). THE PERFORMER IS MARGOT FARRINGTON. "WOW & FLUTTER," EMPAC, 2004. © TONY MARTIN.

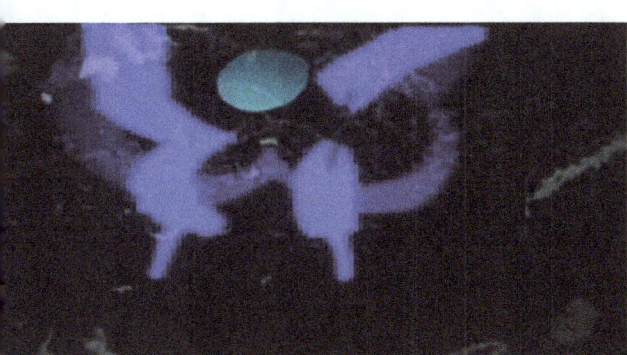 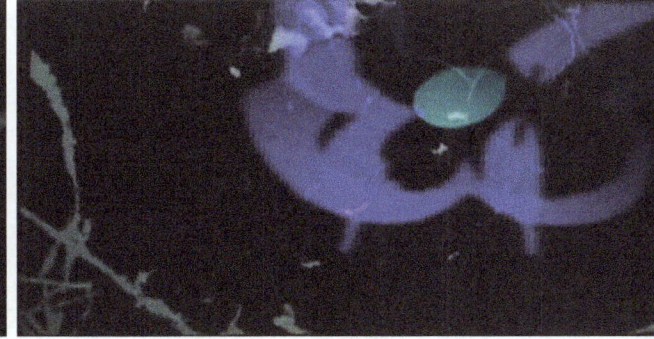

11 TONY MARTIN, STILLS FROM THE VISUAL COMPOSITION FOR *BYE BYE BUTTERFLY* (1965) BY PAULINE OLIVEROS. "WOW & FLUTTER," EMPAC, 2004. © TONY MARTIN.

12 TONY MARTIN, STILLS FROM THE VISUAL COMPOSITION FOR *MANDOLIN* (1963) BY MORTON SUBOTNICK. "WOW & FLUTTER," EMPAC, 2004. © TONY MARTIN.

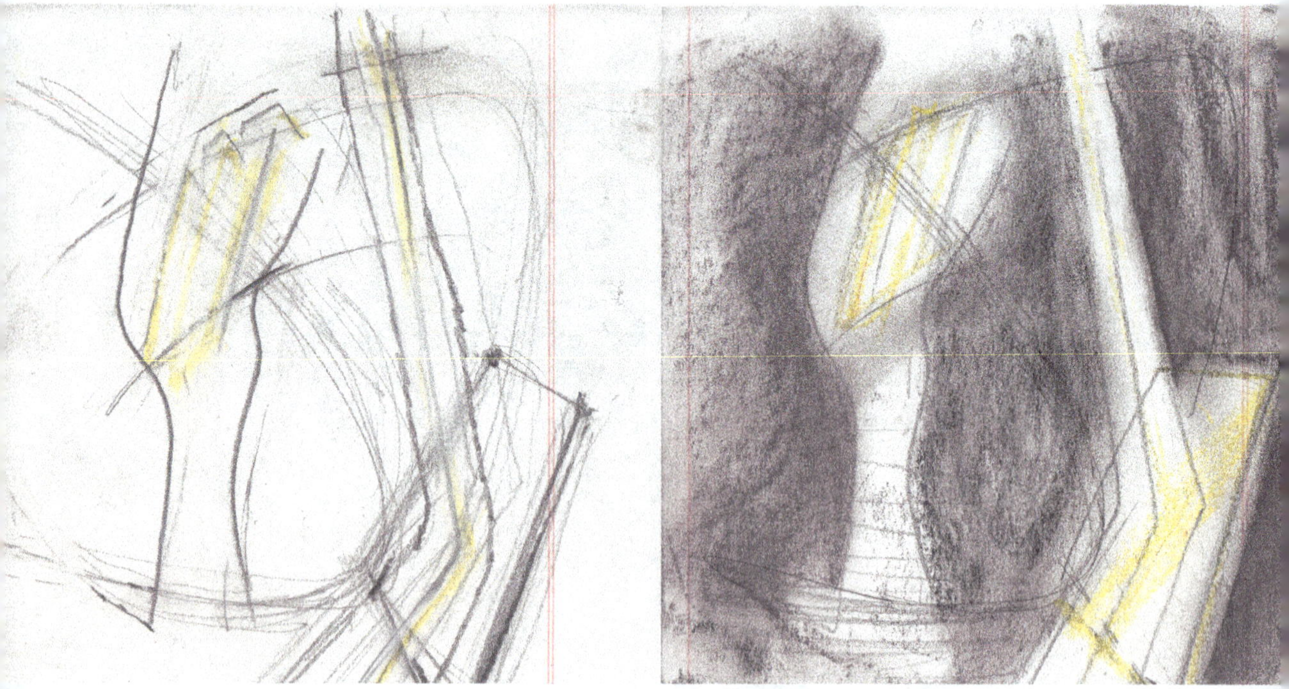

13 DRAWING FOR OPTICAL PROJECTIONS WITH MIRRORS BY TONY MARTIN. © TONY MARTIN.

14 TONY MARTIN, VISUAL SCORE DRAWING FOR A LIQUID PROJECTION IMPROVISATION (1966). © TONY MARTIN.

15 (LEFT) **OVERVIEW OF THE TRIPS FESTIVAL. PHOTOGRAPH © SUSAN ELTING HILLYARD.**

16 (RIGHT) **RAMON SENDER (TOP) AT THE TRIPS FESTIVAL. PHOTOGRAPH © SUSAN ELTING HILLYARD.**

17 TONY MARTIN AT THE TRIPS FESTIVAL. PHOTOGRAPH © SUSAN ELTING HILLYARD.

was the uniquely American handling of light and dark in Albert Pinkham Ryder and Ralph Albert Blakelock. I responded to Arthur Dove's wild and irregular rhythms as well as Mondrian's more modular ones. The eccentrics of early Chinese art made use of a wonderful asymmetrical energy that invigorated me. For as long as I can remember, I've had a need to find a common stage for the tiny and ingoing and the expansive and outgoing. Multiple projection methods gave me new opportunities to explore this. It joined with my love of natural universal phenomena; illumination of water in motion, whorls of atmosphere in clouds, the startling and inviting forms of flowers, the friendliness of leaf shapes. And how humanity fits and doesn't fit with these—our everyday situational drama. In the mid-1960s, I came across the wonderful book *Sensitive Chaos* by Theodore Schwenk.[1] His written and photographic investigations into the dynamics of liquids in motion and biological form broadened and deepened my path. I find something essential in the flow and interdependency of choice and chance: chaos is comprised of the organized, and vice versa. We live in a dynamic, exciting, joining place. An auditorium, a street corner, a single person is a place where the universe and person and the human condition are one arena: filled with threat and beauty in every instant, and with specific form at every moment.

I left the San Francisco Bay Area in 1967, after a year as visual director of the Tape Music Center at Mills College. I went east, to a position with partial income at the New York University School of the Arts Intermedia Program, serendipitously headed by Boyd Compton. Boyd was the man who had worked to shape the grant that funded the newly established Tape Music Center at Mills College. We were all very conscious of the positive and negative aspects of this move, but it felt in some important way as though it was time for a change. The larger, more dynamic visual art world of New York City was a draw for me. Indeed, the triumvirate of the Intermedia Program, the added income for helping to set up the Electric Circus visual system, and the rare and wonderful enthusiasm of Howard Wise for art that applied new media and technology was a powerful lure.

NOTE

1. Theodor Schwenk, *Sensitive Chaos: The Creation of Flowing Forms in Water and Air*, trans. Olive Whicher and Johanna Wrigley (1965; reprint, New York: Schocken Books, 1976); originally published as *Das sensible Chaos: Strömendes Formenschaffen in Wasser u. Luft* (Stuttgart: Verl. Freies Geistesleben, 1962).

Tony Martin

INTERVIEWED BY DAVID W. BERNSTEIN AND MAGGI PAYNE

Although his collaborations with members of the San Francisco Tape Music Center began several years earlier, Tony Martin became the group's visual composer shortly after the center moved to 321 Divisadero Street in 1963. A former "East-Coaster," as he described himself, Martin attended the Chicago Art Institute, where he began his career as a painter. Moving to San Francisco in 1959 initiated a wonderful transformation of his work. The city's dynamic visual environment, ranging from opaque fog to sunny, crystal clear blue skies that cast changing shadows through the windows of his studio, stimulated his interest in light, and particularly in the ways that it developed in time. The Bay Area also provided Martin with a more open cultural climate than he had encountered in the East. These factors served as catalysts, inspiring Martin to move beyond the canvas and ultimately to his pioneering work with light using overhead projectors, films, and slides, and to a somewhat separate arena of art with viewer participation.

Martin's interview documents his artistic development from his arrival in San Francisco to his work at the Tape Music Center. He carefully describes both the techniques and the working methods he employed in his collaborations with Pauline Oliveros, Morton Subotnick, Ramon Sender, Ken Dewey, and Ann Halprin. A unique working relationship existed among these artists. In each project, they worked together toward creating a synergetic whole, a unified artistic conception fusing both the visual and the aural. Martin's influence was a major factor in the evolution of this collaborative aesthetic.

The Tape Music Center was a closely knit community, which would band together to create fully integrated mixed-media works. But each of the artists working in the center always maintained his or her individuality. Martin never conceived of his light projections as accompaniment for the music or theatrical action. He created light compositions that were orchestrations of visual forms in motion inhabiting a discrete parallel universe.

This interview and the preceding essay reveal the personal character of Martin's visual compositions. Drawing is a strong component of his work. He makes assiduous use of dynamic asymmetrical compositional means consistent with his painting. He explores visual forms conveying deeply felt emotions expressed through the development of images applying alternating changes of light and dark, shape, line, color, texture, and scale, and altered photographic material.

BERNSTEIN: When you arrived in San Francisco in 1959 you were primarily a painter, and in fact you've continued to paint for your entire career.

MARTIN: That's right. I began as painter. I came to the Bay Area from the Chicago Art Institute. A lot of what was going on in new music didn't involve much to look at. There were tape recorders, and once in a while a performer to watch, but at any rate, it often lacked a visual component. I was extending my painting to time, being able to use a combination of projectors to make a changing visual presentation. It was an automatic thing to join up with Ramon and Mort and start to do some pieces. Gradually, I became the visual component of the Tape Music Center, continuing as visual director when the center moved to Mills College. It was wonderful for me to be a visual composer in that milieu.

BERNSTEIN: Early on you became interested in finding ways of working visually off the canvas.

MARTIN: Right.

BERNSTEIN: I'd like to try to trace the evolution of that. I've read that you did some light sculptures in your studio around 1959? Can you tell me about those?

MARTIN: Yes, well, I lived in three different places in the first year. One was up in the Twin Peaks area. I used to fool around with lenses there, because the sunlight coming into the back windows was so good. I made shapes with sunlight with lenses and other optical devices.

Soon after that I was in a different environment, in foggy North Beach, on North Point, down near Fisherman's Wharf. I became fascinated with the fog, and wondered how visual things could happen in an environment like fog. So I used to shine a flashlight through the fog. [Laughs]

Later on I got into the large studio I had on the Embarcadero. That was the first place where I started to put together some of these optical things. I had various lenses and some special mirrors I could buy easily on Mission Street and on Market Street near Van Ness. There were some Army-Navy stores where I'd find these strange-shaped mirrors, oval mirrors and half-silvered mirrors, cheap lenses for fifty cents, and prisms. I got a large six-inch prism; it was really a heavy hunk of glass. And I brought these back to my studio on the Embarcadero. At that point I was living alone.

There was a motor that I had that was from a blender, I believe. It had a rheostat, so it had variable speeds. I attached some of these objects to the motor, and it would go around and I would use the sunlight again, from the back windows. I had ten-foot tall windows. It was a huge loft, in the old Bromo-Seltzer warehouse. I never got a headache in there. [Laughs] It was ten thousand square feet. I rented out about five thousand feet to Paul Wonner and James Weeks. (Paul Wonner is well known for his large still-life paintings. James Weeks is a wonderful painter, somewhat in the David Parks / Elmer Bischoff tradition.) [I also rented space] to Robert Hudson, and another sculptor, Bill Geis.

BERNSTEIN: So you all shared that space.

MARTIN: That's right. I put together redwood planks in the place when I got there and made a wall so that my half was separated from the other half. The light coming in over the Rincon Annex was really good in the late afternoon, and I used to play around with these objects and this motor: there was a large piece of round glass that I had that was somewhat frosted, plus the motor to move this roll of painted translucent material behind the glass; I had [made] myself an abstract motion television set of sorts.

It was my own exploration of abstract form in motion. And only a few friends saw that. I never showed it anywhere. It never really became a finalized work. All of these experiments were more of a workshop, an assembly of various light processes that I was exploring. I was painting at the same time, so might have had two paintings going on the wall, and in the evening I could fool around with my optics and the little machine I just described to you.

An addition to all this [there] was an old 16 mm movie projector; it had a variable-speed rheostat. I could vary the speed of the film as it was playing. I had some old discarded film I found in a trash can, and I would play around with projecting this film faster and slower, sometimes with other things that were going on the wall, either with city light through the window, or with some optics turning around on a turntable.

Those were the kinds of things that I was doing in my studio pretty much on my own. It was during this same time period that I met Ramon Sender and then Morton Subotnick. The excitement I was feeling for extending beyond the canvas was, I guess, almost a subliminal motive to get together with them, because I didn't have a big plan for how to exercise these ideas. We became friendly, and I learned they were starting to do some things at the San Francisco Conservatory. The time period I'm talking about is about a year and half.

BERNSTEIN: What's interesting about this is that not only were you moving beyond the canvas, you were also moving into a temporal world where things changed and moved in time.

MARTIN: Yes, absolutely. Coming to the Bay Area was a little like a Pandora's Box for me. I think I was a bit repressed by New York City, where I grew up. I think I felt [the Bay Area] would be more of an open [environment] for me.

And that's why I went to the Bay Area. When I got there, it seemed natural to go beyond the canvas, to pick up things that were different, to think about assemblage, to put things together in different kinds of ways. Different ways of making monoprints—that was a similar experience. I built a printing press out of old farm parts, and I was using oil and water on paper, just the way I used oil and water on clock faces later on. So you know these things were all part of the same opening out for me. And I really enjoyed being in the Bay Area. There was nobody to answer to, in a way. I didn't feel that there was a cultural authority hanging over my head the way it did in New York City. It was a time period for me when I tried out a lot of methods and different mediums.

BERNSTEIN: Was it all instinct? You mentioned the words instinctual and subliminal. Were you familiar with other, earlier work . . .

MARTIN: I didn't know a lot about many of the things I know now. I was not overly exposed to a lot of the things we talk about as being the sources for light shows. I remember seeing Gabo's sculptures with plastic and wire and I thought those were interesting and wonderful. I'd seen a Tinguely piece in motion, but I never felt that I was in the same path, necessarily, as those things. Do you see what I mean?

BERNSTEIN: Yes.

MARTIN: There I was in the Bay Area, feeling a little bit alienated, like this was another world for me, and picking up things and using them, trying to find some ways of painting that made sense to me. I was happy to be less connected, you might say, exploring in my own way, and in my own time, nobody telling me it should be this or that, or this is better than that.

BERNSTEIN: We understand that you were visual director of the Tape Music Center for a while?

MARTIN: Yes. The work I started to do with Ramon, Morton, Pauline, Terry Riley,

Ann Halprin, and other people in 1962 and 1963 was mostly a visual contribution to what was going on.

PAYNE: How did you come to know that group of people?

MARTIN: I have a hard time remembering exactly when I first met Pauline. I haven't tried to pinpoint it. I knew the Landors, and the Landors knew Ramon.[1] That's fairly certain. And they said, "Hey, you ought to meet Ramon, because he's doing some interesting things with tape recorders and banging on car bumpers and mixing unusual sounds."

So I met Ramon, and we had an immediate kind of empathy in terms of sound experiments and visual experiments. Ramon knew Mort already, who had come from Denver, I think, and was at Mills. Just a short time later, I met Mort. They formed the Jones Street group, and I was immediately included. Then Pauline showed up. I liked her right away. We have been artistically sympathetic to each other for forty years now. I think we were all on similar paths that were also individual.

Michael Callahan was our first technician, capable and inventive. Later on Bill Maginnis was there, and I really liked Bill. He was good at putting together wires, and ultimately we all became quite good at tearing apart and putting together wires. And then other people would come into the Tape Music Center. Steve Reich showed up and . . .

BERNSTEIN: He did a lot of multimedia things, right?

MARTIN: More like film, such as *Oh Dem Watermelons.* And then Terry showed up. Terry and I had some similar roots; I was a musician as a young person and played jazz. Terry had played jazz, so he was close to that, and to some of the classical music I loved from my childhood, because I'd learned classical music as well. And I also felt simpatico with Terry because in 1955 I built a sarod after going to a concert of Indian music, which I fell in love with. I guess I was nineteen at the time.

For the first concert of *In C* [1964], I did a light event. During that time, there were also pieces by Mario Davidovsky and James Tenney; many concerts started to occur at the Tape Music Center, first at Jones Street and then at Divisadero. Basically, the five of us put it all together: Pauline, Ramon, Mort, Bill, and I.

BERNSTEIN: You worked with Ann Halprin as well.

MARTIN: Yes. That was another important thing for me, working with Ann Halprin. I guess I had instincts for a kind of polysensory art form from the beginning, and that may have to do with my love of music and theater and nature and painting. Ann for me was a catalyst for that, so I did some kinds of physical surroundings, "dance ecologies," at her place in Kentfield. I made some tree houses for the dancers and strung ropes, and came up with the cargo net that she used with dancers [in her piece *Esposizione* (1963)]. I would go over there and make environments for the dancers, joining up a particular piece with a certain environment. I liked her approach: it was very open, very horizontal. In fact, San Francisco for me, aesthetically, was not vertical, it was horizontal, which meant incorporating; it meant interdependence, nothing above anything else. That was a nice thing for me, extremely refreshing. New York was hierarchical, very much so, and still is.

BERNSTEIN: Didn't you do some work at the San Francisco Conservatory, when they were doing the Sonics concerts in 1961–62?

MARTIN: Yes.

BERNSTEIN: And one piece that was performed in the garden of the conservatory.

MARTIN: Yes. The things that I used there were varied. I had a nice big truck, a GMC van—they didn't call them vans in those days—it was a covered truck and it had a large bed in the back. When I went over to the conservatory, I put everything I had in there: that movie projector, some flashlights, some mirrors, and a prism. I don't know if I had Mylar or not. I had also bought an overhead projector: a big old Besseler. I bought it used and I'd put that in the back of my truck. I think I got it toward the end of the conservatory time. I can't remember if I had it with me for that outdoor courtyard concert or not.

I didn't use any liquid projection that I can remember. I used some film in the film projector, a turntable with some optics on it, the flashlight; using my hands, I would refract the light and make different kinds of shapes. I used pieces of glass in the light beams to make a mixture of abstract pure light and texture. A lot of textural elements were from the film. I'd change the lens on the film projector from in focus to out of focus.

So I used the film projector as a kind of instrument. I didn't use it as a refined film projector. I had old film in there, and some of my own that I had joined with it. I mostly used old film and sometimes the projector with no film in it! I changed the speed of the film and the focus. At the conservatory, I shot it out the window at one point, into the garden. So, it was improvisatory, loose—a combination of textures, and dark and light.

BERNSTEIN: When was the first time you used liquid projections?

MARTIN: That's a good question. You know, it wasn't with either one of those pieces. I think it was with [a work by] Davidovsky.

BERNSTEIN: At Jones Street?

MARTIN: No, not at Jones Street, at 321 Divisadero. I didn't start directly from liquid [projections]; I took a slightly different path. I started with different kinds of things on the light table, on the overhead projector, including liquid. I never wanted to use liquids alone, I guess.

BERNSTEIN: Perhaps we could talk a little bit more about the Jones Street year.

MARTIN: Right. There are a couple of things I recall since we talked last about Jones Street. One thing I remember more clearly is [the period during which we did] *City Scale* [1963], which was at Jones Street. Ken Dewey and I got together there in the fall, before *City Scale*. I first remember sitting around Jones Street with Ken Dewey and Ramon, and later just myself and Ken Dewey. That would have been November 1962.

I found Ken to be an interesting guy. He had a good sense of theater. He was an inquiring, sensitive guy, and I got along with him quite well. We talked a lot during these meetings, about how theater can be one thing or another—how it can make use of a stage or not; or make use of anything—he had a strong point of view about that. We met now and again over a couple of months. *City Scale* did not spontaneously occur. It had some good background [based on] our getting together informally and then a bit more formally. In particular, Ramon, Ken, and I would sit down and actually map out what we thought would be exciting use of the whole environment: meaning a large part of the whole city of San Francisco.

BERNSTEIN: It was an extremely intricate piece.

MARTIN: Yes, it was, and it really was wonderful how it came together. Most of what we thought of we put into play in some form. *City Scale* represented an intensely concentrated period of time. We put in a lot of energy, a lot of work—physical work.

We put butcher paper all around the walls of the living room at Jones Street. The paper was there for people to write words on, or paint or draw on. We provided a pair of scissors so they could cut off a piece of somebody else's effort: like a little poem that was written on the wall, and take it with them if they wanted. There was tape, so they could tape up another piece if they wanted. Or I could. I added paper in the early part of the evening. Some people did use the butcher paper, and I did some things myself; I was trying to get it going. And this relates to . . .

BERNSTEIN: Your *Theater for Watchers, Walkers, Touchers* [1962]?

MARTIN: Yes, the word wall, which was a more formal use of the same ideas. They were both a group "participational" approach. It wasn't determined; it wasn't set up in an ideological kind of way, the way some of the uses of these ideas were taking place in New York later on. It was quite open-ended, providing people with not only a way to express themselves, but also [opportunities] to exchange feelings, thoughts, and expressions between each other. I think this was part of our aim. Certainly, Ken's, Ramon's, and my aim was partly to provide a joining place where people could come together in a creative way to find meaningful events and experiences.

BERNSTEIN: That's wonderful.

MARTIN: We scored the course of the evening to begin in the Jones Street place and to spiral out into the entire city over a period of six hours.

BERNSTEIN: Now, on another occasion, you also did an installation with plastic that was hung away from the wall in the living room at Jones Street?

MARTIN: Yes, that piece I did in the living room of Jones Street was not on the program schedule. It was done during an improvisation of some sort. That was when I got behind plastic; it was three feet away from the wall, and I painted on it and set up lights behind it.

BERNSTEIN: Around all four walls?

MARTIN: On three walls.

BERNSTEIN: So the facility at Jones Street was basically a multiple-story building?

MARTIN: Yes, we used the ground floor. A wall was taken out; it was one large space—almost like a storefront. Upstairs there were some apartments that I think were rented. I don't know the exact arrangements that were made.

PAYNE: Can you tell us about the visuals for Terry Riley's *In C* [1964]?

MARTIN: Yes. For *In C,* I felt I didn't want to be projecting from the outside in, I wanted to be projecting from the inside out. So I sat in the middle [of the performers] and had a group of simple projection things: I had a prism, a couple of lenses, three or four projectors that were modified so I could dial the light up and down (one, a columnated beam), and I moved shapes through the people and into the environment. The visual event combined large and small lines and shapes of light in motion with the shapes and shadows of the musicians. There were about six musicians, or eight, in that first performance. It was concentric. That was also the way I liked to work with Pauline, from the inside out.

BERNSTEIN: That's Pauline's whole philosophy really.

MARTIN: Yes. I've always been sympathetic to the kind of joining of humanity in music that Pauline believes in. That first performance of *In C* was easy and low-key in a way. I wanted it to rise and have a feeling of opening out, and I didn't use any images—just the shadows of people and beams of light and shapes of light.

BERNSTEIN: Did you have any contact with members of the Once Group?

MARTIN: It's curious, I went to the University of Michigan in 1956–57. I met Gordon Mumma at some point. I didn't meet him again until 1964, almost a decade later. But I never did anything with them. I was aware of them as a student. I don't think they were the Once Group yet. We invited David Tudor to come for a festival [the "Tudorfest"] in 1964. He came to Divisadero Street. Pauline knew him well. We also did pieces from New York, and we may have done something of Ashley's, I am not sure.

This brings up a certain thing I was thinking about yesterday. I always felt that I was using "chance plus choice" and that most of my visual music was generated out of that feeling. It was nature plus me as a piece of nature. So I couldn't just go with random ideas. I loved improvising, and a lot of that was chance, such as, when should the film go on? Well, leave that up to the way this piece of yellow is crossing that photocell. I loved that! That was being like nature. But also I was making choices; I wanted the film to start over here at a certain time because this material was going to be developing because of a certain performer. That was a choice. I realized again later that I was not "Cageian" completely. I somehow wanted to make choices and use randomness. And even to use chaos. It was so available visually to combine things, not just layer them but actually to combine them. The light was doing it automatically. I would use pure light along with lenses and film.

I thought about that; at that time I was first aware of what Cage was about, and what others were bringing to new music. I was a little bit aware of Black Mountain College already; I grew up in an environment where, one morning I woke up (when I was twelve years old) and there was this big guy sleeping on the couch, and it was Charles Olson. My father was friendly with him.

BERNSTEIN: There is a lot of choice in Cage's methods too.

MARTIN: There really is. That's a good point.

BERNSTEIN: I'd like to discuss some of your other work at 321 Divisadero. I'll start with Subotnick's *Play! no. 1* [1964]. Did you create a film for that?

MARTIN: Yes, I borrowed a Bolex 16 mm camera and I got film for it, which I really liked, black-and-white film that had a really wonderful gray scale and good blacks and whites, like those really good Hitchcock movies. So I went around with Morton; we had the idea to be in different kinds of places and just to film them. And maybe doing something and maybe not doing anything. It finally got honed down to Morton and I going around to different doorways in San Francisco, and Morton coming out of the door or going into the door, usually the front door of a building. I would film this. Now, I don't think it was a lot of time, actually, on film. I think we spent more than one session doing this, but ultimately I had shot about, let's see 400 feet of film, maybe ten minutes of film.

We had done quite a bit of walking around, and somehow I felt we had really gotten something that was going to be spliced together fairly easily without much editing. When I took it to a lab and got the film back, it hardly needed any splicing at all. I was delighted, partly because I didn't have a whole studio for film work. I had my hand-splicers and a couple of winders that I picked up at an Army-Navy store. I put that film together pretty easily and had it printed. Mort and I would just start the tape and the film together—the sound was not put on the film. [We just counted] "1–2–3 Go!" and I turned on the projector and he turned on the tape recorder and there was *Play! no. 1.* It was orchestrated in more than one way. Mort had live performers . . .

BERNSTEIN: Right. It was a quintet.

MARTIN: Yes, a quintet, exactly. So it was a combination; it was always a performance piece. The film was never meant to be shown alone. I think that's something people don't understand about the way we worked in those days. The ingredients were not the end result. The film was not a film, it was part of a piece. The quintet was not a quintet without the film.

BERNSTEIN: Do you remember the visual components for *Play! no. 3* [1965] and *Play! no. 4* [1965]?

MARTIN: *Play! no. 3* was very short—I think it was three minutes long?

BERNSTEIN: That was with Leonard Stein, I believe.

MARTIN: Yes, exactly. Now it had a very distinct beginning and end. I don't remember now. I think it was three minutes exactly. I had made an entirely different kind of film for this. I had shot a lot of materials in my studio with color film. And I moved objects and I shot it frame by frame. I would shoot three frames, two frames, one frame. I used entirely different methods of filmmaking than I used for *Play! no. 1.* So it's a different kind of piece; it's a very fast moving, rhythmic scoring. I got some really good color film and made an animated film for it, mostly in my Embarcadero studio. It was very easy to set things on the floor and use a tripod with a camera and many kinds of light. It was easy to set up, very improvised, but a very effective animation setup that I made for myself with the tripod and the Bolex. Putting it together was a completely different kind of framework at the time, with color, using objects, cutouts, collage material that I placed on the floor and recorded frame by frame for most of it. I would make ribbons of the frame numbers and shoot three frames, three frames, then one frame, one frame, one frame, and then six frames, six frames, and I would repeat that over and over again, achieving certain kinds of rhythms appropriate for the images and the music, which I often didn't listen to while I was working on the visual part of it. I'd heard Mort's tape, and I would play it once in a while in the studio, and finally ended up with about, probably, about six minutes of film that had been shot in this frame-by-frame kind of way. Then I processed it and got the film back and realized it wasn't quite right. It had two rhythmic structures. I felt right away that was not what was needed here and I started splicing, cutting and splicing the animated sequences I had made. But then it came together very easily. Cutting and splicing quite a few times—I must've spliced a hundred splices to make the color 16 mm print. I put it all together and played it with the sound and it worked! It functioned very meaningfully with the sound.

Play! no. 4 was entirely different. It was illuminated entirely by two reels of film. They were long films, not short, fifteen, sixteen minutes of film, two large reels of film, which, as you can imagine, are no easy task to make. The film was put together mostly from film that I had already shot and some that I was shooting at that current time, some of which I actually shot of people dancing in the Fillmore Auditorium.

BERNSTEIN: It was for orchestra, wasn't it?

MARTIN: No, but it had an on stage performer setting, entirely lit by the two films. So it was a very interesting setup; it was truly music theater.

BERNSTEIN: The musical score is very theatrical. The musicians had to do all sorts of things.

MARTIN: Yes, I still have it on two rolls of film. I should save it for the record. You know, we didn't record our pieces, which is a big mistake because it could have been done one way or another. We did not film the work at Divisadero Street or when we were on tour. And that's really a missing part of the whole decade, but we did manage. Well, the case that I'm trying to make here is that I either willingly or unwillingly saved everything from the time. So, I have the original slides that I painted on for *Desert Ambulance;* I have the original pieces of film that went into *Play! no[s]. 1, 3,* and *4.* I've got all the ingredients, in other words, to do these pieces exactly the way they were done then.

I'd like to speak about another piece that I think I should mention right away.

BERNSTEIN: Of course.

MARTIN: I'm thinking of the *Tarot* [1965] piece, which was really an interesting piece for me because I felt I could join a couple of things with that piece. One thing I did was to film Luciano Berio's head in black space. I filmed him and John Graham. Berio was working at Mills College for at least one semester. He was at Divisadero Street; we were talking about the *Tarot* piece that Mort was doing then, and that I was going to be doing a visual composition for it. It would be easy to turn all the lights off and turn on one projector with a pinhole illuminating his head, and to film that. So I did that. [Laughs] I don't know if I have that actual film except maybe on one print of the *Tarot*. There may be a piece of it.

John Graham was working with Ann Halprin as a dancer and textual performer. He was very good at speaking. His voice was wonderful. I asked him if I could film his head, so we did the same thing and turned the lights off. I illuminated his head and filmed his head turning slowly back and forth and scanning from one side of the frame to the other side of the frame. I combined that with some other footage.

BERNSTEIN: We were talking about Kandinsky before we turned on the tape, thinking about the idea of the total work of art, how it has come back many times during the twentieth century, early on with Wagner, later with the things you are describing, and in a sense it is coming back again with all the new discoveries in computer technology and multimedia.

MARTIN: I think you are right, I think there are some major cycles. To me they go back to the cave man. A tribal art is an inclusive art, such as painting your face and singing, and joining fire with some sounds from primitive drums and plucking of strings. Early religious music in practically every country has some extra things, even incense with music. What I was doing was not exactly new, just trying to incorporate sound and tactile and visual media together. The opportunities to do it are cyclical as you were saying.

I hope I don't sound too analytical here, but I feel that there is a real human need to come together through our expressions that can be very horizontal, joined up and interdependent so that our eyes and ears and taste become one thing. That has been cyclical in our century, as you say, and sometimes that is funneled through someone like Kandinsky. For me he is a wonderful art producer because he was essentially composing time and almost as well, a kind of music. He was very tuned to sound and to music, he talked a lot about that and wrote about it. His paintings were for me an incorporation [of the two].

The lineage from Kandinsky incorporated a spiritual point of view, the physical and the spiritual come together through his paintings. And the physical and the spiritual were coming together through using light in such a natural way sometimes to a point where I didn't feel I was doing it all, it was doing itself. I would provide the projectors with these materials and try to allow it to happen. A lot of Kandinsky's paintings are called "Improvisations" for the same reason. Trying to develop feeling, to allow feelings to occur because a big mass of yellow is slowly going this way and a piece of black comes up and grows in three minutes' time and meanwhile a whole group of green specks suddenly comes out of somewhere in space and then an image of somebody's face comes and goes and part of that green becomes a blob and disappears—for me, that was in the lineage of Kandinsky. At least I can say this now. I was somewhat aware of that then. I was painting the whole time through that period of time. There were two shows of my paintings at the Batman Gallery.

PAYNE: Could you tell us more about the equipment you used?

MARTIN: [I had some lenses and] slide projectors I had taken apart and put back together to make them function more flexibly. I took the lamp wires out and made them available for transformers, made some lenses with cardboard, and purchased others at an Army-Navy store on Market Street. A couple of projectors [I used] were 16 mm film projectors that you could regulate to go down to three frames a second. They had rheostats on them, old Bell and Howells. I had wanted some kind of equipment where I could join up projectors through low voltage and truly make [them] interdependent through direct means. [To accomplish this] I got together with Carl Countryman.

PAYNE: Countryman Associates?

MARTIN: Not at that time. But the same guy. Carl and I got along great. This was 1965, we got together, and I said what I really want to do is to have the low-voltage ability to join everything up, the sound and the light and other things using proximity detectors, or switching from photocells. I wanted to be able to patch this together, everything on common ground. But also I needed some filters, because I wanted to be able to select. It was chance with choice. I wanted to be able to refine the spectrum of how things went on and off.

The SCR [silicon-controlled rectifier] unit he came up with was beautiful. It had tiny preamps and SCRs. I could control ten related 1,000-watt circuits through high-impedance one- to three-volt banana plugs, that was exactly what I wanted to do.

I could patch from the Buchla or from microphones or preamps or through my own photocells, I could externalize all these functions through photocells, because the voltage was so small and the impedance was right; I could regulate intensity with photocells. I liked photocells a lot, because they offered a natural feedback, pure direct natural feedback. Arrange a group of photocells around, and they could tell each other and related equipment what to do. They could feed each other information from lenses, which change the placement of light [creating an interactive system]. I had big elliptical mirror dishes and parabolic dishes, and [I] would put beams of light in motion, reflecting on those focusing mirrors, with photocells in them, to gate signals. I started to buy frequency-selective photocells, photo resistors that would pick up different parts of the color spectrum. It was easy to separate blue and red or violet and green for discrete signals.

Finally, Carl was able to put together the basic low voltage–high voltage unit. That winter at Mills, he housed it in two briefcases—20,000 watts of projection ability in one briefcase and all the filters in the other briefcase. So I could travel with two briefcases to do performances. It was a real miniaturization for that time. I also wanted memory, so he built a memory device. I could make a pattern of on and off, using from ten-second pulses up to ten thousand per second, this was the amazing range of rate for that tiny device.

BERNSTEIN: So then you could program your piece?

MARTIN: Yes. I should talk about that a little bit. I was scoring my visual pieces to some extent. After hearing Ramon's *Desert Ambulance* (1964), I went home and orchestrated what I thought would be a successful visual event with some of Ramon's ideas. I worked it out on my own, back in my loft and decided to combine handmade slides that were cross-fading with film that illuminated Pauline. I used a half-inch cutout of her shape that I put in the gate of the film projector.

Ramon had a really good time with it. I loved the sound of the piece. Ramon played the tape part [for me], then I went home and did my part, and we brought it together. This tended to be a modus operandi for us. I would either hear a piece or we would talk about it. I would go back into my life, which was partly a painting life, and Ramon would go back to his. [The same was true when I worked with] Pauline or Mort.

We had enough empathy that when we came back together it was usually what we wanted. We really loved each other and liked what the other was doing, and we thought that what the other was doing was conducive to our own contribution.

BERNSTEIN: Did the machines make a lot of noise?

MARTIN: Yes, they did make a little noise. That was a problem. 321 Divisadero didn't have the greatest acoustics. Fortunately, the back absorbed a lot of the projector sound. I had to keep my fans down; they were so loud I had to put cardboard boxes around them to keep them quieter. But you know, sometimes the sound was almost an ingredient. In *Desert Ambulance* that Bell and Howell went "click click click." It wasn't bad at all. A little rhythm fit right in. Somehow the light on the accordion keys, which was actually other people's hands that I had projected onto Pauline's hands, an image going down the middle of her accordion, that was some people marching down a street, and the sound of the projector joined up nicely. *Desert Ambulance* is a good example of what our pieces looked like in 1963 and 1964.

For Mort's *Mandolin* [1963], I used more overhead projection and more liquids, some dry things I had found, and drawings I had made. These acetates I combined with the plates for liquids and using the condensing of the water so it would form a kind of mist that I projected. And the mist would dissolve and make rain in the projector, so the mist would slowly occur, and the mist would slowly form down into the next plate and radiate out waveforms, so here was a projected natural phenomenon. I loved incorporating natural phenomena into the compositions.

I would go out into the woods and collect decaying leaves, different earth for shapes and textures to project. I also made my own improvisations during this time that were solely composed by me as visual compositions. One time a beetle crossed a projection, making a beautiful journey crossing about twenty feet of the screen. A bug crawling through my little swamp of ingredients. The bug was making its journey followed by a little piece of red food coloring.

[In 1962] I did an installation piece that Ann Halprin commissioned. I made a polysensory maze that was part sculpture, part sound, part words, and part visual. It was called *A Theater for Watchers, Walkers, Touchers*. It took place in an octagonal room in the San Francisco Museum of Art (the room next to the rotunda) about thirty feet across, and the piece was about twenty feet across, which I made as an octagon that spiraled in, and in the middle was a swing that you could sit on that was hung with harp strings, so if you were heavy it sounded high and if you were light it sounded low. You could swing on the swing and open a little window in front of you and see people in the beginning of the maze. So it combined beginning and ending, sound and reverie, and looking and touching. There was a touch piano where just for the sense of touch, you touched keys on one part of the wall. They would feel different, like sandpaper, rubber bands, or liquid.

There was part that was a "word wall." It was a poetry wall where strings came down that held pencils and I had layered paper and I would go in every other day and add more paper, not covering up anybody's words, and people would rip holes and they made little books so it was a continuously written poem by the viewers who came to see the piece. They would add their words and phrases on this poetry wall. That was very early, 1962 perhaps. It was an interactive, polysensory piece and truly viewer-participational.

BERNSTEIN: Sounds a little like Fluxus.

MARTIN: Maybe. This was a little more of a set installation than they would do, but I don't know. So this was in the museum, and I didn't even take a picture of it. I think probably some effort should be made to increase the information about these pieces.

BERNSTEIN: You were so involved in the moment that . . .

PAYNE: Things were of the moment in those days. It was a rebuttal against all the scores. It was more experiential.

MARTIN: Exactly. We were feeling a freedom of doing things that was different from the formal formulation of things that is so much a part of our culture. We loved the doing of it and the making of it and seeing where it could go. We didn't write it all down and write it up. [We were] too busy doing it.

One piece I did on my own was called *Room* [1964–65]. I made a film of my loft on the Embarcadero that went for some minutes with no change, suddenly things did change in certain parts of it, things would happen: a lamp would go on and go off. Or suddenly a whole group of people was frolicking and throwing things at each other on a large old Spanish couch I had there, the action actually appearing mostly inside the cushions, as if existing in the couch's memory. Then at another time a rhinoceros comes out of a painting and goes back into the painting. I put all these things into one film as a kind of stage set for a performance, whereby I could arrive at an auditorium with my can of film and immediately do the concert.

I had fixed everything into the film (16 mm, color). I took it to the printers, mixed ABCD rolls, the cost wasn't bad then, a $50 lab fee or so. I put performers onstage when I performed it. I had a TV set facing away from the audience with two performers watching the TV. One had a percussion instrument and the other had a violin; they played according to what light was coming to them from the TV, which was tuned to a no-picture channel so it would flip and turn into snow. They were lit from the TV set. The room projection around them was as big as an average living room.

Another composition I made was called *Floorlamps* [1964–65], six musicians onstage with six floor lamps. They each had a score on a music stand that was pie-shaped, and they would progress around the pie shape and choose to play what each section indicated or not when their floor lamp went on. It was a closed system with photocells I set up to work by itself. It turned its own lamps on and off through the SCRs,

I wired an information loop of the sounds the performers made with the circuits for the floor lamps that went on or off from those sounds. That was a set piece with no projections. It was interactive electronics. I guess I would have to say that was pretty early for that. It was another piece I did all on my own without collaboration. After 1967, I began to create more interactive pieces, employing direct means for incorporating the individual character of the viewer into the artwork. This direction, like many of the ideas I developed during my time in San Francisco, continues to inspire me.

NOTE

1. Jo Landor was a painter who served as artistic director for the Ann Halprin Dancers' Workshop.

Don Buchla

INTERVIEWED BY DAVID W. BERNSTEIN AND MAGGI PAYNE

Don Buchla, a legendary figure in the history of electronic music, earned a bachelor's degree in physics from the University of California at Berkeley in 1959. He began graduate studies and worked in the university's Lawrence National Laboratory, but he soon got caught up in the whirlwind created by the social, political, and artistic revolutions taking place in the Bay Area during the early 1960s. His scientific knowledge, musical background, and talent in electronics allowed him to become one of today's leading electronic instrument builders. As the discussion below illustrates, Buchla's interests are not limited to sound; they engage the entire range of human perceptions. He specializes in building unique interfaces between humans and machines. As a participant in the 1960s counterculture, Buchla cultivated an antiestablishment "edge" that naturally led him to the San Francisco Tape Music Center and to Morton Subotnick and Ramon Sender, for whom he developed the Buchla 100 series Modular Electronic Music System.

BERNSTEIN: I have read that you composed some music while training to be a physicist. You were working on accelerators? At Berkeley? You had a tape recorder and created some musique concrète pieces. Is that when you first started getting into electronic music?

BUCHLA: Yes, my first work was with tape.

BERNSTEIN: Were you familiar with the repertory, pieces by Stockhausen and other composers?

BUCHLA: Some of them, yes, certainly with Stockhausen.

BERNSTEIN: And then you went to a Tape Music Center concert in the 1960s?

BUCHLA: Yes.

BERNSTEIN: Was that at one of the Sonics concerts? Do you remember? Was it at the San Francisco Conservatory?

BUCHLA: No, it was an early concert at 321 Divisadero. I just had a one-track Wollensack and they had a three-track recorder. So I talked Mort into letting me use their three-track.

BERNSTEIN: Do you still have your pieces?

BUCHLA: Many of them, yes.

BERNSTEIN: And what kind of sounds were you using?

BUCHLA: Found sounds, mostly.

BERNSTEIN: And you worked with tape splicing? You didn't work in real time like Pauline Oliveros?

BUCHLA: Well, I didn't like splicing. But . . .

BERNSTEIN: . . . but you did it?

BUCHLA: . . . to a certain extent, yes. That's all we had.

BERNSTEIN: You didn't really have mixers or anything like that either?

BUCHLA: No.

BERNSTEIN: The spirit behind the Tape Music Center was different from other electronic music studios such as those at Columbia-Princeton, Bell Labs, and all those other places. And I think that you were coming from a direction politically and socially similar to the composers working at the Tape Music Center. Berkeley was a pretty interesting place to be in the early 1960s. It seems to me that you and the others became part of the counterculture. And that's the way you approached electronic music.

BUCHLA: I'd say so, yes.

BERNSTEIN: For one thing, many of you participated in the Trips Festival. Can you tell us about that? I understand that there was a plan to feed Big Brother and the Holding Company through the Buchla that never was realized. But the Buchla was used during that festival. Is this so?

BUCHLA: Yes. I switched bands on and off, toy projectors, and so on and did all the interlude music. I was also in charge of the lighting.

BERNSTEIN: Did you run that through the Buchla as well?

BUCHLA: No, the lighting was done with specialized equipment.

BERNSTEIN: When you say lighting—there were light shows, projections, and all of that?

BUCHLA: Well, we brought in Tony Martin for the projections. We had other lighting, too by various artists of one sort or another.

BERNSTEIN: Did you know about the kinds of electronic sounds that were being played at the Acid Tests?

BUCHLA: I was playing them.

BERNSTEIN: What were you playing?

BUCHLA: My system.

BERNSTEIN: The Buchla?

BUCHLA: Yes.

BERNSTEIN: So the Buchla was there, with Ken Kesey and all the others?

BUCHLA: Oh, yes.

PAYNE: I'm so curious as to what came together to spark the idea of a modular voltage-controlled synthesizer? I personally learned in a classical studio with all the knobs; you operated every oscillator and every filter by hand. The voltage-controlled synthesizer was such a major innovation. It really turned the music world on its end. So how did it come to mind that this was what to do?

BUCHLA: I guess I was basically looking for a replacement for tape.

PAYNE: But still, the possibility of using voltage control, was it that the technology was now in place that enabled you to design this system?

BUCHLA: It sort of was.

PAYNE: Were there other applications where voltage control was happening? How did you hook together music, engineering, and physics and put this all together to arrive at this concept?

BUCHLA: I don't know. I just did it.

PAYNE: I am curious about how the development of the voltage-controlled synthesizer came about. What was the design process? I assume Mort may have been primary in working with you.

BUCHLA: Yes.

PAYNE: The idea of having a live performance instrument was unique. That was one of the criteria for the Buchla 100 series. Was it mostly Mort driving it and asking for possibilities and your going back and forth, or . . . ?

BUCHLA: There was a lot of back and forth. We had a lot of discussions.

The Genesis of the Buchla 100 Series Modular Electronic Music System

MORTON SUBOTNICK, RAMON SENDER, AND MAGGI PAYNE

PAYNE: What sparked the idea of building a voltage-controlled synthesizer, especially since the concept of voltage-controlled modules was so innovative?

SUBOTNICK: Ramon and I both had realized the financial implications as well as the portability of the new emerging transistor technologies.

PAYNE: What was the design process for the Buchla in the early stages? Did all the Tape Music Center members meet and collaboratively work out the configuration or was Mort the composer most interested in the development of the synthesizer? What was the nature of the interaction? Lots of back and forth?

SUBOTNICK: A number of meetings with Don, Ramon, and me occurred, during which we spoke of our musical needs. We wanted to be able to control amplitude and frequency, etc. I used the Boulez, *Le marteau sans maître* [1953–55], first page as an example. I would imagine patching the Boulez and see something was missing and we would add another knob.

SENDER: As a pianist, I held out for a real keyboard, but Mort kept pushing for the etched approach and Don also wanted that. Frankly, I think Mort had more to do with the ultimate design.

PAYNE: How long did it take from the first design meetings to come to fruition? I had read that this process had its seed around 1963 and that by 1964 it was well under way?

SUBOTNICK: There were a lot of meetings and talk about what we needed. I started reading the navy book on electronics, and then I realized I didn't know any electricity so I got the navy book about electricity. I got addicted to aspirin in the process because I had such headaches. We read the Helmholtz book first.[1] Ramon and I were talking hours daily about this.

PAYNE: Buchla's interfaces have always been nontraditional (non–keyboard oriented). How did you arrive at the touch-controlled voltage source, with individual A and B control outputs per touch-sensitive area (pad) and the remarkable pressure-sensitive C control output that could be used to control amplitude, frequency, and so forth?

SUBOTNICK: I wanted a neutral keyboard and Ramon wanted a black and white. Don wanted a neutral, so we went that way. The ten-note keyboard [Don made earlier] everybody thought was because we have ten fingers, but it was because we had ten Viking loop decks. The finger pressure was in order to be able to do musique concrète and to control the amplitude on the Viking loop machines.

PAYNE: Could you tell me when the Buchla first arrived at the Tape Music Center?

SUBOTNICK: Well. Let's see. Terry Riley's *In C* was premiered in November 1964, is that right?

---

1. Hermann von Helmholtz, *On the Sensations of Tone as a Physiological Basis for the Theory of Music*, trans. Alexander J. Ellis (London: Longmans, Green, 1875; reprint, New York: Dover, 1954).

PAYNE: Yes.

SUBOTNICK: I'm 99 percent sure we had the Buchla around that time and demonstrated it. I didn't write it down, so I can't tell you for sure. If it was after that, it had to be right after that. It would have to be January 1965. It couldn't have been much later than that. I was just with Moog, and he remembers it in 1964. He said that it predates anything he did, and that the Moog came out in 1965. He said it was a year before him.

PAYNE: So he would specify how many oscillators he thought would be needed . . . and all the gates and sequencers? Where did all these ideas come from because I don't think there were sequencers at that time?

BUCHLA: No, but when you invent voltage control, you invent ways of generating voltages for control.

PAYNE: Right. So it was just a natural hooking together of ideas after that.

BUCHLA: Yes.

PAYNE: You were searching for an innovative interface between humans and instruments. Your interfaces are unique. It's a really different approach, rather than sticking with keyboards all the time. Even with the very first system, you were already thinking very differently. So I was just wondering, was that something that came up from your side of the equation in trying to develop this system? Was it something that Mort was also interested in? Or, how did that idea . . .

BUCHLA: I was never tempted to build keyboards into synthesizers. To me, that was unnatural.

PAYNE: It puts a mind-set on that system when it's really an instrument of its own.

BUCHLA: Yes. I didn't use keyboards for many years. It wasn't until I could do polyphony that I regarded the keyboard as a potential input.

PAYNE: Interesting. Your device, the touch-control voltage source, was also polyphonic in a way. It had the A, B, and this wonderful pressure-sensitive C control voltage out.

BUCHLA: Yes, that's true. It was tunable, malleable, and not in a twelve-tone array.

PAYNE: Right. There was no system implied other than that you can derive two control voltages plus a third pressure sensitive on each of the twelve, what would you call them, keypads? No, that's not right, touch-sensitive areas perhaps? [Laughs]

BUCHLA: OK. [Laughs]

THE MODULAR ELECTRONIC MUSIC SYSTEM

27 **THE BUCHLA MODULAR ELECTRONIC MUSIC SYSTEM, OR "BUCHLA BOX" (PICTURE FROM MANUAL).**

PAYNE: I think that's a major innovation. And you certainly continued that with all the other interfaces. You mentioned that you went to a concert at the San Francisco Tape Music Center. Did you already know Pauline or Ramon or Mort? What got you interested in going to that concert? Or were you just interested in new music at the time?

BUCHLA: Oh, I went to a lot of concerts.

PAYNE: But how did you get involved in the Tape Music Center so deeply?

BUCHLA: I asked Mort what type of resources they had. And he said to come on up and look at the studio. So I saw the three-track there and that did it.

PAYNE: Do you remember who their technical person was at the time? Was Bill Maginnis already there?

BUCHLA: It was pretty much . . .

BERNSTEIN: Michael Callahan?

BUCHLA: No, I didn't know Callahan. But Maginnis was already there, if not then, shortly thereafter.

PAYNE: It appears that he was probably the first person to actually produce a piece on the Buchla.

BERNSTEIN: We have recordings of his piece called *Flight*. The first Buchla was completed in late 1964. Is that right?

BUCHLA: I don't know the dates. That sounds right.

BERNSTEIN: During the time before that, had you invented anything else? Were you working on any other kinds of electronic music instruments?

BUCHLA: No. I started on the modular system in 1963.

BERNSTEIN: So that's before, isn't that before you started working with Mort?

BUCHLA: No, that's when I started.

BERNSTEIN: Oh, in 1963, that early?

PAYNE: That's the date I have.

BERNSTEIN: So it probably took it about a year to bring it all together.

BUCHLA: Well, it didn't occur all at once. It was a modular system. One module developed into the next.

BERNSTEIN: Did you start off with the idea that you wanted to make it portable? I know that you weren't interested in its commercialization, but you wanted to be able to disseminate it, to be able to allow other people use it.

BUCHLA: Yes.

BERNSTEIN: I've read the original brochure. It's visionary because it says these instruments are going to be available to all sorts of musicians, from rock to classical.

BUCHLA: One instrument that I brought in hadn't previously been used musically, it was called an ORB and was for optical ranging for the blind. Cage was particularly fascinated by it.

PAYNE: What is it? Can you describe it?

BUCHLA: Yes, I remember it quite well. It employed one of the first LEDs made by RCA. They gave me a bunch of them, they were $450 each, so . . .

PAYNE: . . . for an LED?

BUCHLA: Yes, [laughs] and they probably consumed a lot of power.

PAYNE: They were very inefficient. Right?

BUCHLA: Yes, but I managed to make a beam out of it, and the device could be carried by a blind person, and it would translate distance into pitch.[1]

PAYNE: Oh, that's so interesting.

BUCHLA: I taught at the blind school for some time, so . . .

PAYNE: The one at UC Berkeley?

BUCHLA: Yes, it didn't used to be so associated with the university. It was private. I found that congenitally blind people had enormous ranges for learning, enormous centers for basically doing pitch discrimination and acoustic analysis of their environment. So I built this gadget, and John [Cage] liked it simply because he put his hand in it, moved it around, and it made all kinds of funny squeals.

PAYNE: I forget the name of the devices that I believe Alvin Lucier used, the clickers, right? This was a kind of echo-location device where you'd hear the echoes bounce off the walls and other surfaces. He did a really wonderful piece called *Vespers* [1968]. [Your device] is even more sophisticated, and it has a continuous tone, I presume . . .

BUCHLA: Yes.

PAYNE: . . . that would change in frequency, that would give you feedback at all times and not be so complicated by bouncing the signal off so many walls.

BUCHLA: Yes.

PAYNE: Because you could aim it.

BUCHLA: Well, they're different functions of that sort of thing. Eventually, we combined it with ultrasound, in which we could discern the nature of surfaces as opposed to the discrete terrain-avoidance problems.

PAYNE: Sort of mapping the surface? The texture?

BUCHLA: No, we didn't try to map it.

PAYNE: But it was refined enough that you . . .

BUCHLA: Well, you don't have to refine it very much. People didn't understand what the blind brain was all about. They still don't. But they can learn far better discrimination than we can.

BERNSTEIN: Did you have contact with David Tudor?

BUCHLA: He was my first customer for the modules.

BERNSTEIN: What year was that? Do you remember? Just around when it was first invented?

BUCHLA: Must have been in 1964.

BERNSTEIN: Do you know what he used it for? Which pieces?

BUCHLA: No, I don't. I have no idea. I know what he got.

PAYNE: Which is?

BUCHLA: One was a series of circular pads [which Tudor apparently used to change the spatial location of sounds]. I think there's one—maybe Mills has one—I guess not. People are trying to trace these things down. They're in pictures.

PAYNE: It's too bad that we don't have one.

BUCHLA: There's one that exists that we know of. There were five channels, four on the periphery and then one in the center of this controller. And there were four such pads, so one could take a sound, and take your hands like this, and manipulate them. And then that hooked up to a pretty amazing voltage-controlled mixer, a matrix mixer.

PAYNE: I think we have a voltage-controlled matrix mixer.

BUCHLA: You do?

PAYNE: Yes, but I'm not sure it's working.

BUCHLA: So it has five signal outputs and five control voltage inputs for each pad—so it has twenty inputs. And . . .

PAYNE: . . . and they're controllable. Each one of them, right?

BUCHLA: Mmm-hmm.

PAYNE: For amplitude?

BUCHLA: Yes. Well, I just imagined this one application, but later on we added other modules, and a lot of other things went with it that were automated. But my own studio had the four channels plus one overhead, so, it was a four point one. [Laughs]

BERNSTEIN: So leading up to the "[Buchla] Box," you were working with all these modules, and there were a lot of different tributaries in the development.

BUCHLA: Yes. My modules have been cataloged, most of them. They still find one once in a while that wasn't in the catalog, but there is a rather large number. I was amazed at how many modules I've done over the years.

BERNSTEIN: After the Tape Music Center, where did you work? You had a studio at the Alameda Naval Base? Is that where it was?

BUCHLA: No, it wasn't in Alameda. It was in Oakland at the big shipyard, the Kaiser— or the ex-Kaiser shipyard.

BERNSTEIN: And you were making music there and building more modules?

BUCHLA: Lots of music and some modules. That's where I developed the [Buchla] 200.

BERNSTEIN: And I think Ramon Sender came out there.

BUCHLA: Yes.

PAYNE: He did several recordings?

BUCHLA: Yes, he was a frequent visitor, along with all kinds of people.

PAYNE: Do you remember anyone specifically?

BUCHLA: I remember I had a quad mix down situation before it was common in the studios, and one of the funniest scenes was Wally Heider driving up in his portable recording studio and passing cables through my windows to get to my basement studio.

PAYNE: Yes, Heider was a major recording engineer. He was also a very generous person.

BUCHLA: And I did a lot of recording with the Hell's Angels.

BERNSTEIN: What did they want?

BUCHLA: They were a little bit associated with Kesey's bus and were involved in drug distribution. [Laughs] It all seemed fine to me. I got some interesting tapes from that source.

PAYNE: They were musicians as well?

BUCHLA: No, you don't have to be a musician to make a tape.

PAYNE: Were they using your synthesizers?

BUCHLA: No. Well, Ken did, but that was just in the bus. But the Hell's Angels were just a funny scene.

BERNSTEIN: So Kesey was interested in electronic music and got into making tapes.

BUCHLA: I'm not so sure that he was interested in electronic music.

BERNSTEIN: I mean sounds for the Acid Tests.

BUCHLA: I don't know the background there. I just showed up at the places with my instruments, took some acid, played some music.

BERNSTEIN: And they had lights going on, too.

BUCHLA: Sometimes, yes. There was quite a variety there.

BERNSTEIN: I've read that you were working with randomness in some of the machines that you built?

BUCHLA: Yes.

BERNSTEIN: When did that start?

BUCHLA: Oh, from the beginning.

BERNSTEIN: Did Cage influence that?

BUCHLA: Yes, for sure.

BERNSTEIN: That's very different from the Moog, right?

BUCHLA: Well, the whole approach is pretty different, even though they had common elements.

BERNSTEIN: Well, the Moog seemed to go totally toward the commercial side.

BUCHLA: Well, that's what he [Robert Moog] wanted to do . . .

BERNSTEIN: . . . with the rock groups, and the whole thing.

BUCHLA: Yes.

BERNSTEIN: Do you remember the Chamberlin music master?

BUCHLA: Very well. I got my fingers dirty on that one quite a bit.

PAYNE: We had the Chamberlin Rhythmate as well. I don't know if you knew that box; it was a . . .

BUCHLA: It had a lot of heads in it?

PAYNE: Yes, right.

BUCHLA: I do. I forgot what you called it, the Rhythmate?

PAYNE: Yes, the Rhythmate, I think.

BUCHLA: There was an Echoplex built along the same lines.

PAYNE: I remember there were voices and some instruments, and I think I remember some sound effects on that Chamberlin? Do you remember? Wasn't there a rhythm section as well?

BUCHLA: Yes, and there were chickens cackling, too.

PAYNE: Yes, and the dog barking, which the Beatles used, I believe.

BERNSTEIN: Those were pre-programmed tape loops that were in the machine, right?

BUCHLA: Yes.

PAYNE: Yes, you could send the Chamberlin sounds, and I think they could record them.

BUCHLA: Yes, it wasn't that easy to make the recordings.

PAYNE: Yes, there were three tracks, and I think you had like nine seconds or so before it would spring back or something.

BUCHLA: Then you had six locations.

PAYNE: There were three heads.

BUCHLA: Yes, there were three heads this way and then six locations that you could start at and move the tape up and start somewhere else. So it was quite powerful, the number of sounds you could put in it.

PAYNE: Oh, I just remember that you'd had to move your hands after nine seconds or else. [Laughs]

BUCHLA: Yes. It would go into the next track.

BERNSTEIN: I thought you couldn't program those.

BUCHLA: Yes, we could.

BERNSTEIN: Oh, you did.

BUCHLA: As I said, it was with difficulty. The tapes were not standard format, and there was no recording yet on the Chamberlin per se.

PAYNE: Yes, I remember using it at Mills. And finally it just got so crotchety . . .

BUCHLA: Yes, it squeaked a lot. It was pretty crotchety when I worked on it, too. [Laughs]

PAYNE: [Laughs] Yes, it was barely usable. But it was so great when it was. And "Blue" Gene Tyranny used it a considerable amount for all sorts of films.

BERNSTEIN: The Chamberlin has a wonderful sound in *Desert Ambulance;* it's beautiful.

BUCHLA: Yes, it is.

BERNSTEIN: Did you work with Tony on the Buchla? Did you use the controls on the light sources?

BUCHLA: Not very much, no.

BERNSTEIN: Was the Buchla used at any time for controlling light?

BUCHLA: There were some modules that were specifically designed for lighting control.

BERNSTEIN: And were they used at the Tape Music Center? Or did that happen later?

BUCHLA: No, I had—I lived a life outside the Tape Music Center, too.

PAYNE: Were they interfaceable?

BUCHLA: Oh, yes.

PAYNE: So you could have the audio . . .

BUCHLA: It was the same control voltages that controlled lighting.

BERNSTEIN: Did you use it at any of the ballrooms? Or the Fillmore?

BUCHLA: I used it extensively; I did all the Electric Circuses.

BERNSTEIN: In New York?

BUCHLA: In New York and Toronto. Well, two in New York actually. And [the lighting] was quite elaborate. I built each console for controlling all the projectors. I put in forty projectors into the . . .

PAYNE: Are these film and slide projectors or . . . ?

BUCHLA: . . . forty slide projectors and quite a few film projectors as well, and projection strobes, once that caught on.

BERNSTEIN: That is in the late 1960s, right? After Mort left the Tape Music Center.

BUCHLA: There were two Electric Circuses, and I'm a little confused with the dates there.

BERNSTEIN: One of them was in Toronto, you were saying?

BUCHLA: Well, there was that one, too. There were two in New York at the same place. And I did the Playboy Club and places like that in Los Angeles.

PAYNE: Yes, I remember that David Rosenboom had been involved with you in the Electric Circus.

BUCHLA: I brought him in.

BERNSTEIN: I once went there. I saw the Chambers Brothers perform. It was great. It was in the East Village. And it had a light show. But that was probably in the 1970s.

BUCHLA: Well, that was the later one. The earlier one was done in a big tent, a monstrous tent made of stretch fabric. I liked it a lot. And the later one had a finished projection surface that was optically correct. Unfortunately, it wasn't acoustically correct too, so that you could be down on the floor and you could hear, very distinctly, conversations coming from the projection gallery. And they had to put up a sheet of Lucite across the whole gallery, which was fifty feet long.

PAYNE: That's expensive.

BUCHLA: It was an inch thick—it was very expensive. But they had to do that for the sound. But it was a fabulous projection surface. And I built the very high-powered carousel projectors—modified them for registrations, so we could have eight projectors covering the whole surface and could have them all registered so we'd take 8 × 10 pictures and cut them up and make slides of them. We had 1,200-watt bulbs in each projector, and they had to have that cooling, of course. By the time you put the fans in . . .

BERNSTEIN: . . . lots of noise!

BUCHLA: Well, we had organ pipes—ten-inch organ pipes—coming down from the huge blowers above the ceiling, so the noise wasn't too bad. And then we used two-inch vacuum cleaner hoses into each projector. And then there were thirty-two projectors, four stacked from each location on the eight subdivisions, so we could overlap four pictures. So, as you can gather, there's a lot of power there. But it took a full-time five-man light show just to feed the whole thing.

BERNSTEIN: So you've been interested in both light and sound from the beginning.

BUCHLA: All the perceptions.

BERNSTEIN: And that's actually gone into your instrument building over the years, a multisensory approach. That's another thing that you have in common with the whole Tape Music Center milieu.

NOTE

1. Ramon Sender recalls that "during the buildup to the Trips Festival, [Don] put the ORB in the window of [the] City Lights [bookstore] with rotating (dental?) mirrors in front of it. The distance of a person in front of the window dictated the melody it played, and people would quickly [realize] that they were making the music and start to move back and forth on the sidewalk." Ramon Sender, e-mail to David W. Bernstein, December 28, 2006.

Michael Callahan

INTERVIEWED BY THOMAS M. WELSH

Michael Callahan became the first technical director of the San Francisco Tape Music Center when it moved to its permanent location at 321 Divisadero. A shy and withdrawn teenager, he was a classic self-taught tinkerer who disassembled everything in the house. Truancy was an ongoing problem, but the homemade security alarm he had rigged up while hiding under the stairs reading electronics magazines from the local market on Haight Street kept the real world at bay.

Attending the first Sonics concert on a lark, Callahan immediately found kindred spirits. He was sixteen at the time, still in high school, and more than ten years younger than the composers who would go on to found the Tape Music Center. Nevertheless, Ramon Sender, Pauline Oliveros, and Morton Subotnick were welcoming and glad to make use of his technical expertise. Throwing himself into the creation of what would become the preeminent electronic music studio on the West Coast, Callahan abandoned a brief flirtation with a career in psychology and affirmed a life in electronic arts. In addition to his work at the Tape Music Center, he worked closely with the poet and media artist Gerd Stern, an early proponent of the theories of Marshall McLuhan. Their creation of the "Verbal American Landscape" and other mediacentric events were pioneering in vision and execution.

Callahan moved to Rockland County, New York, in 1964 to join Stern and Stephen Durkee in forming the multimedia group USCO (as in "company of us"), making their official performance debut at the University of Rochester that October at McLuhan's invitation. In 1977, Callahan joined Harvard University as supervisor of film studios and electrical engineer in the Carpenter Center for the Visual Arts, where he remained for seventeen years. He founded the company Museum Technology and is a devoted historian of radio and electronics.

CALLAHAN: I was born in San Francisco on October 8, 1944, in St. Mary's Hospital. My parents, Alfred and Eleanor Callahan, had just recently moved from Los Angeles. My father was an electrician, and we lived on Clayton Street. Then I lost my father around 1949, and my Aunt Edith Phillips, my mother's sister, came to live with us.

I missed a lot of school. I basically dropped out. I was studying on my own. And then I went to Lowell High School for three years, graduating fall 1962; Carl Koenig was my mentor. He was a physics teacher and he took me under his wing. I started working on the school sound system and various things. He also ran a surplus scrounge business on the side, and that was my connection to the surplus at the Lawrence Radiation Laboratory, which came to serve the Tape Music Center quite well.

WELSH: Were you a tinkerer?

CALLAHAN: Oh, yes, I'm hard-core.

WELSH: Is this a vestige of your father, or what?

CALLAHAN: Probably, because I was just fascinated by electricity, by how things work, from earliest memory. I was reminded by my late Aunt Edith a couple years ago about my security lamp. I would drag this little gooseneck lamp around instead of a blanket. And I think the house rule was I could take it apart, but I'd have to put it back together.

WELSH: Did you find other people who shared this interest?

CALLAHAN: Not until high school. Not until Mr. Koenig. Basically, I was on my own. There were two radio places on Cole Street: Lockhart and Curley's. And I'd go over there, endlessly fascinated. I'd just stand and look in the window (preferably when they were closed) and look at the workbench. I bought a radio from Lockhart for ten dollars.

WELSH: When you got a radio into the house did you immediately take it apart?

CALLAHAN: I was nine then, that was 1954. It was a nice Packard Bell console, not a huge one, but it was easy to take apart. I think also about this time I realized that perhaps some of the books in the library were not totally au courant. One of them must have been from around 1915. It was really pre–vacuum tube—I mean, a picture of Marconi and his spark transmitter.

Then my mother and Aunt Edie bought a tape recorder, a Pentron. They bought it from a gentleman named Mr. Kopf—Kopf Sound Supply. I think one time I even got off the bus to look in the window because he was doing more commercial audio installation. He went out of business and called up and asked Mother if I'd be interested in some of the things he was about to throw away.

WELSH: How did he know you, from looking in his window all the time?

CALLAHAN: Yes, well, from buying the tape recorder, I guess. So I took the bus there, and I think I had several trips on the bus—just marvelous—because I had amplifiers, tubes, an intercom, and that was my real stash—and oh, yes, some speakers. That was right around 1953 or 1954, so I was nine or ten. I started trying to build speaker cabinets out of orange crates and built an amplifier—a simple vacuum tube amplifier—out of some parts there. Aunt Edie played the piano, and I would record the piano. And then I started building a mixer for it, because it just had one input. Then I started modifying it.

WELSH: What were you doing, music or . . . ?

CALLAHAN: Well a little, but I think I'd be recording off the radio. There was an elaborate radio chassis from Mr. Kopf. I finally got it to work. And then I would record. A lot of the time I was just using it as an amplifier. I'd record piano and that's also when I started realizing, you know, playing things backward and changing the speed. In 2005, it doesn't seem like any big deal, but I was thinking the other day in the course of preparing for the retrospective performance Gerd Stern and I did at the Anthology Film Archive in New York at Jonas Mekas's invitation, up until tape, everything was real time. There was no "slow-mo." Maybe film, but that was exotic. But everything we saw and heard was real time. Today, hardly anything [is]—[we have] instant replays on TV and slow motion and whatever. But any manipulation of the time frame, any manipulation of the time order electronically, was something new. And I, for whatever reason, really found that fascinating, to be able to shift time—to slow things up, to speed things up, change the timbre somewhat.

There's something about being able to record and then play it back and mix it with something else. We got TV in 1955, and I really liked turning the volume down on the TV and turning the radio on or playing a tape while watching the TV. Which might have been a harbinger of things to come.

WELSH: Sounds like early moves toward collage work.

CALLAHAN: Yes, I remember Eisenhower was giving some speech, and [I] had some soap opera on the radio. I found it more compelling than Eisenhower.

WELSH: In high school, did you have a chance to indulge in electronics?

CALLAHAN: I think my senior year the PTA bought an Ampex and a couple of those speakers in a suitcase. I built a mixer, but I was really equipment-limited. Carl Koenig had oriented his physics class toward electronics. I certainly learned a few things in there and was reassured that a lot of things I'd learned on my own were valid. I really wanted to work with the real thing. It wasn't toys. And I just found the city fascinating—the railroad tracks, the power lines going into the trolley barn on Masonic. I just loved looking at power lines. At the Southern Pacific Hospital on Hayes and Baker, it was so beautiful; there was a powerhouse. They generated their own electricity. You could stand on Hayes Street and look in this big window at the generators, the instruments, the control panels, and all the polished brass rails—it was just absolutely immaculate.

So at this point in high school, I reworked the sound system. They had put in a new sound system, and it didn't really quite do what was needed, so that was kind of my senior project. Mr. Koenig said, "Look, I'll give you an 'A' if you straighten this out."

WELSH: How was it that you ended up at the first Sonics concert on December 18, 1961?

CALLAHAN: I delivered the *Chronicle* for a year in high school. Looking at it one morning, there was a picture I believe of Ramon and Mort, or Pauline, and in the corner of the picture I recognized the electronics panel of a professional Ampex recorder. So I basically went to the concert, not to hear so much, but to see the recorder. I would probably have gone if the little corner of the Ampex hadn't been there, but as soon as I saw that, I definitely was. Because I had built some oscillators and had gotten a World War II surplus piece of test equipment, an oscilloscope that had several oscillators in it, so I could mix those sounds together, so I could get three tones at a time. [It had] a primitive little panel of three volume controls, and I think three telegraph keys. So I was interested in it.

WELSH: But that was basically a concert announcement that you saw in the newspaper.

CALLAHAN: Yes, and that really sent me on the path that I've been on. That had to be one of the most influential events of my life. I remember taking the bus out there—high school geek, shy, going into this avant-garde [event], not knowing anything except I'd heard of John Cage and Tinguely. I was fascinated by Tinguely—you know, his machines. Oh, those were absolutely so cool, self-destructing machines!

I remember the room was dark and it was downstairs, kind of a small room. There was a lot of hiss. Technically, it wasn't perfect, and maybe I thought that if this is recorded on an Ampex, that it must be perfect. These people, they're grown-ups and they have an Ampex. They must know what they're doing. I guess that initially I was listening for the technical, because I hadn't really heard that much other audio equipment and so I was interested in comparing what I'd built. But then I started *listening* after a few minutes. I started listening to these squeaks and squawks and pings.

WELSH: It was a surprise to you?

CALLAHAN: Yes, not a total surprise, but it was a reach. I was straining. And also not knowing what to listen for, not knowing where it was coming from really, but still, above all, being a card-carrying teenager, having to appear cool.

WELSH: But you didn't know the people who were performing their tape music.

CALLAHAN: No, I don't think I'd heard of any of them. It was a seminal moment for me.

WELSH: Did you introduce yourself?

CALLAHAN: Yes, after, because they had this little open house. It was upstairs in this closet. It was tiny. And wow, they're doing all this with equipment—aside from their Ampex—this is really on my level. I mean, there's no magic here, but there's a lot of inspiration and hard work.

WELSH: Did you ask some questions about their technical abilities?

CALLAHAN: I was basically looking, and chatting with them. I could see that they had these tape recorders and it was funky beyond belief, even by my standards. But I loved it because I could see what they were doing with very limited resources.

I must have said that I had hooked up a few oscillators. I guess I might have expressed somehow to Ramon my disappointment that I hadn't been able to really get my circuitry to sound like a violin. And he said, "Well, you know, if you want something to sound like violin, I'd recommend playing the violin. See what other sounds you can get." Boom—a light went off.

WELSH: There were more Sonics concerts at the conservatory. It was a series.

CALLAHAN: I know I went to one other. I remember hearing the washing machine, seeing the washing machine, and saying this is really cool, because this is sort of the Tinguely fascination with the machine.

WELSH: What was in the Jones Street house setup?

CALLAHAN: Ramon had an Ampex 601–2—far and away the best recorder on the scene for a long time. There were, I think, various tape loops, a little audio mixer, some Ampex speakers in wooden cabinets. There was nothing really too fancy there at all. It was bare bones. I guess the capability today would be a modest stereo. You know, a few tape recorders in this ornate living room, which was crowded and piled up.

WELSH: In the spring of 1963 . . .

CALLAHAN: . . . I was out of high school and was going to City College.

At that point I'd decided on psychology. My sister Patricia had a friend, Wayne

Coykendall; he was a research assistant at Langley Porter Clinic, a psychiatric institute up on Parnassus. I would help Wayne in the research lab; they had a lot of nice electronic equipment. I thought it would make sense in a way to go into engineering. But I really was more interested in people, so I thought experimental psychology would be a way of combining humanities and technology. And it really allowed me to get my hands on some real equipment, because this was the University of California. Rather than home-built or Heathkit, they had Hewlett-Packard and Tektronix, and they had a big Ampex tape deck. This was the real stuff.

WELSH: Were you involved in moving equipment to 321 Divisadero?

CALLAHAN: Yes, I remember the Tape Music Center when it was a totally empty building. It was pretty wild. Here's finally some room to make some noise. I was quite excited. I don't remember the exact arrangement, but I had a key.

Morton and Ramon had arranged to lease one of the studios to [the listener-sponsored public radio station] KPFA and the other to Ann Halprin. The rent on the building I believe was $175. I wound up writing checks, paying some bills later on. The building was owned by Mr. Ayres, who lived around the corner on Page. We never met him. He had an elderly factotum who collected the rent.

WELSH: You never met the owner?

CALLAHAN: Another mystery, right? I remember Mort asking Ramon, "Where's this Mr. Ayres?" And Ramon said he figured he was just floating in some saline solution around the corner—typical Ramon, you know.

WELSH: You said that Jones Street was a primitive setup. Did you set about to acquire equipment [for 321 Divisadero]?

CALLAHAN: At this point, it was all a pooling of Mort's equipment, Ramon's equipment, Pauline's equipment, and my equipment. And also there was this freight salvage, which Ramon had arranged somehow. There was a lot of junk there, but then there were also some useful things: microphones, some amplifiers, a Western Electric line amp.

I don't remember exactly how it got there, but it was a big pile from Western Railroad Salvage or whatever. Some of it had tags on it saying "Electrical Communications—A Corporation." It might have been some commercial sound company or something that also did intercoms and paging systems. I never could find out anything about them. But there were a number of things like some rack cabinets, hardware, and switch panels that were useful. Basically, we were starting from scratch.

One thing that came out of that salvage sale was a number of Viking tape cartridge endless loop machines. I think they'd been used for background music because they would play over and over. That's probably what motivated Ramon, the thought of these endless loops. I set those up; this is all just general wiring infrastructure. And that was the summer. I think at that point I started designing some things.

WELSH: What did you get into building?

CALLAHAN: I was attempting to respond to either requests or if I saw that some piece of equipment would allow Mort or Ramon or Pauline to do something, I'd try and build it. I built some filters to separate the frequencies out. Modulation was one of the first effects we had, because up until this point, the manipulation was all in editing and mixing. But now we were starting to actually manipulate the signal.

WELSH: So, did you say, "I have an idea for a modulator and let me show you something I've done"?

CALLAHAN: It was all very collegial. It was collaborative, the best way of working. It was really the best of times. . . . At this point, I was eighteen. I'd taken Ramon's statement of a year or two before—"If you want a violin, get a violin; what else can this do?" The interesting thing here is what else can be done. At that point I was priding myself on designing amplifiers with vanishing low distortion and flat frequency response. I had to loosen up a little bit and say, "Hey, wow, I'm designing an amplifier intentionally to distort." And even though it's a classic studio in the way it was wired, some of the elements going into the racks were definitely not traditional, because they were modifying and distorting.

WELSH: Can you tell me about the ring modulator that you worked on?

CALLAHAN: It's basically where you have two inputs and one output, and the output is the product of the two inputs. It's a multiplier, in effect. So, if one took some audio and fed it into one input and then, say, one took the output of one of the oscillators, a sine wave at a few cycles per second, it would be modulated so the volume—woooOOOoooOOOoooOO—would control the volume. And this also would produce sidebands so it would produce all these nonharmonically related tones. It would produce some interesting sounds.

WELSH: Where did the development of that come from?

CALLAHAN: In high school I was designing audio equipment, and I had an interest in feedback systems, which was reasonably new then. I was intrigued by servo systems, which is all it is. Like cruise control in a car, if you start going down a hill that sensor sort of lets up on the gas. But on the other hand, if you change the sense

28 FROM LEFT: RAMON SENDER, MICHAEL CALLAHAN, MORTON SUBOTNICK, AND PAULINE OLIVEROS (SEATED). PHOTOGRAPH BY ART FRISCH, COURTESY OF THE *SAN FRANCISCO CHRONICLE*.

of it, [it] could get interesting, because when you start going downhill the car will speed up! So that was also the leap: rather than designing the systems to be linear and well-behaved, what happens if we change the sense so it gets chaotic? The modulator was a general utility piece of equipment, and I think they tried building some others, according to Bill Maginnis, but they couldn't quite get the sound. That's because I didn't really know what I was doing!

And then the filters, I got intrigued by that at Langley Porter because of the speech research. Over in San Leandro with Mr. Koenig, there was Lawrence Radiation Surplus, [and] I picked up a whole box of inductors, which are essential elements, coils for making filters. Filters were basically composed of, in those days, inductors, a coil of wire and a capacitor, and some fairly nasty math. I remember being quite delighted that I'd calculated it out on a slide rule and it matched very closely, so that was a nice moment. A filter is kind of a general-purpose thing, and Ramon, Mort, and Pauline were checking the capabilities to see what was possible, because there were a lot of combinations. We had a lot of inputs and outputs now, and things were used in various combinations and sequences.

WELSH: KPFA installed a radio broadcast booth?

CALLAHAN: Interestingly enough, the broadcast booth was there. It was made to order. I remember the old-timer from the telephone company came to equalize the line. I was watching him sending a tone out and seeing that it needed to be boosted a little at this frequency. He was very meticulous, and I remember him saying another thing that made an influence on me. I was commenting on his work, "That's really quite a job you're doing." He said, "Well, if you're going to do it, you might as well send only the best." And he was talking about the signal—but that really got me. You know, if you're going to send it, if you're going to do it, do the best.

WELSH: In October of 1963 at the San Francisco Arts Festival, the Tape Music Center did something downtown in the Civic Center.

CALLAHAN: That was the big plaza in front of City Hall. We arranged to get a couple of Marantz amplifiers, which were high-end, and four Electro-Voice Musicaster speakers. They could put out some volume. We put them at each end of the plaza, and we were playing over the plaza tapes from the Tape Music Center collection, which was growing at that point.

So there was enough sound to sufficiently seriously irritate the people who would like to nap on the benches at City Hall Plaza. It was a little strange. I mean it was a little surreal. This music, the sound, the echoing—we weren't doing rock 'n' roll loudness or anything. This was all fairly modest equipment, but you could hear it all over. And I was really into it because hey, wow, I'm finally getting to do it. This is a kid's dream come true. Here I am at the controls with speakers at City Hall Plaza.

I detected some shift, maybe the high frequencies disappeared because a speaker had been rotated 180 degrees. I glanced over, and we had the equipment about halfway up in the midpoint of the plaza on the north side, and one of the fellows who had been trying to nap (he was up visiting I think from Third and Howard for the day), he's got this speaker, holding it over his head, and he's staggering toward the fountain, toward the water with it. That was action theater. Ken [Dewey] would have loved it. We got there in time. I think he dropped it.

WELSH: You were preparing for the season opener in November 1963, but you were doing an outside project as well with Gerd Stern.

CALLAHAN: I met Gerd Stern for the first time through Michael McClure, who was a neighbor of Morton's. Gerd was planning this fund-raising event. He had done some sculpture and was having a show at the Museum of Art, and George Culler, a wonderful man, the director of the museum then, offered Gerd, "Well, if you want to use the auditorium for a reading or whatever, go ahead." Gerd cooked up quite an elaborate event with many live participants.

WELSH: What was the name of that event?

CALLAHAN: "Who R U?" and "What's Happening?" [1963]. Alfred Frankenstein reviewed it in the next morning's *Chronicle*. It's entitled "Landmark of a Flop." "Some horrendous eggs have been laid in the public halls of San Francisco in my time, but none so horrendous as to score a kind of success."[1]

WELSH: How did you get pulled into Gerd Stern's event?

CALLAHAN: Gerd came by the Tape Music Center, I think maybe with McClure, and approached Morton. So Gerd was really soliciting assistance from the Tape Music Center, not me. I subsequently wound up working with Gerd and continue to work with him forty years later. "Who R U?" and "What's Happening?"—the Tape Music Center was central to [it]. It was Gerd's production, but the Tape Music Center was there in full force.

Gerd had just read an early manuscript copy of what was to become *Understanding Media* written by Marshall McLuhan and was quite taken by McLuhan's work.[2] I think it was basically taking some of McLuhan's theories and putting them into practice. Television was new, [and] long distance wasn't all that common. I mean, it was technologically, compared to today, nowhere. But McLuhan was contending that communication at the speed of light was profoundly changing patterns of human association. And we'd better come to grips with it, because this was really going to threaten our sanity, if not our existence. I think that is bearing out forty years later.

Onstage there was a panel of sociologists and psychologists—Howie Becker from Stanford, and some others. They were at a table at the front of the hall, and in the auditorium on each side there were two kinds of niches in the wall, and we enclosed those with clear plastic. Each one had a table and a microphone in it. There were four guests, who didn't necessarily know each other, who were put in there [in each of the niches]. So there were sixteen people. And there was also a telephone. I rigged the telephones up to telephones on the sociologists' table. All of these microphones went into a mixer, and we would mix the conversation, which would go over the public address system. The sociologists would monitor the conversations and periodically ring up the table to direct the conversation. This might actually be the first instance of television in an art museum. We had closed-circuit television, and the phones all belonged to the phone company. It was basically illegal to have one, because it was prima facie that you stole it. But we got the phones out of the phone company with some PR stunt—you know, we want to teach kiddie science or whatever, I don't remember. But they went along. "Oh, yes, certainly, for the museum this is fine. Of course Pacific Bell supports the arts." There were a total of sixty-four people on the two evenings. It was an interesting list: Allen Ginsberg, Michael McClure, Rene deRosa, Jeremy Ets-Hokin, Harry Hunt . . . heavy-duty San Francisco society, plus the poets.

WELSH: So it was a sound-collage piece?

CALLAHAN: Yes, that was part of it. Simultaneous to all this was the first performance of the "Verbal American Landscape" [1963], which was slides of close-ups of words. Here in big red neon is the word "Temple," and "Stop," and "Yield," and "Do Not Enter." Really, it's beautiful. (We just restaged it at Anthology Film Archives in March down in New York. It's still lovely.) And while that was going on, the sound broke into feedback, because it was a marble hall, and it would squeal. Also we had prepared some tape loops recorded off the telephone of the time service—"The time is . . .

WELSH: Even though it was critically panned by Frankenstein, do you recall what the public's reaction was?

CALLAHAN: It was pretty well attended, and the audience was by and large good-natured. I remember at one point they were stomping their feet and at other points maybe there was a little more singing along or hooting and hollering. Some of them were getting increasingly irritated. At one point I was starting to think that maybe it might get a little ugly, but it never really did. It was quite an event. And as Alfred Frankenstein said, "It will be repeated, God help us, on Thursday."

This was a Tuesday night. And Monday night had been the opening concert at the Tape Music Center, which was what we had all been preparing for that year.

WELSH: The first concert of the season in the new space, 321 Divisadero, was on November 11, 1963.

CALLAHAN: Yes, this [was] my coming-out party, because I was on the line. But it worked. I think it went off without a hitch. I remember being, like many teenagers, self-conscious of clothes, and I didn't know what to wear. KPFA had had a rummage sale a few weeks before at 321. Across from the broadcast booth was a big closet, and KPFA was storing the things at the rummage sale that didn't sell. So I found a suit. I remember Steve Reich saying, "Hmm, Michael, you're looking downright funereal."

WELSH: On the opening night, there were tape pieces as well as live performance.

CALLAHAN: The tape machines were upstairs on the third floor, and there were wires run down to the speakers. I think I stuck upstairs, which was the responsible thing to do—you know, a pilot doesn't leave the cockpit. But I do remember the light show. Because that didn't have tape, did it? It was *Improvisation No. 1* with Subotnick, Oliveros, Sender, and Elias Romero. And that was the first time I really saw this liquid show. I think it was the first time a lot of people saw the liquid show.

WELSH: This experience was new for you and your friends?

CALLAHAN: I think it was new for all of us. I'm not saying this is absolutely the first or anything, but it was a new space, an interesting space. You'd walk up; it's on the second floor, and it had that particular San Francisco turn-of-the-century feel to it. It had been the California Labor School; it wasn't a commercial theater. It wasn't an academic institution. It was independent. I mean, there were no affiliations. [People] were very taken with Elias, with the visual element. The first pieces, you'd basically sit there in the dark, and you're listening to, as my sister says, "a squeaky-squawky music." That's not everybody's cup of tea. But to all of a sudden have visual accompaniment of a magnitude equal to the music, to the sound. These were both very powerful, and they potentiated [each other]. And it was chilling to me.

At this point, I was becoming more familiar with the music. Because, as I mentioned, a few more tapes were being added and exchanged. So we were building up a library. I'm not a musician, not trained as one, but I would listen when I was there working on something. That's when I really became aware that it was possible to really listen. Not just hear, but to listen. Pauline with "Deep Listening" has taken that much farther. And that was one thing that was another major turning point in my life. I was now in an environment where there were things worth listening to very carefully and intently—just the sound and then the emotion. What is that sound? Why does it trigger that emotion or that association?

This was all an education for me, because I wasn't taking City College seriously at all. I was learning a lot [here]. I mean, this was my education. It was also just fascinating to meet people who I'd heard about.

WELSH: The people who dropped by, did they take an interest in what you'd rigged up upstairs?

CALLAHAN: No, but that also gave me an appreciation of people actually *using* technology, as opposed to people who were just in it *for* the technology. I've met a few who were really in love with the technology. You know, when we should've been out chasing girls, we were out chasing surplus oscilloscopes or something. But to see people using it, and appreciating the technology, that gave me an appreciation of the craft, the precision. And I would see that in the exquisite detail of the composition and the struggle with the beast to realize it.

WELSH: The February show was tape pieces plus *Desert Ambulance* [1964].

CALLAHAN: I never thought of Ramon as a *Desert Ambulance* chaser, but he really wanted this Chamberlin. I forgot who told him about it or where he saw it, but he really had this need to acquire a Chamberlin. The local dealer was the Pacific Organ Company out in the Richmond [district] as I recall, owned by a surgeon. And one Saturday morning, Ramon asked me to go along, and we went to this guy's home, in that private enclave off of Arguello right before the Presidio, on a Saturday morning.

Here's me from the Haight-Ashbury, and Ramon, who'd probably been delivering the western edition of the *New York Times* on his motor scooter, and came straight from work. The guy says that he had bought the organ company because a surgeon's hands are only good for so many years. I remember him asking to see our prospectus. Prospectus? I think he was probably used to investing or something where there would be a prospectus. I think Ramon was obviously angling for him to just lay one on us for publicity. But I don't think that the Tape Music Center publicity was the type that this guy was seeking if he was selling kind of sing-along organs as a retirement safety [net]. The whole scene was a little bizarre. But anyway, Ramon somehow acquired it, in maybe December.

Under each key was a tape head, same as in a tape recorder. And when one pressed on the key, it pressed the tape head down, and under that running from keyboard level down to the floor inside was a tape loop. And all these tape loops were rotating at the same speed. Each tape loop had a particular note, which was recorded off a real pipe organ or whatever to make it authentic. But that was certainly not the intent of Ramon, who loved looping. We'd gotten those loop machines surplus, but I mean this was nirvana. You could play it like, well, an organ. It solved a lot of problems. But then there were also a lot of problems. You'd have to record the loops and splice them. Loading it was a real bear. And that took him quite a while. And you couldn't change them easily. It didn't record; they'd have to be recorded on an external machine, on one of the Ampexes, and then trimmed to length, and hope the splice held. You had to get them just right, because they all had to be the same length and the same time. But Ramon did it. That was a major project going on in the winter.

WELSH: Ramon actually prepared new loops?

CALLAHAN: Yes, he took out the pipe organ. Because this is just exactly what Ramon was saying. "If you want an organ, why don't you play an organ." Because you see that's basically eighty-eight tape playback machines. I mean, it's not trivial. Ramon wanted to see what else he could do with it.

Also, in January, the University of British Columbia was having an arts festival, and McLuhan was going to be there. This was the first performance of the "Verbal American Landscape" without the live characters [of "Who R U?" and "What's Happening?"]. And for that, Gerd and I had prepared four tapes, which were played on four tape machines that the university had, and there were our slides.

WELSH: We were talking about composers and other artists [who] came to the Tape Music Center.

CALLAHAN: Yes, it was a happening place. And I think it influenced the neighborhood a little, too. Because the Magic Theatre for Madmen Only [boutique and head shop] opened up in an empty storefront a few doors away. I remember Ramon was sort of chuckling and quite pleased that, in effect, there goes the neighborhood.

WELSH: Let's go on to the spring of 1964. How does the Tudorfest come to be?

CALLAHAN: There was a lot of interplay between New York and San Francisco. People like Ken [Dewey] and Steve Reich, a lot of people. That's where the action was. (One time when we were leaving the Arts Council down in Civic Center, I remember after the door closed and we were on the street, Ramon saying, "You know, San Francisco really is a provincial little clod hole.") This was going to be a big event, because John Cage was certainly well known. And I remember being a little curious at the time, not having met David Tudor, why John Cage wasn't getting top billing. Knowing more now and having met and gotten to know (because I ended up living in Rockland County) David a little better, I see why it was called the Tudorfest, because he was performing. It's like [Glenn] Gould might be playing Bach, but you're after the Gould. The reason I mention this is to show my lack of experience, if not ignorance, in this area. But this was big time; a major production because it was a number of evenings. And there was a lot of rehearsal. Unlike tape-based performance, you know; what's to rehearse? And [it was on] a much higher level, because [of] John Cage and David Tudor. I just remember a lot of preparation.

Also the technical setups with David were elaborate. That took a lot of attention.

I performed in one of the pieces. This was my first public performance, in [John Cage's] *Atlas Eclipticalis* [1961–62].

WELSH: You didn't consider yourself a musician and now you're performing John Cage's music. Did you get pulled into this?

CALLAHAN: Yes, I enjoyed it. It was a natural anyway, because *Atlas Eclipticalis* [included a part] for electronics, for a sound mixer, and there were microphones scattered amongst the musicians, which fed into a mixing panel I built. And John Cage prepared the score for the person playing the electronics. There was a star chart, and he took some clear acetate, and I remember John putting black marks on the acetate. Maybe there was another piece of acetate, which had an outline with the mixer, the knobs or at least the knobs drawn on it. And my instructions were to shuffle the star chart and the acetate. There were general guidelines on shuffling, but nothing radical. And when one of the dots lined up on a star chart, which lined up on a knob, I was to turn the knob to the position.

I asked John, "What happens if it gets so loud that it breaks into feedback?" He said, "Don't hurt anyone." I had a little dilemma here because we had these lovely JBL Olympus speakers. Bart Locanthi, who was vice president of JBL down in Los Angeles, responded to an invitation and sent up these nice, nice, nice speakers. We had those when we moved in.

WELSH: A summer tour was organized, which I believe was the first time that the Tape Music Center goes on the road. But you didn't go on tour.

CALLAHAN: Right, I did not go. I was invited and I was really tempted because I hadn't seen the country. I mean, I had only been up and down California and [to] Vancouver.

WELSH: They took some of the equipment?

CALLAHAN: I think maybe a tape recorder or two. Eldon Coral had reclaimed the big Ampex, because Ampex had promised that to the Republicans, who were holding their convention in July in San Francisco at the Cow Palace. I was less than pleased. I knew that it was on loan sort of, but I wasn't expecting Ampex to come take it back, much less to loan it to the Republicans! I mean that was a bit much!

WELSH: You had some other outside activities going on. You worked with Harry Partch at that time?

CALLAHAN: Yes. Harry had just finished composing *And on the Seventh Day Petals Fell in Petaluma* [1964] and was living in Petaluma. It was still sort of rural California. And Harry wanted to record this.

WELSH: How did you meet Partch?

CALLAHAN: Probably through Gerd Stern because Gerd had done work for Harry. Harry was living in this chicken hatchery. They had already torn part of it down, and Harry had to get out. So there was some serious time pressure. I rented some equipment and on the weekends would go up to Petaluma and record. Not having a multitrack machine, this was quite complex. I built a circuit as a metronome basically, which fed the headphones and they're listening to a click track, which was the master sync for everything.

WELSH: Was that an idea of yours?

CALLAHAN: It's an electronic metronome, yes. Harry had already spent some time trying to figure out how to pull this off. That's one maybe slight advantage to being young and inexperienced, because in retrospect, given the equipment, even given the state of the art in 1964, it was damn near impossible. But you know, here it is!

WELSH: When were these recordings with Partch?

CALLAHAN: That was March and April 1964. That was all in that time. It was very busy, and going to school full-time just wasn't happening.

WELSH: You edited it at the Tape Music Center?

CALLAHAN: Harry came by the Tape Music Center a few times, and what we were doing there was making safety copies. So I only had one machine up there [in Petaluma] and we just took the masters and just made straight dubs. We might have done some editing, because I remember Harry's displeasure when I was splicing the tape, splicing a note, which was a couple of inches long on the tape—and the whole floor, the whole place is covered with tape—and I dropped a note! I had to crawl around on the floor, and it was so short that it was very difficult to play because you need a few feet to thread it. I finally took my Ampex, pulled the playback head off and extended the wire so I could crawl along the floor and rub the head over all these thousands of little scraps of tape until I found the right one and spliced it back in.

WELSH: [When you decided to leave the Tape Music Center], did you announce to your colleagues, "I need a change—I'm going to go to New York"?

CALLAHAN: I was torn, and I wasn't quite sure what I really wanted to do. Yes, I told them, certainly, at some point. I don't exactly remember when. Probably before the tour, because I knew they were coming back sometime in July. I was preparing to go to New York sometime in August.

With Gerd, we had been invited to do ["Verbal American Landscape"] again with

McLuhan in Rochester in October. It was a good invitation, one that I didn't want to pass up. I wouldn't totally agree with Ramon about San Francisco being a provincial little clod hole, but that's not totally lost on a nineteen-year-old. As I said, endless people just came in from New York or [were] going back to New York.

[My replacement was] Bill Maginnis, a very sweet dude, a musician. I don't remember exactly what the introduction was. He's from Northern California, but lived in San Francisco a long time with his family, and grew up in San Francisco, I guess. His father owned a radio station in Northern California somewhere. So he knew audio and was interested in it, and I spent some time going over things with him. I got to know Bill a bit. Maybe somewhere in the back of my mind, I realized that it might be time for someone who was more experienced in electronic design. I was still using vacuum tubes, because they were cheap and plentiful, and I had tried designing a nonclassic studio. I remember getting butcher paper and just spreading it out on the floor in my room just trying to figure out how to get away from this classic studio mold. But there had to be a better way of going about this. It was beyond me and I struggled with it. I didn't come up with it. Robert Moog and Don Buchla did, with voltage control—brilliant, absolutely brilliant.

WELSH: When you came home to visit, did you drop in again to see what was going on?

CALLAHAN: Yes. I flew back to San Francisco in February. I was there for a month. So this was 1965 now. I was by Divisadero Street several times.

WELSH: Had the studio itself or any of the facilities changed in any way? Did you notice anything different?

CALLAHAN: Yes. I'm trying to [remember] whether that was the time I first saw the Buchla. I realized that this was exceeding the capability and indeed intended function of the classic studio. And I [also] had been struggling with the way of the next step. And the Buchla was up above the mixer against the Divisadero Street wall. If you're standing in the upstairs studio, the door would be on the right. Well, the racks and then the door. The Buchla was there. I remember staring at it, and I wouldn't say [I experienced] every possible emotion, but a lot simultaneously. One was . . . a profound elation that it had been done and I didn't have to worry about it. But on the other hand, somebody else did it!

WELSH: Can you describe in general terms the advance that was made?

CALLAHAN: Yes, one advance was made possible by transistors. [At] the Tape Music Center up until that point, what I had been doing was largely with vacuum tubes, since there was so much surplus and no money. Solid state and transistors were too new to be readily available surplus.

But in a nutshell, in the classic studio, one would have various sources, like microphones [or] whatever the signal sources were. It could be a phonograph or a tape machine playing back. And the outputs of these would go into a big patch panel. Then the patch panel would also have jacks on it where the output of a device, like a tape machine, could be patched into the input of a mixer, and then another output from a phonograph or whatever could be patched in. And these two could be mixed together. Then the output of the mixer was patched into the input of a machine to record on. Then the output of that machine was patched into an amplifier connected to the speakers so you could hear. But the key thing here is its signal path. It's [that] the actual audio signal is being switched about, patched about, routed. That's a whole routing process of the actual analog signal, and any modification of the signal was done in a box with an input and an output.

Buchla and Moog's implementation, their breakthrough, was that they separated the audio signal (what you were hearing) from the signal which was controlling it. There was a control signal which acted upon the audio signal. So instead of patching the audio signal, one would patch the control signals. And since one control signal could control multiple [signals]—this was another big, big thing—you could have one control signal from one of Buchla's touchpads or Moog's keyboard or whatever. You could take this control signal, which technically was, I believe, in the range of zero to ten volts direct current, and the standard was one volt per octave.

So if you wanted to change the pitch of an oscillator in the Buchla system, you would change the voltage going into it. The beauty was that you could take the same voltage and run it to as many oscillators as you wanted. And so you could make the settings on the oscillators—let's say one of them was centered at A440 and another at 880 or whatever—you could set them, but then when you changed the control signal, manipulate the control signal, they would all change. That's where it got beyond the classic studio, because to do that, how would you change all the oscillators at once? They were mechanical. You'd put your hand on a knob, and inside there would be a big capacitor that would move.

It's like tuning a radio. I can make a quick analogy. Let's say you had five radios and you wanted to tune them all the same. You'd need to turn the five knobs. There's no way—maybe some huge mechanical monstrosity of gears and pulleys tuning them all, but forget it. But in the Buchla system, where you have a control voltage, you just plug your control voltage into the five radios and when you change the control voltage, all five tune.

And it wasn't just the pitch of the oscillators. It could control the cutoff frequency of a filter, among many other things. All the Buchla modules had a common control. They were all zero to ten volts.

WELSH: When you visited the Tape Music Center and saw [it] sitting there, did you know it by looking at it? Did you know what it was?

CALLAHAN: I studied it. Yes, I knew what it was, because the controls and the jacks and everything are labeled. I knew it was a synthesizer. I mean, the term "synthesizer" was in use because there was the Columbia-Princeton synthesizer—the RCA [Mark II designed by] Harry Olson. I studied the Buchla quite intently, looking at the various modules. That's all I needed to see: voltage-controlled oscillator, voltage-controlled filter. These were engineering, technical descriptors of things I was familiar with. Buchla really had the packaging and the manufacturing and printed circuit boards . . . very, very sophisticated.

WELSH: Did you have any contact with Buchla or the others who knew this was in development?

CALLAHAN: I think I must have known it was in development. As I said earlier, there was a lot of back and forth between New York and San Francisco, and I would run into people in New York. So it's not that I was totally out of touch. There's no way I can really recall, but this was not a total shock to me. It's not like it just landed from outer space. There was very little written about all this, but there were occasional articles or papers in the *Journal of the Audio Engineering Society*.

But I really got to hand it to him. I didn't know Buchla. I didn't really meet him until 1967. I really want to [express] though my admiration for Don's technical ability dealing with transistors in those days, the early silicon transistors. The transistor [was first developed] in 1948, the first transistor radio in 1955.

If you connect a transistor a certain way, it's logarithmic, and that characteristic was employed, I believe (I don't know, I've never seen any of Don's circuitry), to get this logarithmic function. But the transistors were terribly, terribly temperature-sensitive. For every degree centigrade, the voltage across the transistor changes about $2/1{,}000$ of a volt, which might not sound like big deal, but you change ten degrees, and that's twenty millivolts, and you might be dealing with one millivolt to begin with, so all of the sudden the change has been twenty times larger than we're dealing with. So it takes some very sophisticated circuit design, which was way, way beyond me then. Moog got that also. I mean that's very sophisticated. I just wanted to go on the record as saying that I hand it to Buchla.

WELSH: Basically, by this time you're living in New York. Obviously, you're a San Franciscan, come home to visit. Any recollections of the city?

CALLAHAN: When I left in August, I figured I might go for a few months, but I realized then that I was going back to New York. So I packed up some more stuff, like the big Ampex downstairs, which I had not taken the first time, but I think I packed that up. It was still painful for me, and I had the feeling that I was abandoning people. It was a very, very tense time of my life. I took a night flight. First time across the country, leaving home. I took the airport bus from downtown. It was a TWA flight around 10:30 at night. And I flew across the country uneventfully, but I was looking out at the country. It was night, and seeing all the cities. You know, a young person leaving home and all that.

NOTES

1. Alfred Frankenstein, "A Landmark of a Flop," *San Francisco Chronicle,* November 13, 1963, 6.
2. Marshall McLuhan, *Report on Project in Understanding New Media* (New York: National Association of Educational Broadcasters, U.S. Department of Health, Education, and Welfare, 1960), was an early version of *Understanding Media: The Extensions of Man* (New York: McGraw-Hill, 1964).

The Great Grand Kludge!

WILLIAM MAGINNIS

I must have arrived at the San Francisco Tape Music Center in the summer of 1964. Michael Callahan had done a great deal of very fine work. The basic layout of the studio was really classical and classy as well. It centered around a patch bay, once part of a cryptograph, I think, and was logically laid out. Each row or patch strip was essentially dedicated to an equipment rack in the room. All lines were supposedly balanced, 600 ohms, and line level + 4 dbm, at least that was the idea. In reality, that was the problem. Most of the equipment we had was not balanced or 600 ohm, line level. Hum of the 60 Hz flavor was a common problem. We never really had a mixer, and the lack of a common mixing point was a very large problem. My first project was to build a keyboard system that served as a mixer of sorts, and caused other problems that might have been solved with a real mixer. Something like 16 × 8 × 4 × 2 would really have been a help. The building of the mixer is a story in itself. The result almost destroyed the studio!

Each equipment rack had a dedicated patch strip of thirteen balanced points. The patch strips were of the Western Electric double plug, double row type. The upper row, as I remember, was for bridging, and the lower row was for patching. The racks themselves were made from two-by-fours and right-angle aluminum stock, drilled and tapped for rack screws, oval head 10–32's with cup washers. The inside edges of the two-by-fours were, of course, spaced nineteen inches apart. The patch bay itself was in an enclosed rack. I believe it was of military origin and was poised at a 45-degree angle to the proposed mixer and keyboard area. To the left of the patch bay stood a large rack containing a homemade three-channel multispeed tape machine, a difficult device to operate even on its good days, which were few. Continuing to the left were more tape machines: an Ampex 401 full track and an Ampex 351–2 two-track. Next to the 351–2 was the Chamberlin Music Master. This was the general layout of the work space. It should be noted that nothing was really permanently installed. Various pieces of equipment were placed in the two-by-four rack spaces. We had acquired an Ampex PR-10 tape duplicating system through Ampex

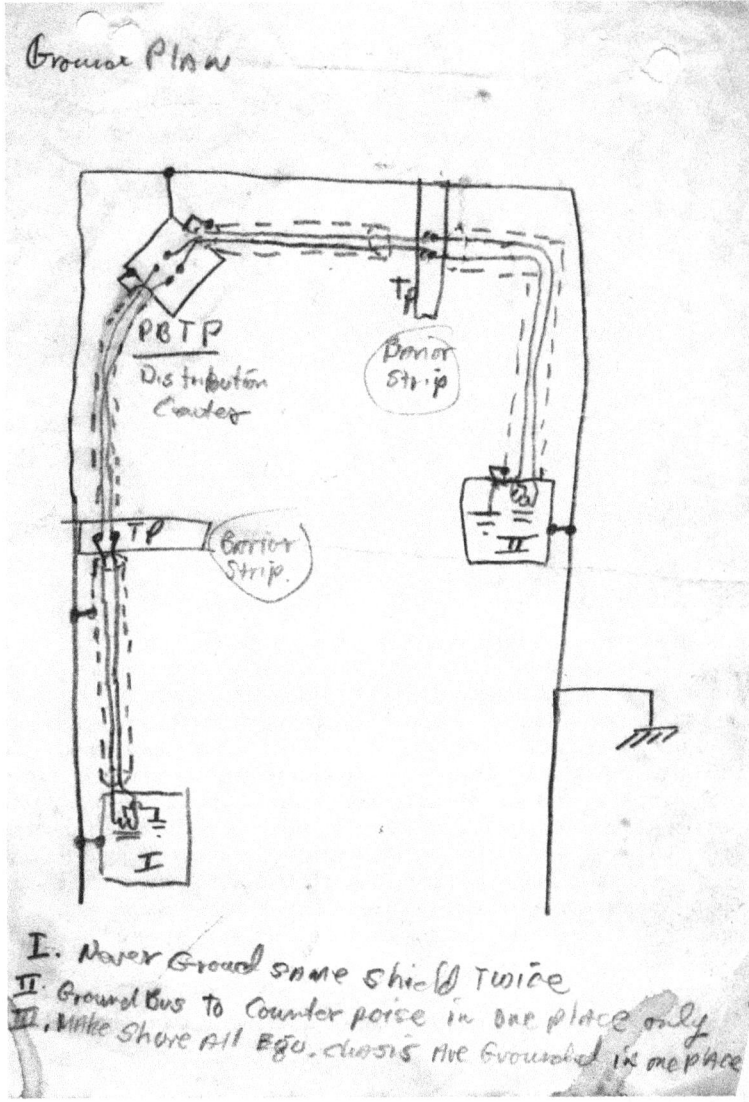

29 DRAWING SHOWING THE GENERAL OUTLINE OF THE STUDIO WORK SPACE AT 321 DIVISADERO STREET AND TWO WAYS OF GROUNDING THE EQUIPMENT (FROM WILLIAM MAGINNIS'S NOTES MADE IN 1964, COMPLETE WITH COFFEE STAINS). THE IDEA WAS TO REFRAIN FROM GROUNDING IN MORE THAN ONE PLACE, BUT CARRY THE GROUNDED SHIELDS AS FAR AS POSSIBLE. PBTP (PATCH BAY TIE POINT) IS THE MAIN DISTRIBUTION AND CROSS-CONNECTION POINT. OTHER TIE POINTS INCLUDED BARRIER STRIPS IN EACH RACK OR RACK SPACE/SECTION. THE IDEA BEHIND THIS CONFIGURATION WAS TO DISCONTINUE OR "BREAK" THE SHIELD AT THE STRIP TO PREVENT GROUND LOOPS. THE EQUIPMENT WAS MOUNTED IN SUCH A WAY AS TO ALWAYS CONNECT THE CHASSIS TO THE FRAME OF THE RACK, WHICH WAS GROUNDED BACK AT THE PATCH BAY. IT WORKED MOST OF THE TIME.

30 FOUR AND A HALF RACK SPACES IN THE STUDIO AT 321 DIVISADERO STREET. THERE IS A SHELF OR WORK SPACE SIMILAR TO A TABLE THAT RUNS THE LENGTH OF ALL THE RACK SPACES. FROM LEFT TO RIGHT, RACK 1 (TOP TO BOTTOM): A SINGLE TONE GENERATOR (PERHAPS WITH THE REMOTE CONTROL FOR THE AMPEX 315-2 AND THE 401/350 ON THE SHELF BELOW THE GENERATOR); RACK 2 (TOP TO BOTTOM): AN AMPEX "DIRECT RECORD TEST UNIT," WHICH COULD BE FREQUENCY MODULATED; A HEATHKIT (?) SINE/SQUARE GENERATOR; A HEWLETT-PACKARD SINE WAVE GENERATOR AND A HEWLETT-PACKARD SQUARE/PULSE GENERATOR WITH VARIABLE PULSE WIDTH; AN EICOKIT SINE/SAWTOOTH (?) GENERATOR AND A HEWLETT-PACKARD SINE WAVE GENERATOR (PRE-BUCHLA 100 ELECTRONIC SOUND GENERATORS); RACK 3: AN AMPEX PD 10 TAPE DUPLICATING SYSTEM; RACK 4: A HAMOND SPRING REVERBERATION UNIT AND INPUT AMPLIFIER. (THE OUTPUT AMPLIFIER IS IN RACK 5.) BEHIND THE RACK SPACES, THE BACK SIDES OF THE VIKING LOOP DECKS ARE VISIBLE. ONLY HALF OF RACK 5 APPEARS IN THE PHOTOGRAPH. IT INCLUDES AN S-100 HALLICRAFTER COMMUNICATIONS RECEIVER (SHORT WAVE, ETC.) AND THE HAMOND REVERBERATION OUTPUT AMPLIFIER. PHOTOGRAPH BY WILLIAM MAGINNIS.

International. It had apparently fallen onto the dock while being loaded onto a ship. The transport decks of the PR-10 were supposedly designed to shatter at high stress and not bend. Well, this did not happen, and we were somehow allowed to salvage this wondrous device. I managed to get it operational. Other strange things began to happen. The SFO airport radio direction beacon would mysteriously record itself onto tape copies, but only on Mort Subotnick's copies. I contacted the FCC and, at their suggestion, started installing low pass filters on the inputs. However, I discovered that none of the wires to the terminals on the circuit boards had ever been soldered, and were beginning to corrode, and form little diodes, perfect little radio receivers. Needless to say, solder, not low pass filters, solved the problem.

The rack area contained other amplifiers, tone generators, and sound processors. The mixer area was never finished. The story of the "MIXER" is one almost not to be believed. It all started with the appearance of this fellow, whom I shall call Joe

31 THE SFTMC STUDIO (SOMETIME BEFORE SEPTEMBER 1966). FROM LEFT TO RIGHT: (1) A PATCH BAY; (2) A SMALL EQUIPMENT RACK WITH (A) AN ACTIVE (TUBE-TYPE) BALANCED RING MODULATOR, BUILT BY MICHAEL CALLAHAN; (B) A PASSIVE RING MODULATOR, BUILT BY DON BUCHLA AND WILLIAM MAGINNIS; (C) A GRAPHIC EQUALIZER; (D) A HI/LO PASS FILTER (CAL AUDIO COMPANY TYPE 500); (E) A FAIRCHILD AUTOTEN, WHICH COULD BE USED TO AUTOMATICALLY ATTENUATE A SIGNAL ON A PROGRAM CHANNEL OR AS A LIMITER (OTHER FUNCTIONS WERE ALSO AVAILABLE); (3) EV STUDIO MONITOR SPEAKER AND MONITOR AMPLIFIER CONTROLS (NOTE RCA 77B MICROPHONE) AND A PASSIVE MIXER OF SORTS JUST BELOW THE MONITOR SPEAKER AND CONTROLS; AND (4) A SMALL EQUIPMENT RACK WITH 3 PREAMPS (W/VUS) AND ENVELOPE CONTROLS FOR THE KEYBOARD BELOW. PHOTOGRAPH BY WILLIAM MAGINNIS.

McGee. Joe claimed to have a degree in electronics from McGill University. He suggested that we build a 16-in / 4-out mixer to occupy the appointed mixer location. This was to be done using discarded telephone company repeat coils (one-to-one transformers) and would be completely passive—no amplifiers needed! "Wow!" I thought. "If only we could!"

"We can," he said. He did get gain through a network of repeat coils! I discovered that the band pass of the coils however stopped at 3 kHz. "No problem, we can EQ that with RC networks." To work he went and disassembled the whole studio. When he was through, he disappeared for a long period of time. Meanwhile, after some experiments with the repeat coil network and further consultation with an electronics engineer, I knew this scheme was just as impossible as I had thought. Yes, there was voltage gain, but there was also current loss! The whole mess went dead as a doornail as soon as any load was placed at the output end! Well, it also turned out that Mr. McGee's degree was not from McGill but from crystal meth, good old crank strikes again! It took several weeks to restore the studio

32 SFTMC STUDIO WORK AREA (LATE 1965 OR EARLY 1966). FROM LEFT TO RIGHT: RACK 1 (TOP TO BOTTOM): BALANCED RING MODULATOR, PASSIVE RING MODULATOR, GRAPHIC EQ, HI-LO PASS FILTER, AND "AUTOTEN" SETUP; RACK 2 (TOP TO BOTTOM): EV MONITOR SPEAKER, PART OF A TEMPORARY MIXER, MONITOR LEVEL CONTROLS; RACK 3 (TOP TO BOTTOM): MIXER OUTPUT AMPS, KEYBOARD ENVELOPE CONTROLS, KEYBOARD RELAYS; TABLE TOP (BELOW RACK 2): TEMPORARY MIXER CONTROLS. THE MICROPHONE IN THE FOREGROUND IS AN RCA 77B. THE OBJECT DANGLING BETWEEN RACKS 1 AND 2 IS AN EXPERIMENT! PHOTOGRAPH BY WILLIAM MAGINNIS.

to "normal" operation. Soon after the mixer fiasco, maybe four to six months, the first Buchla 100 prototype made its appearance, complete with mixers and all kinds of new goodies.

From all of the above one might assume that I was always building this thing or that. Building stuff was really not what I did most of the time. Most of the time I tried to keep the "GRAND KLUDGE" running. General maintenance was the usual order of the day. This included cleaning tape heads, pathways, and alignments, fixing this or that piece of equipment, preparing for whatever concert was coming up, and generally helping other composers with what ever technical problems came up. One of my jobs was to try to translate from composerspeak to engineerspeak (no small task I might add!). Sweeping the floor in the work area was another of my duties. One day, while I was sweeping up little bits of tape, David Tudor walked in, and when he saw that I was about to dump it all in the trash, he suggested I instead splice it all together and write a piano part, and promised to perform it. What a great idea, thought I, and went right to work. After several weeks went by, I had spliced about two or three minutes of cast-off tape. It was nearly completely silent

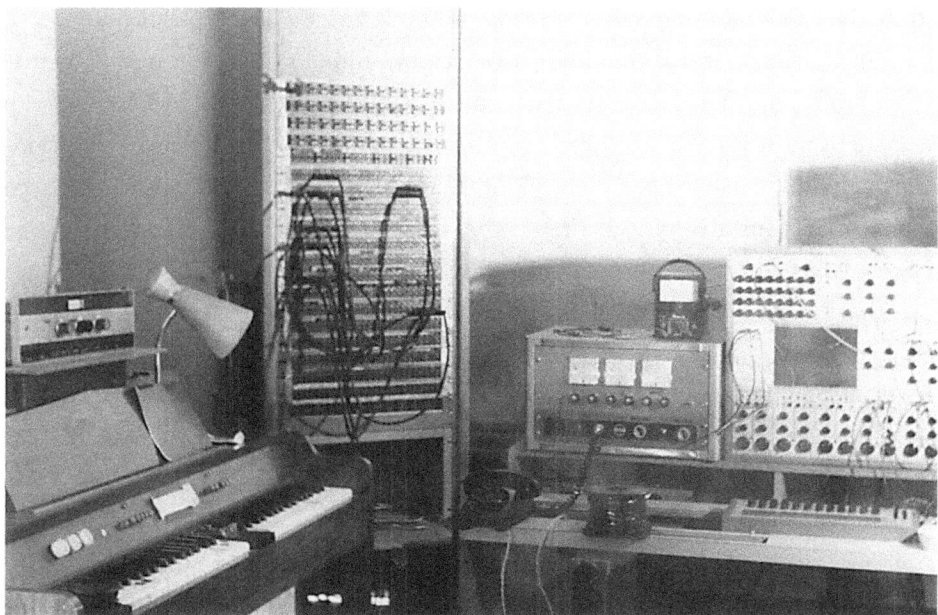

33 SFTMC STUDIO WORK AREA WITH THE FIRST BUCHLA SYSTEM AT THE RIGHT (LATE 1965 OR EARLY 1966). FROM THE LEFT: CHAMBERLIN MUSIC MASTER, PATCH BAY, AUXILIARY AMPLIFIERS, BUCHLA BOX. PHOTOGRAPH BY WILLIAM MAGINNIS.

with an occasional click or pop or short bit of almost inaudible hiss or hummmmm. Needless to say, that work never really got off the ground, or floor for that matter.

There were other projects and experiments I played around with to some degree of success. There was my sequencer that used a telephone dial and stepping relay, a set of filters operated by the black keys of the keyboard. The keyboard started out as a multi-input one-out mixer of sorts. The white keys were connected to relays that connected whatever was connected to the input to be switched to the output. It was a pure on/off arrangement—no envelope whatsoever, just annoying clicks and pops. Well, we soon discovered the cadmium sulfide photo resistor. I put a pot on the light source, and we were able to generate some primitive envelopes. It worked well for most audio sources, but not for the passive filter part of the keyboard, and for obvious reasons, it changed the R-C-L [resistance-capacitance-inductance] relationship as the envelope decayed. Back to the drawing board! Once again the Buchla 100 prototype solved that problem to some extent.

After the great grand mixer mess, Don Buchla became the projects development man at the Tape Music Center. Don had his place in Berkeley and did very little work at 321 Divisadero, or at Mills after the move. Needless to say things went smoother with Don Buchla than with Joe McGee! Don's first contribution to the studio was a passive ring modulator that we built one night out of selenium rectifiers, of all things. It still works and I use it from time to time even now. The major contribution Don made before the Buchla 100 was the amplifiers for the loop decks. His most wonderful contribution was, of course, the Buchla 100 series Modular Electronic Music System. The night it arrived, I stayed at the studio and played and worked with it until well after 4 A.M. I even completed a short piece entitled *Flight.* Even at 4 A.M., I was feeling so good about what was now beginning to happen that I played a little joke on Pauline Oliveros, who was to start working that morning around 9 or 10 A.M. I programmed the sequencer to play the first eight notes of "Yankee Doodle" over and over again as soon as the main power was turned on. This plan backfired; the joke was on me. Pauline called at 8:30 A.M., woke me out of a sound sleep, and I had to go back to the center and stop it.

The 321 Divisadero San Francisco Tape Music Center was one of the most creative spaces I have ever seen, heard, or otherwise experienced. I must admit that I did not realize it at the time. It seemed we were just having fun in an underfunded and ill-equipped experimental music studio. It is only now that I realize it was the most creatively productive time of my life. It was there that I really learned how to listen. How could I help it working with people like Ramon Sender, Mort Subotnick, Pauline Oliveros, Tony Martin, John Cage, David Tudor, Shep Shapiro, Terry Riley, Steve Reich, Folke Rabe, Jan Bark, Arne Mellnäs, the list goes on and on!

Terry Riley

INTERVIEWED BY DAVID W. BERNSTEIN AND MAGGI PAYNE

Along with Steve Reich, La Monte Young, and Philip Glass, Terry Riley was one of the founders of musical minimalism. He was also, and remains today, a prominent member of the Bay Area new music scene, an esteemed colleague and close friend of many composers who worked at the San Francisco Tape Music Center. In the following interview, with his characteristic generosity, Riley emphasizes how his colleagues influenced his development as a composer. Although he left the Bay Area for Europe from February 1962 to February 1964, the evolution of the Tape Music Center's aesthetic during its formative years owed much to his influence.

It was Riley who initiated the improvisation sessions with Loren Rush and Pauline Oliveros in 1958 at the Berkeley public radio station KPFA, providing Oliveros with an invaluable opportunity to hone her skills as an improviser, which she put to such good use when improvisation later became an integral element of performances at the Tape Music Center. Along with La Monte Young, Riley helped introduce Bay Area composers to John Cage's "total field of sound" with such radical "noise" works as Young's *Poem for Chairs, Tables, Benches, etc.* (or other sound sources) (1960) and Riley's *Concert for Two Pianos and Five Tape Recorders* (1960). Very much in the spirit of the avant-garde, these works included theatrical elements, a stylistic feature later employed by Tape Music Center composers.[1]

The premiere of Riley's *In C* on November 4, 1964, was among the most significant events presented at the Tape Music Center. It brought musical minimalism into the limelight, and challenged distinctions between so-called serious and popular music. The spirit of *In C* was very much aligned to the freethinking aesthetic inclusiveness cultivated at the Tape Music Center. It serves as an important reminder that although the minimalist movement thrived at the center of the New York "downtown" scene during the 1970s, it had actually begun a decade earlier on the West Coast, in a cultural environment that provided the ideal conditions for its emergence.

34 **TERRY RILEY (CA. 1964).**
PHOTOGRAPH © WARNER JEPSON.

BERNSTEIN: It would be good if we could start with the 1950s. We have recordings of improvisations with you, Pauline Oliveros, and Loren Rush from that period. They're fantastic.

RILEY: Where did they come from? KPFA?

BERNSTEIN: KPFA in 1958 I think.

RILEY: Right.

BERNSTEIN: And I was wondering if you would talk about that aspect of your music. Your improvisations in the 1950s don't sound like jazz. I would call them free improvisation. And it seems to me that you, Pauline, and Loren Rush were doing that quite early in its development.

RILEY: That's a good place to start. When I came to San Francisco in 1955, I was living up in Redding, California, and got into a composition class at San Francisco State. Pauline and Loren Rush were in the class and Ken Benshoof and Joseph Weber, and a whole bunch of really interesting musicians. Pauline, Loren, and I became really close friends and used to hang out on weekends a lot and, you know, have parties, play music, and get together whenever we could. I think the improvisations at

KPFA, at least some of them, one of them in particular, came about because I'd been asked by the sculptress Claire Falkenstein, who had made a film called *Polyester Moon*, to make a soundtrack for it. So I asked Loren and Pauline if they wanted to do it with me and do it as an improvisation. I remember in particular that was one of the ones we did. We probably did more. Loren [brought] kotos and different instruments to the sessions. Pauline would play French horn and possibly accordion, and I would play piano. They were based a lot on the kind of compositions we were doing in those days. So I think we were bringing a lot of the spirit of that music [into our] improvisations, which were quite free. I'd call it musical abstract expressionism [rather] than jazz.

BERNSTEIN: I have listened to some of those early works you composed, and some of them a little bit later, some of Pauline's as well, like her *Outline* for flute, double bass, and percussion [1963]. And your two piano pieces, they are from the late 1950s, I think?

RILEY: Those were [composed in] 1958 and 1959. I started in 1958 and finished in 1959.

BERNSTEIN: Are they in the style that you're talking about?

RILEY: Well, that was around that time, a little bit later, but it was. You know, I must say I was very influenced by Pauline and Loren in those days, because I had been previously writing in a more neoclassic style before I met them. I was really into Poulenc and Milhaud. Oddly enough, I kind of came back more to that after this period of working with them. Pauline and Loren introduced me to music by Schoenberg and Webern, and this was a world that really blew me over when I first heard it. And I really wanted to do it too. I really wanted to do this kind of music. I wrote several pieces between 1957 or 1958 and around 1961 that were kind of in this more abstract expressionist style for lack of a better way to describe it. I also had been playing some of Loren's piano music at UC Berkeley. He'd invited me over to perform at Wheeler Hall. So learning his piano music also influenced me in terms of what I was writing. This was a really exciting period for me, because it was opening me up to a wider range of musical ideas than I'd previously had.

BERNSTEIN: I was just listening to the two piano pieces and was impressed by their virtuosity. They reminded me of Schoenberg, maybe a little of Stockhausen.

RILEY: Yes, of course, by that time I was already a little bit familiar with Stockhausen, too, and Boulez. But I'd say Schoenberg got me onto the track. Looking at his early piano music was a revelation for me. I really found it quite beautiful. I think some of my favorite music of Schoenberg's is his piano music.

The 1958 KPFA Tapes

FRED FRITH

The 1958 improvisations by Pauline Oliveros (French horn), Terry Riley (piano), and Loren Rush (koto, bass) bear fascinating witness to the musical issues and concerns of the times.[1] Of course, they were not alone. In 1957, Lukas Foss founded the Improvisation Chamber Ensemble, a quartet devoted to what he described as "un-notated music." This group was instigated and led by Foss, and based on his own rather particular ideas. It disbanded in 1962, and Foss subsequently made statements questioning the efficacy of improvisation, complaining about the traps and pitfalls that it presented to the musicians:

> In ensemble improvisation you can't take certain chances like you can in composition. You've got to make it work, you've got to be sure that it will work. So what do you do? You play very soft, because you realize it's going to sound sensitive, that's safe, or you play very loud, it's going to be powerful, so that's safe. But *mezzo-forte* improvisation, that's much harder . . . so improvisation became playing safe—as it most always is for jazz musicians also.[2]

To the contemporary improviser this sounds perplexing, given how far the practice of non-idiomatic improvisation has come in the intervening fifty-odd years, but such statements were not unusual at the time and highlight the difficulties faced by those wishing to experiment but perhaps unwilling to carry the experiments to their logical conclusions.

The fundamental issues for many composers at that time were threefold: how to "articulate ideas without passing through the medium of written parts";[3] how to *control* the exciting and vital interchanges that arise from improvisation; and how to distance that kind of practice from jazz. George Lewis has, to a certain extent, addressed the subtle and not so subtle racist attitudes underlying statements made by some of those in agreement with the latter objective.[4] There are other issues, though, that touch on questions of authenticity and ownership, which have rarely been openly articulated. If we look at the musicians in Britain who made the transition from jazz to improvised music a few years later (Joseph Holbrooke, Derek Bailey's group with Tony Oxley and Gavin Bryars began this transition in 1963), there is clearly a motivation to find a personal expression that could be more relevant to their own context, and that could belong to them rather than being perpetually seen as an imitation of something else. As Bailey puts it in his book on improvisation, they were embarked on "an emotional, or instinctive, search to find something that was logical and right, or at least appropriate, to replace the inherited things which we found stilted, moribund, and formal."[5] During the same period, others took this

---

1. A recording of a selection of the 1958 improvisations is housed at in the F. W. Olin Library, Center for Contemporary Music Archive, Mills College, Oakland, California.
2. Lukas Foss interviewed in Cole Gagne and Tracy Caras, *Soundpieces: Interviews with American Composers* (Metuchen, N.J.: Scarecrow Press, 1982), 198–99.
3. Luc Ferrari interviewed in *Mouvement*, special nos. 33–34 (March–June 2005). The quotation is translated by Fred Frith.
4. George Lewis, "Improvised Music after 1950: Afrological and Eurological Perspectives," *Black Music Research Journal* 16, no. 1 (Spring 1996): 91–121.
5. Derek Bailey, *Improvisation: Its Nature and Practice in Music* (New York: Da Capo Press, 1993), 87.

shift away from (jazz) tradition even further,[6] by searching for a radically new and unprecedented musical language and sound world. As Victor Schonfeld trumpets on the sleeve notes of John Stevens's Spontaneous Music Ensemble's 1968 LP *Karyobin,* SME "created nothing less than a revolutionary form of improvisation of which its own style is only one of innumerable possible examples, a form which challenges other musics as well as defining the next stage of jazz itself." Similarly, Eddie Prévost describes the beginnings of AMM:

> Out of these attempts to make small group and orchestral jazz musics there grew an unease with emulation, and a desire to have a more creative relationship with music. In 1965, AMM began a radically different kind of music-making. The prevalent notions of musical theory, practice, hierarchy, and structure (thematic reference, jumping-off points—for example the "head" arrangements from which improvisation lifted off—and even the relatively informal criteria of the then "free jazz" movement) were replaced by the creation of, and engagement with, a sound-world in which there was not even a formal beginning or ending. And from its first raucous explosions, it knew too that it was not only speaking a new language but that it was talking about things not perceived in any music the member musicians had heard elsewhere.[7]

We can now see two distinct tendencies, both doing their best to distance themselves from the improvisational lingua franca of the day, jazz, but with very different apparent motivations, and each anxious to establish its credentials as being or having been at the forefront of a radical new movement. It is at this intersection that the work of Oliveros, Riley, Rush, and others from the West Coast scene of the late 1950s seems both prescient and refreshing. This is experimental music in the purest sense of the word—the results are not necessarily predictable in advance—which doesn't seem to be situating itself self-consciously in relationship to jazz or anything else, or making any exaggerated claims for itself. If anything, it seems to anticipate Fluxus, still a few years away. The musicians are clearly not concerned with the "successful" performance, so this is not about establishing or upholding careers. These tapes are recordings of work in progress, as the players attempt to establish the parameters for an improvisational practice free of idiomatic rules and seek only to create a narrative space that reflects the moment of listening. I find it noteworthy that unlike the composers of the time who experimented with performer freedom and rather decided against it—Foss, Feldman, and others—Oliveros, Riley, and some of their cohorts are still (almost fifty years later) at the center of that practice of improvisation perhaps best defined by Cornelius Cardew:

> Discipline is not to be seen as the ability to conform to a rigid rule structure, but as the ability to work collectively with other people in a harmonious and fruitful way. Integrity, self-reliance, initiative, to be articulate (say, on an instrument) in a natural direct way; these are the qualities necessary for improvisation. Self-discipline is the necessary basis

---

6. Alfred Nieman's legendary improvisation group, which started in Hampstead as an adult education class in 1961 and continued at least until 1968 should be mentioned here. Most of its members were music students at the Guildhall School of Music, where Nieman taught. Clearly, this had nothing to do with a transition from jazz practice, but was more in line with ideas of the day about performer freedom, the absence of notation, and so on.

7. Edwin Prévost, *No Sound Is Innocent: AMM and the Practice of Self-Invention, Meta-Musical Narratives, Essays* (Harlow, Essex, UK: Copula, 1995), 9.

> for the required spontaneity, where everything that occurs is heard and responded to without the aid of arbitrarily controlled procedures.⁸
>
> This seems like a perfect description of the music on these fascinating archival recordings. While there are inescapable references to the musical practice of the 1950s academy, especially in the atonal intervallic material iterated by the piano from time to time, the music is primarily characterized by an overwhelming lack of interest in either specific musical style or personal virtuosity. The 1958 recordings provide an encyclopedia of improvisational strategies in which density, pointillism, abrupt stops and starts, manic skitterings, all possible instrumental combinations including solos, and the inventive use of physical space are contained within one long unfolding narrative structure. Silence is important, and tension is also created by the implication (in continuous bouts of laughter) of a small audience that is not sure how to react. Above all, and this seems to set the music apart from everything else I've heard and read from this period, there is a welcome warmth and humor to the proceedings. The players are having fun, and aren't afraid to show it. In other words, this is music that doesn't take itself too seriously, that is not concerned with its place in history, and that has nevertheless formed the basis of a lifetime of practice. As such it represents a serious, historic, and curiously practical lesson.
>
> 8. This quotation appears in Michael Nyman, *Experimental Music: Cage and Beyond* (New York: Schirmer Books, 1974), 107.

BERNSTEIN: Did you use serial techniques in those pieces?

RILEY: I didn't. I was aware of serial technique, but there was only one period in my life when I tried to use it. It was a little bit later. Most of the pieces I wrote in that time, I threw away. I just did them as exercises to try and control everything: dynamics, measure numbers, and, you know, pitches and rhythms. Everything was totally serialized. It actually was a lot of fun to do. I just wanted to see how it worked and how it would feel to do it myself. But my piano pieces were written just intuitively.

BERNSTEIN: Didn't you write a piece in the style of Stockhausen's *Zeitmasse* [1955–56]?

RILEY: It's called *Spectra* [1959]. And it's for six instruments: flute, clarinet, bassoon, violin, viola, and cello. Actually, Morton Subotnick conducted a performance of it. It was a piece [in which] I took Stockhausen's idea of a multitempo polyphony.

BERNSTEIN: Was it performed at the Tape Music Center?

RILEY: No, it was before the Tape Music Center was happening. It was, I think, performed in around 1960 or 1961.²

BERNSTEIN: What's really interesting to me, thinking about all this music that you did from 1957 to around 1970, is all the different things you were doing: your written out "abstract expressionist" music, improvisation, which I now am learning is related—as kind of an improvisational manifestation of that music—and then the music with long tones, like the *String Quartet* [1960] . . .

RILEY: Right.

BERNSTEIN: . . . being another style. There was also music involving noise recorded on tape or performed live for Ann Halprin with La Monte Young . . .

RILEY: Right.

BERNSTEIN: . . . and the tape music with loops and delay. It's interesting in those years you were doing all these different things sometimes at the same time.

RILEY: Well, the spheres of influence or sources for me during that time, as I have said, were always my colleagues or friends or fellow students during those days that were making the biggest impact on me. You know it started out with Pauline and Loren when I came to the Bay Area, and then when I went to UC Berkeley, I met La Monte Young, and I sort of got into his gravitational field. He'd already been working with long tones and he'd also been a jazz musician. La Monte and I became kind of inseparable; I just remember that we were never apart. He'd come over to my house and we'd be always listening to records or transcribing stuff or talking about different things. He was into Coltrane, early Coltrane, before anybody knew John Coltrane. And he also had had experience listening to Asian music earlier than I had and introduced me to gagaku [Japanese court music] and even Indian music. This really became a focus for me and influenced a lot the way I was composing.

Performing with Ann Halprin was another opening thing. La Monte and I had our biggest period of improvising together because we had this whole form that she brought, the dance form and everything, to work within. And I think we both grew a lot while working with her. She's a very inspiring and visionary person, and all three of us started hanging out together over at Ann's place. That was the period when I was doing the piece for five tape recorders and two pianos that La Monte and I performed several times in Berkeley and in Provo, Utah, for a student composers' conference. During that period, I was really getting into noise, but I was also starting to get into repetition. During some of Ann's pieces, I would do things like play a Bach chorale endlessly while La Monte was banging on garbage cans and Ann would be dancing. I was starting to get into the feeling of cycles and repetition just working with the dance. I started making my first tape pieces also working with her. I feel like that was the opening of my career that kind of showed me what I really wanted to do in music.

35 LA MONTE YOUNG AT ANN HALPRIN'S STUDIO, KENTFIELD, CALIFORNIA (CA. 1959–60). PHOTOGRAPH © WARNER JEPSON.

BERNSTEIN: One of those pieces was Halprin's *The Three-Legged Stool*?

RILEY: Yes, I thought it was called *The Four-Legged Stool* [1961] when I did it. But I think it's been called *Three-Legged* . . . *Four-Legged* . . . *Five-Legged*. [Laughs] I guess I did the first music for it before I went to Europe, and that became *Mescalin Mix* [1960–61]. *Mescalin Mix* was the background tape that she used. Some of the *Mescalin Mix* actually has, you can hear me playing the piano, kind of small fragments of blues riffs and other things that I was playing. Yes, that was the beginning of the "how many legged stool series." I think Morton [Subotnick] then wrote some music for it, and they might have called it *The Five-Legged Stool* [1962].

And it was a high point in Ann's career, the early 1960s. After that she got into a lot of other things. It was kind of a culmination of her work with A. A. Leath and John Graham, who were really wonderful dancers and collaborators for her. And they had worked together so many years that their intuitive interaction on the stage was phenomenal. They'd come up with things that I just couldn't believe.

BERNSTEIN: Was Lynne Palmer part of it, too?

RILEY: And Lynne Palmer was part of it too, yes.

BERNSTEIN: And *2 Sounds* [1960] is another piece from this period?

RILEY: Yes, *2 Sounds* was created on the windows of Ann's studio. La Monte was really into friction sounds during this period. That's when he composed *Poem for Chairs, Tables, Benches, etc.*, a piece that [also] uses friction sounds. And I think *2 Sounds* was created using metal objects and things to drag across the windows of Ann's studio.

BERNSTEIN: The piece for two pianos and five tape recorders uses similar sounds.

RILEY: Right. I used an old piano, just the insides of a piano, the sounding board and strings, standing up against a wall to make *Concert for Two Pianos and Five Tape Recorders*. I took a bunch of metal ball bearings and rolled them across the floor and crashed them into the sounding board, and yes, it resonates. It would sound almost like a bowling alley, a combination bowling alley–piano, with keyboard sounds.

BERNSTEIN: Were the two pianos prepared?

RILEY: No. They weren't prepared in that sense, but we used a lot of things inside the pianos, like ashtrays. Just things that were lying around. La Monte would often be under the piano, or almost inside it lying down, because he's not so big. The use of the piano was kind of brutal at times. I don't think I would be able to do that to a piano today. [Laughs] I remember one time tossing an ashtray, a metal ashtray, halfway across the stage, landing on the strings. Things that were quite harsh, but when you're a student, sometimes you don't think about consequences.

There was quite a bit of this in the air, you know. One of the concerts that La Monte and I did was with Walter de Maria, one of the minimalist sculptors in New York, who was working with us a lot in those days. We were kind of a trio. We worked a lot with Walter. Walter did a premiere at the Old Spaghetti Factory of a piece called *Bats*. The Old Spaghetti Factory, did you ever go there? I used to play ragtime piano there, and we talked [the owner] into letting us do a new music concert. It was a very tiny room with a little stage on one end with a piano. Walter brought a table up and a baseball bat and he announced to the audience, "The world premier of *Bats*" and he started hitting, breaking the table up. Wood was flying all over the audience, and people were running for the exits. I mean, it was scary! It was actually quite violent. So there could be an element of danger to the audience and [to] the performers. This was a field of art which frightened me when I saw where it could go, where it was headed. I didn't want this kind of violence in my own [work]. But I was involved, and to me, it was an important thing, although I couldn't do it myself. It was an important thing to do, to make art so scary that the audience would be very alert. [Laughs] Because their lives depended on it! [Laughs]

BERNSTEIN: There are pieces by Nam June Paik called *Danger Music* . . .

RILEY: Yes.

BERNSTEIN: . . . and I remember reading that John Cage was horrified by all these new developments. They were going a little bit too far.

RILEY: I think I heard a story about Paik; I think it was in Stuttgart. He had a classroom somewhere and he put a motorcycle in there and invited the audience in, locked the doors, and revved up the motorcycle full speed, so there was carbon monoxide, noise, and panicking people. Another interesting thing about this was when I went to these concerts in Germany. During the early 1960s, Germany wasn't quite reconstructed yet, so you'd walk around and the streets were full of rubble. If you think about all this in terms of Fluxus going to Germany, which is the place where violence had been enormous, and doing violent things, it's pretty astounding! I could almost understand it more in a place where there hadn't been a war to awaken people to the fact that there is violence being committed in world. Just so people would be aware. But in Germany, it almost seemed too much.

BERNSTEIN: Getting back to *Mescalin Mix*. Did you compose some of that work in your own studio at home using long tape loops extending around wine bottles?

RILEY: Yes.

BERNSTEIN: And then you later worked on it in Ramon Sender's studio at the San Francisco Conservatory?

RILEY: Yes, well, Ramon had this little studio setup at the conservatory, and he had a, what do they call it, this looping machine?

BERNSTEIN: An Echoplex.

RILEY: Echoplex! Thank you. He had a little studio setup. All I was doing was sound on sound. I had a couple of mono Wollensak tape recorders, and I'd use one to run the loop on and the other one to record on, and I'd do sound on sound, because there was no multitrack. So all the noise would build up at the same time. [Laughs] You know, the source material would build up. It was very funky. But Ramon invited me up to the conservatory to finish [*Mescalin Mix*] up there and to actually put it all together. I can't remember what he had there, but I know it was a lot more than what I had. I think he might have had an Ampex or something that was better quality, and that's probably where we made the master, the so-called master. And we did use Ramon's Echoplex, which I really loved. I remember that now. So that's about all I remember about just working with him up there, and I think there were a couple of versions. There was one that kind of stuck and survived. I had many versions, but they've somehow gotten lost over the years. They were different mixes of that piece. You know, different combinations of the loops.

BERNSTEIN: So the one that's on your CD is . . .[3]

RILEY: . . . the one we mastered at Ramon's, yes.

BERNSTEIN: As you know, other composers were working with limited equipment. I'm thinking of two other works, one by Pauline Oliveros, entitled *Time Perspec-*

tives, [1961], [in] which she used a bathtub as a reverberation chamber and recorded all the sounds in real time. And then there's another work by Sender called *Traversals,* also created with fairly simple equipment. These pieces were performed in the first Sonics concert along with *Mescalin Mix.*

RILEY: At the conservatory?

BERNSTEIN: Yes, on December 18, 1961.

RILEY: I don't have a clear memory of that. I might have been there.

BERNSTEIN: So you left for France in 1962?

RILEY: It was February of 1962.

BERNSTEIN: While you were in Europe did you continue composing tape music?

RILEY: Well, actually, I didn't have a studio or anything when I was in Europe, most of the time I was there. So I wasn't actually doing any tape music until just before I came back. What I was doing was hanging out with a lot of beat poets, who were living in Paris. I lived in Paris much of the time, and during this time I was meeting people like Brian Gyson and William Burroughs, who were living at the Beat Hotel in Paris. I had a band that I was playing in that was a bunch of American expatriates. We worked on the American bases, and I was learning to play jazz piano.

I was thinking about composition all the time, but I was not actively doing anything. I was trying to dream up what my next move was going to be. But it was really a period of doing something else. Mainly, I had to support myself, because it was hard to live in Europe as an American. The only way I could do it was playing in bars and playing on the American bases, which were there because the Strategic Air Command was in France. I hooked up with some agents who could book me into these places. And I'd play for floor shows and travel with circus acts, which actually I enjoyed quite a bit. But there was always this idea that I was going to do something; I was going to create some kind of thing as soon as I could figure out what it [was] I wanted to do. I'd just gotten out of school. I didn't like the academia of UC Berkeley. I knew I wanted to go as far away as I could from anything like that. Playing for floor shows was about as far [laughs] as I could get from academia. So it was a good place to be for a few years.

And what happened, what finally brought it all back was this: Ken Dewey, whom I'd met out here in California, and who was a little bit associated with Ann Halprin and the Tape Music Center, came to France. He brought John Graham, who was one of the dancers working with Halprin, Lynne Palmer, and some of the members of the Living Theater. Dewey was commissioned to do a piece for the Théâtre Récamier. There was a festival called Théâtre des Nations in Paris. He'd gotten a two-night date for a piece of his called *The Gift*. And he wanted me to be the musical director, and the Living Theater, actors. Coincidentally, Chet Baker had just arrived in Paris. I had seen him at a pool hall while I was waiting to take some of these floor show acts out to eastern France. I told Ken that "Chet Baker's in town and why don't we get him involved in this piece?" So Ken approached him, and he agreed to do it. Ken got me into a small recording studio at the Sarah Bernhardt Theater in Paris. We took Chet Baker and his band in, and I gave him some ideas about what to record. Mainly, I wanted him to play, a modal piece, and they picked *So What?* by Miles Davis. I told them to play the solos separately, without the whole band. So that I could cut it up and put it back together later. And so this was the first project I'd done in two years. Up until that point I had not been in a studio. I had not had any equipment, nothing. So it was very exciting for me to finally hit something that I could put my teeth into and feel real exhilarated about working on.

BERNSTEIN: Was the studio part of the French National Radio?

RILEY: Yes, it was the French radio, but they had studios in different places. It just happened to be the Sarah Bernhardt studio where we did the recording and used their studios for mixing.

BERNSTEIN: And they showed you a way to do tape delay?

RILEY: Yes, the recording engineer . . . it was funny because I had *Mescalin Mix* and the Echoplex loop in my mind. I think I first asked the engineer, "Do you have an Echoplex?" and he said, "No." So I said, "Well I want this kind of sound: RRRRRRRRrrrrrRRRRRR that's got a long loop, and do you know how you can do that?" and he said, "Oh, yes!" He stretched the tape between two tape recorders and voilà! and I thought, oh, this is incredible, exactly what I want.

BERNSTEIN: I really like the way you use tape delay in *The Gift*.

RILEY: I used some small tape loops, of course, and John Graham's voice. It was interesting because I was working with an engineer who was a very straight guy in a white jacket, you know [laughs] who looks like he's wearing a lab coat. I had to tell him what I was trying to do without having my hands on the machine, which is a little bit frustrating. But it was so wonderful to have really high quality, even though in those days I guess it was mono, but just to have these really high-quality machines to work with, where you really could hear what you were recording.

BERNSTEIN: Pauline Oliveros was also interested in the delay effect, in *Bye Bye Butterfly* [1965], for example.

RILEY: Yes, well, you know it was one of the things that were very musical that you could do in those days. It was pre-synthesizer days, pre–most electronic technique days. We had loops and delays, which we could get from the head gaps of machines. I remember David Tudor turned me on to this place in San Francisco where you could buy all these tape heads, and when he was out here once, I built this little box, even though I'm not very good at electronics. He showed me how to string a bunch of tape heads together, and I made this jerry-rigged thing that I could put between two tape recorders and get several tape heads and could move them, even though the alignment was horrible. [Laughs] But that was part of the sound, too. And that definitely was one of the things that was available to us and was definitely in the air. Tape delay has a kind of psychological effect. It has this kind of mystical quality that echoes and things have for us. And I think we were, a lot of us were drawn to that. We were looking at music and mysticism together.

BERNSTEIN: Then you really took delay effects a long way in subsequent years with *Dorian Reeds* [ca. 1965] and similar pieces?

RILEY: Yes, from that period in Paris, which was 1963, when I worked with Ken Dewey, until about 1980, I was pretty heavily involved with tape delay.

PAYNE: When did you come back from Europe?

RILEY: I came back in February of 1964. I was gone just exactly two years.

PAYNE: Why did you decide to come back?

RILEY: Well, I was going to stay in Europe. I was really happy there. But my existence there was a little precarious, because I was working on these American bases and was living month to month. You know, I'd contract with the booking agent how many gigs I'd get a month, so if I missed a paycheck, I didn't have anything to rely on, no money beyond that. And in November of 1963, John Kennedy was killed, and they put a moratorium on all entertainment on American bases. The agents that owed me money refused to pay me, so I found myself suddenly broke in Paris. By that time maybe I felt it was a good sign that I should come back and check it out here.

PAYNE: Where did you decide to settle?

RILEY: Well, I came back to New York again. We came back on a boat. We came back from Tangiers to New York City and La Monte picked me up at the dock. I was pretty broke, and I'd written him and told him when the boat was getting in, and he met me. I really wanted to get back to San Francisco. But I really was excited about what La Monte was doing. He had his Theater of Eternal Music going then with Tony Conrad and John Cale. I'd gone to some rehearsals and it really was tempting to stay and play in the band.

But we got one of those "drive-away cars"—you know, you can deliver a car for somebody—and we drove back to California. I had a job waiting for me here, because I'd played piano at the Gold Street Saloon, and they'd kind of kept the job open for me. When I came back, they hired me right away. So I was able to resume my life in San Francisco.

BERNSTEIN: And San Francisco was really a great place then.

RILEY: Yes, and of course Ramon had been storing my piano for me, and I started collecting my things again and could start working. Plus, you know, having the experience of working with Chet Baker, and working on music for *The Gift,* I felt was really a new direction for me and was something that was going to nurture my whole career for quite a while. So I started trying to write a piece—another piece, but without using electronics. I wanted to write an instrumental piece that could have the same effect. I was taken by the modality of [the music] that Chet Baker [had played] in conjunction with tape loops, and I wanted to do something like that for other musicians. I had this kind of weird abstract dream about doing that. And I kept trying to write it, and I could not find a solution that I was happy with until the idea for *In C* came along, which was a few months after I'd been back. And it was a solution that I hadn't been looking for, that just came, so . . .

PAYNE: What a solution!

RILEY: . . . I wrote *In C* in the spring of 1964. I don't remember which month, I just remember it was springtime. Must've been like around March, April, May, something like that. I'd been sitting around for a few months when Ramon and [Tony] Martin asked me to come up and do a one-man show at the Tape Music Center.

It was like I was trying to write it all out in a big score from my memory. I had this thing where it was kind of like an orchestral piece and all the patterns were written. Writing it out might have worked, I don't know.

PAYNE: How did you decide to modularize it?

RILEY: Well, the idea came intact. The whole piece, all the patterns, everything came intact. I didn't have to think about it. It was the only thing I've ever written that came to me like that. I say that now, but in retrospect, I didn't really know what to do with it after it came to me. I saw it all on the page, but I didn't really have a plan of how it would be performed. I knew kind of vaguely what it would all do, and I knew that it would create a lot of interesting polyphony and combinations of patterns just because of my experience with tape loops.

PAYNE: How did you work that process through?

RILEY: Steve Reich was in town. He had moved out here while I was in Europe. And it turned out that I moved into a place right near where his house was in Bernal Heights, so we became friends. And I showed him *In C,* and he got real excited about putting it together. He'd formed a group to perform with the San Francisco Mime Troupe, with John Gibson and some other musicians, including Jeannie Brechan. I don't know all the other people who were working with him. He said, "Let's do this; I'll bring John in, and I'll play in it," and then Warner [Jepson] and Pauline said they'd do it. And oddly enough, some of the guys that I'd played with in France came back to the States and ended up in San Francisco. Sonny Lewis, this great tenor saxophone player, ended up playing. It was kind of fun. Here were some of the people that I'd known from my former life in Europe that came to play in *In C.*

BERNSTEIN: Is there a recording of that first performance?

RILEY: There is! Yes, but it's only good for historical curiosity because the mic . . . I don't know if we only used one mic, but it sounds like all you can hear is the tenor saxophone with some other instruments kind of vaguely in the background. So it must have been a mic right in front of the bell of the saxophone or something. [Laughs]

BERNSTEIN: During the first performance, Tony Martin created a visual component projected from among the performers?

RILEY: Yes, he did light projections. Yes, Tony was lighting—I think—almost every show I saw up there. This was another interesting development, a prelude to all these rock concerts with light shows. It was, I think, where a lot of that came from. Later, Tony started working for the Fillmore. And then they had the Trips Festival and all that.

BERNSTEIN: That program included some other works by you? One was called *I* [1964]?

RILEY: Yes, that was a piece I did when I got back. I had two tape recorders, probably both borrowed, and I started trying to set up a little studio in my home. I wanted to see if I could stretch the tape across the two tape recorders like the engineer did in France. Well, it was a lot funkier when I did it at home in my little studio in San Francisco, but I did this piece *I* and *Shoeshine* [1964], [which was] a cut up of a Jimmy Smith blues organ solo.

BERNSTEIN: There was another piece, I think, *In B♭ or Is It A♭?* [1964].

RILEY: Yes, which was an early version of *Poppy No Good and the Phantom Band.* Actually, Sonny Lewis was playing; this is before I started playing saxophone. At that time I was working with Sonny, having him play, you know, record patterns for me, and I put them through the tape delay, just like I'd done with Chet Baker and his band. Later, I learned to play saxophone when I went to New York in 1966, and I started playing it myself, developing and expanding it.

BERNSTEIN: There was one final piece, was it *Coule* [1964]?

RILEY: *Coule,* yes. That was the beginning of *Keyboard Study No. 1,* which was called *Coule.* A lot of times I'll change titles over the years as the piece develops. But yes, I think that was about it. Was there anything else on that program? *Music for "The Gift"* [1964] was played. What we decided for the first concert [at which] *In C* was played [was to start] out with all the recorded tape stuff, then at the end of the first half I played solo piano. We put all the chairs in the room of the Tape Music Center—they were folding chairs—against the wall. We didn't put them out for the audience, because I told Ramon and Tony I wanted to see people come in and sit where they want and organize themselves. "We have this big empty room. Let's not put them in rows." And it was really interesting because the way people came in and organized themselves. That was almost as much fun for me as the piece. [Laughs] You know, how they would put the chairs, not everybody was even facing the stage when the music was playing. The music with Chet Baker started about ten minutes before the concert started. So people walked into the room, and it started very informally. That was a little bit unusual for starting a concert in those days. But the people really seemed to like it. And even Alfred Frankenstein came to review it and liked it! You know, I mean, it was like a lot of the stuff we did there, at the Tape Music Center; I think [it] set the style, a kind of a "downtown" approach to presenting your work.

BERNSTEIN: What interests me about that whole period is how open it was. The new stuff that was happening there was unique. The counterculture and the whole scene in San Francisco, even rock music, played important roles. It was a sort of an alternative culture which included pieces [such as] *In C* and then later *Rainbow in Curved Air* [1968] and was intended for a broader audience. Is that right?

RILEY: Yes, the 1960s were a renaissance period in music and all across the spectrum. It was a very amazing time for musical creation, an exciting time to be living. I listened to the radio, AM radio all the time. I'd never listen to AM radio all the time today. Maybe it's who I was then and who I am now, but it was exciting! The newest releases coming from England were always playing on the Top Ten and were some interesting music that you had to listen to! A lot of things were happening—the formation of new rock groups, [for example]. Phil Lesh was always around the Tape Music Center, and he and Steve Reich bought a tape recorder together and shared it. Phil was writing orchestral pieces before he started playing with the Grateful Dead. There was a lot of crossover. I was connected with a lot of local jazz musicians, like Mel Martin. We had a rehearsal band together. John Gibson was in it. There weren't these strictly defined categories of serious musician, jazz musician, and rock musician. And psychedelic drug culture was mixed up with it all. Everybody had usually taken at least one trip, if not many, and that was an eye-opener for most people. How we were listening under the experience of mushrooms or LSD was not the way we were listening when not under that spell.

BERNSTEIN: Were you around for the Trips Festival?

RILEY: No. That was one of the things I really regretted that I missed.

BERNSTEIN: It must have been amazing to have so many members of the underground arts scene and the counterculture all in the same place.

RILEY: Yes, and remember, we had a war going on during that time. That's why I wonder if we'll have another renaissance. If we're going to be in an eternal war now, we better get another renaissance going.

NOTES

1. Both Young and Riley continued their associations with the avant-garde. For example, shortly after arriving in New York in the fall of 1960, Young began the famous concert series presented at Yoko Ono's loft on 112 Chambers Street that later led to the founding of Fluxus. As Keith Potter points out, Riley later intersected with the Fluxus movement, performing his *Concert for Two Pianos and Tape Recorders* in Wiesbaden, West Germany, in 1962. See Keith Potter, *Four Musical Minimalists: La Monte Young, Terry Riley, Steve Reich, Philip Glass* (Cambridge: Cambridge University Press, 2000), 101.

2. *Spectra* was performed on April 30, 1961, in a Composers' Forum concert at the California Palace of the Legion of Honor. See the chronology by Thomas M. Welsh in the present volume.

3. Terry Riley, *Music for "The Gift," Bird of Paradise, Mescalin Mix* (compact disk), Organ of Corti 1 (Malibu, Calif., 1998).

Anna Halprin

INTERVIEWED BY DAVID W. BERNSTEIN

Anna Halprin (formerly Ann) lives in a house built on a five-acre site on the slopes of Mount Tamalpais, surrounded by redwoods and other trees. The house has a large dance deck extending out into the woods, which she uses for teaching, rehearsals, and research. Halprin lives and works in harmony with nature.

Halprin's Dancers' Workshop moved to 321 Divisadero Street when the Tape Music Center relocated there in 1963, and she remained there after the Tape Music Center moved to Mills College in the summer of 1966. Her connections with composers at the Tape Music Center began several years earlier. When she moved to the Bay Area in 1945, Halprin brought with her a strong background in multidisciplinary work, which began with her early exposure to Walter Gropius and the Bauhaus School. An important influence on the Bay Area arts community, she created many opportunities for dancers, artists, and musicians to work together and, above all, provided them with a model for how to work collaboratively with artists from other disciplines. As the following interview shows, Halprin also did pioneering work using improvisation and forms of audience participation—new directions that became crucial elements of the aesthetics developed at the Tape Music Center.

BERNSTEIN: When did you first start working with composers at the San Francisco Tape Music Center?

HALPRIN: I worked with Morton Subotnick at the Venice Biennale in 1963. Morton was working with Luciano Berio, and we got to know each other through that connection. And when they found the building at 321 Divisadero, he asked if I wanted to move there as well. So that's how it started. It was really through my connection with Morton. I was just thrilled; it was a wonderful big old building, with lots of space for all kinds of activities, and it had one room that could be used as a studio for teaching. There was a huge auditorium, which we all used for performances, and a wonderful big lobby where we could exhibit our work. It was a facility that enabled us to do a variety of activities, which included having many guest musicians and guest dancers. I remember Julian Beck and the Living Theater visited us, and we had events with the Dancers' Workshop and the Living Theater. John Cage [attended] performances there, and sculptors [such as] Seymour Locks collaborated with us. He would have us build an environment [in which] people [would] move. Together we would create these wonderful, spontaneous . . . what Allan Kaprow called "happenings." But I never called them happenings; I always called them "events." I didn't even know about happenings. It was a wonderful time for a kind of Bauhaus type of experimentation by multidisciplinary artists working together. As a matter of fact, that word "multidisciplinary art" was really invented during that period. That was not a way that artists worked. In the past, a dancer might create a dance and then hire a musician to write the music. But this new collaborative method was very different. It was more about mixing up who did what. So [as was the case in our work with Locks], we became the sculptors because we were building the environment. But it was his "score"; it was his idea.

BERNSTEIN: Much of what you're saying about the way you worked parallels the way the musicians at the San Francisco Tape Music Center worked, combining lighting and theatrical elements as well. It was a matter of collaboration, not a matter of one person writing a piece and putting a name on it and having some assistance from others. In fact, there's an interview with Ramon Sender, Tony Martin, and Morton Subotnick in which they talk about not associating a specific composer's name with a piece because it was a collaborative effort. This is similar to what you are describing.

HALPRIN: Yes, it reminds me of the Bauhaus. My husband [Lawrence Halprin] is an architect and a landscape architect who studied at Harvard where [Walter] Gropius was the director. I was there at that time. For me, the idea of collaborating with other artists was a very natural way of working, because I always collaborated with Larry and was introduced to the Bauhaus and Oskar Schlemmer and his work in theater, in which he, too, worked with architects. [I also worked] with Fritz Perls, the Gestalt therapist, who was on the fringe of the Bauhaus and was bringing his Gestalt work into that scene.

It was a period when there was this desire to find new possibilities. It was right after World War II. I came to San Francisco with that background, which I brought with me from Harvard. And it was just a natural way of working for me by that time. I didn't even realize that we were doing anything avant-garde. It was just a natural way to work. And it was just a stroke of luck that through Morton I found this facility in which the Tape Music Center and—you know KPFA [the Berkeley public radio station] was there too.

BERNSTEIN: Yes, they shared it as well.

HALPRIN: As I mentioned to you earlier, I met Morton in Venice. The proscenium arch at the Opera House there was like a fireplace in a big living room. The audience was seated vertically, with only 150 people on the floor. But most of the audience was up and down. [At first] I didn't know how I would approach the space. At that time, I was already thinking architecturally, and already in a multidisciplinary way. Berio was also very multidisciplinary in his approach. So we got a cargo net and hung it. And that's where I collaborated with Tony Martin on hanging that cargo net and getting [it] in place and organized. [Tony and I] did a lot of work out in the woods here.

BERNSTEIN: The piece you are describing, *Esposizione,* is from 1963. In the spring of 1963, the Tape Music Center was located at 1537 Jones Street. Earlier, before they were formally called the San Francisco Tape Music Center, they were doing work at the San Francisco Conservatory . . .

HALPRIN: Yes, I remember that.

BERNSTEIN: . . . and some of the dancers that worked with you were involved in their performances, including John Graham, A. A. Leath, and Lynne Palmer.

HALPRIN: Yes.

BERNSTEIN: Do you remember the Sonics concerts at the San Francisco Conservatory?

HALPRIN: No.

BERNSTEIN: One of the pieces for the first Sonics concert was Terry Riley's *M . . . Mix* [1960–61], which I understand was used for either your *Four-Legged Stool* [1961] or *Five-Legged Stool* [1962].

HALPRIN: There's a *Three-Legged Stool* and a *Four-Legged Stool* and a *Five-Legged Stool.*

BERNSTEIN: [Laughs] I think Riley created the music for *The Four-Legged Stool?*

HALPRIN: I don't remember. [Did you know that] David Tudor took over *The Five-Legged Stool* in Yugoslavia? Morton was supposed to do the performance. He had to come back [to the United States] for some reason. He turned it over to Tudor. And Tudor, I remember, was under the piano most of the time; I don't know what he was doing under the piano. Tudor came into the scene through Morton. It was quite a community, wasn't it?

BERNSTEIN: Yes. A. A. Leath, John Graham, and Lynne Palmer participated in the

321 Divisadero
A Staircase to 1960s Dance Experimentation
JANICE ROSS

Three twenty-one Divisadero Street was an extraordinary incubator for dance as well as avant-garde music in San Francisco in the 1960s. The three-story Victorian building at this address housed the Tape Music Center and the San Francisco Dancers' Workshop, the radical group of dancers working with Ann (later Anna) Halprin. Both groups of artists were pushing the boundaries of their disciplines, and their collaborations helped chart the course for dance, music, and performance for the next several decades.

This association between dance and the Tape Music Center formally began in the fall of 1963, when Ann accepted an invitation to join the Tape Music Center in the building Ramon Sender had just rented at 321 Divisadero. Sender had been interested in Halprin's task-based dance work since his arrival in San Francisco in 1960, and three of her dancers, John Graham, A. A. Leath, and Lynne Palmer, often improvised on the concert series titled "Sonics" that Sender, Morton Subotnick, and Pauline Oliveros produced at the San Francisco Conservatory during 1961–62. "I was very enthused about Ann's work," Sender said, also noting that the 100-seat capacity of the main studio at 321 was just right for the center's experimental music concerts as well as San Francisco Dancers' Workshop events.[1]

Halprin's association with composers active in the Bay Area experimental music scene began in the summer of 1960 when La Monte Young, then a graduate student in music at UC Berkeley, contacted Halprin at the suggestion of John Cage. "I played her some of my music, including my *Trio for Strings* (1958), which had been recently recorded for me by Dennis Johnson for a performance called 'Avalanche No. 1' at UCLA," Young remembered. "I don't exactly recall the details, but she became interested in my work and my ideas and invited me to become the musical director." Within a couple of months, Young was eagerly recommending Halprin's work to other artists, many of whom would work at the Tape Music Center. Over the next six years, she would make eleven dances to scores by a half dozen composers (Luciano Berio, Morton Subotnick, Folke Rabe, and Pauline Oliveros, in addition to Young and Terry Riley). Until Young left for New York in late 1960, and Riley departed for Europe in February of 1962, their musical aesthetic dominated the sound environment for Ann's influential summer workshops. "These sounds were ancestors of the wild sounds—natural sounds, abstract sounds—interesting material juxtapositions such as metal on glass, metal on metal," Young said of the music he and Riley collaborated on extensively from late 1959 through 1960 for Halprin, beginning with her *Stillpoint* (1960) and *Visions* (1960). "Terry and I started making incredible sounds; they were very long and very live, and we'd really go inside of them, because they filled up the entire room of the studio."[2]

Late in 1960, over a period of three months, Halprin pulled together the previous two

---

1. Janice Ross, telephone conversation with Ramon Sender, San Francisco, 2004.
2. Richard Kostelanetz, "La Monte Young," in *Theatre of Mixed Means: An Introduction to Happenings, Kinetic Environments, and Other Mixed-Means Performances* (New York: Dial Press, 1968), 193.

years' experiments in improvisation to present her first long work, the fifty-minute *Birds of America, or Gardens without Walls. Birds* was structured as a series of seven directives for five dancers (Halprin, A. A. Leath, John Graham, and Daria and Rana Halprin). A large chart Halprin made listed the task-like actions each section was to encompass, which dancers were to perform them, and the encumbrances of props to be paired with these actions. Halprin was exploring the use of fragmented narratives in works of this period, which also included *The Four-Legged Stool,* for which Riley created what would come to be known as his *Mescalin Mix.* While Young and Riley were on a path that would lead in a few years to the launching of music minimalism, Halprin was unhinging dance from traditional narrative logic, not so much in quest for minimalism as out of a desire for stripped-down functional realism. Their sensibilities paired up well. Young once described his *Trio for Strings* as "a series of single sounds, each surrounded by silence and produced independently of melody."

Not all of Halprin's collaborations were as smooth. On May 4, 1964, Halprin collaborated with Jo Landor, Morton Subotnick, and Patric Hickey on *Yellow Cab,* an odd little surrealist solo set to a signature score of babbling, sighs, coughs, and brief fragments of conventional melody by Luciano Berio. The piece flummoxed the two local critics who covered it. "Miss Halprin was the solo performer, although it was not easy to find her under the mobile mess of paint-stained fabric that first covered her and under the sub-human, drippy dressing of her ogre-like make-up and costume," Alexander Fried wrote in the *San Francisco Examiner.* "When the ogre put on sunglasses, brushed its teeth, and lit a cigarette, the expressive value of the performance caved in."[3] Fried described the score as "agonizedly frustrated stammerings over guttural syllables that gradually emerged into freer sounds including laughter, sobs and chatter in an unknown language."[4] Berio's sound collage of the human voice made a tight parallel to physical collages of human actions and relations Halprin was also exploring.

The 1965 *Parades and Change,* the dance that would become Halprin's signature piece and solidify her reputation as a pathbreaker in the American dance avant-garde, was her last major work with Tape Music Center composers, in this instance, its cofounder, Morton Subotnick, and Folke Rabe, a Swedish musician who had been working at the center. The raison d'être of *Parades and Changes* was the setting up of certain structures to allow for spontaneously vital, what Halprin called "unarmored," moments. Each of the work's five sections was designed as a set of instructions containing parameters rather than the specifics of stage behavior. The most controversial was the "Undressing and Dressing" section, where the instructions were to undress in a smooth, slow, uninflected manner while maintaining eye contact with a member of the audience, and then to dress in the same consciously de-eroticized way. Morton Subotnick's score of ambient sounds, which for the dressing and undressing section included turning on a portable radio, undergirded the work's aura of fresh invention. "There was no chance in *Parades and Changes,*" Subotnick once remarked of its intent. "Everything was done by choice, but there was a

3. Alexander Fried, "A Tape Center Novelty—Is It a Parlor Trick?" *San Francisco Examiner,* May 1964; press clipping in Anna Halprin's archives, San Francisco Performing Arts Library and Museum.
4. Ibid.

great freedom in choice."[5] That freedom in choice was also one of Halprin's great legacies to American dance, influenced incalculably by her early shared tenancy with the Tape Music Center.

5. Janice Ross, "Interview with Morton Subotnick," Santa Fe, New Mexico, 1992.

Sonics concerts. One of the last concerts included a piece entitled *Smell Opera with Found Tape*. Do you remember that? It involved some of the dancers in your workshop going around with perfume bottles spraying the audience.

HALPRIN: [Laughs]

BERNSTEIN: Could you tell me about those dancers?

HALPRIN: Lynne Palmer and John Graham were, like so many of the dancers that I used, essentially trained as actors. And when they joined us, they came as students, and of course they were so talented, we immediately began to work together. John was teaching at San Francisco State, in the drama department, and Lynne just came as a student.

BERNSTEIN: What about A. A. Leath?

HALPRIN: I invited him to San Francisco. He came from the University of Wisconsin; that's where I studied dance. I wanted another teacher for [my school] at 1821 Union Street. And so I contacted Margaret H'Doubler, who was our [former] professor, and said, "Do you have somebody who would like to come out and teach with me?" And so she sent A. A. here. We started working together since about 1948. And I worked with A. A. and John for about eighteen years. So we really kind of grew up together artistically, the three of us.

In *Esposizione,* we were given lines to read—John, in particular, was given lines to read in Latin—and we spoke and we sang, and we were like acrobats. There's a lot of information about that piece. It was done with an [orchestra]. It was a really interesting piece because we never heard [the music] until the performance. The whole thing was done with timing. I brought a group of teenagers and stationed them at different places in the Opera House. At specific times, the dancers had to be at specific places. But the most important thing was, at a specific time, we had to be at the top of the cargo net, because the music was going to absolutely explode at that moment, and we all were to fall down and roll down the net.

We had a basket of tennis balls. And the basket was released and hundreds of

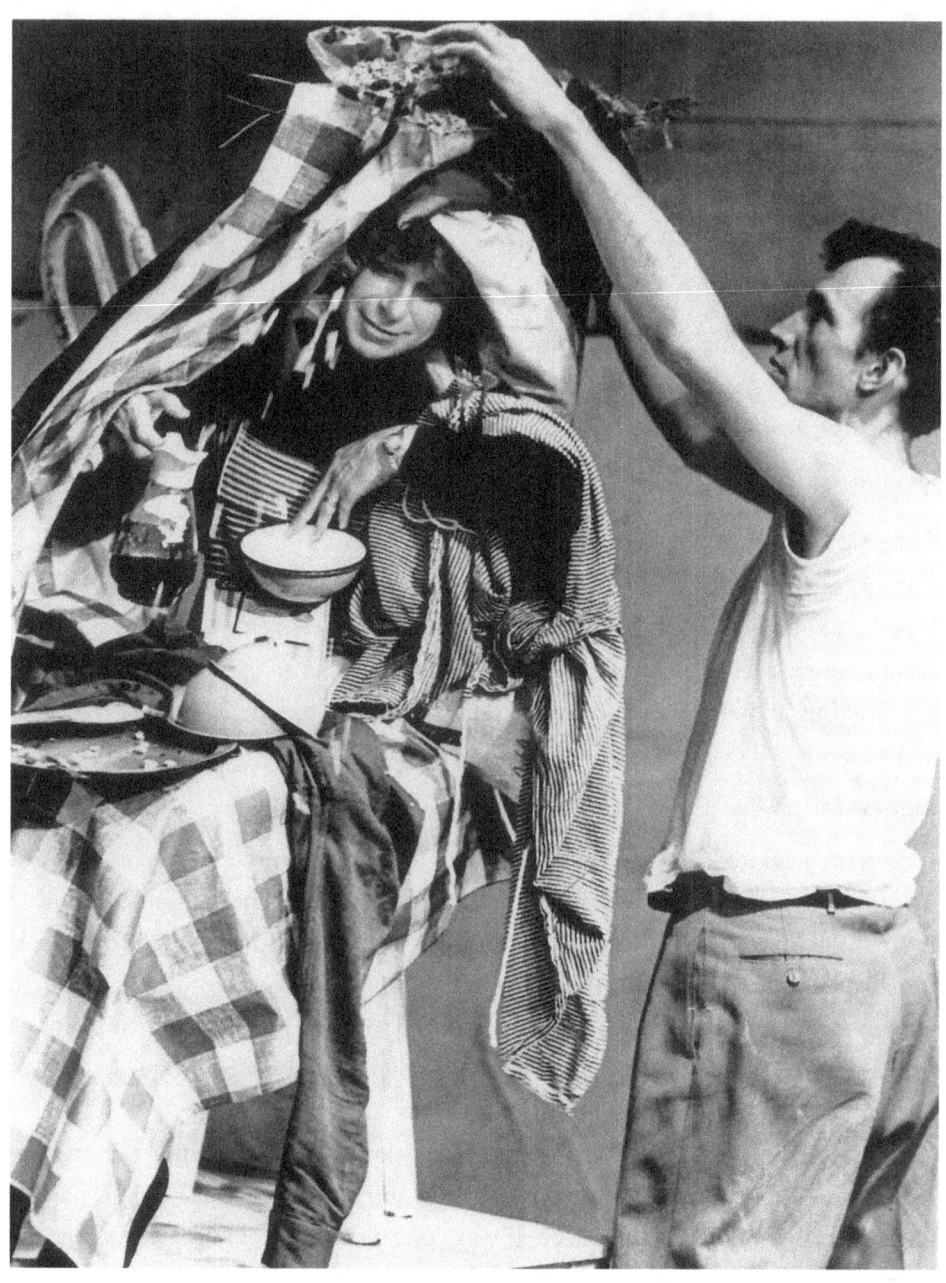

36 ANN HALPRIN AND JOHN GRAHAM PERFORMING *APARTMENT 6* (1965). PHOTOGRAPH BY HANK KRANZLER.

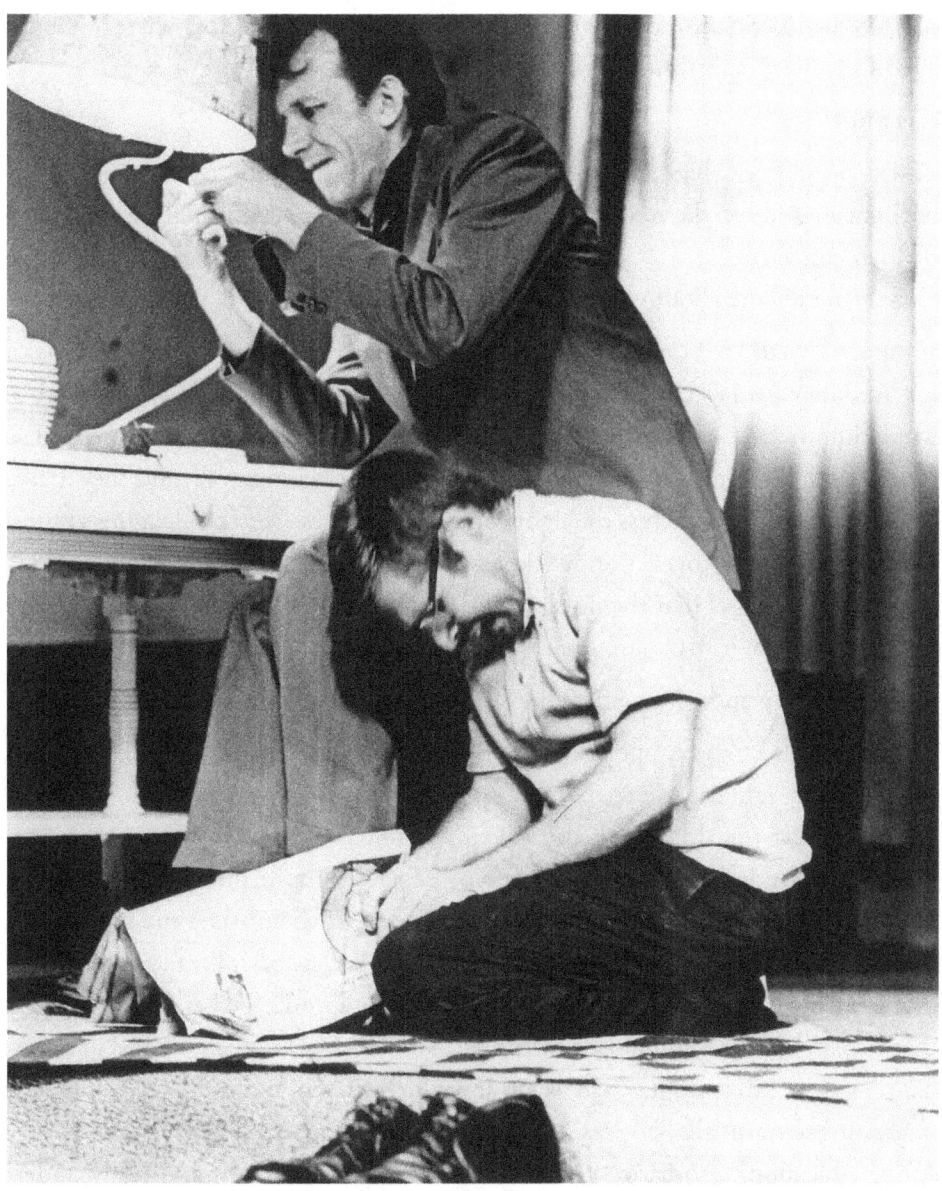

37 JOHN GRAHAM AND A. A. LEATH (ON FLOOR) PERFORMING *APARTMENT 6* IN SAN FRANCISCO (1965). PHOTOGRAPH BY HANK KRANZLER.

tennis balls came down with us and bounced out into the audience. So that was a very experimental piece that created quite a furor. As you know, in Italy, they love things that are controversial. We started the dance out in the plaza and then moved in and throughout the whole environment. And that's where we used that cargo net. It was a very interesting piece of collaborative work with Berio. John [Graham] was really quite remarkable in that piece.

BERNSTEIN: Berio came over to the United States in the early 1960s, where he taught at Mills College, substituting for Darius Milhaud.

HALPRIN: Yes.

BERNSTEIN: Berio had a very strong influence on the Tape Music Center. He brought in a lot of the new electronic works, which were featured during many of their concerts.

Can you tell me about your work with La Monte Young and Terry Riley?

HALPRIN: Well, La Monte and Terry were like partners. They worked together a lot. And they used to come to the studio down here. We would improvise and they would improvise. Some of the things that they would do would be to use the glass [doors] and just run their fingers down the glass or down the wall, and they'd take chairs and [drag them across the floor] until you get these very challenging sounds. While we would improvise, they would have their backs turned to us, so they wouldn't see us. The idea was that the music and the dance were going on [independently] at the same time. It may have been influenced by John Cage.

BERNSTEIN: I wonder how much they would have known about Cage at that time?

HALPRIN: I don't know, but you know that question comes up [for me]. I was not influenced by John or Merce, not one single bit. I just thought what they did was interesting and fun. I even asked them to teach here. But my influences were just being in nature and noticing that there'd be a foghorn in the distance and then the red berry would fall and a bird might fly overhead. It was at the time when I was first trying to reinvent movement, and to find a different basis for movement than modern dance, which was based on an idiosyncratic approach where all the dancers that were in Graham's group [for example] all looked like Graham, moved like Graham. I thought this was just like ballet. It was no different philosophically. It wasn't interesting to me at all. So I was searching for a new way to move. And I had a very strong education in somatics. I did human dissection for a year and really understood how the body works on a very objective level. I have a skeleton in my studio to this day, where I keep showing students: this is what a scapula looks like, and these are the trapezius muscles, and when you contract them, it does this. And then when it does this, it makes you feel a certain way that's different when you relax.

So I was really looking to the natural world to find out how nature operates. And this is where my information came from. John's came from philosophy [and especially from] Zen. He and Merce did a lot of meditation. They would stay here, when they visited San Francisco. They'd live with us. And John would go out and look for mushrooms in the woods. I think that there's a very important distinction,

38 ANN HALPRIN PERFORMING *APARTMENT 6* IN FINLAND (1965). PHOTOGRAPH BY OVE ALSTROM.

and sometimes I think historically that the idea is lost. That living in this area, you're close to nature. It's not an urban environment. Even San Francisco back in the 1960s was not as [it is now]. You didn't have shopping centers. It wasn't so consumer-oriented in an urban way. I can't speak for the musicians, but for me, my ideas came from being in nature and having a studio that was outdoors. I didn't have the indoor studio until fifteen years later. We worked in the rain. We just were like animals. We got used to being able to work outdoors. If it rained, it rained. So what if it rained. And that's where my ideas came from. And then they began to grow and change.

I called [working with chance] working with independent elements that could be organized in the way I deliberately chose to organize them. I didn't just throw pennies down and just say anything goes. I organized those independent elements in a way that was evocative to me. It wasn't really left totally to chance. However, having said all that, I understood where John and Merce were coming from, so we could speak the same language. We always respected our differences. And consequently,

39 ANN HALPRIN PERFORMING IN *BRANCH DANCE* (1957). PHOTOGRAPH © WARNER JEPSON.

we went in very different directions. We may have started out in a very similar direction, because we were trying to discard the cause and effect, and all the mythology that went with the art of that era. But where I developed it and where Merce developed it are very different.

I started from working with nature and trying to find what is the difference between a human, in terms of how we organize ourselves, and the natural world. Well, the difference is that human beings have images and feeling-states, and this connects us to real-life issues. And my work with Fritz Perls gave me the skills to be able to work with the emotional responses that come from movement. Merce doesn't work with that at all.

BERNSTEIN: Big difference.

HALPRIN: Big difference!

BERNSTEIN: Cage wanted to get away from emotional expression . . .

HALPRIN: . . . and I wanted to say, but that's what makes us human. And that's our nature. So I began to want to go to the next step for me, which was beginning to understand the aesthetics of nature. I'm surrounded by it. I live with it. That's why I took all my clothes off. I didn't take my clothes off because it was a sexual act. I took them off because I kept saying to myself, "Well, you know, a tree doesn't wear anything. [Laughs] It's just a tree."

BERNSTEIN: [Laughs]

HALPRIN: There's nothing more beautiful than seeing the human body. Artists have been working with nude bodies since time immemorial. There's nothing more beautiful than the natural state of a human body. That's why, when I introduced nudity, it wasn't meant to be anything shocking. I was surprised that I was arrested! I thought, "Why are you arresting me? It's not a sexual thing! There's nothing pornographic about this."

BERNSTEIN: We live in a very repressive society.

HALPRIN: Yes. It was when we went to Sweden and worked with Morton and Folke Rabe that we introduced nudity. Because the Swedes said this was a great ceremony of trust.

BERNSTEIN: The work you are describing is *Parades and Changes* [1965–67]?

HALPRIN: Yes. And when we came back to the States, we were arrested. [The *New York Times*] said that "the no-pants dancers return." [Laughs]

BERNSTEIN: Improvisation comes up a lot in discussions about your work. One thing that's really striking is how important improvisation was to many of the composers and performers active during the 1960s who were not directly connected to the jazz tradition. So this is another interesting parallel development.

HALPRIN: Definitely, we were all searching for new ways to compose. And there were no rules and there was no precedent. We were working with "There's no beginning and there's no end. There's no A-B-A form." When we went to school, you would study preclassic music with Louis Horst; that's not relevant anymore. So then what takes the place of that? We didn't know. So we improvised to find new possibilities. And invented all kinds of possibilities. So I think that's why improvisation happened. And it wasn't going on in the East Coast in dance. As a matter of fact, I was considered a nondancer because of that. And the director at UCLA—oh! Terry and La Monte and the Dancers' Workshop did a performance at UCLA [laughs] that was absolutely wild! And we used improvisation. At one point, the director of the dance department said that I had thrown dance back a hundred years. I mean, I was crucified by dancers! It was so bad, and they were so ugly about it, I didn't even align with dancers, with the dance world any more. I completely separated myself from the dance world and aligned myself with the Actor's Workshop, with [Herbert Blau and Jules Irving]. That there was an Actor's Workshop was really interesting because we were a Dancers' Workshop. The word "workshop" was new; now, everything's a workshop. But in those days the word "workshop" meant experimentation, collaboration. The Actor's Workshop was very experimental at that time.

[As I was saying] improvisation just came out of trying to find what new forms are possible. And that's where John [Cage] was very, I think, helpful to the musicians and to some of the more intellectual, we called them, the conceptual dancers. He offered some kind of a method. There was nothing to hang on to. And he offered a method. I think the young composers felt very anchored and grounded by that. But at the same time, they still weren't completely satisfied. They wanted, all of us wanted, to find our own way.

I think *Parades and Changes* was remarkable because there we changed roles. We would be musicians for Morton. He'd organize the whole idea of the piece. He actually was in many ways a co-choreographer. He worked with . . . did he ever tell you what the system was?

BERNSTEIN: No, he didn't.

HALPRIN: The idea was that there were all these different artists and each one of us would have a series of cell blocks, with different activities within [each of them]. And every time we went to a different environment, we would be able to relate to that particular environment—whether it was a stage or outdoors—and organize our cell blocks. I had, say, 10 × 10 cell blocks. Each cell block was a different activity. The lighting man would have different lighting possibilities, and each lighting idea would have its own cell block. And Charles Ross, a wonderful sculptor by the way, who is doing some remarkable things right now today, would have his activities. But when we went into a theater, we could order them any way we wanted, so you'd never have the same performance twice. I might have a piece of music with the dressing and undressing scene in one theater, but if I did it in another theater, I might have a different piece of music and a different lighting and a different landscape. Morton designed this system.

Parades and Changes was really a turning point where we began to find new methods of organizing material in a collaborative way, that had an open score feeling, but wasn't totally improvised. There was a structure to it. So out of the sort of improvisation which was "come into the room and do anything you want," we gradually began to find containers and structures that didn't box us in, but gave us opportunities to focus and to deepen and to refine.

And then Larry [Halprin] came along and designed RSVP ["Resources-Scores-'Valuaction'-Performance"] cycles. Larry wrote a book entitled *The RSVP Cycles: Creative Processes in the Human Environment.*[1] He was so important in the avant-garde scene because he evolved a scoring method, a way of working collectively, creatively, because collaborators didn't have a grounded way of working together. [Our work] was very improvisational, and consequently, we wasted a lot of time. I [remember] we would be up until four in the morning trying to figure out what we're going to do in this theater that's different than what we did in that theater.

Larry saw what we were doing and realized that what we needed was a [new] creative process. So he developed a system of scoring for theater that is really remarkable. The idea was that he made the creative process visible externally. So everybody could feed in ideas, and these were called "resources." So you could get a collection of ideas under "resources." And nothing was right or wrong; you could come up with any idea that you wanted, but you also needed to have an intention. So the resources would come from what your intention was. If your intention is to find new possibilities, then you keep the score very open.

Well, what is a score? A score is a series of activities over space, in time, with people. That simple. Now, what are your activities? How do you want to use people? How do you want to use the space and how much time do you want to give to this? Well, you can have scores ranging from one to ten; one being totally open, ten being totally closed. So, if you want really to use a score to generate new ideas, you keep it very open.

I do a thing called the *Planetary Dance,* which is now being done in about thirty-six different countries. It's very closed. You run in a circle. The people that want to run bigger and faster run in an outer circle; the people who want to move not so fast move in a center circle. The older people or disabled people move in the center circle. The only thing that's open is what you're running for. Because you're always running for something; you dedicate it to something. We just did it Sunday—we did a run for somebody in your life that needs your thoughts, your prayers. Then the second run was for something that you want to put out in the world. Then the third run is for your future, for the children—it's the children's run. But it's very closed, so everything, everybody has to run on the beat, but what you're running for is open. Because it's very closed and very simple, this score can be sent all around the world, and everybody can do it and adapt it to the needs of their own community. Every year, we take a different community theme, whether it's violence in schools, or cancer, or AIDS, or the environment.

So [Larry] worked out this system so that we could all collaborate in a very efficient way . . .

BERNSTEIN: . . . that was also free.

HALPRIN: It allowed everybody to be in the same "place." We all had this thing that we could work with that was externalized. And that was a big, big breakthrough. And he started introducing scoring when we were doing *Parades and Changes*.

BERNSTEIN: Your description reminds me of indeterminate scores, another parallel development in music.

HALPRIN: Yes.

BERNSTEIN: And again what you were saying about the need for freedom to try to move to another level reminds me of something that John Cage said, "Experimental activity is an activity the outcome of which is unknown."

HALPRIN: Well, I think that John, in music, is a little bit more abstract. But when you're in theater, and you're a human being out there and you are the instrument, not just sound, but you're a human instrument, you begin to get into content. And he wasn't interested in content. But you must be interested in content, if you're a human being out there with your instrument that feels things. You can't do a movement like this [gestures] and not feel anything, or a movement like this [gestures] and not feel anything. So you have to go somewhere else. You can't, I can't . . . I can't as a human being work abstractly.

BERNSTEIN: There is a very important point that most people miss about Cage. Because when they see his indeterminate scores, they compare them to improvisation, to a certain kind of spontaneity. But it's not true. David Tudor would go over those scores and measure every little nuance and then make his own score.

HALPRIN: Yes.

BERNSTEIN: And then perform it as if it were a normally notated piece.

HALPRIN: Yes.

BERNSTEIN: So it's very different. It's not spontaneous. It's not a way to channel improvisational activity. But others, during the 1960s, began to experiment with that and now of course there are many types of real-time scores, similar in spirit to what you're talking about.

I think all of this trying to break away from artistic traditions and trying to look for different aesthetic worlds during the 1960s was also part of the broader picture of breaking away from the conservativism prevalent during the 1950s.

HALPRIN: We called it the "establishment."

BERNSTEIN: So there was this political aspect to what artists were doing at that time. More specifically, there was also a kind of intersection between the counterculture and the avant-garde.

HALPRIN: The Living Theater was the epitome of that.

BERNSTEIN: And the Mime Troupe.

HALPRIN: And the Mime Troupe.

BERNSTEIN: It seems to me you were also that way. And your work continues to be politically, socially conscious.

HALPRIN: The newest piece I did, *Intensive Care,* is really all about my response to the Iraq war. Well, we were doing a lot [back in the 1960s]. We were taking to the streets. We marched down Market Street carrying placards that were blank, telling people to put their protest on the placard. So we didn't say what the protest was, but people would say, "Well, what are you protesting? " Because it was blank. And we would say, "What would you like to protest?" So that was one of the things. We were arrested when we were doing some street theater during the Vietnam War. So most of our political stuff was done on the streets, and was designed specifically as protest. And then just being antiestablishment was a political statement. Not following the rules of the game.

We were also doing street theater when we were at 321 Divisadero. People would be interested in what we were doing and then we would invite them to the studio to work on *Citydance* [1976–77]. So we were trying to break the barrier between the performer and the viewer. We spent . . . years, and I'm still now breaking that barrier.

BERNSTEIN: Do you remember the Trips Festival?

HALPRIN: Yes.

BERNSTEIN: Maybe I could get you to say a little bit about that.

HALPRIN: Well, . . . they used me a lot to work the audience, and give them things to do in movement. And that's what I did. I don't remember any specific performance. I was like a catalyst who helped the participants—[gave] them ideas of what to do.

And what about the Straight Theater? Do you know about the Straight Theater? That was interesting because they brought in Janis Joplin, the Butterfield Blues Band, and the Jefferson Airplane. They were all there. The Straight Theater was in the Haight-Ashbury district, right around the corner from the Tape Music Center. They put on these big rock events, and they would use very wonderful lighting. I don't know if Tony Martin did lighting for them. But they worked with all these avant-garde projectionists and lighting people. And I worked with them.

Also, across the street from the Tape Music Center was this nightclub with John Handy.

BERNSTEIN: The jazz player.

HALPRIN: Yes. There were no boundaries. There was so much interaction between what was going on that there were absolutely no boundaries. What was popular art, what was fine art, what was experimental art all got kind of moved together, which I thought was quite exciting. I thought the rock scene was magnificent, and I was very excited to be invited to participate with them.

NOTE

1. Lawrence Halprin, *The RSVP Cycles: Creative Processes in the Human Environment* (New York: George Braziller, 1969).

Stewart Brand

INTERVIEWED BY DAVID W. BERNSTEIN

A Swiss chemist named Albert Hofmann discovered the hallucinogenic properties of LSD (lysergic acid diethylamide) in 1943.[1] LSD found its way to America during the 1950s, when it attracted the attention of psychologists interested in exploring the nature of mental disorders, particularly schizophrenia. Around the same time, the Central Intelligence Agency assessed the drug's potential as a mind-control agent. In the late 1950s and early 1960s, researchers employed the drug in LSD-based therapy sessions.

The British novelist Aldous Huxley, who had earlier experimented with mescaline and first took LSD in 1955, saw these drugs as a means to attain higher levels of consciousness.[2] But it was not until the 1960s, when ex–Harvard professor Timothy Leary and the novelist Ken Kesey and the Merry Pranksters arrived on the scene that LSD use began to escalate around the country. Both Leary and Kesey were interested in the drug's transformative potential. But while Leary saw LSD as a means to achieve spiritual growth through an exploration of an individual's inner self, Kesey used the drug to create uncontrolled and often chaotic situations within which participants could move beyond traditional social norms.

In the early 1960s, Stewart Brand was among the first participants in a study of the effects of LSD conducted at Myron Stolaroff's International Foundation for Advanced Study in Menlo Park, California.[3] He later became one of Kesey's close associates, participated in the latter's acid parties and several of Kesey's so-called Acid Tests, and produced the Trips Festival. Brand's visit to the Warm Springs Indian reservation in Oregon in 1962 inspired a deep appreciation for Native American culture that led to the creation of "America Needs Indians," a multimedia presentation extolling the virtues of Native American civilization, which he presented at the Trips Festival and at other venues. In the late 1960s, his interest in the writings of Buckminster Fuller led him to create the *Whole Earth Catalog,* a compendium of information on alternative lifestyles and technologies and environmentalism, which served as a "survival manual" for the counterculture.

BERNSTEIN: I understand that you graduated from Phillips Exeter Academy [in New Hampshire] in the 1950s . . .

BRAND: Yes.

BERNSTEIN: . . . and then you went to Stanford and studied biology.

BRAND: Right.

BERNSTEIN: In 1958, Ken Kesey enrolled in the Stanford writing program; did you know him then?

BRAND: No, not at all. I did not realize he was there in 1958.

BERNSTEIN: Do you remember Vic Lovell?[4]

BRAND: Only later through Kesey and Jim Fadiman.[5]

BERNSTEIN: Apparently, Kesey volunteered to do some drug testing at Menlo Park Veterans' Hospital.

BRAND: Right.

BERNSTEIN: Was that connected to the International Foundation for Advanced Study?

BRAND: No, that was a different scene; that was charging for sort of therapy-based LSD trips. There's actually quite a good description of the whole process in a new book by John Markoff called *What the Dormouse Said: How the Counterculture Shaped the Personal Computer Industry*. Myron Stolaroff was the keeper of that thing. He was inspired by Harry Rathbun [who taught business law at Stanford] and some of the other turned-on engineers around Stanford. So he started that operation. It's quite different from what Kesey was doing.

BERNSTEIN: So you meet Kesey much later, probably after 1963, maybe 1964?

BRAND: Yes, right in there 1963–64, I think I had already photographed Indians up in Oregon at that point. I had a mutual friend who knew him, Jim Fadiman, and that's how we hooked up.

BERNSTEIN: In 1962, you were at the San Francisco Art Institute . . .

BRAND: Right

BERNSTEIN: . . . studying photography.

BRAND: That's right. I was at the Art Institute a couple of times. Once I was there right after Stanford studying photography. Somewhere in there, I took Kenneth Rexroth's course on poetry. After the army, I was studying photography again at San Francisco State College with Jack Wellfons. That was in 1962–63.

BERNSTEIN: How did you first meet Kesey?

BRAND: I got his mail address and sent him some photographs and he called me by telephone and said, "Come on by," and I went on by at Perry Lane.

BERNSTEIN: Perry Lane was a bohemian community near Stanford University?

BRAND: Yes.

BERNSTEIN: You weren't living there, were you?

BRAND: No, I think I was in San Francisco by then, in North Beach.

BERNSTEIN: In July 1964, Kesey took that bus ride to the South and up the East Coast. Were you on the bus?

BRAND: I was on and off the bus at various times. I did not take part in the famous trip to the World's Fair that went cross-country.

BERNSTEIN: So you were not at [Leary's estate at] Millbrook [near Poughkeepsie, New York].

BRAND: I had been at Millbrook separately on my own before that, but I was not there for the peculiar intersection between Kesey and Leary at Millbrook.

BERNSTEIN: So was the story factual that Kesey and the others were sort of snubbed at Millbrook and just left?

BRAND: I think so, by and large. I wasn't there, but Tom Wolfe described it quite accurately, at least in impressionistic terms.[6]

BERNSTEIN: Can you tell me about "America Needs Indians"? Was it first presented at the Committee Theater?

BRAND: It was certainly there in a public way. There were couple of Taos Indians in town that were part of it. A photographer named Walter Chappell plugged into it at some point. And then I did it on and off until the Trips Festival in 1966, which was the last time I did "America Needs Indians." It was presented at colleges and in people's homes; they did it at one or two of Kesey's Acid Tests, a short version. I also did it at Berkeley.

BERNSTEIN: Could you describe it? I understand it was a multimedia event.

BRAND: It was a multimedia show with two slide projectors, two eight millimeter film projectors, sound, and tape, which was separate from those, and a certain amount of live action.

BERNSTEIN: Who did the sound?

BRAND: I did.

BERNSTEIN: Were you interested in Marshall McLuhan back then?

BRAND: Yes, we were all reading his works. I did not meet him until years later. There was also a group back East called USCO that was much influenced by McLuhan

BERNSTEIN: That included Gerd Stern.

BRAND: Yes, Gerd, Steve Durkee, and the whole crowd . . .

BERNSTEIN: . . . and Michael Callahan, who also worked at the San Francisco Tape Music Center.

BRAND: Michael Callahan and John Brockman. It's nice to hear Michael Callahan's name. I haven't heard that in a while.

BERNSTEIN: Did you attend any of the San Francisco Tape Music Center concerts?

BRAND: I don't know. I am trying to recall how in fact I intersected with Ramon [Sender] and those guys. Most of the creative people in the Bay Area seemed to know each other then.

BERNSTEIN: Were you involved in Kesey's Acid Parties?

BRAND: I was.

BERNSTEIN: The Acid Tests came after that. Were you at the one in Palo Alto?

BRAND: I was at the one at Palo Alto and one or two others.

BERNSTEIN: They did have one at the Fillmore. Isn't that true?

BRAND: Yes, that's right. I was at that one. I remember Neal Cassady at that one.

BERNSTEIN: Donald Buchla told me he brought the Buchla [synthesizer] to the Acid Tests. Do you remember that?

BRAND: Yes.

BERNSTEIN: So he supplied some of the music.

BRAND: Yes.

BERNSTEIN: Who was the sculptor who did the "Thunder Machines"?

BRAND: Ron Boise. Ron Boise was a sheet-metal sculptor who created large and humorous, and on several occasions, noisy sculptures. Kesey loved him; he was big part of [the scene] for a little while.

BERNSTEIN: There was also Ken Babbs. Was he responsible for the so-called edge during the Acid Tests and Parties, kind of getting people "off guard"?

BRAND: Kesey was usually in charge of the "edge." Babbs was in charge of motivation; getting people on and off of the bus or organizing things in some way. There were a few ex-military people involved—I was one, Babbs was another, a marine helicopter pilot—who were responsible for getting things done.

BERNSTEIN: He used the term "Briefings"?

BRAND: I wouldn't be surprised.

BERNSTEIN: [Laughs] Were the Hell's Angels involved?

BRAND: Yes, out at La Honda. Kesey kept a nice connection with them for a number of years. There was one in particular that I liked named "Gut."

BERNSTEIN: So what inspired you to organize the Trips Festival?

BRAND: I really didn't intend that should happen, but [it turned out that] the Pranksters were not going to be able to pull it off, but hopefully I could. So I picked up the phone and started organizing stuff. Ramon Sender was one of the first people I called and he waded into it. And later we put together his group, Ben Jacopetti, "America Needs Indians," the "Congress of Wonders," and everyone else.

BERNSTEIN: Before the Trips Festival there was another event on January 8th at the Fillmore. Around 2,400 people showed up.

BRAND: That was probably the Fillmore Acid Test.

BERNSTEIN: I noticed that you advertised the Trips Festival very well.

BRAND: We took the bus around downtown and received quite a bit of press from that.

BERNSTEIN: In a sense, wasn't there a meeting of the San Francisco avant-garde arts scene and the counterculture at the Trips Festival?

BRAND: Yes, it was a brief intersection.

BERNSTEIN: It was pretty amazing.

BRAND: Kesey's major connection with the avant-garde was the beatniks, primarily through Cassady and Allen Ginsberg. He did not particularly connect with the other acts in the Trips Festival I would say. The Trips Festival was like "a changing of the guard" in the Bay Area [arts scene]. The Pranksters and the Grateful Dead pretty much stole the show. Bill Graham, whom we hired late in the game to help produce it, grabbed that and ran with it. As far as I know, the "Congress of Wonders" did hardly any acts after that. There wasn't that much more Tape Music Center. There was no more "America Needs Indians." Sandy Jacobs was never heard from again. [Laughs] It was the beginning of the Grateful Dead and the end of everybody else.

BERNSTEIN: I was thinking about that when I read some of the accounts of what happened. The program was very impressive. You have "America Needs Indians." You have "Revelations," Ann Halprin, and the San Francisco Tape Music Center. Did you have the chance to present all of this, or was there more chaos and pandemonium?

BRAND: They all were put on; they all were fine. And people sort of applauded politely, and then they wanted to dance. Nobody booed or walked out or anything like that. They all were having a "high old time." We added a number of things that did not exist as their own acts. One I invented was getting a trampoline artist to dive off the balcony onto a trampoline in the strobe lights. He was doing tricks in the strobes [that seemed to be] impossibly high in the air. It was one of the finer "mind blows" there, because people were not sure whether they saw it or imagined seeing it, because it seemed beyond what was humanly possible. [Laughs] And he wore a ski mask, because I paid him $100, or something like that, so he could keep his amateur standing.

BERNSTEIN: On one day you scheduled a series of what was called "side-trips." The first one featured Chloe Scott and Lou Harrison.

BRAND: Chloe Scott was avant-garde and really was best buddies with Kesey and that whole scene. That was really probably more of an intersection than any other. Chloe was really tight with the Pranksters.

BERNSTEIN: Another side-trip featured Pauline Oliveros's *A Theater Piece*. Do you remember that?

BRAND: No, I'm sorry, I don't.

BERNSTEIN: It included a collage of rock music with tape delay.

BRAND: I used tape delay when I was doing my tape stuff on the East Coast to cause phase effects, so you could make a sound go through a person's head by going in and out of phase, driving from one side of their head to the other like a freight train.

BERNSTEIN: [Laughs]

BRAND: One piece using tape delay that I haven't yet heard, but wanted to hear was by Ramon Sender, where he took Beethoven or something and ran a read-write loop on it so the loop was going around. As it plays it, it's recording it and you get the gradual degradation. It very, very gradually goes to white noise. What I wanted to hear was basically to do that backwards, take a piece of music on tape, run it back-

San Francisco Underground Rock

DAVID W. BERNSTEIN

In the wake of the Trips Festival (January 21–23, 1966), the vibrant San Francisco experimental arts scene began to lose steam. Many of the avant-garde acts in the Trips Festival never performed again; the Actor's Workshop had already moved to New York; and the San Francisco Tape Music Center disbanded the following summer, taking a new form within an institutional setting at Mills College. But the dynamic interplay between experimental art, avant-garde aesthetics, and popular culture that culminated with the Trips Festival contributed to another exciting development.

As the Trips Festival organizer Stewart Brand observed, "the Grateful Dead stole the show," a fact duly noted by Bill Graham, who shortly after the festival began to present rock concerts accompanied by light shows at the Fillmore. An amalgam of folk and rock 'n' roll had already supplanted jazz and folk music as staples of the "neo-beatnik" community in San Francisco. The Beatles and the Rolling Stones had taken the world by storm. Bob Dylan had "gone electric"—much to the chagrin of folk music "purists"—by plugging in an electric guitar on July 25, 1965, at the Newport Folk Festival, performing "Maggie's Farm," with keyboardist Al Kooper and guitarist Michael Bloomfield.[1] A month earlier, at the Red Dog Saloon, a remodeled turn-of-the-century hotel in Virginia City, Nevada, a San Francisco rock band called the Charlatans had taken the stage, dressed in western garb. A wave of rock bands—including the Jefferson Airplane, the Grateful Dead, the Mystery Trend, the Great Society, Quicksilver Messenger Service, Big Brother and the Holding Company, and Country Joe and the Fish—had begun to appear at various venues such as the Matrix, Mother's, the Avalon Ballroom, the Longshoremen's Hall, and the Fillmore Auditorium. As the Great Society guitarist Darby Slick observed, looking back on this period in San Francisco:

> And what was going on here that was new? It was the dance drama transformation of the young beatniks into hippies. We had read the new poets: Allen Ginsberg, Lawrence Ferlinghetti; seen the new movies: Truffaut, Fellini; had heard the music of Miles and 'Trane and Stockhausen and John Cage, and, most recently the Stones and the Beatles. We were alive, for Christ's sake, and the fifties had to end.[2]

The San Francisco bands sought to develop a distinct sound, free, as much as this was possible, from the powerful influence of the "British invasion." At the beginning, the new sounds of San Francisco rock had a somewhat restrained style, drawing from its roots in folk music and the blues, sometimes including extended improvisations loosely resembling Indian classical music (as in, for example, the Great Society's rendition of "Sally Go 'round the Roses" and the opening of that band's version of "White Rabbit"). The folk-rock scene in San Francisco was very much a local phenomenon popular in the dance halls; it had not yet attracted the attention of major record companies.

In 1965, San Francisco rock was still in its formative stages, but a new, far more dy-

---

1. Dominick Cavallo, *A Fiction of the Past: The Sixties in American History* (New York: St. Martin's Press, 1999), 174.

2. Darby Slick, *Don't You Want Somebody to Love: Reflections on the San Francisco Sound* (Berkeley: SLG Books, 1991), 12.

namic style was emerging with lightning speed. After attending Ken Kesey's first Acid Test in Soquel, a band called the Warlocks (later renamed the Grateful Dead) played at the Acid Tests in San Jose, Palo Alto, Muir Beach, and at the Fillmore. Phil Lesh recalls that typically there were tape loops, tape delay effects, and sophisticated setups with mixers, microphones, and Möbius-strip speakers, several projection screens with film clips and liquid projections, and Ron Boise's "thunder machine," a metal sculpture adorned with contact mics.[3] (It was also very likely that Don Buchla was present, creating sounds from his "Buchla Box.") Describing the Fillmore Acid Test, Lesh compares the event to music by Berio, Stockhausen, and Cage, remembering it as a varied and "finely sculptured, and very dense sonic landscape," in which musical and so-called nonmusical sounds had equal status.[4] Lesh had classical training as a composer and, along with his friend Tom Constanten, whom he had met at UC Berkeley in 1961, studied composition with Luciano Berio at Mills College (where Steve Reich was a graduate student). Constanten, who performed with the Grateful Dead for several years in the late 1960s, attended Stockhausen's seminars at Darmstadt.[5] Both Lesh and Constanten were active participants in the Bay Area new music scene. Taking on dual roles as rock musicians and composers of "serious" music was a natural thing to do in San Francisco's open cultural environment at that time, especially during the period leading up to the Trips Festival's convergence of rock 'n' roll, the counterculture, and experimental music. It is thus certainly not surprising that Lesh and Constanten crossed over between rock and electronic music, and that Grace Slick, Janis Joplin, the Charlatans, and Big Brother and the Holding Company all attended concerts at the Tape Music Center.

By 1966, a new style called psychedelic rock, integrating disparate musical sources—including the blues, Indian ragas, jazz, musique concrète, Stockhausen, and Cage—had taken root in Los Angeles and London. But San Francisco, the "Liverpool of America" as the *San Francisco Chronicle* critic Ralph Gleason put it, was at the center of this development.[6] Although rock musicians were experimenting with various studio techniques and forms of distortion on the electric guitar as early as the 1950s, the new genre inspired further exploration for new sounds. Feedback, no longer an accident to be avoided, became musical material, such as in the opening of the Jefferson Airplane's "The Ballad of You and Me and Pooneil" (1967) (and, of course, in the legendary guitar solos by Jimi Hendrix, arguably the greatest master of this technique). Another example occurs at the end of the Grateful Dead's "Caution (Do Not Stop on the Tracks)" from their second album *Anthem of the Sun* (1968), where the band builds an extended closing passage lasting close to four minutes by exploring various harmonic inflections created with feedback. Both the Grateful Dead and the Jefferson Airplane used tape collage. For example, Tom Constanten's *Electronic Study no. 3* (1962), a tape piece created in the APELAC electronic music studio in Brussels,[7] appears in "We Leave the Castle," at the close of the first section of *Anthem of the Sun*. (Constanten also plays prepared piano on the same album.) The Jefferson Airplane's *After Bathing at Baxter's* (1967) includes a tape com-

3. Phil Lesh, *Searching for the Sound: My Life with the Grateful Dead* (New York: Little, Brown, 2005), 66ff.
4. Lesh, *Searching for the Sound*, 70–71.
5. Tom Constanten, *Between Rock and Hard Places* (Eugene, Or.: Hulogosi, 1992), 35ff.
6. Ralph J. Gleason, "Dead Like Live Thunder," *San Francisco Chronicle*, March 19, 1967.
7. Constanten, *Between Rock and Hard Places*, 176.

> position entitled "A Small Package of Value Will Come to You, Shortly," ending with the poet John Donne's phrase "No man is an island," repeated with tape delay. The first section of *Anthem of the Sun* uses a subtle application of delay, superimposing four live performances of "That's It for the Other One," which become minutely out of phase.[8]
>
> The two albums by the Grateful Dead and the Jefferson Airplane appeared after the often recognized early examples of psychedelic rock such as the Beatles' "Tomorrow Never Knows" from their album *Revolver* (1966) and several tracks (most notably on "The Return of the Monster Magnet") from *Freak Out!* (1966) by Frank Zappa and the Mothers of Invention. However, all the elements of psychedelic rock were already in place in San Francisco in 1965 when psychedelic rock was an underground phenomenon.
>
> The San Francisco bands arose independently from mainstream rock 'n' roll, and had much in common with community-based artists' collectives such as the San Francisco Tape Music Center. Many of bands were by and large more concerned with making music than with selling large numbers of records. Later, several bands rebelled against the recording industry, demanding not only artistic control over their music and performances but also to oversee the packaging and distribution of their records.[9] This was the case with the Grateful Dead, who refused to sign a recording contract until they persuaded Warner Brothers to agree to their demands.[10] Adopting an artistic and a social agenda shared by avant-garde artists and musicians, bands like the Grateful Dead saw themselves as members of an independent musical subculture. Some of the bands, like Country Joe and the Fish, articulated a more oppositional political stance. They all sought to break down the barriers between audience and performers in order to advance a vision of a new society expressed through the shared experience of music and dance.
>
> 8. Lesh, *Searching for the Sound*, 128.
> 9. Cavallo, *Fiction of the Past*, 146.
> 10. Ibid., 161.

wards as a loop so that I could start with absolutely pure white noise, which would very, very gradually—you would never know exactly where it started—become this recognizable piece of music. As far as I know, no one ever did that.[7]

BERNSTEIN: After the Trips Festival things began to wind down and change. The Tape Music Center, by the end of the 1966 season, received a grant from the Rockefeller Foundation, which stipulated that they had to affiliate with an institution in order to get the funding. At this point, the Tape Music Center moved to Mills College.

BRAND: Yes, that's right. I sort of remember that.

BERNSTEIN: Ramon Sender went to Morning Star [Ranch, a commune in Sonoma County], and I guess you went there too?

BRAND: No. Lou Gottlieb, who was doing a newspaper column at the time in the *San Francisco Chronicle*, . . . wrote about us. This may have been how he and Ramon hooked up. Anyway, Lou started Morning Star, and Ramon went off to that. That was the main event for a while for those guys.

BERNSTEIN: So you weren't at Morning Star?

BRAND: I don't think I ever went there.[8]

BERNSTEIN: Didn't you go to a commune in New Mexico?

BRAND: Yes, I was early on in the founding of Lama Foundation, which I guess is still there. I was in Drop City for a while in Colorado. I probably stopped by a few other places when I was selling *Whole Earth Catalog*s in 1968, but I don't remember much else.

BERNSTEIN: Getting back to the changes. I noticed looking back over the history that the Diggers had their famous dispute with the merchants in the Haight.[9]

BRAND: I was not much part of the Haight action, and I did not know the Diggers. At the time, I was aware of what they were doing. Later, I became friends with Peter Coyote. That was many years later. By the time the Haight-Ashbury was really happening, I was down at the Peninsula on Alpine Road.

One thing that did persist in terms of avant-garde art from the Trips Festival on, and through the Fillmore and everything else, was the light shows. The Trips Festival was pretty much the first or one of the first places where light shows, which had become a medium then for a few years, were really put together with rock 'n' roll. And so the Grateful Dead was blasting away and images were blasting away somewhat in synch with them on the wall. That whole aspect of the show was so much more effective than anything else. That's what took off. And so then, within a couple weeks, Bill Graham was taking over the Fillmore and advertising shows that include "the sight and sounds of the Trips Festival," by which he meant Buchla, Tony Martin, and Bill Hamm.

BERNSTEIN: I understand that Bill Hamm worked with you at San Francisco State.

BRAND: Yes, I did a thing called "Whatever It Is" when Kesey was a fugitive and we hid him there secretly in a back room talking live over a tape. I don't remember all of the elements for that one, but that was a kind of follow-up to the Trips Festival.

BERNSTEIN: Was that when you staged an "apocalypse"?

BRAND: Yes, Buchla was in the thick of that one.

BERNSTEIN: . . . and there was a countdown?

BRAND: I forget whether we did it live or on tape, but it was a countdown to nuclear missiles coming in, and at zero we popped a bunch of flashbulbs and the electricity went out and people were left alone in the dark. That was nice. It was a bright idea to interrupt a rock 'n' roll show in case anyone was having a good time. [Laughs]

BERNSTEIN: Everybody was having a good time, but I get the sense that there was another aspect to all these activities, an inspiration to change the world in some way.

BRAND: The Diggers were more political than the others. Remember in the thick of all this was the Mime Troupe. In fact, Bill Graham got his start doing benefits for them. They were really an inspiration for what I did at the Trips Festival. They were a political agitprop theater group. So theater, propaganda, and political ideas were woven all together a fair amount. You had the Committee doing very good satire, some of which had a bit of that edge, Scott Beach, and everybody.

There also was a divergence and Kesey [and I were] part of this. Sort of a New Left was emerging as a political force ever since the Free Speech Movement in 1964 at Cal, and increasingly as an anti-Vietnam movement. I had been in the military and didn't believe what people said about soldiers. I was [also] inspired by Buckminster Fuller, who said pay no attention to politics. Kesey, for what reasons I do not know, pretty much walked away from the political frame entirely. Here's what Kesey was not: Kesey was not, by and large, avant-garde. He connected with a few things like light shows and Chloe Scott. He was not spiritual. He did not take on Tim Leary's, Dick Albert's approach to what psychedelics were all about. And he was not political. He was invited to be part of Vietnam Day. It must have been in Berkeley or Oakland or the border between them, and he went, but he disappointed people. He just played the harmonica. That was when I was along, and I remember going over on the bus, and he was dubious about the whole thing. So he pretty much made whatever was going on with his kind of art and his kind of psychedelics much more personal and much less either political or artistic-movement oriented—personal in the sense of beatnik personal. I suppose some quasi-existential get out there and be brave and do incredibly brave things and see what happens.

BERNSTEIN: It's an idea of personal transformation rather than societal.

BRAND: Yes.

BERNSTEIN: Weren't the Diggers reacting against a certain form of parochialism? You can tune in, turn on, and have a great community, but what do you do after it's all over? What kind of improvement will you offer the rest of the world?

BRAND: That was the standard critique of the recreational approach to drugs. It was not politically engaged enough, and we were not reading Mao Tse-tung. [Laughs]

What freaks me out a little bit still is that nobody ever apologized for that. Nobody ever said that [they were] out there promoting one of the three monsters of the twentieth century and never said, "Oops." I think we had ways to know what the Cultural Revolution and the Great Leap actually were, but we didn't take the trouble to find out or act on the knowledge. It's a blot on that memory.

BERNSTEIN: It's interesting that you mentioned Buckminster Fuller.

BRAND: We were all reading [Fuller's collection of essays] *Nine Chains to the Moon*[10] and going to Fuller's lectures and reading Marshall McLuhan carefully and at length.

BERNSTEIN: So Fuller was one of the inspirations you had for *The Whole Earth Catalog*?

BRAND: Yes, I think a primary one.

BERNSTEIN: I am thinking that you moved on from the drug culture, which I'm not thinking of in a negative sense at all.

BRAND: In retrospect, I realized that I stopped drugs before most people started taking them. I had my last LSD at a Prankster occasion in New Mexico in 1969. That was the great "bus race" when the Pranksters and the Hog Farm got together above Santa Fe and raced their buses. It was a lovely trip and I hitchhiked to get there and that was the last I did of that. I continued to do nitrous oxide on and off for a few years after that, but that was pretty much it.

NOTES

1. Jay Stevens provides an exhaustive account of the history of LSD in *Storming Heaven: LSD and the American Dream* (New York: Grove Press, 1987).

2. Aldous Huxley's account of his experiments with mescaline appears in *The Doors of Perception and Heaven and Hell* (New York: Harper & Row, 1954).

3. For a detailed discussion of Myron Stolaroff's activities, see John Markoff, *What the Dormouse Said: How the 1960s Counterculture Shaped the Personal Computer Industry* (New York: Viking Penguin, 2005), 20ff. Stolaroff was an engineer who helped Alexander M. Poniatoff design the first magnetic reel-to-reel tape recorder. Poniatoff founded the Ampex Electric and Manufacturing Co. The name "Ampex" derives from the initials of his name, with the "ex" added at the end standing for excellence.

4. Vic Lovell was a graduate student in psychology at Stanford who lived on Perry Lane from 1957 to 1963. He received his Ph.D. in 1964 and later helped run the Free University, an alternative educational institution modeled on the Freie Universität in Berlin. See Markoff, *What the Dormouse Said*, 112–13.

5. Jim Fadiman received his B.A. at Harvard, where he was a student of Richard Alpert (who

gave him his first dose of LSD), and subsequently a graduate student in psychology at Stanford. According to Markoff, *What the Dormouse Said,* 58, Fadiman was Brand's guide on his first LSD trip.

6. Tom Wolfe, *The Electric Kool-Aid Acid Test* (New York: Farrar, Straus & Giroux, 1968; reprint, New York: Bantam Books, 1999), 105–7.

7. Brand is referring to a tape piece by Sender, which uses a loop of the opening phrase of Wagner's *Siegfried Idyll,* which gradually becomes white noise as it records over itself. Sender later took Brand's suggestion to make another piece trying the opposite: beginning with white noise and allowing the theme to emerge gradually in his *Great Grandpa Lemuel's Death-Rattle Reincarnation Blues in F Sharp* (1981).

8. Ramon Sender maintains that "Stewart and his wife Lois were on the first visit to Morning Star with me, my then-partner Joan, and Lou, on or about Easter of 1966. Sometime later, when Stewart was running his Whole Earth Truck Store, he drove in with his truck for a brief visit."

9. The Diggers were an anarchist collective consisting of former members of the San Francisco Mime Troupe. Their inspiration was the seventeenth-century group of English millenarians of the same name who attempted to establish a cooperative of craftsmen and peasants in the aftermath of the English Civil War. See Michael William Doyle, "Staging the Revolution: Guerilla Theater as a Countercultural Practice: 1965–68," in *Imagine Nation: The American Counterculture of the 1960s and '70s,* ed. Peter Braunstein and Michael William Doyle (New York: Routledge, 2002), 78ff.

10. R. Buckminster Fuller, *Nine Chains to the Moon* (1938; reprint, Garden City, N.Y.: Anchor Books, Doubleday, 1963, 1971).

Stuart Dempster

INTERVIEWED BY THOMAS M. WELSH

Stuart Dempster is a groundbreaking virtuoso of the avant-garde on an unlikely instrument, the trombone. He managed a career as a working musician, playing everywhere from the Oakland Symphony to Chinese funerals, German bands, hotel gigs, and civic park bands, while studying composition with Roger Nixon at San Francisco State College. Dempster credits his undergraduate classmates Pauline Oliveros, Terry Riley, and Loren Rush with encouraging his interest in new music, which, together with a chance encounter with Ramon Sender at the San Francisco Conservatory of Music, would bring him into the orbit of the founders of the San Francisco Tape Music Center. "The trombonist in the tunnel" remains one of the paradigmatic memories of *City Scale,* the citywide happening that was an early Tape Music Center production.

Dempster participated in many concerts at the Tape Music Center and commissioned works by Oliveros, Luciano Berio, and Robert Erickson, among others, that featured his radical playing techniques. These pioneering efforts are codified in his book *The Modern Trombone: A Definition of Its Idioms,*[1] and in the many recordings Dempster has made since the 1960s. In 1967, Dempster left the Bay Area to accept an invitation to serve as creative associate at SUNY Buffalo, where he promptly invited Terry Riley to lead a performance of *In C.* With the assistance of David Behrman, he then organized Riley's recording of this piece with the Buffalo ensemble (including luminaries such as David Rosenboom, Jon Hassell, and Jan Williams), released the following year by Columbia Records and marking a new era in music. Dempster's perspective as a premier interpreter of new music gives a unique insight into the musical life at the Tape Music Center.

DEMPSTER: I was born in Berkeley [in 1936 and] lived in what is now known as Kensington. I studied piano with Hilda Weagant, who lived down the street fairly close to me. I went to San Francisco State College in 1954 and believe I met Pauline [Oliveros] either in the fall of 1954 or the spring of 1955 in the state college orchestra. She was playing French horn, I was playing trombone, literally meeting with our bells facing each other. I got interested in the Composers' Workshop run there by Dr. Wendell Otey because of Joe Weber—Joseph F. Weber, a composer who taught me how to listen to music (courtesy of Green Death—that's Rainier Ale to the uninitiated) and [had] lots of access to important records he thought I should know about, such as *Wozzeck* and Webern and stuff I'd never heard.

WELSH: So Terry Riley, Pauline Oliveros, and Loren Rush were all classmates of yours?

DEMPSTER: Yes.

WELSH: You graduated from San Francisco State in 1958?

DEMPSTER: Yes, June of 1958, and from there I went into the service. I volunteered for the draft; ended up fortunately in the Seventh Army Symphony in Germany, which toured in France and Italy as well as throughout Germany, and came back as it turned out to San Francisco State for a master's in composition.

WELSH: So you returned to the Bay Area in the summer of 1960?

DEMPSTER: Yes.

WELSH: At that time, late 1950s into 1960, there were a number of presenting organizations in the Bay Area doing contemporary music concerts. Were you aware of these concerts going on around town?

DEMPSTER: It seemed that during the 1960–61 season, there were school groups, the Composers' Forum, and things at the San Francisco Museum of Art. But the real catalyst, I think, was when the Tape Music Center was formed. It seemed to drive other people into thinking, "Gee, this is good stuff"—or, they just were so excited there was something like this going on.

WELSH: You went out to the San Francisco Conservatory at some point?

DEMPSTER: I ended up with three teaching jobs, and the first one was at the San Francisco Conservatory in the fall of 1961. My trombone studio turned out to be the costume attic near this little room where someone was dragging in electronic things and plugging stuff in and booping and beeping. I started talking to him, and it turned out to be Ramon Sender. He was very talkative then, as he is now, and was quite willing to chat with me in between lessons. And when I had nothing to do, I'd listen at the door. He'd hear me teaching my lessons, while I was hearing boop-beep come out of the electronic studio—which I thought being in the costume attic with boop-beep at one end and bloop-bleeping trombone sounds at the other end was rather special.

WELSH: In 1961, Ramon and Pauline presented the first in a series of concerts called the Sonics series.

DEMPSTER: I remember the Sonics series and think that I went to some of those concerts.

WELSH: The first Sonics concert was December 18, 1961. The concert featured tape pieces and culminated in a group improvisation. Were you interested in improvisation at this point?

DEMPSTER: Yes, well, I didn't *do* much except in jazz contexts. I hadn't really come to grips with the idea that there was improvisation other than jazz. It didn't get through to me that that was something I should know about or care or think about. But that changed over time.

WELSH: Talking about improvisation in this time period, the end of the 1950s to 1960 and 1961, this program we're talking about, Sonics, was half a program of tape pieces and half a program of free improvisation.

DEMPSTER: Yes, I think that would certainly seem to be a real point of change—getting more public about [improvisation], even if it was going on otherwise, elsewhere.

WELSH: Then Lukas Foss came to town with his improvisational group on tour [to San Francisco State College].

DEMPSTER: I was ending my second year of grad school.

WELSH: And these are not improvisations in the jazz sense that we are talking about.

DEMPSTER: No. It was probably my first realization that, "Hey, this is really pretty serious stuff. I think I should really pay attention." And a lot of my friends were there. We had a lot of excitement about that. I'd love to figure out who the other players were in that group sometime.

WELSH: At the end of that academic year, after having done apparently six of these [Sonics] concerts, they were invited not to come back.

DEMPSTER: Yes. I don't know any details about why they felt they had to leave, but it certainly wouldn't surprise me, because it was a pretty traditional space. And I can't see the conservatory at that time getting excited about anything that was that "out there." It was one thing to have it in the attic, but to have it start spilling down into the main space, it was certainly suspect. And I guess that's when they went to Jones Street.

WELSH: There's a piece that happens in the spring of 1963, which would have been the end of the first season [at Jones Street] called *City Scale*. Can you talk about how you heard about this and who designed it.

DEMPSTER: I believe it was Ramon, it could have been Mort, who asked me to play trombone in the Broadway Tunnel. It was this real "happening" kind of thing, with lights on buildings. [The audience traveled to] different parts of town to look at this and hear that. I was appointed to go play trombone in the Broadway Tunnel. There was a lot of traffic there, I remember, and there was that little kind of a sidewalk where you can walk along and do whatever I did.

WELSH: Were you instructed to do a certain thing?

DEMPSTER: Well, I think I just did stuff and played with the echo and amused myself as I pretty much wished to. I don't think that I dressed in anything special for the occasion. I don't remember anything like that. After I played a sufficient amount of time—it seemed like there was a score time, a half hour, forty-five minutes—then I was done, and I had an indicator of where I should go to see the [other] events [from] certain viewpoints in the city, like Russian Hill. It seemed it was mostly off Pacific Heights somewhere.

WELSH: When did you start performing in the Tape Music Center?

DEMPSTER: Probably in 1964 [*sic*] in *Pieces of Eight* [1964].

WELSH: Can you tell me about *Pieces of Eight?*

DEMPSTER: Yes, Pauline Oliveros's piece, it's really a wonderful piece. It was a kind of life-changing event for many, and certainly for me. It [used] eight alarm clocks, which presumably meant there were eight seated performers, plus this huge packing crate. I think Warner Jepson was the one working with the packing crate.[2] And then there was a big scale, presumably a railway express–type scale. It was a huge thing about three feet square with a big upright thing, all the balances and all. How they dragged that thing into the hall I'll never know. And a cash register—this gorgeous old cast-iron cash register was used, as well as collection plates, borrowed from a church somewhere, and the bust of Beethoven that had flashing lights. It was really special, because there was this blur on the wall, and the bust of Beethoven comes down, the collection plates are going around, and so it's like this big religious service going on and you're donating money (which the program says goes to the composer, but . . .). The bust of Beethoven must have been four feet tall, carried by two people. I don't think it was all that heavy, but it was kind of awkward. As the piece ends, the blur on the wall gradually comes into focus and it turns out it's a bust of Beethoven—Beethoven's head. Some picture of a statue somewhere, this great god

Beethoven. You've got to remember it was the time of Charles Schultz doing the *Peanuts* thing, and there was a big Beethoven component, which goes all the way through his strips of the pianist studying music, and Lucy leaning on the music staff, and all the notes fall off, and all kinds of jokes around that. But it was quite often Beethoven themes, and Beethoven's birthday was big. There really was this kind of great god Beethoven. I think that was Pauline's way of asking, "OK, well, where are the goddesses? And is there anybody else? Anybody new that we can talk to, or are we stuck [with] Beethoven forever?" I think that was sort of a subplot, but just on the surface level, it was incredible, let alone the deeper issues. And the alarm clocks were designed to go off at the same time, which of course they didn't. They were all kind of Big Ben–looking things, quite funny, really gorgeous.

WELSH: Was there traditional instrumentation in there as well?

DEMPSTER: Oh yeah! We all had our instruments, the eight of us that had clocks, and I don't know, the list is in [the program], but [the instrumentation] was clarinet, trombone, maybe Robert Moran, Stan Shaff on trumpet, and various players that were seated that could deal with the alarm clocks. And then there were the other performers that were doing packing crates.

WELSH: When did this element of theatricality come into performance?

DEMPSTER: Well, that was a defining moment for me. I certainly don't think it's [Pauline's] first theater piece, but it was certainly the first one that really took me somewhere and I've never recovered.

WELSH: It seems that among the regular programming, one of the defining moments at 321 Divisadero was the Tudorfest, which was three repeated concerts [in 1964 focusing on] David Tudor and John Cage. Was this a big deal at the time?

DEMPSTER: It was a big deal. A lot of people knew about it and there was quite a bit of publicity. And things were pretty well attended.

WELSH: You played in some of these pieces?

DEMPSTER: Yes, I played in [Toshi] Ichiyanagi's *Sapporo* [1962].

WELSH: Can you describe that piece?

DEMPSTER: That's the one I played *shakuhachi* on. That was my one and only *shakuhachi* debut and um, well, whatever the other end of it is—retirement.

WELSH: Had you met Cage before this time?

DEMPSTER: I think this would have been my first meeting. And so that was really interesting to meet him. Tudor, of course, I sort of worked with, because he rehearsed us in the *Concert for Piano and Orchestra* [1958] in particular. I had various instruments in my quiver for that, including the garden hose.

Loren Rush [played] bass and he also had a big water jug, that broke in the middle of one of the performances. I made the mistake of turning around, and there was Pauline. She was playing horn, but I think she also had her sousaphone with her and was making these roaring sounds into the sousaphone—and I kind of lost it. So I got quite a dressing-down from Tudor for losing my concentration, which was really good because it really focused me in on [the fact that] you just can't do that. I mean you just have to be in the moment all the time. And not become unglued over something relatively trivial. But what a sound it was, all that breaking glass! It was unbelievable.

WELSH: Tell me about the piece that Pauline wrote for her[self] and Tudor, the *Duo for Accordion and Bandoneon with Possible Minah Bird Obbligato* [1964].

DEMPSTER: That was incredible. The seesaw was built by Elizabeth Harris, and presumably designed by her, and it was on a big circle pedestal. It was quite huge. I would say it was twelve feet across, at least. It was built so that it went up and down like a teeter-totter normally does, but it also would go around in a circle at the same time. So you get these kinds of "ellipticals." Each seat was also able to turn around on its own. Well, [during] the first rehearsal, Pauline fell off, so they put seat belts on the seats after that. And it was really dramatic. I remember going to the rehearsal and the concert and I sat fairly far down front so the teeter-totter would actually come right over my head, so it was kind of this revolving stereo sound. You had this left-right stereo and what I call front-back stereo and then suddenly back-front stereo and up-and-down stereo as well. So it was as close as you could get to what we would now call spherical stereo. I don't think there was anything like it that I've ever run across since.

WELSH: And there was a bird in this piece.

DEMPSTER: And then there was this mobile-looking tower thing with the mynah bird in a cage. The rehearsal was incredible; [the bird] made all this racket! But at the formal concert, with a crowd present, it was as quiet as could be. It didn't make a peep. I was so happy I'd attended one of the rehearsals.

WELSH: Are there other pieces on the Tudorfest that were particularly memorable moments or really important moments for Bay Area music?

DEMPSTER: Well I think all the Cage stuff, like *Atlas Eclipticalis* [1961–62] and the *Concert for Piano and Orchestra, Cartridge Music* [1960], and *Music Walk* [1958]. I didn't play in *Cartridge Music,* as I recall, but I did play in *Concert for Piano and Orchestra*. It was a big deal. People had read about [and] knew about [Cage and Tudor] more than I did, actually. But, still, I could somehow appreciate the fantastical nature of this event, even if I didn't really know why. I could just sense that it was something—I knew I was in the presence of something really special.

WELSH: One of the big events was a concert in November 1964 dedicated entirely to the music of Terry Riley. It was the premier of *In C.* And [the following May] you played [in a series of concerts that also featured *In C*]. What happened in those later concerts?

DEMPSTER: We had some rehearsals to get the piece happening. But they certainly were not extensive. And I doubt if we had everybody at every rehearsal. Of course, some [performers] were more experienced and needed only one. I would have needed two and I think I was at two. And then we just did it. And we just started this thing off and it was as transcendent as everybody writes about it. And that was another big moment for me, of another kind of way to make music that was as incredibly dramatic in its own way for me as *Pieces of Eight*.

WELSH: What was it about *In C* that startled you or gave you that feeling?

DEMPSTER: It was just that you go into this space somehow, this mental space as you played it. Certainly, as a listener, it seemed to be apparent enough, but as a player you could also enter, too, and still play. It wasn't either/or. I guess you could say it pulled you in, drew you in. And it was a beautiful space to be. It was like watching a kaleidoscope turn really, really slowly. Things would kind of drop into place a little differently, and these little musical fragments would then merge together, and they'd be constantly changing, always moving, always changing, but in a special way.

In C by itself probably took ninety minutes. It's designed to go forty-five to ninety minutes. We probably didn't do ninety minutes; it might have been an hour, easily, just for that piece alone. And it might have been an hour and a quarter, because we all loved it. We loved stretching it out. It wouldn't surprise me if somebody said, "Hey, that took ninety minutes to perform." So that's what made it so interesting when it came time for the recording.

WELSH: The critics loved that event as well. Terry's piece was instantly well received.

DEMPSTER: Yes, Frankenstein was in particular outspoken about this being a defining moment, which turned out to be quite true.

WELSH: With all these defining moments happening under the roof at 321 Divisadero, did you have a sense that nonmusical people were stumbling in and having these experiences, too? Or was it only in the contemporary music community that these discoveries were being made?

DEMPSTER: To me it seemed a lot more mixed. I always thought that there were, you know, poets, dancers, and of course there was the Halprin studio right there. Sometimes some of the dance people might come and hang out. There was a lot of curiosity on a lot of different fronts.

WELSH: Sometime in 1965, Robert Erickson worked at the Tape Music Center on *Piece for Bells and Toy Pianos*. Robert Erickson was, as you mentioned, the grandfather to a lot of these ideas and to the people involved.

DEMPSTER: Yes, I think he was really a catalyst. As much as a single person could be, I think he was a great catalyst. And the fact that he was ten to fifteen years older than most of the other major players we're talking about made a difference. He was so open about sound and about his willingness to mentor. And the fact that the people were willing to be mentored I think was significant too.

WELSH: So I think there is kind of an interesting moment here when Robert Erickson comes into the Tape Music Center to do some of his work—as if the teacher has come back to learn from the students.

DEMPSTER: Yes, I think he wanted to get into some other stuff and needed some assistance. So he spent a fair amount of time there and learned a lot about the equipment and recording, which was still quite new at that time.

WELSH: There were other visitors who came up to join you—this group of composers from overseas, three Swedish composers [Folke Rabe, Jan Bark, and Arne Mellnäs] came specifically to work in this [artistic] community.

DEMPSTER: Yes, I'm particularly remembering knowing Jan Bark and Folke Rabe because they had written and performed this piece called *Bolos* that they had recorded two [of the four] parts and then recorded the other two parts. I've since done it live with students and other people who've then done it live. A lot of the sounds in *Bolos,* and this is 1964, really were kind of a precursor for the sounds Erickson got interested in and found their way into *Ricercar* [1966], which he wrote for me.

WELSH: Were Bark and Rabe trombone players?

DEMPSTER: Yes.

WELSH: I think you mentioned you did a trombone piece with Folke and Ann Halprin?

DEMPSTER: Yes, it was some piece that Folke had done; I don't know whether you could say, it was sort of composed, I guess. Folke asked me to join him; it was done over at Wheeler Hall at UC Berkeley. They used those big kind of scaffold things that you wheel around on stage that are six by eight feet, maybe something like that with the dancers doing whatever it is they do when they're on things like that. There was a great big weather balloon that was being tossed around the audience.[3] It was gorgeous. And that's a pretty big space.

WELSH: Was it an improvised piece?

DEMPSTER: Certainly my part of it was improvised. I might have been cuing off of things that Folke was doing. We were on opposite sides of the back of the hall. We weren't onstage. We were in the back of the hall doing our sounds. Whether there was an electronic component I don't remember.

WELSH: You also prepared your own full recital of solo pieces for trombone.

DEMPSTER: Yes, by this time I knew Pauline, and I knew Erickson and Berio well enough that I'd asked them for commissions, for a concert on March 21 and 22, 1966, that I wanted to do at 321 Divisadero. Berio wrote *Sequenza V* [1966]. I'd met him earlier, in 1961 or 1962, and sent him a tape, a little tape of sonic fragments I sent composers who were interested in my stuff, which later became some kind of a version of what was eventually done for my trombone book. Talking about that now seems like my life going by at fast forward, hearing all those sounds: one A: "bbbgggghh," one B: "bblllcchhhh," one C: "whowho," you know, silly sounds through the trombone. Of course, there are hundreds of them.

WELSH: You were pioneering in this regard! So it was a solo trombone concert with extended techniques?

DEMPSTER: Yes, and it was sort of a parallel development [related to what] Folke Rabe and other instrumentalists like Bertram Turetzky on bass and William O. Smith on clarinet [were doing].

WELSH: Were all these composers interested and anxious to write for solo trombone, which was kind of an avant-garde thing in itself?

DEMPSTER: I think anxious to write for trombone would be optimistic. But they seemed to be willing to put up with my requests. And Erickson got particularly interested, and we spent long hours [together], days, that is. He recorded my playing over many Tuesdays and Thursdays and built what became the tape accompaniment to *Ricercar,* and then in looking back on it I realized, "Wait a minute—we could do this live." And so later on I was able to assemble some trombone players and teach them how to do enough of this stuff.

WELSH: The other pieces on that program at the Tape Music Center included something by Pauline.

DEMPSTER: *Theater Piece for Trombone Player and Tape* [1966]. The title she wanted, now regained, is *In the Garden: A Theater Piece for Trombone Player and Tape.* It's an incredible piece with these garden hose sculptures. One was the "candle trumpet." I was so intrigued with these funnels and the candles in them, because the way I played would affect the lighting of a space. The candles would almost go out if I did the air just right. I could make the sound and the lighting be integrated. I was really fascinated by that. And just how we discovered that was probably Elizabeth Harris's doing, because she really designed those instruments, I guess you could say.

Then the sprinkler flower was six foot tall, with three sprinklers that we could spin around. One of the great stories that I'll never forget was when I blew a note and this huge cloud of dust came flying out of the sprinklers and hoses and stuff. And we were just hysterical. So then we used talcum powder so it would kind of poof out as these things would spin and we were playing. I did a lot of stuff under the piano, crawling around; it's a great piece. There again I think [it was] really quite, you could almost say, religious, spiritual, in its energy even though there are lots of animal sounds. As a garden can be spiritual, [Elizabeth] put it that way. [Pauline] told me to go study the gibbon monkey to learn this piece, before I had access to the tape.

WELSH: Then the third premiere, third world premier on that program was Berio's *Sequenza V.* How did that come about?

DEMPSTER: Yes, I'd written him, asking him to commission this piece. Vinko Globokar had played a piece called *Essay* at Carnegie Recital Hall, which I found out later was the inner part of the second section of the *Sequenza*. And then the remaining piece was, what was the remaining one?

WELSH: The Childs . . .

DEMPSTER: . . . Barney Childs' *Solo Sonata*. That's a nice little piece. It has a fairly straight-ahead allegro movement, a slower movement, then the last one was a do-it-yourself rondo! The A [section] had three choices, [and] you chose one. Then the B had three, and then the C, and then the D. And so you could choose any one of three. Maybe line one of A which could go to line two of B or line one of C and back to line three of A. So it kept me awake. I never did write out a plan. I always tried to do it on the fly.

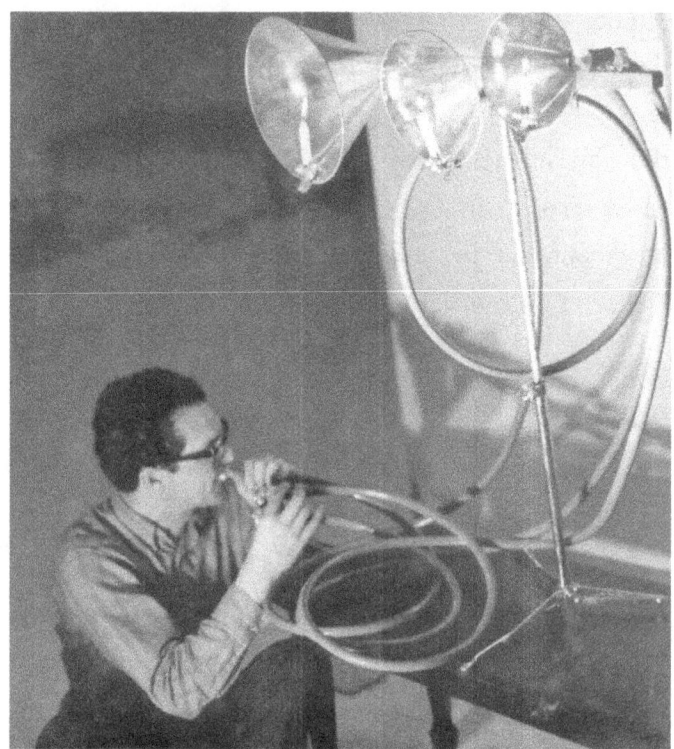

40 STUART DEMPSTER PERFORMING *IN THE GARDEN* (MARCH 1966). PHOTOGRAPH COURTESY OF STUART DEMPSTER.

WELSH: This concert was very well received. The press was very positive.

DEMPSTER: I don't think I would have done what I'd done had I not met Pauline and Erickson. All the stuff that was going on at the Tape Music Center was so inspirational to me. And I think one of the reasons it excited me [was that] those electronic sounds didn't sound very good. [I thought] I can do that better. And I'd imitate electronic sounds. That's really how I got started making funny sounds, rather than just being "Spike Jonesy," which is one of my other inspirations, but that's another story. I was arrogant enough to think that I could do these things better, and sometimes I think I got away with it. Erickson and I were kind of similar thinkers in that way that he really wanted that live, all that little funky stuff that's in there. As he said later on, when computers came along, he said, "I think they left those widgets out of the digits." The widgets were what he was really interested in. All the little junk.

WELSH: To a degree, the motivation around *In C* was very similar. [Riley] thought he'd already done tape looping and repetition in loops, which is the machine-oriented music, but felt that he could capture some of that in live playing.

DEMPSTER: He was a performer. He really was a performer, as am I. And the orientation stays that way. I think for Pauline, too, for as much electronic music as she did, she was always looking for the junk to make it very interesting. I think *Bye Bye Butterfly* [1965] is a classic example, a wonderful example.

WELSH: Why?

DEMPSTER: Well, there's live input from the *Madame Butterfly* recording, which I don't think she was intending to use at the time. But in other pieces she'd get the tone generators and then find the "garbage" that they would do together. This makes it like they're living somehow, in a way that straight electronic music to me never did, for my ear. It's hard for me to get into that.

WELSH: By 1966, the Tape Music Center had been active and vibrant for a few years (four or five years, if you go back to the conservatory days), and people began to look in other directions, to move away. People had opportunities to go elsewhere. And the Tape Music Center itself moved over to Mills. In other words, it was winding down. Do you remember what the tone was at the time? I know there was a conversation about whether the Tape Music Center should move.

DEMPSTER: It was amazing. There was this peak period, which is why I think the Tape Music Center itself was such a symbol, let alone their significant output of actual music. It was just a symbol of what things could be. And so, yeah, as that moved to Mills, it was being institutionalized. No matter what the philosophy was, it was still going to an institution. Thank goodness it was Mills rather than somewhere else. I mean, would we still be complaining about it now? If it had been somewhere else, it would have been buried long ago in some budget cut somewhere. Yes, thank goodness it's there to complain about.

And so people started leaving. Pauline had gone her way. Mort had gone to New York. Ramon was, I think by that time, about to or already living in a commune up in Sonoma County. I was, just by chance, not that I had any great significant anything to do with the Tape Music Center in the first place, but I was off on my big tour thing that turned into the Creative Associates thing, which turned into the teaching job at the University of Washington, a year after that. So there was this big exodus. There was a loss of energy of some kind.

WELSH: Well, the energy started to change in San Francisco in 1966–67, didn't it?

DEMPSTER: Yes, it could have been more that music was going in a more pop-type direction that I wasn't interested in. And that's what you read about in the paper. You don't read about new music, you read about pop stuff. You never hear about "no-goods" like Tape Music Center people or me.

NOTES

1. Stuart Dempster, *The Modern Trombone: A Definition of Its Idioms,* New Instrumentation 3 (Berkeley: University of California Press, 1979; repr. Athens, Ohio: Accura Music, 1994).

2. Warner Jepson (b. 1930) is a composer and pianist who performed and had his own works performed at the San Francisco Tape Music Center. Jepson composed music for the Ann Halprin and the Welland Lathrop Dance Companies.

3. The work described here is Halprin's *Parades and Changes* (1965–67).

CHRONOLOGY

THOMAS M. WELSH

The roots of the San Francisco Tape Music Center took hold in the disparate but intermingled activities of various artists in the years leading up to 1961, the beginning of the Sonics series. Through the late 1950s, a number of presenters had been hosting contemporary or experimental art events that in retrospect clearly seem to have prepared the ground for what was to come. The San Francisco Museum of Art was home to concerts by living composers produced by the prestigious Composers' Forum, in addition to its own programming of what was exotically referred to as ethnic music. The Actor's Workshop, led by Herbert Blau, utilized experimental scores by young composers. And Ann Halprin's Dancers' Workshop, at locations in the city and at her rural home in Kentfield, regularly interacted with musicians and light artists before the decade was out. The creative cross talk, from music to dance to theater to film, was active and getting ever more so. By 1959, all the major figures of this history were in the Bay Area and finding their paths. Morton Subotnick, a young composer and first-rate clarinetist, was teaching at Mills College. Pauline Oliveros had left the state college master's program to strike out on her own, while William Maginnis remained. Terry Riley, in the graduate program at UC Berkeley, teamed up with La Monte Young to turn the academy on its ear. Ramon Sender arrived from New York to study at the San Francisco Conservatory of Music, and Anthony Martin moved from Chicago to pursue a life in visual art. The long-term Bay Area residents, including Halprin, Michael Callahan, and Stuart Dempster, had all been pushing up against the limitations of academic environments or teaching independently.

Indeed, that summer, the University of California Extension hosted a conference on the San Francisco renaissance in the arts, where a rather colorful panel, including Darius Mihaud, Dave Brubeck, Robert Erickson, Gregory Millar, and the *San Francisco Chronicle* music critic Alfred Frankenstein, who would report on the occasion, came to the conclusion that "there really is a musical renaissance in the Bay Region, and that it stems mostly from the colleges—and that San Francisco's major musical institutions are remiss in not recognizing it sufficiently."* But it was precisely the major institutions' failure to embrace this change that led Oliveros, Subotnick, and Sender to create their own determinedly noninstitutional center around their common interests.

What follows is a chronology of selected events before and during the lifespan of the Tape Music Center in the context of experimental music, theater, and dance in the Bay Area, as well as historic events of the day. The shading of the dates divides the entries into three categories: the darkest shading highlights performances at the Tape Music Center; the medium shading highlights performances and other events at other venues, primarily in the Bay Area; and the lightest shading highlights important historical events that occured during the period. While comprehensive, the chronology cannot pretend to be complete. There were a number of activities, for instance, that took place at 321 Divisadero Street during its busiest period, including composition seminars, lecture series, and virtuoso concerts put on by outside presenters, not to mention innumerable impromptu events and chance encounters, but space limitations necessitate setting ancillary events aside. And then there were events that now at best conjure up only vague memories, which they evidently will remain.

Everyone interviewed in this book gave generously from their personal archives and recollections, the reward for which was endless follow-up questioning and cross-examination. I am in their debt. Many others responded enthusiastically to inquiries and deserve thanks, including Folke Rabe, Warner Jepson, Stanley Shaff, Gordon Mumma, Tom Constanten, Alden Jenks, Philip Winsor, Roger Hillyard, Susan Hillyard, Robert Moran, Gayathri Rajapur Kassebaum, Fumi Spencer, and Bill Ham. Several university archives were tapped for original documentation of events, as well as supporting materials. These include the University of California, Berkeley, the University of British Columbia, Ball State University, and the Yale University Oral History of American Music. Other resources that preserved parts of this story include the David Tudor Papers at the Getty Research Library, the Los Angeles County Museum of Art archives, and the archives of the Composers' Forum, which reside in the UC Berkeley Music Library. Special appreciation goes to Barbara Rominski, head librarian of the San Francisco Museum of Modern Art, and to Robert Battaly at the Rockefeller Archive Center, both of whom certainly sped things along. Finally, Richard Geiger at the *San Francisco Chronicle* graciously abetted the search along a well-documented trail. It turns out that even at the farthest reaches of the avant-garde, the daily newspapers were there to bear witness. The astounding amount

---

* Alfred Frankenstein, "Jazz vs. 'Classical': A Matter for Study," *San Francisco Chronicle,* June 10, 1959.

of continuous and thoughtful coverage of developments in modern music and art over an impressively long period of time by Alfred Frankenstein made this chronology and this period in Bay Area history come to life.

MAY 28, 1957 Vortex, a twelve-speaker arrayed sound experience accompanied by visual images created by the electronic musician Henry Jacobs and the filmmaker Jordan Belson, premieres at the Morrison Planetarium in Golden Gate Park.

SUMMER 1958 Pauline Oliveros, Terry Riley, and Loren Rush play and record free improvisations at the listener-sponsored Pacifica radio station KPFA 94.1 fm, Berkeley, for the soundtrack to a film by the artist Claire Falkenstein.

SEPTEMBER 28, 1958 The Ann Halprin Dancers' Workshop presents two new dances, including *The Branch,* with tape music by Warner Jepson, and another with tape music by Pieter Van Deusen, plus *Earth Interval,* with percussion score by Doris Dennison, and *Opening and Closing Ceremonies,* with music by Alan Hovhaness, on Halprin's Dance Deck in Kentfield; dancers include A. A. Leath, Simone Morris, Sunni Bloland, John Graham, Erv Dill, Sherry Gowgil, and Sandy Piezer.

NOVEMBER 7, 1959 Enormously popular at the Morrison Planetarium, where the sound-and-image experience had expanded to include more than three dozen speakers, Vortex moves its weekend programs to the San Francisco Museum of Art.

DECEMBER 2, 1959 La Monte Young organizes a program for the UC Berkeley Department of Music "Noon Concerts" series, including Dennis Johnson, *The Second Machine* (1959), John Cage, *Imaginary Landscape No. 4* (1951) or *March No. 2 for 12 Radios,* La Monte Young, *Vision* (1959), and Richard Maxfield, *Cough Music* (1959); performers include Young, Johnson, Terry Riley, Anna Carol Dudley, Paul Epstein, and Gardner Rust.

APRIL 22, 1960 The Ann Halprin Dancers' Workshop performs *Still Point* (1960), *The Flowerburger* (1959), and *Visions* (1960) at Schoenberg Hall, UCLA, with musical accompaniments by La Monte Young and Terry Riley.

MAY 11, 1960 The UC Berkeley Department of Music "Noon Concerts" series presents "Music from the Composition Seminar": Douglas Leedy, *Trio for Flute, Horn, and Piano,* Paul Epstein, *True and False Unicorn* (1960), Loren Rush, *Three Movements from Serenade for Violin and Viola,* Terry Riley, *Concert for Two Pianos and Five Tape Recorders* (1960), La Monte Young, *Poem: A Chamber Opera in One Act* (1960); performers include Riley, Young, Rush, Marvin Tartak, and Walter De Maria. Young adapted his *Poem for Chairs, Tables, and Benches, etc. (or other sound sources)* (1960) to a chamber opera, where onstage activity included frying eggs, a game of marbles, a pianist playing Beethoven, a broadcast of his tape piece *2 Sounds* (1960), students walking in the aisles reading from textbooks, Young shouting "Green!" and Bruce Conner passing out literature.

MAY 12–14, 1960	The House Un-American Activities Committee meets in the San Francisco City Hall supervisors' chambers. Picketing and demonstrations get unruly, and police turn hoses on student protestors.
JULY 23, 1960	The Ann Halprin Dancers' Workshop presents *Visions* (1960) at the "San Francisco Renaissance" series on contemporary arts at the University of California Extension, with electronic music by Stanley Shaff, lights by Seymour Locks and Fred Blackman; artistic director Jo Landor.
JULY 30, 1960	The Ann Halprin Dancers' Workshop presents "An Afternoon Dance Demonstration and an Evening of Dances" in Marin County, with a poetry reading by Richard Brautigan, art exhibit by Manuel Neri and Joan Brown, dancing by Ann Halprin, A. A. Leath, John Graham, and others, new musical works by Stanley Shaff and Douglas McEachern, lighting by Pat Hickey; artistic director Jo Landor.
SEPTEMBER 13, 1960	The John Coltrane Quartet opens at the Jazz Workshop, Coltrane's San Francisco debut as bandleader.
FALL 1960	La Monte Young moves to New York City.
NOVEMBER 29, 1960	The Ann Halprin Dancers' Workshop presents *The Flowerburger* (1959), *Mr. and Mrs. Mouse* (a selection from *Rites of Women*) (1959), and the premiere of *Birds of America, or Gardens without Walls* (1960), music by John Cage, at the Contemporary Dancers' Center.
DECEMBER 16, 1960	Composers' Forum concert at the California Palace of the Legion of Honor program includes Milton Babbitt, *Woodwind Quartet in One Movement* (1953), La Monte Young, *Study I for Piano* (1959), performed by Marvin Tartak, Robert Basart, *Four Variations for Piano* (1959), Jerome Rosen, *Five Pieces for Wind Quartet and Piano* (1960), Roger Sessions, *First Piano Sonata* (1930), and Gunther Schuller, *Woodwind Quintet* (1958).
APRIL 17, 1961	Cuban rebels supported by the CIA make failed attempt to invade Cuba at the Bay of Pigs.
APRIL 28, 1961	Student Composers' Symposium at UC Berkeley program includes Terry Riley, *String Quartet* (1960); William Maginnis, *Three Pieces* (1960), for piano; Stuart Dempster, *Sonata* (1961), for bass trombone and piano; Joseph Weber, *Sonata* (ca. 1960–61), for piano; Robert Moran, *Two Songs on Chinese Texts* (1961); Dexter Morrill, *String Quartet ("to my father")* (1961); and Paul Epstein, with poems by James Broughton, *Three Songs* (1960), for soprano and clarinet, and *Two Autumn Songs* (1961), for soprano, flute, bass clarinet, trumpet, violin, viola, and cello.
APRIL 30, 1961	Composers' Forum at the California Palace of the Legion of Honor program includes Richard Swift, *Eve, Cantata for Soprano and Five Instruments* (1959); Terry Riley, *Spectra for Six Instruments* (1959); Bruno Maderna, *Serenata no. 2 for Eleven Instruments* (1954, rev. 1957); and Pierre Boulez, *Le marteau sans maître* (1954).

MAY 3–5, 1961	Actor's Workshop presents William Shakespeare's *King Lear* at Marines' Memorial Theater, with music by Morton Subotnick.
JUNE 13, 1961	Robert Erickson's Composers' Workshop at the San Francisco Conservatory program includes Morton Subotnick, *Three Preludes* (1956, 1961), for piano, performed by Marvin Tartak; Istvan Anhalt, *Electronic Composition #3 "Birds and Bells"* (1960); Milton Babbitt, *Composition for Synthesizer* (1961); Richard Maxfield, *Piano Concerto,* for 2-channel tape, mono tape, and piano, performed by Terry Riley; and Ramon Sender, *Four Sanskrit Hymns* (1961), for four sopranos, instrumental ensemble, and three tape recorders; Gerhard Samuel, conductor.
AUGUST 13, 1961	The Soviet Union and the German Democratic Republic begin the construction of the Berlin Wall.
SEPTEMBER 1961	Steve Reich arrives in the Bay Area to study at Mills College.
SEPTEMBER 24, 1961	Ann Halprin Dancers' Workshop premieres *The Four-Legged Stool* (1961) at the Playhouse Repertory Theater, with music by Terry Riley.
SEPTEMBER 24, 1961	Music of Morton Subotnick at Opus Too program of works for instruments and tape includes *Caves* (1961), *Three Preludes* (1956, 1961) for piano, and the premiere of *Sound Blocks: An Heroic Vision* (1961), performed by Marvin Tartak, Bonnie Hampton, Nathan Rubin, and Jack and Anne Van der Wyk.
OCTOBER 1961	Ramon Sender builds an electronic music studio in the attic at the San Francisco Conservatory.
OCTOBER 4, 1961	Lenny Bruce is arrested on obscenity charges for performing material of a "lewd nature" at the Jazz Workshop.
NOVEMBER 18, 1961	The R. G. Davis Mime Troupe stages *Event I* (part of the Midnight Mime Show series) at the Encore Theatre; participants include Mia Carlisle, Larry Lewis, Norma Leistiko, William Raymond, Barbara Melandry, Yvette Nachmias, Ron Poindexter, Wally Hedrick, Lee Breuer, William Wiley, Robert Hudson, and Ken Dewey.
DECEMBER 18, 1961	The Sonics series begins at the San Francisco Conservatory. Sonics I includes Ramon Sender, *Traversals* (1961); Pauline Oliveros, *Time Perspectives* (1961); Terry Riley, *M . . . Mix* (1960–61); Philip Winsor, *Sound Study I* (1961); and *Improvisation for Mixed Instruments and Tape* (Oliveros, Sender, Winsor, and Laurel Johnson).
FEBRUARY 1962	Terry Riley moves to Europe.
FEBRUARY 23, 1962	The Merce Cunningham Dance Company, featuring John Cage and David Tudor, performs at Wheeler Hall, UC Berkeley; the program includes music by Cage and Conlon Nancarrow.
MARCH 4, 1962	The Lukas Foss Improvisation Chamber Ensemble performs in the "Artists' Series" at San Francisco State College; the program includes excerpt of Foss's unfinished work *Echoi.*
MARCH 8–18, 1962	Ken Dewey presents *The Gift,* featuring Lynne Palmer and John Gra-

ham; Lee Breuer and the American Cooperative Theater (ACT), a short-lived cooperative that included Dewey, Breuer, Ann Halprin, and Ronnie Davis, present Jean Genet's *The Maids,* featuring Graham, Palmer, Susan Darby, Ruth Breuer, Bere Boynton, and William Spencer, at the Mission Neighborhood Playhouse, 362 Capp Street.

MARCH 24, 1962 Sonics II includes Bruno Maderna, *Serenata No. 3,* for flute, marimba, and tape (1961); Luigi Nono, *Omaggio a Vedova* (1960), *Improvisation #1 Birthday Piece for L. L.* (Oliveros, Sender, Subotnick, Palmer, and Graham); Luciano Berio, *Momenti* (1960); James Tenney, *Analog #1* (1961); Henri Pousseur, *Trois visages de Liège* (1961), *Improvisation #2 "Opera Not by Bruce Conner"* (Subotnick, Sender, Oliveros, Graham, and Palmer); technical assistance by Charles Shaefer.

APRIL 13, 1962 Sonics III, copresented by the Composers' Forum program, includes Mauricio Kagel, *Transition I* (1959–60); Luciano Berio, *Thema (Omaggio a Joyce)* (1958); Ramon Sender, *Kronos* (1962); and Karlheinz Stockhausen, *Gesang der Jünglinge* (1955–56).

APRIL 20, 1962 Sonics IV includes Gordon Mumma, *Vectors* (1959) and *Densities* (1960–61); Morton Subotnick, *Mandolin* (1962); James Tenney, *Collage #1 ("Blue Suede")* (1961); Ramon Sender, *Parade* (1962); and *Opera Three* and *Opera Four* improvisations by A. A. Leath, Lynne Palmer, Oliveros, Sender, and Subotnick, with set and lighting by Anthony Martin; technical coordination by Charles Shaefer.

MAY 7, 1962 Ann Halprin Dancers' Workshop premieres *The Five-Legged Stool* (1962), featuring Ann Halprin, Lynne Palmer, John Graham, and A. A. Leath, at the Playhouse, with music by Morton Subotnick.

MAY 13, 1962 Composers' Forum concert at UC Berkeley program includes Steve Reich, *Composition,* for piano; Luciano Berio, *Due pezzi* (1951); John Cage, *Winter Music* (1957), for two pianos; Tom Constanten, *Sonatina, Part 1* (1962); Joseph Weber, *Movement No. 5;* Robert Kuykendall, *Music for Two Pianos;* and Elsor von Illosovay, *Eine Kleine Chance-Musik* (1962).

MAY 15, 1962 Luciano Berio, visiting professor at Mills College, conducts a concert of his work at Mills featuring Cathy Berberian; the program includes *Thema (Omaggio a Joyce)* (1958), *Momenti* (1960), *Differences* (1958–59), and *Circles* (1960).

MAY 18, 1962 Sonics V includes works by André Boucourechliev, Roberto Gerhard, and Gottfried Michael Koenig; no program has been found.

JUNE 11, 1962 Sonics VI, entitled "An Evening of Improvisation Operas," includes *Tropical Fish Opera* (Oliveros, Sender, Subotnick, and Rush), *Interlude [Smell Opera with Found Tape]* (John Graham, Norma Leistiko, Anthony Martin, and Lynne Palmer), *Opera without Tropical Fish* (Graham, Leistiko, Martin, Palmer, Oliveros, Rush, Sender, and Subotnick), and the "washing machine action-event," which took place throughout the halls and rooms of the conservatory.

SUMMER 1962	Ramon Sender and Morton Subotnick establish the San Francisco Tape Music Center in an old Victorian house in Russian Hill; Pauline Oliveros travels to the East Coast and Europe, where she is awarded the Gaudeamus Prize for *Sound Patterns* (1961).
JUNE 21–24, 1962	The Poetry Center of San Francisco State College presents the Poetry Festival at the San Francisco Museum of Art; the program includes readings by Kenneth Rexroth, James Broughton, Lynn Lonidier, and Elizabeth Bartlett; screening of *Allures* by Jordan Belson; Lee Breuer directing Lawrence Ferlinghetti's *The Allegation,* with sound by William Spencer; Dean Goodman directing Leonard Wolf's *Lulu,* with music by Pauline Oliveros; Morton Subotnick conducting his *Sound Blocks: An Heroic Vision* (1961), with collages by Robert LaVigne and poems by Michael McClure, read by David Meltzer; the Ann Halprin Dancers' Workshop performing *Birds of America, or Gardens without Walls* (1960), featuring Rana Halprin and John Graham, with music by La Monte Young, *The Flowerburger* (1959), and *Mr. and Mrs. Mouse* (1959); the R. G. Davis Mime Troupe performing *Who's Afraid?;* musical performances by the Vince Guaraldi Trio, Jean Cunningham, and many others.
JULY 2, 1962	Ann Halprin exhibition *Theater for Watchers, Walkers, Touchers* (1962), created by Anthony Martin, opens at the San Francisco Museum of Art.
OCTOBER 1, 1962	SFTMC season concert program includes Morton Subotnick, *The Juggler, Part One of TAROT I;* Ramon Sender, *Sound Study 7/30/62;* and the Robert Duncan play *Adam's Way,* including Lewis Brown, Robin Blaser, Helen Adam, Peter Bailey, with paintings by Paul Alexander, Jess [Collins], Tom Field, and Fran Herndon.
OCTOBER 22, 1962	Cuban Missile Crisis begins when President John F. Kennedy announces a naval blockade of the island in confrontation with Soviet forces.
NOVEMBER 5, 1962	SFTMC season concert program includes Morton Subotnick, *Yod* (1962); Ramon Sender, *Kore* (1961); Robert Ashley, *Public Opinion Descends upon the Demonstrators* (1961); poetry by Robin Blaser; collages by Jess Collins; paintings by Paul Alexander and Tom Field; and an improvisation with the dancer-mime Judith Wickware.
NOVEMBER 14, 1962	Mills College presents "An Informal Look at Contemporary Music." The program includes Elsor von Illosovay, *Dialogues* (1962); Morton Subotnick, *Yod* (1962); Ramon Sender, *Information* (1962), with Judith Wickware, speaker (Sender and Robert Moran, pianos); Tom Constanten, *Synthesis III* (1961); and John Cage, *For M. C. and D. T.* (1952), *T.V. Köln* (1958), *4'33"* (1952) in three parts, and *Radio Music* (1956).
DECEMBER 3, 1962	SFTMC season concert program includes Luigi Nono, *Omaggio a Vedova* (1960); James Tenney, *Blue Suede* (1961); Andre Boucourechliev, *Texte II* (1959) *first version* and *Texte II second version;* Mario Davidovsky *Electronic Study #2* (1961); and the Lee Breuer theater piece *Composition*

	for Actors, including Susan Darby, JoAnne Akalaitis, William Raymond, and Ruth Brewer, with lights by Elias Romero.
DECEMBER 14, 1962	Actor's Workshop premieres Bertolt Brecht's *Galileo* at Marines' Memorial Theater with music by Morton Subotnick, projections by Elias Romero, scene design by Judith Davis, carnival mime by R. G. Davis, and lighting by Lyn Fischbein; directed by Herbert Blau.
C. 1963	R. G. Davis creates the film *Plastic Haircut* with Robert Nelson, Robert Hudson, and William Wiley; sound by Steve Reich.
JANUARY 1963	Pauline Oliveros returns to San Francisco.
JANUARY 7–8, 1963	SFTMC season concert program includes Ramon Sender, *Sound Mobile* (1963; collaboration with Morton Subotnick) and *Interstices* (1963); Roberto Gerhard, *Caligula* (1961); Mel Powell, *Sound Study;* and the R. G. Davis Mime Troupe, *Event II,* including Judy Rosenberg, Susan Derby, Daniel McDermott, Tom Purvis, with lights by Elias Romero.
FEBRUARY 4–5, 1963	SFTMC season concert program includes Robert LaVigne, *Transformation,* a work combining paintings by Robert LaVigne, Harold LaVigne, Ronald Cushing, and [?] Fortinberry, set with tape music by Ramon Sender and Morton Subotnick; also on the program Sender, *Kronos* (1962); Subotnick, *Music from "Galileo";* and Henri Pousseur, *Trois visages de Liège* (1961).
FEBRUARY 11, 1963	SFTMC with Robert LaVigne presents *Transformation* plus tape pieces by Sender and Subotnick at the Vancouver Festival of Contemporary Arts, University of British Columbia.
MARCH 9, 1963	SFTMC performs *City Scale,* a citywide happening created by Ken Dewey, Anthony Martin, and Ramon Sender.
SPRING 1963	Fire destroys 1537 Jones Street; Sender and Subotnick lease the old California Labor Hall, the new home of the Tape Music Center, at 321 Divisadero Street; KPFA and the Ann Halprin Dancers' Workshop sublease spaces in the building.
APRIL 18, 1963	The Ann Halprin Dancers' Workshop performs *Esposizione* (1963), with music by Luciano Berio, at the Teatro La Fenice as part of the Venice Biennale; the program includes six dancers, nine musicians, and five tape recorders, scenery and lighting by the sculptors Jerry Walters and Seymour Locks, and costume supervision by Jo Landor.
MAY 26, 1963	The Milhaud Festival at Mills College program includes electronic music plus an "environment and sound mobile" by Ramon Sender, Morton Subotnick, and Robert Dhaemers heard throughout the Music Building, courtyards, and surrounding outside areas.
JULY 8–10, 1963	Ken Dewey presents *The Gift* at the Théâtre des Nations in Paris, with music by Terry Riley in collaboration with Chet Baker.
AUGUST 15, 1963	The San Francisco Mime Troupe premieres Milton Savage's *Ruzzante's*

	Maneuvers at Capp Street Studios; costumes by Marina Sender, music by Steve Reich and William Spencer.
AUGUST 28, 1963	Reverend Martin Luther King Jr. delivers his "I Have a Dream" speech in Washington, D.C., before an audience of 200,000 people.
OCTOBER 4–7, 1963	SFTMC presents electronic music in Civic Center Plaza as part of the San Francisco Arts Festival.
OCTOBER 9, 1963	Anthony Martin solo exhibition opens at the Batman Gallery, 2222 Fillmore Street.
OCTOBER 17, 1963	Audium, a sixteen-speaker experience of "controlled movement of electronic music through space," is presented in total darkness by Stanley Shaff and Douglas McEachern at the San Francisco Museum of Art.
NOVEMBER 11, 1963	SFTMC season concert program includes Mario Davidovsky, *Synchronism no. 1* (1963), for flute and electronic sounds, performed by Walter Subke; Luciano Berio, *Visage* (1961), for voice and tape, performed by Cathy Berberian; and *Improvisation No. 1* by Morton Subotnick, tape, Pauline Oliveros and Ramon Sender, pianos, and Elias Romero, visual projections.
NOVEMBER 12 AND 14, 1963	Gerd Stern presents "Who R U?" and "What's Happening?" multimedia event, including the "Verbal American Landscape," in association with the SFTMC at the San Francisco Museum of Art; participants include Ivan Majdrakoff, Howard Becker, Sheldon Messinger, David Sudnow, Paul Verden, and many others.
NOVEMBER 22, 1963	President John F. Kennedy is shot in Dallas.
DECEMBER 2, 1963	SFTMC season concert program includes pieces by John Cage and Luciano Berio featuring Cathy Berberian, voice; tape pieces by Mario Davidovsky and Györgi Ligeti; and Ramon Sender, *Kronos* (1962), with visual projections by Elias Romero.
DECEMBER 11, 1963	The San Francisco Mime Troupe presents Alfred Jarry's *Ubu Roi*, renamed *Ubu King*, with score by Steve Reich.
DECEMBER 13, 1963	Actor's Workshop presents Bertolt Brecht's *The Caucasian Chalk Circle* at the Marines' Memorial Theater, with music by Morton Subotnick, performed by Pauline Oliveros and Jack Van der Wyk.
JANUARY 6, 13, AND 20, 1964	SFTMC season concert program includes Ernst Krenek, *San Fernando Sequence;* Ramon Sender, *Triad* (1964); Luigi Nono, *Omaggio a Vedova* (1960); Bulent Arel, *Stereo Electronic Music* (1961); and the premiere of Morton Subotnick's *A Theater Piece after Sonnet No. 47 of Petrarch* (1963) for recorded spoken voice and electronics, featuring John Graham, Rana Schuman, mimes, Sender, piano, Linn Subotnick, viola, Elias Romero, visual projections, and Judith Davis, set design.
JANUARY 29, 1964	Stanley Kubrick's film *Dr. Strangelove, or, How I Learned to Stop Worrying and Love the Bomb* opens in theaters.
JANUARY 29–31, 1964	Gerd Stern and Michael Callahan present "Verbal American Landscape"

	at the Vancouver Festival of Contemporary Arts, University of British Columbia, where they meet Marshall McLuhan for the first time.
FEBRUARY 1964	Terry Riley returns from Europe.
FEBRUARY 3 AND 5, 1964	SFTMC season concert program includes Henri Pousseur, *Trois visages de Liège* (1961); Karlheinz Stockhausen, *Zyklus* (1959); Richard Swift, *Domains II* (1963), featuring Stanley Lunetta, percussion; Włodzimierz Kotoński, *Microstructures* (1963); and the premiere of Ramon Sender's *Desert Ambulance* (1964), featuring Pauline Oliveros, accordion, and Anthony Martin, visual composition.
FEBRUARY 9, 1964	The Beatles appear on the Ed Sullivan Show.
FEBRUARY 11, 1964	The Elizabeth Harris Dance Company debuts at Marines' Memorial Theater with *Seven Passages* (1963) for tape and dancer, with music by Pauline Oliveros.
FEBRUARY 27, 1964	The San Francisco Mime Troupe stages *Event III (Coffee Break)* at Capp Street Studios, including visual projections by Elias Romero, sound by Steve Reich and Phil Lesh, and movement by R. G. Davis and Fumi Spencer.
MARCH 8, 1964	Composers' Forum concert at the California Palace of the Legion of Honor program includes Ramon Sender, *Balances* (1963), for string quartet and electronics; Karl Kohn, *Concerto Mutabile* (1962); and Erik Satie, *Socrate* (1917–18).
SPRING 1964	The Magic Theatre for Madmen Only boutique, the first head shop in town, opens a few doors up from the SFTMC on Divisadero.
MARCH 30, 1964	Tudorfest I: program includes John Cage, *34' 46.776"* (1954), for two pianists, David Tudor and Dwight Peltzer, pianos; Pauline Oliveros, *Duo for Accordion and Bandoneon with Possible Mynah Bird Obbligato* (1964), Oliveros, accordion, Tudor, bandoneon, Ahmed, mynah bird, seesaw version by Elizabeth Harris; Toshi Ichiyanagi, *Music for Piano, no. 4* (ca. 1963), Tudor and Oliveros, pianos; Alvin Lucier, *Action Music for Piano, Book I* (1962), Tudor, piano, light composition by Anthony Martin; program repeated on April 6.
APRIL 1, 1964	Tudorfest II: program includes Toshi Ichiyanagi, *Music for Piano, no. 4* (ca. 1963), electronic version, David Tudor, piano; John Cage, *Music for Amplified Toy Pianos* (1960), Tudor, toy pianos and amplifiers; Ichiyanagi, *Sapporo* (1962); George Brecht, *Card Piece for Voice*, for mixed sextet; Cage *Variations II* (1961), Tudor, amplified piano; additional performers included Stuart Dempster, Pauline Oliveros, Loren Rush, Ramon Sender, Morton Subotnick, Milton Williams; program repeated April 8.
APRIL 3, 1964	Tudorfest III: program includes John Cage, *Atlas Eclipticalis* (1961–62), with *Winter Music* (1957), electronic version, *Concert for Piano and Orchestra* (1958), *Cartridge Music* (1960), and *Music Walk* (1958); perform-

ers: Michael Callahan, electronics, John Chowning, percussion, Stuart Dempster, trombone, Warner Jepson, piano, Douglas Leedy, horn, Robert Mackler, viola and viola d'amore, Pauline Oliveros, horn and tuba, Dwight Peltzer, piano, Ann Riley, piano, Loren Rush, double bass, Ramon Sender, conductor, Stanley Shaff, trumpet, Linn Subotnick, viola, Morton Subotnick, clarinet, David Tudor, piano, Ian Underwood, flute and piccolo, Jack Van der Wyk, timpani; program performed twice, 6 P.M. and 8 P.M.

APRIL 22, 1964 Composers' Forum in conjunction with SFTMC presents a concert of electronic music in the San Francisco State College Gallery Lounge; the program includes James Tenney, *Collage #1 ("Blue Suede")* (1961); Ramon Sender, *Kore* (1961); Włodzimierz Kotoński, *Microstructures* (1963); Morton Subotnick, *Mandolin* (1961–63); Aurelio de la Vega, *Co-Ordinates;* and Mario Davidovsky, *Electronic Study #2* (1961).

MAY 4, 1964 The Ann Halprin Dancers' Workshop performs *Yellow Cab* at SFTMC, set to *Visage* (1961) by Luciano Berio; the program also includes Krysztof Penderecki, *Psalmus* (1961); Andrzej Dobrowolski, *Music for Tape No. 1* (1961); and Henri Lazarof, *Quantetti* (1963) performed by Leonard Stein, piano.

MAY 16–17, 1964 Lee Breuer presents *The Run*, an experimental narrative theater piece, at the SFTMC, featuring William Spencer and Warner Jepson, music, Elias Romero, liquid lights, Fumi Spencer, choreography, Norma Leistiko, dance, and Bill Ham, sculpture.

MAY 21, 23, 29–30, 1964 Steve Reich presents "Music Now Koncerts" at the San Francisco Mime Troupe Theatre, including ensemble improvisations and compositions by Reich, Phil Lesh, Tom Constanten, and Jon Gibson.

JUNE 15, 1964 SFTMC goes on tour, performing concerts from late June into early July at the First Unitarian Society in Minneapolis, Central Michigan University in Mount Pleasant, Michigan, College-Conservatory of Music in Cincinnati, Ball State Teachers College in Muncie, Indiana, and Center Harbor, New Hampshire.

JULY 13, 1964 Republican National Convention begins at the Cow Palace in San Francisco. Arizona senator Barry Goldwater gets party nomination.

JULY 24, 1964 The San Francisco Mime Troupe presents Molière's *Tartuffe,* adapted by Richard Sassoon, with music by Steve Reich.

AUGUST 18, 1964 Michael Callahan moves to New York. William Maginnis replaces him as SFTMC technical director.

OCTOBER 1, 1964 Thousands of University of California, Berkeley, students surround a police car after police arrest the civil rights activist Jack Weinberger, a former student. Protesting against the university's ban on political activism, the students form the Free Speech Movement.

OCTOBER 7 AND 9, 1964 SFTMC season concert "Music from the French Studios" program includes Bernard Parmegiani, *Phonosophobe,* and Luc Ferrari, *Tautologos I* (1961) and *Tautologos II* (1961), with visual environments by Anthony Martin, plus improvisation for clarinet, horn, and recorded sounds, followed by commentary.

OCTOBER 12 AND 14, 1964
West Coast Wind Quintet debut concert at SFTMC program includes Carl Nielsen, *Kvintet, Op. 43* (1922); Cage/Harrison/Cowell/Wigglesworth, *Sonorous and Exquisite Corpses;* Bulent Arel, *Stereo Electronic Music;* and Morton Subotnick, *Play! no. 1* (1964), for woodwind quintet, piano, and tape, with film by Anthony Martin.

OCTOBER 15–16, 1964
Additional performances of Audium, a sixteen-speaker experience of "controlled movement of electronic music through space," are presented in total darkness by Stanley Shaff and Douglas McEachern at the San Francisco Museum of Art.

OCTOBER 16, 1964
Stuart Dempster and Robert Moran present a KPFA benefit concert at SFTMC; the program includes Fredric Lieberman, *Card Overture with Promenade* (1964); John Cage, *Atlas Eclipticalis* (1961–62), *Winter Music* (1957), and *Fontana Mix* (1958); Robert Moran, *Bombardments No. 4* (1964, rev. 1968); Roman Haubenstock-Ramati, *Decisions I* (1951); and La Monte Young, *Poem for Chairs, Tables, and Benches, etc. (or other sound sources)* (1960).

NOVEMBER 4 AND 6, 1964
SFTMC season concert "The Music of Terry Riley" program includes *Music for "The Gift"* (1963), *I* (1964), *Shoeshine* (1964), *In B♭ or Is It A♭?* (1964), *Coule,* and *In C* (1964), performed by Riley, Pauline Oliveros, Morton Subotnick, Ramon Sender, Steve Reich, Jon Gibson, Jeannie Brechan, James Lowe, Sonny Lewis, Mel Weitsman, Warner Jepson, Stan Shaff, and Phil Winsor, with visual environments by Anthony Martin.

NOVEMBER 10, 1964
The Ann Halprin Dancers' Workshop performs at San Francisco State College in celebration of the tenth anniversary of the Poetry Center; program includes *The Flowerburger* (1959), *Intermission, Procession* (1964), and *Sound Event,* with electronic music by Morton Subotnick.

NOVEMBER 13, 1964
The Ann Halprin Dancers' Workshop repeats November 10 program as part of improvisation festival at Royce Hall, UCLA.

DECEMBER 2, 1964
Four thousand people hear Mario Savio deliver his famous speech denouncing "the operation of the machine" at a Free Speech rally at Sproul Plaza, UC Berkeley.

DECEMBER 2 AND 4, 1964
SFTMC season concert presents the poet, commentator, and critic Peter Yates in a lecture-concert on experimental music, including poetry, musical demonstration performed on an iron skillet, and color slides and 16 mm film on the Watts Towers.

LATE 1964
Don Buchla brings his Electric Music Box series 100, the electronic instrument commonly known as "the Buchla," to the SFTMC studio.

JANUARY 16, 1965	The San Francisco Conservatory of Music and the Women's Board of the San Francisco Museum of Art present "An Avant Garde Concert by John Cage and David Tudor" at the museum.
JANUARY 20, 1965	Lyndon Johnson is inaugurated as president of the United States. The following month, he orders the first air strike against North Vietnam.
JANUARY 27, 1965	SFTMC season concert "The Music of Steve Reich" program includes *It's Gonna Rain, or, Meet Brother Walter in Union Square after Listening to Terry Riley* (1965), *Music for Three or More Pianos or Piano and Tape* (1964), and *Livelihood* (1964).
FEBRUARY 15, 1965	Chamber Music Society concert in Golden Gate Park's Hall of Flowers, featuring SFTMC; the program includes Morton Subotnick, *Mandolin* (1963), for viola, tape, and 16 mm film, with Linn Subotnick, viola, and Anthony Martin, light projections.
FEBRUARY 21, 1965	California narcotics agents raid the Berkeley home of Augustus Owsley Stanley III, confiscating his laboratory equipment, which they mistakenly thought was for producing methadrine. In April, after he gets back his equipment, Owsley's LSD is available in the San Francisco Bay Area.
MARCH 21–25, 1965	Reverend Martin Luther King Jr. leads 25,000 voting rights advocates in march from Selma to Montgomery, Alabama.
APRIL 2–4, 1965	Charles Shere, Peter Winkler, and Robert Moran present "The Third Annual Festival of the Avant Garde" at SFTMC; program includes works by Moran, Winkler, Earle Brown, Joshua Rifkin, John Cage, Ian Underwood, and Douglas Leedy.
APRIL 12 AND 14, 1965	SFTMC season concert program includes Bruno Maderna, *Le rire* (1962); Steve Reich, *Livelihood* (1964); Earle Brown, *Times Five* (1963), for five instruments and two 2-channel tapes, featuring Jean Cunningham, flute, Stuart Dempster, trombone, Nathan Rubin, violin, Helen Stross, cello, and Ann Adams, harp; and an Anthony Martin–Morton Subotnick–Ramon Sender collaborative event in seven sections, for piano, clarinet, tape, and visual projections, including I. *UCLA*, II. *Improvisation*, III. *Objects*, IV. *Slide*, V. *Two Portraits JOHN, RICHARD*, VI. *Ninety Feet*, VII. *Improvisation*.
APRIL 24, 1965	The Ann Halprin Dancers' Workshop premieres *Parades and Changes* (1965–67) at Wheeler Hall, UC Berkeley, with music by Morton Subotnick, accompanied by Folke Rabe; later performed in Fresno (May) and in Europe (fall), where Rabe becomes co-composer.
MAY 3, 1965	Boyd Compton of the Rockefeller Foundation arrives in San Francisco for a twelve-day visit to research SFTMC grant proposal.
MAY 3 AND 5, 1965	SFTMC season concert program includes Mel Powell, *Second Electronic Study* (1962) and *Improvisation for Viola, Clarinet & Piano* (1962), performed by Linn Subotnick, viola, Morton Subotnick, clarinet, Naomi

Sparrow, piano; Gerald Shapiro, *Antiphonies for Piano and Tape* (1965), performed by Leila Birnbaum, piano; Folke Rabe, *Arg—N.Y. 3.5.65, 1–5pm* (1965), tape piece, and *Impromptu* (1962), performed by Terry Riley, piano, Stuart Dempster, trombone, Baruch Klein, cello, Jack Van der Wyk, percussion, Donald O'Brien, bass clarinet, Rabe conducting; Ramon Sender, *In the Garden* (1965), for two performers and tape, performed by Kiki Nelson, viola, and Morton Subotnick, clarinet, with visual projections by Anthony Martin; Pauline Oliveros, *Pieces of Eight* (1964), performed by Riley, flute, Subotnick, clarinet, Mark Shockman, oboe, Steven Wenrich, French horn, Robert Hughes, contra-bassoon, Donald O'Brien, bass clarinet and cash register, Stanley Shaff, trumpet, Dempster, trombone, Ernest Edwards, Paul Alexander, Robert Moran and Orville Dale, collectors, and Warner Jepson, conducting.

MAY 7, 1965

The San Francisco Mime Troupe presents Bertolt Brecht's *The Exception and the Rule* at the Gate Theatre, Sausalito, with music by Pauline Oliveros; presented with "The U.S. War in Vietnam," a talk by *Ramparts* magazine editor Robert Scheer.

MAY 21–23, 1965

"3 Concerts by Terry Riley" at SFTMC—a three-day festival of tape music and compositions, including *Bird of Paradise* (1964), *M . . . Mix* (1960–61), *Music for "The Gift"* (1963), *I* (1964), *In C* (1964), *Coule, In B♭ or Is It A♭?* (1964), and the premiere of *Tread on the Trail* (1965), featuring members of the Al Bent–Mel Martin rehearsal jazz band, with whom Riley was playing charts at the time; performers include Sonny Lewis, Stephan Pollard, Jeannie Brechan, Jon Gibson, Steve Reich, Mel Weitsman and Robin, Warner Jepson, Robert Mackler, Pauline Oliveros, Ramon Sender, Stuart Dempster, Beat Scherzer, Marvin Mendelow, George Ray, Terry Riley, Hart Smith, George Martin, Al Bent, Mel Martin, John Chambers, and Bill Douglas.

JUNE 7 AND 9, 1965

SFTMC season concert program includes Jan Bark, *Soulway, for Alto and Viola,* performed by Jeannie Brecken, alto, and Linn Subotnick, viola; Stephen Foster and Friends, *Massa's In de Cold Cold Ground, but O dat Watermelon;* Pauline Oliveros and Folke Rabe, *I've Got You under My Skin* (1965), performed by Jack Van der Wyk, percussion; Ramon Sender, *In the Garden with Gayathri* (1965), featuring tape, Anthony Martin, visual projections, and Gayathri Rajapur singing songs of India; Joseph Byrd, *The Ultimate and Plenary Catalysis of the Holy Church, Together with the Communion of Saints, and the Commencement of the Resurrection of the Blessed Martyrs,* featuring visual staging by Martin, Sender, and Don Buchla, based on original production under visual direction of Nancy Daniel.

JUNE 11, 1965

The Rockefeller Foundation awards $15,000 grant to the San Francisco Tape Music Center.

JUNE 17, 1965

The San Francisco Mime Troupe premieres *A Minstrel Show, or, Civil*

	Rights in a Cracker Barrel, with the film *O Dem Watermelons* by Robert Nelson and music by Steve Reich, at the Commedia Theatre, Palo Alto.
SUMMER 1965	Terry Riley, intending to move to Europe, instead ends up in New York City and joins La Monte Young's Theatre of Eternal Music.
SUMMER 1965	Morton Subotnick travels to the University of Illinois at Urbana-Champaign and to the Columbia-Princeton Electronic Music Center in New York City for two months to complete score for Georg Büchner's *Danton's Death,* the opening play at Lincoln Center's new Vivian Beaumont Repertory Theater, Herbert Blau and Jules Irving, directors; work on the electronic score had begun at the SFTMC.
JUNE 29, 1965	The Red Dog Saloon opens in Virginia City, Nevada, featuring the Charlatans, a San Francisco rock band.
JULY 25, 1965	The San Francisco Mime Troupe premieres Giordano Bruno's *Il Candelaio,* adapted by Peter Berg, in Washington Square Park, music by Pauline Oliveros.
JULY 25, 1965	Bob Dylan, performing at the Newport Folk festival, is booed for playing with an electric band.
AUGUST 7, 1965	The San Francisco Mime Troupe performs Giordano Bruno's *Il Candelaio,* adapted by Peter Berg, in Lafayette Park and, in a thinly veiled effort by the Parks Commission to clamp down on the Mime Troupe's left-leaning politics, R. G. Davis is arrested for performing in the parks without a permit.
AUGUST 11, 1965	Riots break out in the Watts section of South Central Los Angeles.
SEPTEMBER 1965	Steve Reich moves to New York City.
OCTOBER 11 AND 13, 1965	SFTMC season concert program includes Mel Powell, *Events* (1963); James Tenney, *Ergodos* (1963–64); Milton Babbitt, *Ensembles for Synthesizer* (1962–64); Mauricio Kagel, *Antithesis* (1962–63); Ramon Sender and Anthony Martin, *After General William Booth Enters into Heaven* (1965).
OCTOBER 14, 1965	The San Francisco Mime Troupe presents Michel de Ghelderode's *Chronicles of Hell* at the Commedia Theatre, Palo Alto, with sound by Pauline Oliveros; presented with Lawrence Ferlinghetti or David Meltzer reading from their own work.
NOVEMBER 6, 1965	"Appeal I" benefit party for R. G. Davis and the San Francisco Mime Troupe legal defense held at Mime Troupe headquarters, 924 Howard Street, San Francisco, produced by Bill Graham; participants include Sandy Bull, the Fugs, Jefferson Airplane, John Handy Quintet, Allen Ginsberg, and Family Dog.
NOVEMBER 8 AND 10, 1965	SFTMC season concert program includes Mario Davidovsky, *Synchronisms No. 3* (1965), performed by Bonnie Hampton, cello, with electronic sounds; Elliott Carter, *Sonata for Cello and Piano* (1948), performed by Hampton and Nathan Schwartz, piano; and Pauline

	Oliveros, *George Washington Slept Here* (1965), *George Washington Slept Here Too* (1965), and *Light Piece for David Tudor* (1965), with visual projections by Anthony Martin.
NOVEMBER 27, 1965	Ken Kesey hosts the first Acid Test near Santa Cruz, including Neal Cassady and the rock band the Warlocks.
DECEMBER 10, 1965	"Appeal II" benefit party for the San Francisco Mime Troupe held at the Fillmore Auditorium, produced by Bill Graham; participants include the Jefferson Airplane, Grateful Dead, Mystery Trend, and the Great Society.
DECEMBER 15, 1965	SFTMC concert program includes Gino Marinuzzi, *Traiettorie,* tape piece; Valentino Bucchi, *Girotondo,* tape piece; Robert Schuman, *3 Melodramas,* performed by the Mills Performing Group, Naomi Sparrow, piano, Anna Carol Dudley, narrator, with visual projections by Anthony Martin; Morton Subotnick, *Serenade #3* (1965), performed by Sparrow, Subotnick, clarinet, Jean Cunningham, flute, and Nathan Rubin, violin and tape; Barney Childs, *Music for Voice and Piano,* performed by Sparrow and Dudley; Richard Swift, *Carmina Archilochi* (1965), performed by Cunningham, Subotnick, Dudley, Sally Kell, cello, and Jack Van der Wyk, percussion.
JANUARY 1966	Morton Subotnick announces he will leave the SFTMC and Mills College later in the year for a position as artist in residence at New York University's new School of the Arts, beginning in the fall.
JANUARY 8, 1966	Ken Kesey hosts Acid Test at the Fillmore Auditorium.
JANUARY 14, 1966	"Appeal III" benefit party for San Francisco Mime Troupe held at the Fillmore Auditorium, produced by Bill Graham; participants include the Grateful Dead, Mystery Trend, Great Society, and the Gentlemen's Band; after this third benefit, Graham and the Mime Troupe part ways.
JANUARY 15, 1966	Bill Ham presents light show with music by William Spencer at SFTMC.
JANUARY 21–23, 1966	The Trips Festival, a weekend of music, light shows, and other recreational events, takes place at Longshoremen's Hall, produced by Ken Kesey, Stewart Brand, and Ramon Sender; participants include the Merry Pranksters, Allen Ginsberg, the Grateful Dead, Big Brother and the Holding Company, the Loading Zone, Henry Jacobs's air dome projections, Don Buchla's sound-light console, "America Needs Indians," Open Theatre, Anthony Martin's visual projections, and many others.
JANUARY 23, 1966	The San Francisco Mime Troupe presents Pauline Oliveros in Concert—"A Side Trip" at the Encore Theatre; the program includes *Apple Box Orchestra with Bottle Chorus* (1964), performed by William Maginnis, Loren Rush, Robert Mackler, Orville Dale, William Spencer,

and "Bottle Chorus," composed of members of the Mime Troupe, with Robert Moran conducting; *A Theatre Piece* (1965), collaboration by Oliveros, Elizabeth Harris, and Ronald Chase, performed by Sandra Archer, Lynn Brown, Ray Davis, Ronald Davis, Bill Freese, Elaine Grosso, Warner Jepson, Jerry Jump, Jane Lapiner, Norma Leistiko, Lomuto, John Robb, Paula Sakowski, Fumi Spencer, and Kenji Spencer; sound by Oliveros, choreography by Harris, visuals and lighting by Chase; slides photographed by Anthony Martin, film by Robert Feldman, sound assistant, Charles MacDermed; assistant on sets and light, Marianne Bodien; light instruments executed by William Maginnis; produced by Bill Graham; program begins with R. G. Davis event, followed by Jane Lapiner Dance Company event.

FEBRUARY 25, 1966 The Rockefeller Foundation awards a $200,000 grant to Mills College to bring SFTMC to Mills and merge it with the Mills Performing Group "as a joint center for creative and performing arts on the Mills College campus."

SPRING 1966 Ramon Sender goes to the desert to meditate and work; upon his return to San Francisco in the summer, he immediately decamps for Morning Star Ranch.

MARCH 21, 1966 SFTMC and Mills Performing Group perform at the Los Angeles County Museum of Art; the program includes Jean-Philippe Rameau, *Cantata: Orphée;* Gerald Shapiro, *Chamber Music;* Ramon Sender, *In the Garden* (1965); Anthony Martin, *Room* (1964–65); Mario Davidovsky, *Synchronism No. 3* (1965); and Morton Subotnick, *The Tarot, Part III* (1965); performers include Subotnick, Martin, and members of the Mills Performing Group.

MARCH 21–22, 1966 Stuart Dempster gives a solo trombone recital at SFTMC; the program includes Larry Austin, *Changes* (1965); Barney Childs, *Sonata;* John Cage, *Solo for Sliding Trombone* (1958); Luciano Berio, *Sequenza V* (1966); Robert Erickson, *Ricercar à 5* (1966); and Pauline Oliveros, *In the Garden: A Theater Piece for Trombone Player and Tape* (1966) (though here presented as *A Theater Piece for Trombone Player and Tape* so as to avoid confusion with *In the Garden* by Ramon Sender).

APRIL 3, 8, AND 9, 1966 Second "Third Annual Festival of the Avant Garde" at SFTMC; program includes John Cage, Christian Wolff, Morton Feldman, Toshi Ichiyanagi, Douglas Leedy, and Ian Underwood.

APRIL 28, 1966 Don Buchla and Anthony Martin present *Sensorium,* an evening of electronic music and light show, at the San Francisco Museum of Art.

MAY 2, 1966 Warner Jepson and Charles MacDermed perform a program of new music with projections by Anthony Martin at SFTMC.

MAY 5, 1966 SFTMC participates in the San Francisco Festival of Contemporary Music, a three-concert series at the San Francisco Museum of Art, featuring works by Oliveros, Subotnick, Sender, Martin, and Henri

	Pousseur; the festival is a collaboration between SFTMC, Composers' Forum, and the Mills Performing Group.
MAY 17–18, 1966	The San Francisco Conservatory of Music presents a "New Music by Robert Erickson" program, including performances by Stuart Dempster, Loren Rush, and Maro Ajemian, plus Warner Jepson premiering *Piece for Bells and Toy Pianos* (1965).
SUMMER 1966	SFTMC moves to Mills College. Pauline Oliveros becomes director; Anthony Martin becomes visual director; Bill Maginnis is technical director.

ARCHIVAL RECORDINGS

The following recordings, now housed in the Archives of the Center for Contemporary Music, F. W. Olin Library, Mills College, Oakland, California, were transferred to CD intact from the original reels by Maggi Payne, sound engineer and transfer archivist.

Ashley, Robert. *Heat*. 1961. Sender Archive, tape 24. Call no. 780.904 M65CD121.

Brecht, George. *Card Piece* (for voice). Recorded at the Tudorfest (April 8, 1964). Call number 780.904 M65CD170.

Cage, John. *34' 46.776"*. 1954. David Tudor and Dwight Pelzter, pianos. Two versions performed at the Tudorfest (March 30 and April 6, 1964). Call no. 780.904 M65CD159.

———. *Concert for Piano and Orchestra*. 1958. Two versions performed at the Tudorfest (April 3, 1964). David Tudor, piano and other unidentified performers. Call no. 780.904 M65CD161.

———. *Cartridge Music*. 1960. Performed at the Tudorfest (April 3, 1964). Call no. 780.904 M65CD157.

———. *Cartridge Music*. 1960. Performed at the Tudorfest (April 3, 1964, second performance). Call no. 780.904 M65CD158.

———. *Music for Amplified Toy Pianos*. 1960. David Tudor, toy pianos and amplifiers. Performed at the Tudorfest (April 1, 1964). Call no. 780.904 M65CD160.

———. *Music for Amplified Toy Pianos*. 1960. David Tudor on toy pianos and amplifiers. Performed at the Tudorfest (April 8, 1964). Call no. 780.904 M65CD161.

———. *Music Walk*. 1960. Two versions recorded at the Tudorfest (April 3, 1964). Call no. 780.904 M65CD165.

———. *Variations II*. 1961. Two versions performed by David Tudor at the Tudorfest (April 1 and 8, 1964). Call no. 780.904 M65CD163.

———. *Atlas Elipticalis* (1961–62) with *Winter Music* (1957). Two versions performed at the Tudorfest (April 3, 1964). Call no. 780.904 M65CD160.

Ichiyanagi, Toshi. *Sapporo*. 1962. Two versions performed at the Tudorfest (April 1 and 8, 1964). Performed by Stuart Dempster, Pauline Oliveros, Loren Rush, Ramon Sender, Morton Subotnick, David Tudor, and Milton Williams. Call no. 780.904 M65CD164.

———. *Music for Piano, no. 4*. Ca. 1963. Four versions performed at the Tudorfest (March 30, April 1 and 6, 1964). David Tudor and Pauline Oliveros on pianos. Call no. 780.904 M65CD162.

Lucier, Alvin. *Action Music* for piano, Book I. 1962. Two versions performed by David Tudor on piano at the Tudorfest (March 30 and April 6, 1964). Call no. 780.904 M65CD165.

Maginnis, William. Three improvisations for electronic sounds: *Flight, Sec,* and *Sweet.* 1965. Created at the San Francisco Tape Music Center. This is the first composition using the "Buchla Box." Call no. 780.904 M65CD24.

———. *Fortune.* 1965; *Awakening.* 1965; *Lifetime.* Call no. 780.904 M65CD25.

———. *Meditation for Ramon Sender.* 1966. Call no. 780.904 M65CD24.

———. *Awakening.* Sender Archive, tape 1. Call no. 780.904 M65CD121.

Martin, Anthony. *Room.* 1964–65. This is the tape component to a multimedia piece, which also includes film, slide projections, and live musicians on stage. Call no. 780.904 M65CD26.

Maxfield, Richard. *Sine Music; Trinity Piece; Pastoral Symphony* (1959); *Cough Music* (1959). Call no. 780.904 M65CD172.

Oliveros, Pauline. *Trio* (French horn, clarinet, and bassoon). 1955. Call no. 780.904 M65CD151.

———. *3 Songs* for voice and piano. 1957. Call no. 780.904 M65CD151.

———. *Time Perspectives.* 1961. Pauline Oliveros's first tape composition. Call no. 780.904 M65CD157.

———. *Trio for Flute, Piano, and Page Turner.* 1961. Two versions. Call no. 780.904 M65CD169.

———. *Tape Chart #1.* 1962. Call no. 780.904 M65CD150.

———. *Before and After Math.* 1963. Improvisation with Ramon Sender, Morton Subotnick, Pauline Oliveros, Michael Callahan, and dancer John Graham. Call no. 780.904 M65CD153.

———. *Outline for Flute, Percussion, and String Bass.* 1963. Source tape. Call no. 780.904 M65CD172.

———. *Seven Passages.* 1963. Call no. 780.904 M65CD156.

———. *Pieces of Eight.* 1964. Tape component only. Call no. 780.904 M65CD153.

———. *Pieces of Eight.* 1964. Two recordings of the same 1965 performance. Call no. 780.904 M65CD173.

———. *Before the Music Ends.* 1965. Call no. 780.904 M65CD149.

———. *Bye Bye Butterfly.* 1965. Two versions. Recorded for a dance work by Elizabeth Harris entitled W*inter Light.* Call no. 780.904 M65CD169.

———. *Chronicles of Hell.* 1965. Call no. 780.904 M65CD172.

———. *The Covenant.* 1965. Call no. 780.904 M65CD172.

———. *The Covenant.* 1965. Film version, October 1965. Call no. 780.904 M65CD155.

———. *George Washington Slept Here.* 1965. Call no. 780.904 M65CD151.

———. *George Washington Slept Here.* 1965. "This is an early remix of appropriated source material and this was in turn used as source material for *George Washington Slept Here.* This is not a composition, only source material."—Pauline Oliveros, April 17, 2004. Call no. 780.904 M65CD155.

———. *Light Piece for David Tudor.* 1965. Source tape. Call no. 780.904 M65CD154.

———. *Light Piece for David Tudor, I-II.* 1965. Call no. 780.904 M65CD149.

———. *Mnemonics I.* 1965. Call no. 780.904 M65CD152.

———. *Mnemonics II.* 1965. Call no. 780.904 M65CD152.
———. *Mnemonics III.* 1965. Call no. 780.904 M65CD152.
———. *Mnemonics V.* 1965. Call no. 780.904 M65CD153.
———. *Rock Symphony (The SSSSSSSSSSSSS).* 1965. Four versions. Call no. 780.904 M65CD158.
———. *A Theater Piece.* 1965. Call no. 780.904 M65CD157.
———. *Big Mother Is Watching You.* 1966. Call no. 780.904 M65CD170.
———. *The C(s) for ONCE.* 1966. Call no. 780.904 M65CD154.
———. *The Day I Disconnected the Record Head and Forgot to Reconnect It.* 1966. Call no. 780.904 M65CD170.
———. *Theater Piece for Trombone Player.* 1966. Call no. 780.904 M65CD156.
———. *Theater Piece for Trombone Player.* 1966. Call no. 780.904 M65CD172.
———. *I of IV.* 1966. Two versions. Call no. 780.904 M65CD167.
———. *II of IV.* 1966. Call no. 780.904 M65CD167.
———. *III of IV.* 1966. Call no. 780.904 M65CD167.
———. *III of IV.* 1966. Call no. 780.904 M65CD168.
———. *III.* Call no. 780.904 M65CD168.
———. *IV of IV.* 1966. Call no. 780.904 M65CD168.
———. *V of IV.* 1966. Call no. 780.904 M65CD168.
———. *Circuitry.* 1967. Two versions. Call no. 780.904 M65CD171.
———. *Engineer's Delight* (for piccolo and seven conductors). 1967. Call no. 780.904 M65CD168.
———. *Feedback Recording I.* Call no. 780.904 M65CD152.
———. *Improvisation 1–2.* Call no. 780.904 M65CD155.
———. Unidentified work. Call no. 780.904 M65CD152.
Oliveros, Pauline, and David Tudor. *Duo for Accordion and Bandoneon with Possible Mynah Bird Obbligato.* Seesaw version. 1964. Two versions performed at the Tudorfest (March 30 and April 6, 1964). Call no. 780.904 M65CD30.
———. *Duo for Accordion and Bandoneon with Possible Mynah Bird Obbligato.* Rehearsal tape. 1964. Call no. 780.904 M65CD173.
Reich, Steve. *Livelihood.* 1964. Call no. 780.904 M65CD48.
———. *The Plastic Haircut.* 1964. Soundtrack to a film by Robert Nelson. Call no. 780.904 M65CD48.
Riley, Terry. *2 Songs.* 1957. #1 (voice and piano). Call no. 780.904 M65CD151.
———. *Piano Pieces,* no. 1–2. 1958–59. Two versions performed by the composer. Call no. 780.904 M65CD165.
———. *Concert for Two Pianos and Five Tape Recorders.* 1960. Performed by Terry Riley and La Monte Young. Call no. 780.904 M65CD165.
———. *Envelope.* 1960. Call no. 780.904 M65CD164.
———. *String Quartet.* 1960. Call no. 780.904 M65CD164.
———. *Mescalin Mix.* 1960–61. Call no. 780.904 M65CD48.
Rush, Loren. *Auden Music* (saxophone, piano, trumpet, trombone?). Call no. 780.904 M65CD151.

———. *Viola + Shhhhh Music* (voice, viola, and piano). Call no. 780.904 M65CD151.

Sender, Ramon. *Four Sanskrit Hymns*. 1961. Sender Archive, tapes 48–50. Call no. 780.904 M65CD127.

———. *Improvisation for Piano*. 1961. Sender Archive, tape 57. Call no. 780.904 M65CD125.

———. *Kore*. 1961. Excerpt. Call no. 780.904 M65CD58.

———. *Kore*. 1961. Call no. 780.904 M65CD68.

———. *Kore*. 1961. Sender Archive, tape 67. Call no. 780.904 M65CD122.

———. *Traversals*. 1961. Call no. 708.904 M65CD32.

———. *Information* for narrator and two pianos. 1962. Call no. 780.904 M65CD35.

———. *Information* for narrator and two pianos. 1962. Call no. 780.904 M65CD69.

———. *Information* for narrator and two pianos. 1962. Sender Archive, tape 7. Three versions. Call no. 780.904 M65CD124.

———. *Kronos*. 1962. Call no. 780.904 M65CD35.

———. *Kronos*. 1962. Sender Archive, tape 44. Call no. 780.904 M65CD122.

———. *Triad*. 1962. Call no. 780.904 M65CD33.

———. *Interstices*. 1963. Call no. 780.904 M65CD163.

———. *Ramon Takes a Bath, or, I Laid Mr. Clean for the F.B.I.* 1963. Sender Archive, tape 3. Three versions. Call no. 780.904 M65CD124.

———. *Balances*. 1964. Sender Archive, tape 38. Call no. 780.904 M65CD121.

———. *Balances,* second movement. 1964. Sender Archive, tape 68. Call no. 780.904 M65CD121.

———. *Desert Ambulance*. 1964. Track 1 is the tape component (music) only; track 2 is the tape component (music) for the audience in the left channel and Ramon Sender's instructions to Pauline Oliveros in the right channel. Call no. 780.904 M65CD33.

———. *Desert Ambulance*. 1964. Sender Archive, tape 2. Call no. 780.904 M65CD122.

———. *Desert Ambulance*. 1964. Sender Archive, tape 31. Call no. 780.904 M65CD122.

———. *Desert Ambulance*. 1964. Tape component. Sender Archive, tape 43. Call no. 780.904 M65CD122.

———. *Worldfood III*. Ca. 1964. Sender Archive, tape 26. Call no. 780.904 M65CD123.

———. *Worldfood XII*. 1964. Sender Archive, tape 16. Call no. 780.904 M65CD125.

———. *In the Garden*. 1965. Call no. 780.904 M65CD124.

———. *Time Fields*. 1965. Sender Archive, tape 34. Call no. 780.904 M65CD125.

———. *Wagner*. 1965. Three submasters. Sender Archive, tape 45. Call no. 780.904 M65CD126.

———. *Hatha Yoga Instructions*. 1966. Sender Archive, tape 52. Call no. 780.904 M65CD128–29.

———. *Ushas*. 1968. Sender Archive, tape 14. Call no. 780.904 M65CD121.

———. *Enoughing*. 1969 [?]. Sender Archive, tape 22. Call no. 780.904 M65CD121.

———. *Great Grandpa's Death Rattle Blues in F#*. 1981. Sender Archive, tape 37. Call no. 780.904 M65CD126.

Subotnick, Morton. *Serenade, no. 1*. 1960. Call no. 780.904 M65CD34.

———. *The Five-Legged Stool*. 1962. Call no. 780.904 M65CD36.

———. *Serenade, no. 2*. 1962. Call no. 780.904 M65CD34.

———. *Yod.* 1962. Call no. 780.904 M65CD68.

———. *Mandolin.* 1963. Call no. 780.904 M65CD34.

———. *Play! no. 2.* 1964. Performed by the Oakland Symphony, 1964. Call no. 780.904 M65CD33.

———. *Serenade, no. 3.* 1965. Three versions. Call no. 780.904 M65CD34.

GROUP IMPROVISATIONS

Improvisations. 1958. Pauline Oliveros, Loren Rush, Terry Riley, and Laurel Johnson. Call no. 780.904 M65CD150.

Improvisations. December 1961. Pauline Oliveros, Ramon Sender, and Laurel Johnson. Call no. 780.904 M65CD150.

Improvisation. Pauline Oliveros, Ramon Sender, Morton Subotnick. Dancers Lynne Palmer and John Graham also performed. Call no. 780.904 M65CD154.

Improvisation (guitar and recorders). Pauline Oliveros, Laurel Johnson, and Mildred Inwood. Call no. 780.904 M65CD151.

Improvisations for KPFA. Pauline Oliveros, Morton Subotnick, Ramon Sender. Call no. 780.904 M65CD31.

Spoken piece with improvisation. Morton Subotnick, Ramon Sender. Call no. 780.904 M65CD33.

MISCELLANEOUS

Tony Martin, Ramon Sender, and Morton Subotnick interviewed by Myron Bennett, College Conservatory of Music in Cincinnati, Ohio, for WGUC-FM, July 13, 1964. Call no. 780.904 M65CD1.

San Francisco Tape Music Center demo. Call no. 780.904 M65CD1.

San Francisco Tape Center demo. Two-channel source tape. Call no. 780.904 M65CD1.

The first printing of this book was issued with a DVD included. The contents of that DVD can be accessed at www.ucpress.edu/go/tapemusiccenter.

DVD PROGRAM NOTES

The San Francisco Tape Music Center reconvened for a festival entitled "Wow & Flutter: The San Francisco Tape Music Center, 1961–Now," sponsored by the Experimental Media and Performing Arts Center and held at the RPI Playhouse, at Rensselaer Polytechnic Institute, Troy, New York, on October 1 and 2, 2004. The DVD accompanying this book contains a video documentation of the "Wow & Flutter" festival, which not only celebrated the artistic achievements of Pauline Oliveros, Ramon Sender, Tony Martin, Morton Subotnick, and Bill Maginnis, but also demonstrated the continuing vitality of their creative work. As Johannes Goebel explained in his opening remarks for the "Wow & Flutter" program booklet: "The SFTMC as such existed for a few years in the 1960s. But its members kept their curiosity as artists as they all went into different directions. Now they meet here in Troy. Not to celebrate the past, but to celebrate the continuity of their artistic practice."

**WOW & FLUTTER:
THE SAN FRANCISCO TAPE MUSIC CENTER,
1961–NOW**

Johannes Goebel	CURATOR
Jason Steven Murphy	PROJECT MANAGER
Karin Hillen and Kim Gardner	ADMINISTRATION
Todd Vos	AUDIO
Jay Maury	LIGHTING AND PROJECTION
Kevin Luddy	LOGISTICS ASSISTANT
Christopher Rines, Kara Janeczko, and Pete Hallsworth	STAGEHANDS
Zulma Aguiar	RESEARCH ASSISTANT
Jennifer Rush and Ryan McAlpine	STUDENT ASSISTANTS
Documentation	
Frans Swarte	AUDIO
Roger Bailey, Eleanor Goldsmith, and Michael DiPaolo	VIDEO
Andy Clark and Dan Ostrov	STUDENT ASSISTANTS

Friday, October 1, 2004
"Three Thirds"

Pauline Oliveros and Tony Martin
Circuitry for Percussion and Light
[20:54]

Morris Lang, Bill Maginnis, Terry Silverlight, Warren Smith, and Brian Willson	PERCUSSION
Tony Martin	LIGHT
Bob Bielecki	TECHNICAL ASSISTANCE

Morton Subotnick
Until Spring Revisited
[13:05]

Morton Subotnick	LAPTOP

Tony Martin
Silent Light
[9:47]

Tony Martin	VISUAL COMPOSITION AND PERFORMANCE
Margot Farrington	FLASHLIGHT PERFORMER

Ramon Sender
Tropical Fish Opera
[7:17]

Bill Maginnis	PERCUSSION
Pauline Oliveros	ACCORDION
Ramon Sender	VOICE
Morton Subotnick	CLARINET

Morton Subotnick
Mandolin
[18:14]

Mark Menzies	VIOLA
Tony Martin	VISUAL COMPOSITION AND PERFORMANCE
Morton Subotnick	SOUND PROJECTION

Pauline Oliveros
Bye Bye Butterfly
[8:22]

Tony Martin	VISUAL COMPOSITION AND PERFORMANCE
Pauline Oliveros	SOUND PROJECTION

Ramon Sender
Great Grandpa Lemuel's Death-Rattle Reincarnation Blues in F Sharp
[8:28]

Ramon Sender	ACCORDION AND VOCALS
Bill Maginnis	DRUMS

Reggie's Red Hot Feetwarmers

Reggie Scanlon	BASS
Tom Shields	TROMBONE
Mike Canonico	TRUMPET
Ron Bill	BANJO
Tony Martin	LIGHT

Improvisation
[6:53]

Pauline Oliveros	ACCORDION
Morton Subotnick	CLARINET
Bill Maginnis	PERCUSSION
Ramon Sender	PIANO

Saturday, October 2, 2004

"Two Halves and Four Quarters"

Ramon Sender
Kore
[9:42]

Tony Martin	VISUAL COMPOSITION AND PERFORMANCE
Ramon Sender	SOUND PROJECTION

Improvisation

[7:43]

Pauline Oliveros	ACCORDION
Morton Subotnick	CLARINET
Bill Maginnis	PERCUSSION
Ramon Sender	PIANO

Pauline Oliveros
Apple Box Double

[12:53]

Pauline Oliveros and Seth Cluett	APPLE BOXES

Ramon Sender and Tony Martin
Desert Ambulance

[16:17]

Pauline Oliveros	ACCORDION
Tony Martin	VISUAL COMPOSITION AND PERFORMANCE

Morton Subotnick
Release

[33:38]

The Ensemble Sospeso

Mark Menzies	VIOLIN
Christopher Finckel	CELLO
Marianne Gythfeldt	CLARINET
Stephen Gosling	PIANO
Nick Williams	COMPUTER OPERATOR

Tony Martin
Silent Light

[10:41]

Tony Martin	VISUAL COMPOSITION AND PERFORMANCE
Margot Farrington	FLASHLIGHT PERFORMER

Pauline Oliveros
Pauline's Solo

[17:59]

Pauline Oliveros	ACCORDION AND EXPANDED INSTRUMENT SYSTEM (EIS) IN EIGHT CHANNELS

NOTES

Circuitry for Percussion and Light (1967)

Circuitry was composed in 1967 in collaboration with the visual composer-performer Anthony Martin. The score is expressed for the performers by lights illuminating a three-by-four matrix score. The matrix contains columns of three choices each for TEMPO, DYNAMICS, METHOD, and STYLE. Four performers interpret the score using percussion arrays, and a fifth performer plays a drum set expressing a variety of popular styles. Each of the five performers plays when cued by his desk light. All lights respond to the players' sounds that are picked up by microphones, filtered, and sent to silicon-controlled rectifiers that turn the desk and score lights on and off. Thus the performers are in a kind of feedback loop that controls the performance and also the artist's lighting for the piece. Tonight's performance has been recreated using the original equipment constructed for the performance in 1966 by Carl Countryman. The equipment was refurbished by Bob Bielecki. William Maginnis, who is performing tonight, was the original drum set player in 1967.

Pauline Oliveros

Circuitry was a joint effort of Pauline and myself when we were the directors of the Mills Tape Music Center in 1967, and performed at the University of Illinois. It carried on my enthusiasm with electronics as a visual tool begun with my *Floorlamps* for sound-visual feedback of 1966. We configured microphone circuits from five percussionists to connect with light sources for scoring and to create various visual events. There is a "scoreboard" with twelve small lightbulbs for the performers to read and determine the character of the sounds they make. Each player also has a light nearby to indicate when to play. There are additional spotlights to light them and the environment in different ways. This is all interconnected in a loop of sound and light information. To do this, we use audio and visual interface electronics, a filter-counter-10-channel SCR unit built by Carl Countryman. The performers, their reflections and shadows, appear and disappear in front of a cyclorama, making a dramatic overlay of the scoreboard lights, colored light illuminating their gear, through drumheads, reflecting off their partial figures: a rich yet articulate amalgam of interdependent sound, imagery, and environmental light.

Tony Martin

Until Spring Revisited (2003–)

Until Spring Revisited is a general title I am using for the development of a full evening laptop event. I hope to premiere the first version of this in February 2005 in New York City. The beginnings of this date back to the development of the Buchla Synthesizer at the SFTMC in the early 1960s, when I had a dream of a "black box"–type electronic tool that would be in the home so that, like a painting easel, it would be a sound/music generator for creating new sound art pieces. This is not the right place for the history of all this, but it relates to the laptop evening I am developing. First, I had imagined that the new technology would allow for people to create new art with sound, and that it would be done in the home and, perhaps, for the home environment. When, a few years later, I had the opportunity to do a work for Nonesuch Records, *Silver Apples of the Moon* (1966–67), I pursued the idea that the Buchla Box, though brilliantly versatile, did not lend itself to the kind of large-scale work I was after. This meant that to make a work thirty minutes long involved tape recorders. The interaction with the equipment was thus limited to only portions of the composing experience. Also, it became clear that my aesthetic understanding about what kind of experience I hoped to end up with was unclear. As time went on, and I was fortunate enough to be commissioned to do more works for the record, I finally came to do a work where I felt that the aesthetic issue had been resolved. That work was *Until Spring* (1976). However, the issue of being able to interact with the medium for long periods of time (and work with the kind of density and variety of materials I wished to use) was still beyond my grasp. Now, with the new generation of laptops, I feel that I can again pursue this and complete what I had hoped to accomplish back on Divisadero Street in the 1960s. The title refers to the work *Until Spring* and where I might have gone with it had today's technology been there in 1976. Some of the materials used in these performances are from the 1976 work, the rest of the materials are new.

There is no ONE version. Rather, it is an ongoing examination of prepared materials that are improvised with each time I perform. In its final form (February 2005) I'll be working with a second laptop performer and a light artist. For now, I'll do a short performance with the materials as they have developed to date.

Morton Subotnick

Silent Light (1967, 2004)

Silent Light was first composed as an attempt at pure light "visual music," first performed in 1967 at NYU. In that early version and the current 2004 version, performers make use of the pure light of flashlights, various lenses, and differently silvered mirrors. Combined with this is imagery from customized projection apparatus. Film and overhead projection were originally used, and now in this version, I perform live, using a stand-alone computer program created for me by Hunter Ochs. This is video-projected on the stage and throughout the auditorium. Specific kinds of individual events of different feeling occur in parts of the space, making a concentric event of center, midspace, and periphery. There is an exchange of high-energy intensity and peacefulness between these areas. The differing character of projected light makes a ten-minute journey that begins in question and provocation and ends in illumination and light as nutrient energy. *Silent Night* was performed on both nights of the "Wow & Flutter" festival.

Tony Martin

Tropical Fish Opera (1962)

During the Sonics series of concerts at the San Francisco Conservatory of Music (1961–62), it became traditional from the beginning to include a live improvisation, and many of these events were named "operas," inasmuch as they frequently included dancers from the Ann Halprin Dancers' Workshop and thus contained a theatrical element. For one of these, I borrowed a tank of tropical fish from a local pet store and placed it as the score center stage. The first performers included Pauline Oliveros on French horn, myself on piano, Loren Rush on double bass, and Morton Subotnick on clarinet. Thus, the *Tropical Fish Opera* was born, and subsequently enjoyed a number of performances, including one that the famed *San Francisco Chronicle* columnist Herb Caen commented on, under the heading "Culture Corner" (see below). Yehudi Menuhin even mentioned it in passing in his public television series on contemporary music during a dour mention of Chance Music, and I paraphrase: "And there even are some composers who use a tank of fish as a score!"

The idea of a three-dimensional score (tank) with movable notes (fish) who can either be pitched high (top of the tank) or loud or soft (close to performer or further away) always intrigued me because the same score was being read from three different directions. Therefore some sort of thematic unity emerges, albeit of an unusual type.

> I suppose you missed the S. F. Chamber Music Society's recital of avant-garde music at Fireman's Fund Auditorium the other night. So did I, dunderhead that I am. Among the "selections" was a piece in which the musicians gathered around a 10-gallon aquarium with five lines painted on it to represent the musical staff. Inside the tank swam three goldfish, whose movements represented "notes" to be played by the gallant musicians. . . . Unfortunately, the fish assigned to Nathan Rubin, concertmaster of the Oakland Symphony, and Clarinetist Larry London settled to the bottom and refused to move. Rubin dutifully played one unvarying low note but London, eventually bored, began improvising a merry tune. At which Rubin swung around and barked, "What's the matter, London? Can't you read fish?" (Herb Caen, "The Rambling Wreck," *San Francisco Chronicle,* sometime in the mid-1970s)

Ramon Sender

Mandolin (1963)

Mandolin is a concert version of the original theater piece, *A Theater Piece after Sonnet No. 47 of Petrarch,* premiered in 1963 at the SFTMC. This was my second large-scale theater (multimedia) work; the first, *Sound Blocks: An Heroic Vision,* was premiered in 1961. The original *Petrarch* theater piece was a full-evening work. The viola part was performed by Linn Subotnick (the viola imbedded in the electronic score was recorded by her as well), the set was by Judy Davis, movement and voice were by John Graham, and the lighting and visual composition were by Tony Martin. I thought that I would step back and say good-bye to the nineteenth century and try to move on from there, rather than thinking of using new media as a "next step" from the modernist sensibility and the early twentieth-century break from the nineteenth century.

I used a work by Franz Liszt, *Transcendental Étude after Petrarch's Sonnet No. 47,* as a focal point in the work. (The grand piano is seen without a performer playing Liszt's piano étude.) In the original version, John Graham read the entire sonnet. In this version, it is left out, as well as the movement and set. The set was the construction of a wall across the front of the stage. I continued to develop my thinking about the nature of a "theater piece." It took many forms and ended with *Intimate Immensity,* premiered a few years ago at Lincoln Center.

The following is an excerpt of a review of the original version:

> Electronic music, living music, visual projections, pantomime, the spoken word, lighting effects, and scenery made up a strange mixture of fantasy in Morton Subotnick's latest avant-garde stage concept, Monday night at the San Francisco Tape Music Center. *A Theater Piece*

after Sonnet No. 47 of Petrarch is the work's title. Whether you choose to call it a composition, a play or merely a bizarre experiment, I myself found it fully absorbing. . . . Its curious complex idiom suggests the possibility that later ventures of the same sort, by Subotnick or other creators, can prove to be significant works of art. (Alexander Fried, "Bizarre Musical Fantasy," *San Francisco Examiner,* January 15, 1964)

Morton Subotnick

Mandolin (1963): I've always performed this visual composition using two overhead projectors. For me, it is an exhilarating painterly and poetic expression of mid-1960s feeling. It became a classic San Francisco Tape Music Center signature piece. Direct configuring of abstract visual language and dynamics is brought into play working with both dry and liquid ingredients together. There is a gradual shift in the work from the worldly stage and piano, applying mostly blue green and bits of light, to an otherworldly bloom of light, yellow and red, rising and expanding out of that. This ultimately evokes what I refer to as a kind of "temple in the sky," and then, as a return, a long passage to a darker mysterious, but inviting, space.

Tony Martin

Bye Bye Butterfly (1965)

Bye Bye Butterfly was composed in 1965 at the San Francisco Tape Music Center studio using two Hewlett-Packard oscillators, two Ampex stereo tape machines, a phonograph and record, and patch bay. The piece was played in real time and recorded. All material was delayed by stringing tape from the supply reel of the first tape deck to the take-up reel of the second tape deck. Signals from the first track were patched from the second machine back to the second track of the first machine and from the second track back to the first track to achieve a crisscrossing delay pattern. There was no mixer.

Pauline Oliveros

Visual composition for *Bye Bye Butterfly:* I first performed with this inspiring work by Pauline at a retrospective concert at the Los Angeles County Museum of Art. I've since developed it into a traveling visual composition package.

Tony Martin

Great Grandpa Lemuel's Death-Rattle Reincarnation Blues in F Sharp (1981)

This piece grew out of a comment Stewart Brand once made to me. I had been describing how I created a loop of the opening phrase of Wagner's *Siegfried Idyll* and fed it through an Ampex PD-10 tape duplication system (one loop through one playback and three slave recorders). Since the recorders had no erase heads, the music merely stacked up over itself until it had randomized the original into white noise. Meanwhile, I had recorded the process onto another machine and used the resulting tape as the source for a tape piece entitled "Wagner" (currently I can't seem to find a copy). Anyway, Stewart said, "Why don't you do it the other way 'round? Start with white noise and have the music gradually emerge?" I was delighted by his comment, and when about ten years later, Mills College invited me to give a retrospective concert, I decided to create a new piece based on Stewart's suggestion. I asked Bill Maginnis if I could record a blues phrase with his Dixieland band. Once recorded, I tried to overdub it several hundred times at Mills on their new 24-track, but the results were disappointing. Gradually, I realized I would have to use a PD-10 tape duplicator. So I searched all over the Bay Area, and I finally found one still in existence—the PD-10 was by now practically an antique—at a school that trained people to become sound engineers. This time I threaded the loop backward through all four machines and punched the start button, recording the gradual decay of the sound into white noise on another recorder. Once finished, I then reversed the reels and voila! Out of chaos gradually emerged a Dixieland band. The lyrics I wrote in an essay titled "Why Nature Grew Humans," part of a series I named "Maybe So Stories" with a tip of my cortex to Rudyard Kipling (they also crop up as chapter starters in my novel *Zero Weather*):

The real reason, the purpose of it all, so long in coming, I will now share with you, dearest of hearts.

Once upon a time, Old Great-To-The-Tenth-Power Grandpa Lemuel, or "Lem" or "Ul" or even "!" famous in certain mystical circles as Yod Unmanifest, Dreamer of All and Everything, was snoozing under his sombrero down by the old fishin' hole, the Pool of All Possibilities. Suddenly the fish line tied to his big toe jiggled. He sat up fast, reeled in a glimpse of his reflection and he saw an old man with a long white beard. Sorry about that, all you more sophisticated religious types. Now this came as a big surprise to Great[10] Grandpa Lem because he had always assumed, quite naturally inasmuch as he was Endlessness Himself, that he was immortal.

"I'm getting old!" he shouted that day beside the Pool of All Possibilities upon the halcyon slopes of Paradise in the Total Perfection of the Absolute Sun. He counted his wrinkles and white hairs in his beard before crying sweet tears. And as he cried, he picked up his guitar or oud or psaltery whatever you call it and sang "The Death Rattle Reincarnation Blues" from start to finish, missing only three Grand Barré's and a high G sharp. These are the verses and chorus as they translate in the current English vernacular.

Oh, I went on down, to the fishin' hole,
All tranquil without a care.
My face stared back, all wrinkled and old,
The marks of death were there.

Oh arrrrrrrrrgh! (gargle in the back of throat)
Pfffffffffffffft! (do a razzberry [or] a "Bronx cheer")
It's the Death Rattle
Reincarnation Blues!

Let me go, let me go, to the ocean sublime,
And ease my aches away.

Let me seed myself through the ages of time,
So death's dues I won't have to pay.

Oh arrrrrrrrrgh!
Pfffffffffffft!
It's the Death Rattle
Reincarnation Blues!

Well, it's just plain hard, to live alone,
And keep yourself in tune.
Much better to find yourself a friend,
To howl with at the moon.

Oh arrrrrrrrrgh!
Pfffffffffffft!
It's the Death Rattle What-in-Tarnation Reincarnation Blues!

Every note of this bluesiest of blues became a ripple in the Pool of All Possibilities and each ripple a universe, and our universe is the third chord in the second line of the final verse (accompanying the word "tune" for you esoteric types). His song quantum'd out in all directions and became manifest as All Time Everywhere in which a light century of ours is but a millisecond, a tachyon, a "zt." Old Ancient of Days Kingfish, crying and laughing and singing out across the waters from his perch, while coruscating galaxies coalesced and dissolved, while even in the coldest, deepest reaches of the pool something that was nothing stirred and resonated to his voice.

Ah, Halcyon the Kingfisher, who combs the water for his water brothers, who completes the fish-to-frog-to-human climb into a circle by preying on us as we pray. His tears are the soul-essence-spirit-spark of our reality, the nothingness-sperm-hydrogen Great-To-The-Tenth-Power Grandma Hattie spins into dust clouds of baby stars.

Great^{10} Grandma Hattie ("Aditi" to you Sanskrit scholars), creator of all us Milky Way creatures, Queen Bee of our heavenly hive, tirelessly giving birth to great ionized clouds of hydrogen trillions of miles in diameter. They swirl out along her arms while she spins the energy from hand to hand

"Ol' Kingfish," she's thinking, "that no-count husband of mine!" Always dropping by for a quickie while she was still dozing before dawn. Well, she bed him and fed him and packed him off to the fishin' hole. Once he was out of her hair, she could get back to the serious business of preserving the realm by her endless efforts. What a cornucopia of good things she was! And Great^{10} Grandpa Lem loved and appreciated her mightily in spite of his roving ways. On their eight billionth anniversary he wrote her a song that actually made it into the Old Testament (check Proverbs 31:10 under "The Sayings of Lemuel"). It's the original alphabet song, which Hollywood transformed into "A you're adorable, B you're so beautiful, C you're the creature I adore! D you're delightful and E you're exciteful and F you are mine forevermore!"

Go for it, Great-Grandpa!

(Ramon Sender, "Why Nature Grew Humans" [1976])

Ramon Sender

Kore (1962)

Kore was created in the small studio I put together in the attic of the San Francisco Conservatory of Music in 1961 and received its first performance on the Sonics electronic music series I produced that winter with the collaboration of Pauline Oliveros and Morton Subotnick, among others. It was the third tape composition I created there and is dedicated to my daughter Xaverie (1955–1989).

The piece utilized an Ampex 403 recorder that had a left-hand drive and a long tension-adjusting arm on the take-up reel. This allowed me to bypass the drive and just control the recording speed by hand-adjusting the tension on the take-up.

Sound sources included scraping bass piano strings with a plastic box and a group of conservatory students whom I invited up to the attic a few times after chorus rehearsal to improvise sounds for me. Kore is the name of Persephone as a young maiden. In the myth, she was abducted into the underworld by Hades (Pluto) who had fallen in love with her. He finally made a deal with her mother, Demeter, that allowed the daughter to return to the world every six months, thus creating the rhythm of springtime rebirth and winter death.

Mircea Eliade recounts how the symbolic death of Persephone had great consequences for mankind: "As a result of it, an Olympian and benevolent goddess temporarily inhabited the kingdom of the dead. She had annulled the unbridgeable distance between Hades and Olympus. Mediatrix between the two divine worlds, she could thereafter intervene in the destiny of mortals." (Mircea Eliade, *From the Stone Age to the Eleusinian Mysteries,* vol. 1 of *A History of Religious Ideas* [Chicago: University of Chicago Press, 1978–85], 290–301.)

Ramon Sender

Visual composition for *Kore:* A few years after Ramon wrote this piece I worked intuitively on overheads and layered slides in performances in the Bay Area and the Divisadero Street space. For a horizontally traveling image of the ancient goddess, Kore, I built a two-direction turntable with a complex prism that defracted the light and multiplied the image as it drifted across the projected environment. The thematic material continues to be exciting to me as a painter much in love with Greco-Roman art.

Tony Martin

Apple Box Double (1965)

Apple Box Double was performed by the composer with David Tudor in 1965 at San Francisco State College and then at the ONCE Festival in Ann Arbor, Michigan. The composer was fond of the resonance of apple boxes. She placed small vibrant objects on the boxes amplified by Piezo contact microphones. Each performer selected his or her own objects and methods of performing. *Apple Box Double* is on New World Records CD 80567, *Music from the Once Festival, 1961–1966,* disk 5, *1964–1966* (2003).

Pauline Oliveros

Desert Ambulance (1964)

Desert Ambulance was composed for Pauline Oliveros. The source tapes were created on a Chamberlin Music Master and then sync'd to a score that I dictated onto tape for the accordionist to hear over earphones. This allowed her to perform in semidarkness, so that the projections could be seen. *Desert Ambulance* was taken on the Tape Music Center tour that same summer, and over time has received more performances than any other piece of mine. The name derives from a marvelous photograph of a missionary ambulance, vintage 1928, that I found thrown away on the street. Some thirty years later, I was able to relate it to the French Red Cross ambulance that evacuated me and my sister to Bayonne from civil war Spain in 1936, and whose looks must have imprinted themselves in my two-year-old brain as impressive. At the time of its first performance, I described the piece as "a vehicle of mercy sent out into the waste-land of (academic) modern music."

Ramon Sender

Desert Ambulance (1964): Hand-painted 16 mm film projected on Pauline and her accordion provides a high-energy visual pulsation as a long dramatic beginning for the piece. Figural connections are made with film collaging of found and filmed magical and humorous animations of children, people walking, and hands that project on the accordion. At a crucial moment, all of this becomes immersed in a larger, more majestic environment by very slowly blending projected hand-painted 2 × 2 glass slides in enormous scale above the performer, arriving ultimately, at the cathartic closing of the piece.

Tony Martin

Release (2004)

I began thinking of this work in 2001. At that time I was beginning to try to understand what it meant to me to become seventy years old. I decided at that time to create a work for this combination to meld my early career as a clarinetist with my later career as a composer using technology. For me, those two worlds were always parallel but distinctly different and, perhaps, opposing realities. I stopped being a professional clarinetist in 1965. Prior to that, maybe in the late 1950s, I frequently performed Olivier Messiaen's *Quartet for the End of Time*. This work had a profound and lasting affect on the evolution of my aesthetic sensibility. Having decided to create a work that would somehow tie my early career with now, the *Quartet for the End of Time* combination seemed natural. And, since my work for the past several years has been developing a series of works for "surround sound," the combination of the quartet and the electronics seemed natural. Around the same time (2002), the death of a boy very close to our family altered my life and all of those close to me. I remember then, and still now, feeling that the moment of dying is a release of life from the body. That sense of release became the first notion for the new work and eventually became the title.

Morton Subotnick

Pauline's Solo (1996–2007)

Listening to this space I sound the space. Listening to the energy of all who are present I sound this energy. Listening to my listening and your listening I make this music here and now with the assistance of all that there is. I dedicate this music to a world without war.

The Expanded Instrument System (EIS) is continually evolving. EIS processes and distributes the sounds of the accordion during the performance. Nothing is prerecorded. Sounds are picked up by internal microphones in the accordion, sent to up to forty delay processors. The delays are modulated by other wave forms and distributed to the eight speakers in geometrical patterns. The ten possible patterns are also determined by algorithms, as well as by the size and speed of the selected patterns. The EIS developed from the composer's work with tape delay that began in the 1960s at the San Francisco Tape Music Center. The evolution of the EIS has moved from multiple tape machines to digital delay processors to the computer. The MAX/MSP interface for EIS was programmed by Stephan Moore with design by Pauline Oliveros.

Pauline Oliveros

BIBLIOGRAPHY

BOOKS AND ARTICLES

Albright, Thomas. *Art in the San Francisco Bay Area, 1945–1980.* Berkeley: University of California Press, 1985.

Bailey, Derek. *Improvisation: Its Nature and Practice in Music.* New York: Da Capo, 1992.

Blau, Herbert. *Take Up the Bodies: Theater at the Vanishing Point.* Urbana: University of Illinois Press, 1982.

Brougher, Kerry, Jeremy Strick, Ari Weisman, and Judith Zicker. *Visual Music: Synaesthesia in Art and Music since 1900.* New York: Thames & Hudson, 2005.

Buchla, Don. *User's Manual for the Modular Electronic Music System.* Buchla Associates, 1966.

Cardew, Cornelius, ed. *Scratch Music.* London: Latimer New Dimensions, 1972.

Cavallo, Dominick. *A Fiction of the Past: The Sixties in American History.* New York: St. Martin's Press, 1999.

Chadabe, Joel. *Electric Sound: The Past and Promise of Electronic Music.* Saddle River, N.J.: Prentice-Hall, 1997.

Constanten, Tom. *Between Rock and Hard Places: A Musical Autobiodyssey.* Eugene, Ore.: Hulogosi, 1992.

Davidson, Michael. *The San Francisco Renaissance.* Cambridge: Cambridge University Press, 1989.

Davies, Hugh. *Répertoire internationale des musiques électroacoustiques / International electronic music catalog.* Paris: Groupe de recherches musicales de l'O.R.T.F.; Trumansburg, N.Y.: Independent Electronic Music Center; Cambridge, Mass.: MIT Press, 1968.

Davis, R. G. *The San Francisco Mime Troupe: The First Ten Years.* Palo Alto, Calif.: Ramparts Press, 1975.

Doyle, Michael William. "Staging the Revolution: Guerilla Theater as a Countercultural Practice: 1965–68." In *Imagine Nation: The American Counterculture of the 1960s and '70s.* Edited by Peter Braunstein and Michael William Doyle. New York: Routledge, 2002.

Duckworth, William. *Talking Music: Conversations with John Cage, Philip Glass, Laurie Anderson, and Five Generations of American Experimental Composers.* New York: Schirmer Books, 1995.

Duckworth, William, and Richard Fleming, eds. *Sound and Light: La Monte Young and Marian Zazeela.* Lewisburg, Pa.: Bucknell University Press, 1996.

Eisen, Jonathan, ed. *The Age of Rock: Sounds of the American Cultural Revolution.* New York: Vintage Books, 1969.

Ellingham, Lewis, and Kevin Killian. *Poet Be Like God: Jack Spicer and the San Francisco Renaissance.* Hanover, N.H.: University Press of New England [for] Wesleyan University Press, 1998.

Erickson, Robert. "Incident in Berkeley." *EAR Magazine,* September 1975, 3, 7, and October 1975, 7–8.

Gagne, Cole, and Tracy Caras. *Soundpieces: Interviews with American Composers.* Metuchen, N.J.: Scarecrow Press, 1982.

Gendron, Bernard. *Popular Music and the Avant-Garde: Between Montmartre and the Mudd Club.* Chicago: University of Chicago Press, 2002.

Grunenberg, Christopher, ed. *Summer of Love: Art of the Psychedelic Era.* London: Tate Publishing, 2005.

Grunenberg, Christopher, and Jonathan Harris, eds. *Summer of Love: Psychedelic Art, Social Crisis, and the Counterculture in the 1960s.* Tate Liverpool Critical Forum, vol. 8. Liverpool, England: Liverpool University Press, 2005.

Halprin, Anna. *Moving toward Life: Five Decades of Transformational Dance.* Edited by Rachel Kaplan. Hanover, N.H.: Wesleyan University Press, 1995.

Halprin, Lawrence. *The RSVP Cycles: Creative Processes in the Human Environment.* New York: George Braziller, 1969.

Henker, James, and Parke Puterbaugh, eds. *I Want to Take You Higher: The Psychedelic Era, 1965–1969.* San Francisco: Chronicle Books, 1997.

Hicks, Michael. *Sixties Rock: Garage, Psychedelic, and Other Satisfactions.* Urbana: University of Illinois Press, 1999.

———. *Henry Cowell: Bohemian.* Urbana: University of Illinois Press, 2002.

Holmes, Thom. *Electronic and Experimental Music.* 2d ed. New York: Routledge, 2002.

Huxley, Aldous. *The Doors of Perception and Heaven and Hell.* New York: Harper & Row, 1954.

Isserman, Maurice, and Michael Kazin. *America Divided: The Civil War of the 1960s.* New York: Oxford University Press, 2000.

Kirby, Michael. "The New Theatre." *Tulane Drama Review* 10 (Winter 1965): 23–43.

Kofsky, Frank. "The Scene." In *The Age of Rock: Sounds of the American Cultural Revolution,* ed. Jonathan Eisen. New York: Vintage Books, 1969.

Kostelanetz, Richard. *The Theatre of Mixed Means.* New York: Dial Press, 1968.

Lesh, Phil. *Searching for the Sound: My Life with the Grateful Dead.* New York: Little, Brown, 2005.

Lewis, George. "Improvised Music After 1950: Afrological and Eurological Perspectives." *Black Music Research Journal* 16, no. 1 (Spring 1996): 91–121.

Markoff, John. *What the Dormouse Said: How the 1960s Counterculture Shaped the Personal Computer Industry.* New York: Viking, 2005.

Marranca, Bonnie, ed. *The Theatre of Images.* Baltimore: John Hopkins University Press, 1977, 1996.

Marwick, Arthur. *The Sixties.* New York: Oxford University Press, 1998.

McLuhan, Marshall. *The Gutenberg Galaxy.* Toronto: University of Toronto Press, 1962.

———. *Understanding Media: The Extensions of Man.* New York: New American Library, 1964.

Miller, Leta. Liner notes in *Music from the ONCE Festival, 1961–1966.* New World Records Box Set 80567 (2003).

Mockus, Martha. "Sounding Out: Lesbian Feminism and the Music of Pauline Oliveros." Ph.D. diss., University of Minnesota, 1999.

Moog, Robert A. "Voltage-Controlled Electronic Music Modules," *Journal of the Audio Engineering Society* 13 (July 1965): 200–206.

Moore, Barbara. *Action Theatre: The Happenings of Ken Dewey.* New York: Franklin Furnace Archive, 1987.

Mumma, Gordon. "An Electronic Music Studio for the Independent Composer." *Journal of the Audio Engineering Society* 12 (July 1964): 240–44.

Oliveros, Pauline. *Software for People: Collected Writings, 1963–80.* Baltimore: Smith Publications, 1984.

Perry, Charles. *The Haight Ashbury: A History.* New York: Random House, 1984, 2005.

Pinch, Trevor, and Frank Trocco. *Analog Days: The Invention of the Moog Synthesizer.* Cambridge, Mass.: Harvard University Press, 2002.

Potter, Keith. *Four Musical Minimalists: La Monte Young, Terry Riley, Steve Reich, Philip Glass.* Cambridge: Cambridge University Press, 2000.

Prévost, Edwin. *No Sound Is Innocent: AMM and the Practice of Self-Invention, Meta-Musical Narratives, Essays.* Harlow, Essex, UK: Copula, 1995.

Rexroth, Kenneth. "Thar's Culture in Them Thar Hills." *New York Times, Sunday Magazine,* February 7, 1965, 28–29, 78–80.

Ross, Janice. "Anna Halprin's Urban Rituals." *Tulane Drama Review* 48 (2004): 249–67.

———. *Anna Halprin: Experience as Dance.* Berkeley: University of California Press, 2007.

Roszak, Theodore. "Youth and the Great Refusal." *The Nation* 25 (March 1968): 400–407.

———. *The Making of a Counter Culture: Reflections on the Technocratic Society and Its Youthful Opposition.* 1969. Reprint. Berkeley: University of California Press, 1995.

Sabatini, Arthur J. "From Dog to Ant: The Evolution of Lee Breuer's Animations." *PAJ: A Journal of Performance and Art* 26, no. 2 (2004): 52–60.

Selvin, Joel. *Summer of Love.* New York: Cooper Square Press, 1994.

Shere, Charles. *Thinking Sound Music: The Life and Work of Robert Erickson.* Berkeley, Calif.: Fallen Leaf Press, 1995.

Slick, Darby. *Don't You Want Somebody to Love: Reflections on the San Francisco Sound.* Berkeley, Calif.: SLG Books, 1991.

Smith, Richard Cándida. *Utopia and Dissent: Art, Poetry, and Politics in California.* Berkeley: University of California Press, 1995.

Stern, Gerd. "From Beat Scene Poet to Psychedelic Multimedia Artist in San Francisco and Beyond, 1948–1978." Oral history conducted in 1996 by Victoria Morris Byerly, Regional Oral History Office, Bancroft Library, University of California, Berkeley, 2001.

Stevens, Jay. *Storming Heaven: LSD and the American Dream.* New York: Grove Press, 1987.

Strickland, Edward. *Minimalism: Origins.* Bloomington: Indiana University Press, 1993.

Tamarkin, Jeff. *Got a Revolution: The Turbulent Flight of the Jefferson Airplane.* New York: Atria Books, 2003.

Von Gunden, Heidi. *The Music of Pauline Oliveros.* Metuchen, N.J.: Scarecrow Press, 1983.
Worth, Libby, and Helen Poynor. *Anna Halprin.* New York: Routledge, 2004.

REVIEWS

Bowe, Edwina. "The Electronic Music Men: Are the Unearthly Screeches and Clangs on Divisadero St. a Cultural Breakthrough?" *San Francisco Examiner,* March 22, 1964.

Commanday, Robert. "A New Type of Artistic Man." *San Francisco Examiner,* April 12, 1965.

Cunningham, Carl. "Exciting Works at Tape Center." *San Francisco Chronicle,* November 12, 1965.

Eichelbaum, Stanley. "Wobbly 'Four-Legged Stool' Performed at Playhouse." *San Francisco Examiner,* September 26, 1961.

———. "Playhouse Dance Bedlam." *San Francisco Examiner,* May 7, 1962.

Frankenstein, Alfred. "Vortex at Planetarium: The Music Goes Round and Round." *San Francisco Chronicle,* May 29, 1957.

———. "Vortex IV Sounds Better Than Ever." *San Francisco Chronicle,* May 19, 1958.

———. "Vortex Experimenter Off to Brussels Fair." *San Francisco Chronicle,* September 13, 1958.

———. "The New Vortex Music at the Planetarium." *San Francisco Chronicle,* January 14, 1959.

———. "Sensorium—Old-New Idea." *San Francisco Chronicle,* April 30, 1959.

———. "Chamber Group Offers Concert Improvisation." *San Francisco Chronicle,* May 6, 1959.

———. "A Composition of Genius: Coats Off for Boulez Work." *San Francisco Chronicle,* May 6, 1959.

———. "Improvisers Make Very Good Music." *San Francisco Chronicle,* May 15, 1959.

———. "Jazz vs. 'Classical': A Matter for Study." *San Francisco Chronicle,* June 10, 1959.

———. "Vortex Concerts Move to Museum." *San Francisco Chronicle,* November 4, 1959.

———. "Works by Two Bay Area Composers." *San Francisco Chronicle,* August 29, 1961.

———. "Subotnick's 'New' Music: An Heroic Vision Is All of That." *San Francisco Chronicle,* September 26, 1961.

———. "Conservatory Test: 'Romantic' Side of Electronics." *San Francisco Chronicle,* December 20, 1961.

———. "Night of Modern Music and Dance." *San Francisco Chronicle,* February 25, 1962.

———. "Lukas Foss Compositions Played." *San Francisco Chronicle,* March 5, 1962.

———. "Stimulating Sounds Too New to Be Named." *San Francisco Chronicle,* March 25, 1962.

———. "Puzzle and Pathos of '5-Legged Stool.'" *San Francisco Chronicle,* May 11, 1962.

———. "Berio Compositions: The Year's Event in Modern Music." *San Francisco Chronicle,* May 17, 1962.

———. "A Milk Can, Tape, and the New Sound." *San Francisco Chronicle,* May 17, 1962.

———. "A Brilliant 'Opera' on Tape." *San Francisco Chronicle,* November 7, 1962.

———. "Composers Similar in New Series." *San Francisco Chronicle,* February 27, 1963.

———. "Partch's Instruments." *San Francisco Chronicle,* June 22, 1963.
———. "A Landmark of a Flop." *San Francisco Chronicle,* November 13, 1963.
———. "Tape Music Center Gives Its Finest Program." *San Francisco Chronicle,* November 13, 1963.
———. "Fine Singing at the Tape Center." *San Francisco Chronicle,* December 4, 1963.
———. "Two Pianists and a Tape Show." *San Francisco Chronicle,* January 8, 1964.
———. "Electronic Music—Mysterious, Romantic." *San Francisco Chronicle,* February 5, 1964.
———. "Modest and Vital Drive: Tape Music Center's New Goal." *San Francisco Chronicle,* March 30, 1964.
———. "The Musical Avant-Garde." *San Francisco Chronicle,* April 1, 1964.
———. "A Concert in the Stars." *San Francisco Chronicle,* April 5, 1964.
———. "Music at Mills: U.S. Musical Experiments." *San Francisco Chronicle,* May 22, 1964.
———. "Magic Images at the Tape Center." *San Francisco Chronicle,* October 9, 1964.
———. "Humor and Daring in West Coast Wind Quintet." *San Francisco Chronicle,* October 14, 1964.
———. "Music Like None Other on Earth." *San Francisco Chronicle,* November 8, 1964.
———. "Gayatri Rajapur's Songs." *San Francisco Chronicle,* June 9, 1965.
———. "Art That Goes Bump in the Night." *San Francisco Chronicle,* January 17, 1966.
———. "Exciting Experiment in Light and Sound." *San Francisco Chronicle,* February 6, 1967.
Fried, Alexander. "A Far-Out Note in Chamber Music." *San Francisco Examiner,* October 23, 1963.
———. "Bizarre Musical Fantasy." *San Francisco Examiner,* January 15, 1964.
———. "Chamber Concert's Avant-Garde Interlude." *San Francisco Examiner,* February 17, 1965.
Gleason, Ralph J. "Dead Like Live Thunder." *San Francisco Chronicle,* March 19, 1967.
Schroeder, Mildred. "Art Lovers Amused by Amazing Mazes." *San Francisco Examiner,* July 25, 1962.
Wallace, Dean. "The Lord High Executioner of Music." *San Francisco Chronicle,* April 3, 1964.
———. "Some Notes on a Frying Pan." *San Francisco Chronicle,* December 4, 1964.
———. "Newcomer to Tape Music." *San Francisco Chronicle,* January 27, 1965.
———. "The Gamut of Sound." *San Francisco Chronicle,* April 14, 1965.
———. "Musical Peanuts and Eden, Too." *San Francisco Chronicle,* May 5, 1965.
———. "Electronic 'Revival' Concert." *San Francisco Chronicle,* October 13, 1965.

ILLUSTRATIONS

COLOR PLATES *(following page 144)*

1. Tony Martin, still from the multiple light projection *Improvisation 1967*
2. Tony Martin, still from visual composition for *Desert Ambulance* by Ramon Sender (1963)
3. Tony Martin, still from visual composition for *Desert Ambulance* by Ramon Sender (1963), with Pauline Oliveros performing
4. Tony Martin, still from *Improvisation* (1963)
5. Tony Martin, image used for *Interior Bloom* (1966)
6. Tony Martin, still from visual composition for *Mandolin* by Morton Subotnick (1963)
7. Ramon Sender, *Tropical Fish Opera* (1962)
8. Tony Martin, still from visual composition for *Desert Ambulance* by Ramon Sender (1963)
9. Pauline Oliveros and Tony Martin, still from *Circuitry* (1967)

10a & b. Tony Martin, stills from *Silent Light* (1967)

11a & b. Tony Martin, stills from visual composition for *Bye Bye Butterfly* by Pauline Oliveros (1965)

12a & b. Tony Martin, stills from visual composition for *Mandolin* by Morton Subotnick (1963)

13. Tony Martin, drawing for optical projections with mirrors
14. Tony Martin, visual score drawing for liquid projection improvisation (1966)
15. Overview of the Trips Festival
16. Ramon Sender at the Trips Festival
17. Tony Martin at the Trips Festival

FIGURES

1. Trips Festival program cover by Wes Wilson 6
2. Trips Festival program (January 21–23, 1966) 7

3. Sonics I program (December 18, 1961)   *10*
4. Sonics II program (March 24, 1962)   *13*
5. Score for *City Scale*   *follows page 16*
6. The San Francisco Tape Music Center location at 321 Divisadero (ca. 1964)   *19*
7. San Francisco Tape Music Center group photo   *24*
8. Program for Tudorfest (March 30 and April 1, 3, 6, and 8, 1964)   *25*
9. Program for Terry Riley concert at the San Francisco Tape Music Center (November 4 and 6, 1964)   *27*
10. Steve Reich (ca. 1965)   *28*
11. Performance at 321 Divisadero of Morton Subotnick's *Play! no. 1* (1964)   *29*
12. SFTMC program by Andrew Hoyem   *32*
13. Ramon Sender   *51*
14. Morton Subotnick and Ramon Sender   *56*
15. Lecture-demonstration at 321 Divisadero   *70*
16. Pauline Oliveros   *81*
17. Tony Martin and Pauline Oliveros at Mills College, Oakland, California (ca. 1966)   *91*
18. Page from score for *Circuitry*, by Pauline Oliveros   *92*
19. Program for the "Tape-athon" of Pauline Oliveros's music in Ronald Chase's loft, San Francisco (1967)   *96*
20. Morton Subotnick   *113*
21. Tony Martin, collage-assemblage for SFTMC season program brochure cover (1964)   *138*
22. Tony Martin, drawings for inward-outward motion for two projectors (1965)   *138*
23. Tony Martin, visual scoring sequence, composition for cross-dissolved projected drawings and liquids (1966)   *139*
24. Tony Martin, drawings for multiple light projections (1966)   *139*
25. Tony Martin, drawing for *Theater for Watchers, Walkers, Touchers* (1962)   *141*
26. Elias Romero (ca. 1960)   *144*
27. The Buchla Modular Electronic Music System, or "Buchla Box"   *168*
28. Ramon Sender, Michael Callahan, Morton Subotnick, and Pauline Oliveros   *185*
29. The general outline of the studio work space at 321 Divisadero   *199*
30. Four and a half rack spaces in the studio at 321 Divisadero   *200*
31. The SFTMC studio (before September 1966)   *201*
32. SFTMC studio work area (late 1965 or early 1966)   *202*
33. SFTMC studio work area with the first Buchla system (late 1965 or early 1966)   *203*

34. Terry Riley (ca. 1964)   *206*
35. La Monte Young at Ann Halprin's studio (ca. 1959–60)   *212*
36. Ann Halprin and John Graham in *Apartment 6* (1965)   *228*
37. John Graham and A. A. Leath in *Apartment 6,* San Francisco (1965)   *229*
38. Ann Halprin in *Apartment 6,* Finland (1965)   *231*
39. Ann Halprin in *Branch Dance* (1957)   *232*
40. Stuart Dempster performing *In the Garden* (March 1966)   *262*

INDEX

Page numbers in italic refer to illustrations.

Abrams, Jerry, 22
Acid Tests, 20, 75, 165, 173, 239, 241, 242, 243, 248, 280
Actor's Workshop, 1, 2, 15, 71, 93, 112, 115, 117, 119, 120–23, 127, 133, 234, 245, 265, 269, 272, 273
Adam, Helen, 271
Akalaitis, JoAnne, 15
Akiyama, Kuniharu, 86
Albin, Peter, 76
Alexander, Paul, 271
American Cooperative Theater (ACT), 15, 270
Amirkhanian, Charles, viii, 82
Ampex equipment, 9, 29, 30, 54, 55, 56, 63, 65, 71, 73, 80, 84, 127, 181, 182, 192, 198, 250n3, 296
Anger, Kenneth, 22
Angerame, Dominic, 37
Anhalt, Istvan, 9, 269
Anker, Steve, 36
Anthology Film Archive, New York, 180, 188
APELAC studio, Brussels, 12, 246
Arel, Bulent, 273, 276
Artaud, Antonin, 15, 16
Ashley, Robert, 39n32, 60, 85, 154, 271
Atherton, Gertrude, 8
Audium, 273, 276
Avalon Ballroom, San Francisco, 20, 34, 143, 245
Ayler, Albert, 12

Babbitt, Milton, 9, 48, 53, 268, 269, 279
Bailey, Derek, 208
Baillie, Bruce, 5, 34, 35–37, 78
Baker, Chet, 17, 216, 218, 220, 273
Bark, Jan, 83, 84, 103, 259, 278
Baron, Rebecca, 36
Barron, Louis and Bebe, 53
Barthe, Fred, 83
Bartlett, Elizabeth, 271
Basart, Robert, 268

Bauhaus, 222, 223
Beatles, 24, 31, 33, 105, 174, 245, 247, 274
beat literature, 8, 15, 215, 243
Beck, Julian, 223
Becker, Howard, 187
Beckett, Samuel, 15, 121
Beethoven, Ludwig van, 256, 267; bust of, 29, 88, 255
Behrman, David, 107, 252
Bell Labs, 12, 164
Belson, Jordan, 20, 21, 35, 37, 143, 266, 271
Benshoof, Ken, 206
Berberian, Cathy, 49, 83, 270, 273
Berg, Alban, 51
Berio, Luciano, viii, 9, 12, 30, 48, 49, 81, 83, 103, 118, 119, 132, 222, 225, 226, 229–30, 246, 260, 261; in chronology, 270, 272, 273, 275, 281
Berry, Chuck, 105
Big Brother and the Holding Company, 5, 75, 76, 104, 164, 245, 246, 280
Blackman, Fred, 268
Black Mountain College, 154
Blaser, Robin, 15, 48, 99, 126, 271
Blau, Herbert, 112, 115, 121, 122, 123, 265, 272, 279
Bloland, Sunni, 267
Boise, Ron, 242, 246
Boucourechliev, André, 270, 271
Boulanger, Nadia, 52
Boulez, Pierre, 118, 166, 268
Brakhage, Stan, x, 34, 35, 66–67, 128, 143
Brand, Stewart, x, 2, 5, 34, 50, 75, 76, 77, 78, 90, 280, 296; "America Needs Indians," 75, 239, 241, 243, 244, 280; interview with, 239–44, 247–50; *Whole Earth Catalog,* 239, 245, 250
Brautigan, Richard, 268
Brechan, Jeannie, 26, 219
Brecht, Bertolt, 15, 88, 107, 108, 110, 121–22, 272, 273, 278

313

Brecht, George, 14, 24, 86, 274
Breuer, Lee, 2, 15–16, 48, 103, 121, 126, 270, 271, 272, 275
Broughton, James, 268, 271
Brown, Earle, 277
Brown, Joan, 268
Brubeck, Dave, 265
Bruce, Lenny, 144, 269
Bruno, Giordano, 108, 279
Bryars, Gavin, 208
Bucchi, Valentino, 280
Buchla, Don: and collaboration with Martin, 281; and collaboration with Sender, 1, 109, 114, 163, 166, 172; and collaboration with Subotnick, 1, 109, 114, 117, 120, 163, 164, 165–67, 169; interview with, 163–76; and involvement in Electric Circus, 175–76; and involvement in Trips Festival, 5, 38n1, 75–76, 164–65, 248, 280; and light projections, 175, 176, 248; modular synthesizer ("Buchla box") developed by, 1, 2, 5, 30–31, 38n1, 50, 75–76, 89, 90–91, 109–10, 114, 115, 117, 134, 163, 164, 165–69, *168*, 171–72, 194–96, 204, 242, 276, 293–94; and ORB (optical ranging for the blind) system, 170–71, 177n1
Burroughs, William, 215
Byrd, Joseph, 278

Caen, Herb, 295
Cage, John, vii, 9, 11, 12, 24, 26, 59, 86, 100, 104, 130–31, 154, 170, 173, 181, 191, 192, 205, 230, 234, 236, 267, 268, 269, 273, 277, 281; works by: *Atlas Eclipticalis,* 26, 40n37, 86, 87, 104, 192, 258, 274, 276; *Black Mountain Piece,* 14; *Cartridge Music,* 26, 258, 274; *Concert for Piano and Orchestra,* 26, 104, 130, 257, 258, 274; *Fontana Mix,* 11, 49, 276; *For M.C. and D.T.,* 271; *4′33″,* 271; *Imaginary Landscape No. 4,* 267; *Music for Amplified Toy Pianos,* 274; *Music Walk,* 258, 274; *Radio Music,* 271; *T.V. Köln,* 271; *Variations II,* 26, 274; *Water Music,* 14; *Williams Mix,* 11; *Winter Music,* 86, 104, 270, 276
Cale, John, 218
California Palace of the Legion of Honor, San Francisco, 221n2, 268, 274
Callahan, Michael, 1, 23, 40n35, 50, 65–66, 69, 127–28, 169, 184, *185,* 242, 265, 273, 275; interview with, 178–97
Callenbach, Ernest, 35, 36
Camus, Albert, 17, 120
Cannon, Terry, 36
Canyon Cinema, 2, 22, 34, 35–37, 85
Cardew, Cornelius, 209
Carter, Elliott, *32,* 50, 53, 54, 279

Case Western University, 107
Cassady, Neal, 8
Center for Contemporary Music at Mills College, 2, 34, 80, 95
Chamberlin Music Master, 24, 26, 70–71, 85, 173–75, 190, 198
Chamberlin Rhythmate, 173–74
Chambers Brothers, 176
Charlatans (rock group), 75, 245, 246, 279
Chase, Ronald, 33, 107, 281
Chicago Art Institute, 136, 146, 147
Child, Abigail, 36
Childs, Barney, 105, 261, 280, 281
Chowning, John, viii, 80, 104, 118, 132, 275
cinema. *See* films and filmmaking
City Lights Books, 17, 64, 177n1
City Scale happening, 17, 19, 63–64, 67, 121, 127, 152–53, 252, 255, 272
Cohen, Milton, 12, 39n21
Coleman, Ornette, 12
Collins, Jess, 48, 99, 271
Coltrane, John, 12, 211, 268
Columbia-Princeton Electronic Music Center, 47, 110, 114, 115, 126, 129, 132, 164, 196, 279
The Committee, 2, 5, 14, 144, 249
Composers' Forum, 40n34, 118, 221n2, 253, 265, 268, 270, 274, 275, 282
Composers' Workshop, 9, 55, 97, 253, 269
Compton, Boyd, 34, 73, 115, 116, 132, 145, 277
Conner, Bruce, 22, 34, 36, 267
Conrad, Tony, 218
Constanten, Tom, 246, 270, 271, 275
Copeland, George, 51
Corl, Eldon, 71, 72, 127, 192
Cott, Jonathan, x
Countryman, Carl, 142, 158–59
Cowell, Henry, 52, 54, 86, 276
Creeley, Robert, 99
Culler, George, 187
Cunningham, Merce, 142, 230–33, 269

dada, 9, 14
Dallapiccola, Luigi, 118, 135n2
dance, 2, 5, 11, 12, 17, 48, 49, 58, 67, 82, 102–3, 110, 111, 142, 144, 212, 265–77 *passim,* 281. *See also* Halprin, Anna (formerly Ann), Dancers' Workshop of
Darby, Susan, 15
Davidovsky, Mario, 30, *32,* 49, 101, 127, 150, 151, 271, 273, 275, 279, 281
Davis, Ferdinand, 51
Davis, Jimmy, 66
Davis, Judith, 20

Davis, Miles, 216
Davis, R. G. (Ronnie), 14, 15, 48, 63, 67, 107, 127, 144, 269, 270, 271, 272, 274, 279, 281. *See also* San Francisco Mime Troupe
De Blanque, Peter, 76
De Maria, Walter, 213, 267
Dempster, Stuart, viii, 2, 17, 64, 97, 102, 104, 110, 130–31, 265, 268, 274, 275, 276, 277, 278, 281, 282; interview with, 252–63
Dennison, Doris, 267
Dewey, Ken, 15, 17, 63, 67, 121, 146, 152–53, 215–16, 217, 269–70, 272
Dhaemers, Robert, 272
Diggers (anarchist collective), 248, 249, 251n9
Dill, Erv, 267
Divisadero Street location of SFTMC, 15, 18, *19*, 30, 34, 36, 49, 50, 62, 67–68, 83, 84–85, 86, 103, 108, 113–14, 129, 135n9, 146, 150, 152, 154, 159, 164, 178, 183, 188–89, 194, 222, 225, 266, 272; technical facilities at, 84, 108, 183, 189–96, 198, *199*, 200–204, *200, 201, 202, 203*
Dobrowolski, Andrzej, 275
Drop City, 78, 248
Dudley, Anna Carol, 267
Duncan, Robert, 15, 48, 63, 79n2, 98–99, 103, 126, 271
Durkee, Stephen, 178
Dylan, Bob, 245

Echoplex, 56–57, 174, 214, 216
Eisler, Hanns, 122
Electric Circus, 115, 145, 175–76
Epstein, Paul, 267
Erickson, Robert, viii, 30, 58, 80, 81, 93, 259, 260, 265, 269, 281, 282; Oliveros as student of, 10, 12, 54, 80, 95, 97–98, 102; Riley as student of, 12, 97; Rush as student of, 12, 53, 80, 97; Sender as student of, 9, 50, 53, 54, 55, 97, 118
Esalen Institute, 75, 77
Expanded Instrument System (EIS), 82, 301
Experimental Media and Performing Arts Center (EMPAC), xi, 3, 93, 289

Fadiman, Jim, 240, 250n5
Falkenstein, Claire, 11, 39n17, 80, 207, 267
Feldman, Morton, 93, 209, 281
Ferlinghetti, Lawrence, 16, 245, 271, 279
Ferrari, Luc, 276
Field, Tom, 271
Fillmore Auditorium, San Francisco, 20, 24, 75, 143, 144, 156, 219, 242–48 *passim*, 280
films and filmmaking, 11, 21, 22, 34, 35–37, 66–67, 69, 80, 128, 143

Fluxus, 14, 33, 161, 209, 214, 221n1
Foss, Lukas, 39n20, 98, 208, 209, 254, 269
Foster, Stephen, 37, 278
Frankenstein, Alfred, viii, 14, 24, 39n21, 64, 71, 79n3, 82, 86, 87, 108, 187, 188, 220, 265–66, 267
Free Speech Movement, 33, 249, 275, 276
Fried, Alexander, 86, 226
Frith, Fred, 2, 208–10
Fuller, Buckminster, 239, 249, 250
futurism, 14, 29

Gaburo, Kenneth, 83
Gaudeamus Festival and Prize, 83, 103, 271
Geis, Bill, 148
Genet, Jean, 15, 67, 69, 270
Gerhard, Roberto, 270, 272
Gerstein, David, 36
Ghelderode, Michel de, 88, 107, 279
Gibson, Jon, 26, 80, 219, 221, 275, 276, 278
Ginsberg, Allen, 8, 16, 188, 243, 245, 279, 280
Glasgow, Glenn, 82
Glass, Philip, 205
Gleason, Ralph, x, 246
Globokar, Vinko, 261
Goebel, Johannes, 3, 289
Goodman, Dean, 271
Gottlieb, Lou, 34, 50, 77, 78, 247–48
Gowgil, Sherry, 267
Graham, Bill, x, 16, 26, 77, 144, 243, 245, 249, 279, 280, 281
Graham, John, 12, 20, 58, 64, 67, 82, 102, 157, 212, 215, 216, 224, 225, 226, 227, 229, 230, 267, 268, 269–70
Grateful Dead, 5, 28, 75, 144, 221, 243–44, 245, 246–47, 248, 280
Gray, Gary, *29*
Great Society (rock group), 135n9, 143, 245, 246, 280
Grenier, Vincent, 36
Gropius, Walter, 222, 223
Gyson, Brian, 215

Haieff, Alexei, 52
Halprin, Anna (formerly Ann): and collaboration with Martin, 140, 141, 146, 150–51, 224, 271; and collaboration with Oliveros, 83, 111, 225; and collaboration with Riley, 2, 11, 62, 83, 211–12, 225, 226, 230, 234, 267, 269; and collaboration with Subotnick, 83, 110, 117, 120, 123–25, 212, 222, 225, 226, 234, 270, 276, 277; and collaboration with Young, 2, 11, 62, 83, 211, 212, *212*, 225, 226, 230, 234, 267, 271; Dancers' Workshop of, vii, ix–x, 2, 58, 62, 64, 67, 68, 82, 83, 85, 102, 114, 121, 129, 144, 162n1, 223, 225, 234, 265–77 *passim;* and

Halprin, Anna *(continued)*
  improvisation, 61, 233–34; interview with, 222–38; and involvement in American Cooperative Theater, 15; and involvement in Trips Festival, 237–38, 244; in photographs, *228, 231, 232*
Halprin, Lawrence, 223
Hamm, Bill, 16, 20, 22, 143, 248, 275, 280
Hampton, Bonnie, 112, 119, 269, 279
Handy, John, 238, 279
happenings, 14, 17, 33, 37, 56, 62, 126. See also *City Scale* happening
Harris, Elizabeth, 5, 26, 33, 86–87, 107, 110, 111, 257, 274, 281
Harrison, Lou, viii, 5, 9, 244, 276
Harvard University, 178
Harvey, Sarah, 20
Hassell, Jon, 252
Haubenstock-Ramati, Roman, 276
Heider, Wally, 172
Heller, Liz, 71
Hell's Angels, 172, 173, 243
Helmholtz, Hermann von, 166
Helms, Chet, x
Hendrix, Jimi, 246
Herndon, Fran, 271
Hewlett-Packard oscillators, 108, 109, 119, 296
Hickey, Pat, 268
Hill, Gerald, 68, 69
Hills, Henry, 36
Hillyard, Roger, 143
Holbrooke, Joseph, 208
Hovhaness, Alan, 267
Hudson, Robert, 148, 272
Hughes, Robert, *29*
Human Be-In, 8, 9
Huxley, Aldous, 239

Ichiyanagi, Toshi, 24, 26, 86, 104, 256, 274, 281
Illosovay, Elsor von, 270, 271
improvisation: and Dempster's work, 254; and Foss's work, 39n20, 98, 208, 209, 254, 269; Frith on, 208–10; and KPFA sessions, 11, 39n17, 80, 205–7, 208–10, 266; and Oliveros's work, 11, 58, 68, 80–81, 82, 84, 85, 95, 98, 102–3, 104, 108, 205–7, 208, 209–10, 266, 269, 270, 273; and Riley's work, 11, 58, 80–81, 95, 98, 205–7, 208, 209–10, 266; and Rush's work, 11, 80, 95, 98, 205–7, 208, 209–10, 266, 270; and Sender's work, 56, 58, 61, 66, 68, 82, 85, 104, 126, 269, 270, 273; and Subotnick's work, 66, 68, 82, 85, 102, 104, 126, 127, 129, 270, 273
The Intersection, San Francisco, 36
Ives, Charles, 59

Jacobs, Henry, 20, 21, 143, 266, 280
Jacopetti, Ben, 15, 78, 243
Jarry, Alfred, 16, 273
jazz, 11, 12, 131, 143, 206, 208, 209, 211, 215, 216, 221, 268, 278
Jefferson Airplane, 131, 238, 245, 246–47, 279, 280
Jenks, Alden, 77
Jepson, Werner, 26, 80, 219, 264, 275, 276, 278, 281, 282
Jess. See Collins, Jess
Johnson, Alan, 80
Johnson, Dennis, 225, 267
Johnson, Laurel, 11, 26, 48, 56, 82, 86, 102, 269
Jones Street location of SFTMC, 14, 15, 17, 30, 48, 50, 61–62, 63, 83, 84, 125, 126, 127, 128, 150, 152, 153, 224; fire at, 18, 50, 62, 84, 103, 128, 272; technical facilities at, 30, 127, 182
Joplin, Janis, 76, 104, 131, 238, 246
Jordan, Larry, 35

Kagel, Mauricio, 86, 270, 279
Kandinsky, Wassily, 157–58
Kaprow, Allan, 14, 64, 223
Kerouac, Jack, 8
Kesey, Ken, x, 5, 34, 75, 77, 165, 172, 173, 239–43, 246, 248, 249, 280
Kirby, Michael, 14
Kirchner, Leon, 14, 118
Kitchen, Diane, 36
Koening, Gottfried Michael, 270
Kohn, Karl, 274
Kotonski, Wlodzimierz, 274, 275
KPFA, ix, 2, 18, 24, 49, 53, 55, 67–68, 80, 81–82, 83, 85, 101, 114, 129, 183, 188, 272, 276; improvisation sessions at, 11, 39n17, 80, 205–7, 208–10, 266
KQED, 67, 119, 128
Kramer, Edith, 37
Krenek, Ernst, 9, 273
Kuykendall, Robert, 270

Lafayette oscillators, 109, 110
Landau, Sol, 69, 70
Landor, Jo, 150, 162n1, 226, 268, 272
Laufer, Robin, 61–62
LaVigne, Robert, 15, 48, 49, 119, 127, 271, 272
Lazarof, Henri, 275
Leary, Timothy, 239, 241
Leath, A. A., 58, 82, 102, 123–24, 212, 224, 225, 226, 227, *229*, 267, 268, 270
Leedy, Douglas, viii, 80, 267, 275, 277, 281
Leistiko, Norma, 16, 82, 270, 275, 281
Leroux, Jean Louis, *29*
Lesh, Phil, 28, 221, 246, 274, 275

Lewis, George, 208
Lewis, Sonny, 26, 219, 220
Lieberman, Fredric, 276
Ligeti, György, 83, 273
light projections, 5, 12, 17, 19–23, 26, 39, 64–65, 280, 281; by Buchla, 175, 176, 248; by Romero, 16, 19, 20, 22, 64, 68, 104, 143, 189, 272, 273, 274, 275. *See also* Martin, Tony, light projections and visual compositions by
Limeliters, 34, 50, 77
Lincoln Center, New York, 1, 115, *123*, 133, 279
Liszt, Franz, 295
Living Theater, 223, 237
Loading Zone (rock group), 5, 75, 280
Locks, Seymour, 20, 21–22, 223, 268, 272
London, Jack, 8
Longshoremen's Hall, San Francisco, 5, 245, 280
Lonidier, Lynn, 271
Los Angeles County Museum of Art, 281, 296
Lovell, Vic, 240, 250n4
Lowe, James, 26
LSD, 2, 5, 72, 75, 77, 90, 173, 221, 239, 240, 250, 277
Lucier, Alvin, 24, 26, 83, 86, 104, 107, 170, 274
Lye, Len, 143

Mabou Mines, 15, 16
MacDonald, Scott, 2
Mac Low, Jackson, 39n15
Maderna, Bruno, 12, 81, 268, 270, 277
Maginnis, William, 1, 20, *24,* 34, 135n9, 150, 169, 185, 194, 198–204, 265, 275, 280, 281, 282, 297; interview with, 3, 50–79; works by: *Flight,* 169; *Three Pieces,* 63, 79n2, 268
Maleczech, Ruth, 15, 16
Mandel, Allen, 71
Manupelli, George, 85
marijuana, 74, 76, 77
Marines' Memorial Theater, San Francisco, 269, 272, 273, 274
Marinuzzi, Gino, 280
Martin, Mel, 221
Martin, Tony: as artist-in-residence at NYU, 115, 145; artists' influence on, 136, 144–45, 157–58; artworks by, 136, *138, 139,* 140, 147, 158; and collaboration with Buchla, 281; and collaboration with Countryman, 142, 158–59; and collaboration with Dewey, 146, 152–53; and collaboration with Halprin, 140, 146, 150–51, 224, 271; and collaboration with Oliveros, 91, 93, 105, 107, 142, 146, 149–50, 153, 159, 293, 296; and collaboration with Riley, 142, 150, 153, 219; and collaboration with Sender, 137, 140, 146, 147, 149–50, 152–53, 159–60, 277, 279, 299, 300; and collaboration with Subotnick, 137, 146, 147, 149–50, 154–57, 160, 277, 295–296; and collaboration with Tudor, 142; interview with, 3, 146–62; and involvement in *City Scale* happening, 17, 63, 152–53, 272; and involvement in Sonics concerts, 48, 151, 270; and involvement in Trips Festival, 5, 34, 165, 248, 280; in photographs, *24, 70, 91;* and SFTMC move to Mills College, 34, 90, 145, 147, 282; solo works by: *Floorlamps,* 142, 161–62, 293; *Room,* 161, 281; *Silent Light,* 290, 292, 294; *Theater for Watchers, Walkers, Touchers,* 140, *141,* 152, 160–61, 271
Martin, Tony, light projections and visual compositions by, 1, 5, 17, 20, 22, 23, 26, 68, 131, 142–45, 150, 151–60, 165, 274, 276, 277, 278, 280; drawings for, *138, 139, 141;* for Oliveros's compositions, 31, 87, 91, 93, 104, 107, 142, 274, 280, 293, 296; for Riley's compositions, 26, 145, 150, 153, 219; for Sender's compositions, 23, 85, 137, 140, 156, 159–60, 274, 299, 300; for Subotnick's compositions, 28, 85, 137, 154–57, 160, 277, 278, 295, 296
Martirano, Salvatore, 132
The Matrix, San Francisco, 20, 245
Maxfield, Richard, 9, 267, 269
McClure, Michael, 15, 120, 144, 187, 188, 271
McEachern, Douglas, 268, 273, 276
McKay, Glen, 22, 143
McLuhan, Marshall, 120, 178, 187, 242, 250, 274
Mekas, Jonas, 35, 180
Mellnäs, Arne, 103, 259
Mellotron, 24
Meltzer, David, 271, 279
Menefee, Emory, 36
Merry Pranksters, 5, 75, 76, 77, 239, 243, 250, 280
Messiaen, Olivier, 118, 300
Milhaud, Darius, viii, 14, 30, 50, 52, 53, 118, 132, 134–35, 207, 230, 265, 272
Millar, Gregory, 265
Miller, Joaquin, 8
Mills College, 3, 26, 59, 83, 93, 112, 118, 230, 246, 270, 271, 272; archival recordings at, 2, 40n37, 80, 208n1; Mills Tape Music Center/Center for Contemporary Music, 34, 90, 94, 293; SFTMC move to, 34, 50, 78, 90, 95, 103, 115, 116, 132–33, 145, 147, 222, 245, 247, 263, 281, 282
Mills Performing Group, 30, 73, 281
minimalism, 205, 226
modular synthesizer ("Buchla box"). *See under* Buchla, Don
Moholy-Nagy, László, 20, 23
Moody Blues, 24
Moog, Robert, 173, 194, 195, 196
Moran, Robert, viii, 74, 80, 83, 90, 256, 268, 271, 276, 277, 281

Morning Star Ranch, 34, 50, 78, 133, 247–48, 251n8, 281
Morrill, Dexter, 268
Morris, Simone, 267
Morrison Planetarium, San Francisco, 20, 21, 143, 266
Mumma, Gordon, 39n32, 85, 154, 270
musique concrète, 18, 20, 48, 81, 112, 126, 163, 166, 248

Nancarrow, Conlon, 269
Nelson, Robert, 27, 34, 36–37, 272, 279
Neri, Manuel, 268
Nerval, Gérard de, 16
New York Times, 1, 94n10
New York University, 34, 73, 90, 115, 133
Nielsen, Carl, 276
Nieman, Alfred, 209n6
Nixon, Roger, 252
Nono, Luigi, 12, 48, 81, 270, 271, 273
Norris, Frank, 8

O'Brien, Donald, *29*
Ogden, Willbur, 67, 82, 93
Old Spaghetti Factory, San Francisco, 119, 213
Oliveros, Pauline: Cage's compositions performed by, 104; and collaboration with Callahan, 184, *185, 186*; and collaboration with Halprin, 83, 111, 225; and collaboration with Harris, 110, 111, 274, 281; and collaboration with Martin, 91, 93, 105, 107, 142, 146, 149–50, 153, 159, 293, 296; and collaboration with Riley, 2, 11, 80, 95, 98, 205–7, 208, 209–10, 266; and collaboration with Rush, 2, 11, 80, 95, 98, 205–7, 208, 209–10, 266; and collaboration with Sender, 20, 54, 58, 68, 81–82, 84, 85, 100, 118; and collaboration with Subotnick, 20, 84, 85; and collaboration with Tudor, 26, 86–87, 89–90, 95, 104, 106–7; Expanded Instrument System (EIS) of, 82, 301; and founding of SFTMC, 82, 95, 100, 118, 266; Gaudeamus prize awarded to, 83, 103, 271; and improvisation, 11, 58, 68, 80–81, 82, 84, 85, 95, 98, 102–3, 104, 108, 205–7, 208, 209–10, 266, 269, 270, 273; interview with, 3, 95–111; and involvement in Sonics concerts, 10, 11, 14, 48, 55, 56, 82, 83, 100, 118, 225, 254, 269, 270; and involvement in "Tape-athon" program, *93*, 95, 96, 102; and involvement in Trips Festival, 5, 34, 90, 107, 280–81; and involvement in Tudorfest, 24, 26, 86, 87, 104, 130, 274, 275; light shows combined with work by, 20, 22, 85, 104, 142, 293, 296; as Mills Tape Music Center director, 34, 78–79, 90–91, 93, 95, 133; in photographs, *24, 70, 81, 91, 185*; Riley's compositions performed by, 26, 87, 219, 276, 278; Sender's compositions performed by, 14, 23, 61, 68, 85, 104, 125, 137, 159, 160, 274, 300; as student of Erickson, 10, 12, 54, 80, 95, 97–98, 102; Subotnick's compositions performed by, 85, 122, 273; as teacher at UC San Diego, 34, 93, 95; works by: *Alien Bog*, 91, 110; *Apple Box*, 89–90, 102; *Apple Box Double*, 90, 102, 292, 299; *Apple Box Orchestra with Bottle Chorus*, 102, 280; *Beautiful Soop*, 91; *Before the Music Ends*, 110–11; *Bye Bye Butterfly*, ix, 30, 31, 89, 94n10, 95, 108, 109, 216, 263, 291; *Circuitry for Percussion and Light*, 91, *92*, 93, 142, 290; *Covenant*, 108, 110; *Duo for Accordion and Bandoneon*, 84, 86, 110, 257, 274; *George Washington Slept Here*, 31, *32*, 105, 106, 280; *George Washington Slept Here Too*, 31, *32*, 33, 106, 280; *Improvisation No. 1*, 68, 189; *In the Garden*, 261, 281; *Light Piece for David Tudor*, *32*, 106–7, 142; *Mnemonics*, 30, 85, 89, 90, 109; music for Brecht's *The Exception and the Rule*, 271; music for Bruno's *Il Candelaio*, 279; music for Wolf's *Lulu*, 271; *Outline*, 207; *Pauline's Solo*, 292, 301; *Pieces of Eight*, 29, 87–88, 94n7, 105, 106, 108, 255–56; *Rock Symphony*, 33, 90, 108; *Serenade for Viola and Bassoon*, 99; *Seven Passages*, 88, 110, 274; *Sonic Meditations*, 29; *Sound Patterns for Mixed Chorus*, 83, 100, 271; *A Theater Piece*, 5, 33–34, 90, 106, 107, 110, 281; *Three Songs for Soprano and Horn*, 98; *Three Songs for Soprano and Piano*, 98; *Time Perspectives*, 10–11, 82, 100, 101, 102, 214–15, 269; *Trio for Flute, Piano, and Page Turner*, 83, 100; *Variations for Sextet*, 99
Olson, Charles, 98, 99, 154
Olson, Harry, 196
Once Festival, 40n32, 60
Once Group, 12, 85, 154
Ono, Yoko, 221n1
Open Theater, 2, 5, 15, 75, 78, 280
Opus Too, 269
ORB (optical ranging for the blind) system, 170–71, 177n1
Orozco, José, 8
Otey, Wendell, 97, 253
Oxley, Tony, 208

Pacific Film Archive, 37
Paik, Nam June, 213–14
Palmer, Lynne, 12, 58, 64, 67, 82, 102, 212, 215, 224, 269, 270
Palmer, Willard, 88
Parmegiani, Bernard, 276
Partch, Harry, 9, 192–93

Payne, Maggi, 2, 3
Peltzer, Dwight, 104, 274, 275
Penderecki, Krzysztof, 275
performance art, 14–17. *See also* theater
Performer's Choice series, 83
Perls, Fritz, 75, 223
Pesanek, Zdenek, 143
Piezer, Sandy, 267
poetry, 8, 15, 16, 48, 98–99, 120, 126, 188, 268, 271, 279
Polta, Steve, 36
Poniatoff, Alexander M., 250
Poulenc, Francis, 207
Pousseur, Henri, 12, 48, 270, 272, 274, 282
Powell, Mel, 272, 277, 279
Prévert, Jacques, 16
Prévost, Eddie, 209
psychedelia, 5, 20, 22, 23, 78, 90, 221, 246, 248–49
Puccini, Giacomo, 30, 89, 109

Quicksilver Messenger Service (rock group), 143, 245

Rabe, Folke, 83, 84, 103, 225, 226, 259–60, 277, 278
Rameau, Jean-Philippe, 281
Rathbun, Harry, 240
Raymond, Bill, 15, 16
Reich, Steve, viii, 26–28, *28,* 36–37, 74, 80, 83, 87, 104, 107, 118, 131, 150, 189, 205, 219, 221, 246, 269, 274, 275, 276, 278; works by: *Composition* for piano, 270; *Four Organs,* viii; *It's Gonna Rain,* 28, 277; *Livelihood,* 28, 277; music for *Ubu Roi,* 273; *Oh Dem Watermelons* soundtrack, 37, 150, 279; *The Plastic Haircut* soundtrack, 27, 28, 36, 272
Rensselaer Polytechnic Institute, 2, 3, 84, 289
Rexroth, Kenneth, 1, 240, 271
R. G. Davis Mime Troupe. *See* Davis, R. G.; San Francisco Mime Troupe
Rich, Alan, 53, 81
Rifkin, Joshua, 277
Riley, Robert R., 2
Riley, Terry, viii; Cage's influence on, 11, 205, 230; and collaboration with Dewey, 215–16, 217; and collaboration with Halprin, 2, 11, 62, 83, 211–12, 225, 226, 230, 234, 267, 269; and collaboration with Martin, 142, 150, 153, 219; and collaboration with Oliveros, 2, 11, 80, 95, 98, 205–7, 208, 209–10, 266; and collaboration with Rush, 2, 11, 80, 95, 98, 205–7, 208, 209–10, 266; and collaboration with Young, 11, 81, 205, 211–13, 221n1, 225, 230, 265, 279; and improvisation, 11, 58, 80–81, 95, 98, 205–7, 208, 209–10, 266; interview with, 205–7, 210–21; and involvement in Sonics concerts, 10, 11, 48, 55, 269; light shows combined with work by, 142, 150, 153, 219, 276; and minimalism, 205, 226; own compositions performed by, 11, 26, 87, 276, 278; in photograph, *206;* Stockhausen's influence on, 118, 210; as student of Erickson, 12, 97; works by: *Bird of Paradise,* 278; *Concert for Two Pianos and Five Tape Recorders,* 11, 39n15, 205, 211, 212, 221n1, 267; *Coule,* 26, 220, 276, 278; *I,* 26, 219, 278; *In B♭ or Is It A♭?,* 26, 220, 276, 278; *In C,* ix, 2, 26, 69, 87, 131, 142, 150, 153, 166, 205, 218–20, 252, 258, 263, 276; *M . . . Mix (Mescalin Mix),* 11, 55, 82, 212, 214, 216, 224, 226, 269; *Music for "The Gift,"* 17, 26, 67, 216, 218, 273, 276, 278; *Poppy Nogood and the Phantom Band,* 220; *Rainbow in Curved Air,* 220; *Shoeshine,* 26, 219, 276; *Spectra,* 118, 210, 221n2, 268; *String Quartet* (1960), 63, 79n2, 211, 268; *Tread on the Trail,* 278
Rivera, Diego, 8
Rockefeller Foundation, 34, 47, 73, 75, 90, 105, 114–15, 116, 131–32, 247, 277, 278, 281
rock music, 5, 20, 24, 33, 75, 76, 104, 105, 131, 135n9, 143–44, 173, 220–21, 238, 245–47, 279, 280
"Roll Over Beethoven" (Beatles remix), 31, 105
Romero, Elias, 16, 19, 20, 22, 64, 68, 104, 143, *144,* 189, 272, 273, 274, 275
Rosen, Jerome, 268
Rosenboom, David, 176, 252
Ross, Janice, 2, 225–27
Roszak, Theodore, 8
Rubin, Nathan, 112, 119, 269, 277, 280
Rush, Loren, viii; Cage's compositions performed by, 104, 257; and collaboration with Oliveros, 2, 11, 80, 95, 98, 205–7, 208, 209–10, 266; and collaboration with Riley, 2, 11, 80, 95, 98, 205–7, 208, 209–10, 266; Erickson's compositions performed by, 282; and improvisation, 11, 80, 95, 98, 205–7, 208, 209–10, 266, 270; and involvement at KPFA, 53, 80, 83; and involvement in Sonics concerts, 11, 48; and involvement in Tudorfest, 274; Oliveros's composition performed by, 280; Sender's compositions performed by, 14, 125; as student of Erickson, 12, 53, 80, 97
Rust, Gardner, 267

Samuel, Gerhard, ix, 269
San Francisco: as haven for counterculture, 8–9; rock underground in, 245–47
San Francisco Art Institute, 36, 39n17, 240
San Francisco Arts Festival, 186, 273
San Francisco Chronicle, 14, 77, 82, 114, 120, 187, 246, 247, 265, 295
San Francisco Cinematheque, 35, 36

San Francisco Conservatory of Music, vii, 9–10, 14, 47, 53, 54, 61–62, 81, 82, 98, 100, 108, 113, 118, 125, 132, 151, 214, 215, 224, 225, 253, 269, 277

San Francisco Examiner, 94n7, 120, 226

San Francisco Mime Troupe (originally R. G. Davis Mime Troupe), 2, 5, 14, 15, 33, 37, 83, 88, 95, 107, 108, 127, 131, 144, 219, 237, 249, 269–80 *passim*

San Francisco Museum of Art, 140, 160, 187, 253, 265, 267, 271, 273, 276, 277, 281

San Francisco Museum of Modern Art, xi

San Francisco State College, 80, 97, 99, 206, 227, 240, 248, 252–53, 275, 276

San Francisco Symphony, 112, 118, 120

San Francisco Tape Music Center (SFTMC): founding of, 9, 14, 42, 47, 50, 61–62, 82, 83, 95, 100, 103, 113–14, 118, 125, 266, 271; and move to Mills College, 34, 50, 78, 90, 95, 103, 115, 116, 132–33, 145, 147, 222, 245, 247, 263, 281, 282; as nonprofit organization, 83, 90, 103, 125, 135n1; technical facilities at, 30–31, 45–46, 48, 69, 71–73, 84, 108, 127, 133–34, 182, 183, 189–96, 198, *199,* 200–204, *200, 201, 202, 203.* See also Divisadero Street location; Jones Street location

Sartre, Jean-Paul, 123

Satie, Erik, 274

Savio, Mario, 33, 276

Saxton, Earl, 29

Schaffer, Pierre, 81

Schlemmer, Oskar, 223

Schoenberg, Arnold, 9, 45, 52, 206

Schuller, Gunther, 268

Schwenk, Theodore, 145

Scott, Chloe, 5, 244, 249

Sears Silvertone tape recorder, 82, 100

Sender, Ramon: Cage's compositions performed by, 104; and collaboration with Baillie, 36; and collaboration with Brand, 5, 50, 75, 77, 90; and collaboration with Buchla, 1, 109, 114, 163, 166, 172; and collaboration with Callahan, 65–66, 183, 184, 186; and collaboration with LaVigne, 49; and collaboration with Martin, 137, 140, 146, 147, 149–50, 152–53, 159–60, 277, 279, 299, 300; and collaboration with Oliveros, 20, 54, 58, 68, 81–82, 84, 85, 100, 118; and collaboration with Subotnick, 1, 14, 20, 49, 55–56, 60, 66, 68, 113–14, 118, 125, 126, 272, 277; and drug use, 72, 74, 75, 77, 78, 90; early musical training of, 50–55; and founding of SFTMC, 9, 14, 42, 47, 50, 61–62, 82, 83, 95, 100, 103, 113–14, 118, 125, 266, 271; and improvisation, 56, 58, 61, 66, 68, 82, 85, 104, 126, 269, 270, 273; interview with, 3, 50–79; and involvement in *City Scale* happening, 17, 19, 63–64, 67, 152–53, 272; and involvement in Sonics concerts, 10, 14, 48, 55–58, 61, 82, 100, 118, 125, 225, 254, 269, 270; and involvement in Trips Festival, 5, 34, 50, 75–77, 90, 244; and involvement in Tudorfest, 86, 274; light shows combined with work by, 20, 22, 23, 65, 68, 85, 104, 137, 140, 156, 159–60, 274, 299, 300; at Morning Star Ranch commune, 34, 50, 78, 133, 247–48, 251n8, 281; "Naked Close-Up" (unpublished ms.) by, 66; own compositions performed by, 14, 68; in photographs, *24, 51, 56, 70, 185;* as student of Carter, 50, 54; as student of Copeland, 51; as student of Cowell, 52, 54; as student of Ferdinand Davis, 51; as student of Erickson, 9, 50, 53, 54, 55, 97, 118; as student of Milhaud, 50, 53; works by: *Balances,* 60, 274; *Desert Ambulance,* 23–24, 37, 45, 61, 70–71, 85, 104, 137, 140, 156, 159–60, 175, 190, 274, 292, 300; *Four Sanskrit Hymns,* 9, 10, 53, 54, 55; *Great Grandpa Lemuel's Death-Rattle Reincarnation Blues in F Sharp,* 251n7, 290, 296–98; *Improvisation No. 1,* 68, 189; *In the Garden,* 28–29, 278, 281; *Information,* 59–60, 271; *Interstices,* 272; *Kore,* 65, 271, 275, 290, 299; *Kronos,* 57, 68, 270, 272, 273; *Parade,* 57, 270; *Ramon Takes a Bath, or I Laid Mr. Clean for the FBI,* 66; *Sound Mobile,* 272; *Sound Study,* 271; *Star Charts for Piano and Tape,* 59; *Time Fields,* 58–59; *Traversals,* 10, 56–57, 82, 269; *Triad,* 273; *Tropical Fish Opera,* 14, 58, 125, 270, 290, 294–95; *Worldfood XII,* 72

Serge synthesizer, 116

serialism, 37, 52, 111n1, 210. *See also* twelve-tone system

Sessions, Roger, 268

Shaefer, Charles, 270

Shaff, Stanley, 26, 104, 256, 268, 273, 275, 276

Shakespeare, William, 112, 119, 120, 269

Shapiro, Gerald, 77, 118, 278, 281

Shere, Charles, viii, 82, 277

Sherman, David, 36

Shifrin, Seymour, 99, 111n1

Shostakovich, Dmitry, 136

Sitney, P. Adams, 35

Six Gallery, San Francisco, 8

Slick, Darby, 135n9, 245

Slick, Grace, 104, 246

Smell Opera with Found Tape (collaborative performance), 14, 125, 227, 270

Smith, Richard Cándida, 9

Snyder, Gary, 8

Sonics concerts, *10,* 10–12, *13,* 14, 40n34, 48, 55–58, 61, 82, 83, 100, 102, 118, 125, 151, 178, 181, 215, 224, 225, 254, 265, 269–70

Sparrow, Naomi, 112, 280
Spencer, Fumi, 16, 274, 275, 281
Spencer, William, 16, 271, 273, 275, 280
Spicer, Jack, 99
Spontaneous Music Ensemble, 209
Stanford University, 118, 132
Stanislavski, Konstantin, 16
State University of New York at Buffalo, 252
Stein, Gertrude, 16
Stein, Leonard, 49, 130, 275
Sterling, George, 8
Stern, Gerd, 40n35, 65, 69, 120, 178, 180, 186–87, 191, 193, 242, 273
Stevens, John, 209
Stevenson, Robert Louis, 29, 87
Stockhausen, Karlheinz, viii, 9, 53, 81, 99, 101, 111n1, 118, 163, 207, 210, 245, 246, 270, 274
Stolaroff, Myron, 239, 240, 250n3
Straight Theater, 144, 238
Strand, Chick, 35, 36
Studio di fonologia musicale, Milan, 12
Subke, Walter, 273
Subotnick, Linn, 74, 104, 273, 275, 277, 278
Subotnick, Morton, viii; as artist-in-residence at NYU, 34, 73, 90, 115, 133, 280; Cage's compositions performed by, 104; and collaboration with Buchla, 1, 109, 114, 117, 120, 163, 164, 165–67, 169; and collaboration with Callahan, 183, 184, *185*, 186; and collaboration with Halprin, 83, 110, 117, 120, 123–25, 212, 222, 225, 226, 234, 270, 276, 277; and collaboration with LaVigne, 49; and collaboration with Martin, 137, 146, 147, 149–50, 154–57, 160, 277, 295–96; and collaboration with Oliveros, 20, 84, 85; and collaboration with Sender, 1, 14, 20, 49, 55–56, 62, 66, 68, 113–14, 118, 125, 126, 272, 277; and founding of SFTMC, 14, 47, 62, 83, 95, 103, 113–14, 118, 125, 266, 271; and improvisation, 66, 68, 82, 85, 102, 104, 126, 127, 129, 270, 273; interview with, 3, 117–35; and involvement in Actor's Workshop productions, 71, 73, 112, 115, 117, 119, 120–23, 133, 269, 272, 273; and involvement in Mills Performing Group, 30; and involvement in Repertory Theater of Lincoln Center, 34, 115, 123, 279; and involvement in Sonics concerts, 14, 48, 55–56, 82, 125, 225, 270; and involvement in Tudorfest, 130, 274, 275; light shows combined with work by, 20, 22, 65, 68, 85, 104, 137, 154–57, 160, 295, 296; Messiaen's composition performed by, 118; in photographs, *24, 56, 113, 185*; Princeton seminars attended by, 131, 134; Riley's composition performed by, 26, 87, 210, 276; Sender's compositions performed by, 14, 68, 125, 278; as student of Kirchner, 14, 118; as student of Milhaud, 14, 118, 134–35; works by: *Caves*, 269; *Improvisation No. 1*, 68, 189; *The Juggler*, 271; *Mandolin*, 40n34, 45, 85, 117, 137, 160, 270, 275, 277, 290, 295–96; music for Brecht's *Caucasian Chalk Circle*, 273; music for Brecht's *Galileo*, 121–22, 272; music for Büchner's *Danton's Death*, 123, 279; music for *King Lear*, 112, 119, 120, 122, 269; *Piece for Four Hands*, 134; *Play!* 130; *Play! no. 1*, 28, *29*, 117, 130, 154–56, 276; *Play! no. 2*, 130; *Play! no. 3*, 130, 155, 156; *Play! no. 4*, 130, 155, 156; *Release*, 292, 300; *Serenades*, 30, 129, 280; *Silver Apples of the Moon*, 116, 134, 294; *Sound Blocks: An Heroic Vision*, 40n34, 117, 119, 120, 269, 271, 295; *Tarot*, 157, 271, 281; television documentary scores, 118–19; *A Theater Piece after Sonnet No. 47 of Petrarch*, 20, 40n34, 49, 68, 273, 295–96; *Three Preludes*, 9, 269; *Until Spring Revisited*, 290, 293–94; *Yod*, 40n34, 126, 271
Swift, Richard, 268, 274, 280

Takemitsu, Toru, 86
Talbot, David, 55
"Tape-athon" program, *93*, 95, 96, 102
tape delay, 15, 26, 30, 33, 90, 111n2, 216–17, 220, 244, 248, 249, 301
tape looping, 27, 37, 190, 214, 262
Tartak, Marvin, 55, 267, 268, 269
Taylor, Cecil, 12
Tcherepnin, Serge, 116
Tenney, James, 12, 48, 270, 271, 275, 279
theater, 2, 5, 14–17, 58, 67, 105, 112, 117, 119, 120–23, 144, 265, 269, 272, 273, 275
Theatre of Eternal Music, 217, 279
Them (rock group), 143
Theremin, 73
Tinguely, Jean, 149, 181, 182
Total Mobile Home, 36
Trips Festival, 2, 5, *6, 7,* 8, 9, 34, 37, 50, 75–77, 90, 107, 164–65, 237–38, 239, 243–44, 245, 248, 280
Tudor, David, 24, *25*, 26, 49, 59, 142, 154, 171, 191, 202, 217, 224, 236, 256–57, 269, 274–75, 277; and collaboration with Oliveros, 26, 86–87, 89–90, 95, 104, 106–7
Tudorfest, 24, *25*, 26, 40n37, 86, 87, 104, 130, 154, 191–92, 256–58, 274–75
twelve-tone system, 52, 99, 118. *See also* serialism
Tyranny, "Blue" Gene, 175

Underwood, Ian, 277, 281
University of Arizona, 105
University of California at Berkeley, 33, 62, 63, 99, 111n1, 118, 130, 132, 163, 170, 207, 211, 225, 246, 260, 267, 268, 269, 270, 277

University of California at Los Angeles, 39n20, 225, 234, 276
University of California at San Diego, 34, 86, 93, 95
University of California Extension, 265, 268
University of Michigan, 154
University of Rochester, 178
USCO multimedia group, 178
Ussachevsky, Vladimir, 110, 115

Vancouver Festival, 49, 191, 272, 274
Van der Wyk, Jack, 269, 273, 275, 278, 280
Van Deusen, Pieter, 267
Van Meter, Ben, 22, 37, 143
Varèse, Edgard, 9, 17, 84
Varsi, Diane, 16
Vigil, Carmen, 36
voltage control, 109, 165, 167, 194
von Gunden, Heidi, 39nn17,20
Vortex concerts, 19–20, 21, 266

Wagner, Richard, 72, 251n7, 296
Wahlberg, Richard, 55
Walker, Junior, 26
washing machine performance piece, 12, 56, 137, 182, 270
Weber, Carl, 122
Weber, Joseph, 206, 253, 268, 270
Webern, Anton, 207
Weeks, James, 148
Wehrer, Anne, 85
Weitsman, Mel, 26
Wellfons, Jack, 240
Welsh, Thomas M., 2, 3–4, 39n17

White, Joshua, 143
Whitney, John and James, 21, 143
Wickware, Judith, 271
Wiley, William, 272
Wilfred, Thomas, 136
Williams, Jan, 252
Winkler, Peter, 277
Winsor, Philip, 11, 26, 48, 55, 56, 82, 269, 276
Wise, Howard, 145
Wolf, Leonard, 271
Wolfe, Tom, 241
Wolff, Christian, 281
Wonner, Paul, 148
"Wow & Flutter" festival, xi, 2, 289–301
Wright, Charles, 36

Yates, Peter, 276
Young, La Monte, viii; *An Anthology* co-edited by, 39n15; Berkeley concert program organized by, 267; Boulez's influence on, 118; Cage's influence on, 100, 230; and collaboration with Halprin, 2, 11, 62, 83, 211, 212, *212*, 225, 226, 230, 234, 267, 271; and collaboration with Riley, 11, 81, 205, 211–13, 221n1, 225, 230, 265, 279; and minimalism, 205, 226; in photograph, *212*; Stockhausen's influence on, 99, 111n1; and Theatre of Eternal Music, 217, 279; works by: *Composition 1960 #7*, 99; *Poem: A Chamber Opera in One Act*, 267; *Poem for Chairs, Tables, and Benches, etc.*, 63, 205, 212, 267, 276; *String Trio*, 99, 111n1, 225, 226; *Studies*, 111n1; *Study I for Piano*, 268; *2 Sounds*, 212, 267; *Visions*, 267

Zappa, Frank, 247

DESIGNER: SANDY DROOKER
TEXT: 11/15.75 ADOBE GARAMOND
DISPLAY: GOTHIC
COMPOSITOR: INTEGRATED COMPOSITION SYSTEMS
INDEXER: ANDREW JORON

www.ingramcontent.com/pod-product-compliance
Lightning Source LLC
Chambersburg PA
CBHW08083523O426
43665CB00021B/2846